THE MODERN LIBRARY
OF THE WORLD'S BEST BOOKS

HELLENISTIC PHILOSOPHY

SELECTED READINGS IN

**EPICUREANISM, STOICISM,
SKEPTICISM AND NEOPLATONISM**

HELLENISTIC PHILOSOPHY

SELECTED READINGS IN

EPICUREANISM, STOICISM, SKEPTICISM AND NEOPLATONISM

EDITED AND INTRODUCED BY

HERMAN SHAPIRO

AND

EDWIN M. CURLEY

DEPARTMENT OF PHILOSOPHY
SAN JOSE STATE COLLEGE

THE MODERN LIBRARY
NEW YORK

THE MODERN LIBRARY
is published by RANDOM HOUSE, INC.

Manufactured in the United States of America

PREFACE

The moral and emotional exigencies obtaining in the first true "Age of Anxiety" suffered in the Western world—the Hellenistic Age—called forth and nourished four great philosophical responses: Epicureanism, Stoicism, Skepticism and Neoplatonism. It is the purpose of this volume to provide a convenient introduction to the philosophical programs of these four schools through the presentation of selected primary source materials in English translation. It is addressed for use not only to those studying this area of intellectual history as part of the standard college course in the history of philosophy, or humanities, but as well to those general readers who may be moved to discover how other men, in other times of extreme trial, attempted to redress the imbalance felt to obtain between their minute selves and the huge world.

Since these four schools form, as it were, a natural unit in the history of thought, it is curious that selections drawn from the writings of Epicurean, Stoic, Skeptic and Neoplatonist have not yet been made available in any single volume. But whatever the reason—and a cogent one is not easy to conceive in an age that has learned the value of a good anthology—it is precisely the satisfaction of this lacuna that constitutes the primary "convenience" of the present introduction to Hellenistic philosophy. But other pedagogically desirable features are herein incorporated as well. Each selection is of such length as to be easily read at a single sitting. Yet, we trust, such editing as this entailed has compromised neither the particular insight nor the general philosophical intent of the original author. In keeping with our conviction that for classroom use it is the instructor's lectures which should properly supply contextual information for each selection, our own introductory remarks have been kept quite brief. For the general reader, however, there is appended to each section a carefully selected list of suggested readings which cites easily available works in English, in which the thought and times of the men represented in the section are authoritatively set forth and examined.

The specialist will recognize at once the value of our special Cicero appendix. It may be employed in any number of ways: as an exhibition of the typically polemic character of philosophy in the Hellenistic Age; as a straight historical document of no little value; as an opportunity to examine the great Roman eclectic's philosophical decisions in their own right; as —but we will presume no further. Each instructor will know best how to exploit this material.

When it came to selecting translations, we found ourselves faced with an embarrassment of riches. Our final choices, embodied in the sequel, were considered most desirable in the light of two stringently applied criteria: general readability and textual fidelity. For the most part the original translations were followed faithfully, with only minor alterations in a few instances.

The editors wish to make grateful acknowledgment to Dr. Morris Philipson of Random House, Inc., not only for his initial interest in this volume, but also for the intelligence, patience and good humor he displayed while seeing it through all phases of its publication.

HERMAN SHAPIRO
EDWIN M. CURLEY

Department of Philosophy
San Jose State College
San Jose, California

CONTENTS

III
SKEPTICISM

IV
NEOPLATONISM

HELLENISTIC PHILOSOPHY

SELECTED READINGS IN

EPICUREANISM, STOICISM, SKEPTICISM AND NEOPLATONISM

I

EPICUREANISM

INTRODUCTION

Like most of the Hellenistic schools of philosophy, Epicureanism owes much to Socrates. Though the physical theory of
the Epicureans was derived largely from that of the earlier
Greek atomists, Leucippus and Democritus, in ethics they
adopted, with some modifications, the hedonism of Aristippus
of Cyrene (c. 435-355 B.C.). Aristippus, a pupil of Socrates
and founder of the Cyrenaic school, held the good to be pleasure and, like the Socrates in Plato's Protagoras, took virtue to
be the art of calculating which course of action will yield the
greatest balance of pleasure over pain.

But Epicurus (341-270 B.C.), the originator of the school
named after him, was not a slavish imitator of anyone. He
interpreted "pleasure" differently from Aristippus, and he
softened the determinism of Democritus to allow for human
freedom. Most important, he brought to his writings on philosophy that fervent opposition to all forms of conventional religion which is the chief characteristic of his school.

Epicurus was a remarkable man. Though his name today
suggests the fastidious search for certain types of physical
pleasure, the man himself led a life that would have done
credit to a medieval monk. Withdrawn from the world into
his famous garden, with only the company of a few friends

and disciples, he dined simply, spoke gently, gave alms to the poor, and preached against wealth, ambition and passion. Though he wrote much, only a few of his writings remain. Apart from some recently discovered fragments, the Vatican Sayings, *there are three didactic letters—*To Herodotus, To Pythocles, *and* To Menoeceus—*and the* Leading Doctrines. *The latter two works, in which Epicurus summarizes his ethical views, are presented below in their entirety.*

The great Roman representative of Epicureanism, Lucretius, lived during the declining years of the Republic. If the legends we have of him are true, he lived a less serene existence than did his master. His wife, jealous of the poet's attentions to philosophy, is supposed to have administered a love potion which drove him to madness, and ultimately to suicide. As Santayana remarks, this story, which comes to us in part from St. Jerome, "attributes too edifying an end to an atheist and Epicurean not to be suspected." In any case, Lucretius died in 55 B.C., with his major work, the poem On the Nature of Things, *unfinished. That poem, still the best introduction to Epicurean physics, is presented below in an abridged version.*

EPICURUS

LETTER TO MENOECEUS*

No one should postpone the study of philosophy when he is young, nor should he weary of it when he becomes mature, because the search for mental

* Reprinted from *The Philosophy of Epicurus* by George K. Strodach, by permission of Northwestern University Press. Copyright, 1963, by Northwestern University Press.

health is never untimely or out of season. To say that the time to study philosophy has not yet arrived or that it is past is like saying that the time for happiness is not yet at hand or is no longer present. Thus both the young and the mature should pursue philosophy, the latter in order to be rejuvenated as they age by the blessings that accrue from pleasurable past experience, and the youthful in order to become mature immediately through having no fear of the future. Hence we should make a practice of the things that make for happiness, for assuredly when we have this, we have everything, and we do everything we can to get it when we don't have it.

The Preconditions of Happiness

[1. You should do and practice all the things I constantly recommended to you, with the knowledge that they are the fundamentals of the good life. First of all, you should think of deity as imperishable and blessed being (as delineated in the universal conception of it common to all men), and you should not attribute to it anything foreign to its immortality or inconsistent with its blessedness. On the contrary, you should hold every doctrine that is capable of safeguarding its blessedness in common with its imperishability. The gods do indeed exist, since our knowledge of them is a matter of clear and distinct perception; but they are not like what the masses suppose them to be, because most people do not maintain the pure conception of the gods. The irreligious man is not the person who destroys the gods of the masses but the person who imposes the ideas of the masses on the gods. The opinions held by most people about the gods are not true conceptions of them but fallacious notions, according to which awful penalties are meted out to the evil and the greatest of blessings to the good. The masses, by assimilating the gods in every respect to their own moral qualities, accept deities similar to themselves and regard anything not of this sort as alien.

Second, you should accustom yourself to believing that

death means nothing to us, since every good and every evil lies in sensation; but death is the privation of sensation. Hence a correct comprehension of the fact that death means nothing to us makes the mortal aspect of life pleasurable, not by conferring on us a boundless period of time but by removing the yearning for deathlessness. There is nothing fearful in living for the person who has really laid hold of the fact that there is nothing fearful in not living. So it is silly for a person to say that he dreads death—not because it will be painful when it arrives but because it pains him now as a future certainty; for that which makes no trouble for us when it arrives is a meaningless pain when we await it. This, the most horrifying of evils, means nothing to us, then, because so long as we are existent death is not present and whenever it is present we are nonexistent. Thus it is of no concern either to the living or to those who have completed their lives. For the former it is nonexistent, and the latter are themselves nonexistent.

Most people, however, recoil from death as though it were the greatest of evils; at other times they welcome it as the end-all of life's ills. The sophisticated person, on the other hand, neither begs off from living nor dreads not living. Life is not a stumbling block to him, nor does he regard not being alive as any sort of evil. As in the case of food he prefers the most savory dish to merely the larger portion, so in the case of time, he garners to himself the most agreeable moments rather than the longest span.

Anyone who urges the youth to lead a good life but counsels the older man to end his life in good style is silly, not merely because of the welcome character of life but because of the fact that living well and dying well are one and the same discipline. Much worse off, however, is the person who says it were well not to have been born "but once born to pass Hades' portals as swiftly as may be." Now if he says such a thing from inner persuasion why does he not withdraw from life? Everything is in readiness for him once he has firmly resolved on this course. But if he speaks facetiously he is a trifler standing in the midst of men who do not welcome him.

It should be borne in mind, then, that the time to come is neither ours nor altogether not ours. In this way we shall neither expect the future outright as something destined to be, nor despair of it as something absolutely not destined to be.

The Good Life

[2. It should be recognized that within the category of desire certain desires are natural, certain others unnecessary and trivial; that in the case of the natural desires certain ones are necessary, certain others merely natural; and that in the case of necessary desires certain ones are necessary for happiness, others to promote freedom from bodily discomfort, others for the maintenance of life itself. A steady view of these matters shows us how to refer all moral choice and aversion to bodily health and imperturbability of mind, these being the twin goals of happy living. It is on this account that we do everything we do—to achieve freedom from pain and freedom from fear. When once we come to this, the tumult in the soul is calmed and the human being does not have to go about looking for something that is lacking or to search for something additional with which to supplement the welfare of soul and body. Accordingly we have need of pleasure only when we feel pain because of the absence of pleasure, but whenever we do not feel pain we no longer stand in need of pleasure. And so we speak of pleasure as the starting point and the goal of the happy life because we realize that it is our primary native good, because every act of choice and aversion originates with it, and because we come back to it when we judge every good by using the pleasure feeling as our criterion.

Because of the very fact that pleasure is our primary and congenital good we do not select every pleasure; there are times when we forego certain pleasures, particularly when they are followed by too much unpleasantness. Furthermore, we regard certain states of pain as preferable to pleasures, particularly when greater satisfaction results from our having submitted to discomforts for a long period of time. Thus every pleasure is a good by reason of its having a nature akin to our own, but not every pleasure is desirable. In like manner every state of pain is an evil, but not all pains are uniformly to be rejected. At any rate, it is our duty to judge all such cases by measuring pleasures against pains, with a view to their respective assets and liabilities, inasmuch as we do experience the good as being bad at times and, contrariwise, the bad as being good.

In addition, we consider limitation of the appetites a major good, and we recommend this practice not for the purpose of enjoying just a few things and no more but rather for the purpose of enjoying those few in case we do not have much. We are firmly convinced that those who need expensive fare least are the ones who relish it most keenly and that a natural way of life is easily procured, while trivialities are hard to come by. Plain foods afford pleasure equivalent to that of a sumptuous diet, provided that the pains of penury are wholly eliminated. Barley bread and water yield the peak of pleasure whenever a person who needs them sets them in front of himself. Hence becoming habituated to a simple rather than a lavish way of life provides us with the full complement of health; it makes a person ready for the necessary business of life; it puts us in a position of advantage when we happen upon sumptuous fare at intervals and prepares us to be fearless in facing fortune.

Thus when I say that pleasure is the goal of living I do not mean the pleasures of libertines or the pleasures inherent in positive enjoyment, as is supposed by certain persons who are ignorant of our doctrine or who are not in agreement with it or who interpret it perversely. I mean, on the contrary, the pleasure that consists in freedom from bodily pain and mental agitation. The pleasant life is not the product of one drinking party after another or of sexual intercourse with women and boys or of the sea food and other delicacies afforded by a luxurious table. On the contrary, it is the result of sober thinking—namely, investigation of the reasons for every act of choice and aversion and elimination of those false ideas about the gods and death which are the chief source of mental disturbances.

The starting point of this whole scheme and the most important of its values is good judgment, which consequently is more highly esteemed even than philosophy. All the other virtues stem from sound judgment, which shows us that it is impossible to live the pleasant Epicurean life without also living sensibly, nobly, and justly and, vice versa, that it is impossible to live sensibly, nobly, and justly without living pleasantly. The traditional virtues grow up together with the pleasant life; they are indivisible. Can you think of anyone more moral than the person who has devout beliefs about the gods, who is consistently without fears about death, and who has pondered man's natural end? Or who realizes that the goal of the good life is easily gained and achieved and that the term of evil is brief, both in extent of time and duration of pain? Or the man who laughs at the "decrees of Fate," a deity whom some people have set up as sovereign of all?

The good Epicurean believes that certain events occur deterministically, that others are chance events, and that still others are in our own hands. He sees also that necessity cannot be held morally responsible and that chance is an unpredictable thing, but that what is in our own hands, since it has no master, is naturally associated with blameworthiness and the opposite. (Actually it would be better to subscribe to the popular mythology than to become a slave by accepting the determinism of the natural philosophers, because popular religion underwrites the hope of supplicating the gods by offerings but determinism contains an element of necessity, which is inexorable.) As for chance, the Epicurean does not assume that it is a deity (as in popular belief) because a god does nothing irregular; nor does he regard it as an unpredictable cause of all events. It is his belief that good and evil are not the chance contributions of a deity, donated to mankind for the happy life, but rather that the initial circumstances for great good and evil are sometimes provided by chance. He thinks it preferable to have bad luck rationally than good luck irrationally. In other words, in human action it is better for a rational choice to be unsuccessful than for an irrational choice to succeed through the agency of chance.

Think about these and related matters day and night, by yourself and in company with someone like yourself. If you do, you will never experience anxiety, waking or sleeping, but you will live like a god among men. For a human being who lives in the midst of immortal blessings is in no way like mortal man!

LEADING DOCTRINES*

[1. The blessed and indestructible being of the divine has no concerns of its own, nor does it make trouble for others. It is not affected by feelings of anger or benevolence, because these are found where there is lack of strength.

[2. Death means nothing to us, because that which has been broken down into atoms has no sensation and that which has no sensation is no concern of ours.

[3. The quantitative limit of pleasure is the elimination of all feelings of pain. Wherever the pleasurable state exists, there is neither bodily pain nor mental pain nor both together, so long as the state continues.

[4. Bodily pain does not last continuously. The peak is present for a very brief period, and pains that barely exceed the state of bodily pleasure do not continue for many days. On

* Reprinted from *The Philosophy of Epicurus* by George K. Strodach, by permission of Northwestern University Press. Copyright, 1963, by Northwestern University Press.

the other hand, protracted illnesses show a balance of bodily pleasure over pain.

[5. It is impossible to live the pleasant life without also living sensibly, nobly, and justly, and conversely it is impossible to live sensibly, nobly, and justly without living pleasantly. A person who does not have a pleasant life is not living sensibly, nobly and justly, and conversely the person who does not have these virtues cannot live pleasantly.

[6. Any means by which it is possible to procure freedom from fearing other men is a natural good.

[7. Some men have desired to gain reputation and to be well regarded thinking in this way to gain protection from other people. If the lives of such men are secure, they have acquired a natural blessing; but if they are not, they do not possess what they originally reached for by natural instinct.

[8. No pleasure is bad in itself. But the things that make for pleasure in certain cases entail disturbances many times greater than the pleasures themselves.

[9. If all pleasures could be compressed in time and intensity, and were characteristic of the whole man or his more important aspects, the various pleasures would not differ from each other.

[10. If the things that produce the debauchee's pleasures dissolved the mind's fears regarding the heavenly bodies, death, and pain and also told us how to limit our desires, we would never have any reason to find fault with such people, because they would be glutting themselves with every sort of pleasure and never suffer physical or mental pain, which is the real evil.

[11. We would have no need for natural science unless we were worried by apprehensiveness regarding the heavenly bodies, by anxiety about the meaning of death, and also by our failure to understand the limitations of pain and desire.

[12. It is impossible to get rid of our anxieties about essentials if we do not understand the nature of the universe and are apprehensive about some of the theological accounts.

Hence it is impossible to enjoy our pleasures unadulterated without natural science.

[13. There is no advantage in gaining security with regard to other people if phenomena occurring above and beneath the earth—in a word, everything in the infinite universe—are objects of anxiety.

[14. The simplest means of procuring protection from other men (which is gained to a certain extent by deterrent force) is the security of quiet solitude and withdrawal from the mass of people.

[15. Nature's wealth is restricted and easily won, while that of empty convention runs on to infinity.

[16. Bad luck strikes the sophisticated man in a few cases, but reason has directed the big, essential things, and for the duration of life it is and will be the guide.

[17. The just man is the least disturbed by passion, the unjust man the most highly disturbed.

[18. Bodily pleasure is not enlarged once the pains brought on by need have been done away with; it is only diversified. And the limit of mental pleasure is established by rational reflection on pleasures themselves and those kindred emotions that once instilled extreme fear in human minds.

[19. Infinite time contains no greater pleasure than does finite time, if one determines the limits of pleasure rationally.

[20. The body takes the limits of pleasure to be infinite, and infinite time would provide such pleasure. But the mind has provided us with the complete life by a rational examination of the body's goal and limitations and by dispelling our fears about a life after death; and so we no longer need unlimited time. On the other hand, it does not avoid pleasure, nor, when conditions occasion our departure from life, does it come to the end in a manner that would suggest that it had fallen short in any way of the best possible existence.

[21. One who understands the limits of the good life knows

that what eliminates the pains brought on by need and what makes the whole of life perfect is easily obtained, so that there is no need for enterprises that entail the struggle for success.

[22. It is necessary to take into account both the actual goal of life and the whole body of clear and distinct percepts to which we refer our judgments. If we fail to do this, everything will be in disorder and confusion.

[23. If you reject all sensations, you will not have any point of reference by which to judge even the ones you claim are false.

[24. If you summarily rule out any single sensation and do not make a distinction between the element of belief that is superimposed on a percept that awaits verification and what is actually present in sensation or in the feelings or some percept of the mind itself, you will cast doubt on all other sensations by your unfounded interpretation and consequently abandon all the criteria of truth. On the other hand, in cases of interpreted data, if you accept as true those that need verification as well as those that do not, you will still be in error, since the whole question at issue in every judgment of what is true or not true will be left intact.

[25. If at any time you fail to refer each of your acts to nature's standard, and turn off instead in some other direction when making a choice to avoid or pursue, your actions will not be consistent with your creed.

[29. Some desires are (1) natural and necessary, others (2) natural but not necessary, still others (3) neither natural nor necessary but generated by senseless whims.

[26. All desires that do not lead to physical pain if not satisfied are unnecessary, and involve cravings that are easily resolved when they appear to entail harm or when the object of desire is hard to get.

[30. If interest is intense in the case of those natural desires that do not lead to physical pain when they are not satisfied, then such desires are generated by idle fancy, and it is not because of their own nature that they are not dissipated but because of the person's own senseless whims.

[27. Of all the things that wisdom provides for the happiness of the whole man, by far the most important is the acquisition of friendship.

[28. It is the same judgment that has made us feel confident that nothing fearful is of long duration or everlasting, and that has seen personal security during our limited span of life most nearly perfected by friendship.

[31. The justice that seeks nature's goal is a utilitarian pledge of men not to harm each other or be harmed.

[32. Nothing is either just or unjust in the eyes of those animals that have been unable to make agreements not to harm each other or be harmed. The same is true of those peoples who are unable or unwilling to make covenants not to harm or be harmed.

[33. Justice was never an entity in itself. It is a kind of agreement not to harm or be harmed, made when men associate with each other at any time and in communities of any size whatsoever.

[34. Injustice is not an evil in itself. Its evil lies in the anxious fear that you will not elude those who have authority to punish such misdeeds.

[35. It is impossible for a person who underhandedly breaks the agreement not to harm or be harmed to feel sure that he will escape punishment, even though he manages to do so time after time; for up to the very end of his life he cannot be sure that he will actually escape.

[36. In its general meaning, justice is the same for all because of its utility in the relations of men to each other, but in its specific application to countries and various other circumstances it does not follow that the same thing is just for all.

[37. In the case of actions that are legally regarded as just, those that are of tested utility in meeting the needs of human society have the hallmark of justice, whether they turn out to be equally just in all cases or not. On the other hand, if somebody lays down a law and it does not prove to be of advantage in human relations, then such a law no longer has the true character of justice. And even if the element of utility should undergo a change after harmonizing for a time with the conception of justice, the law was still just during that period, in the judgment of those who are not confused by meaningless words but who look at the actualities.

[38. In cases where the surrounding conditions are not new and where laws regarded as just have been shown to be inconsistent with the conception of justice in their actual workings, such laws are unjust. Again, in cases where the circumstances are new and where the same laws, once deemed to be just, are no longer serviceable, the laws in this case were just as long as they were useful to the community of citizens, but later when they were no longer useful they became unjust.

[39. The person who is the most successful in controlling the disturbing elements that come from the outside world has assimilated to himself what he could, and what he could not assimilate he has at least not alienated. Where he could not do even this, he has dissociated himself or eliminated all that it was expedient to treat in this way.

[40. All who have the capacity to gain security, especially from those who live around them, live a most agreeable life together, since they have the firm assurance of friendship; and after enjoying their comradeship to the full they do not bewail the early demise of a departed friend as if it were a pitiable thing.

LUCRETIUS

ON THE NATURE OF THINGS*

Book I

*Invocation
of Venus*

Parent of Rome, chief joy of men and gods.
Venus, the life-giver . . .
Nature's powerful ruler, without whom
Nothing that's lovely, nothing gay can come
From darksome chaos' deep and ugly womb,
Thee, now I sing of nature, I must choose
A patron to my verse—be thou my muse!
Polish my lines, while I to Memmius write,
Thy choice, thy most deserving favorite!
Inspire my breast with an unusual flame,
Sprightly as is his wit, immortal as his fame.

*Prayer for
peace*

Let war's tumultuous noise and labors cease,
Let earth and sea enjoy a quiet peace!
Peace is thy gift alone, for mighty Mars,
The only governor and god of wars,
Conquered by the wound of love, does oft resort
To taste the pleasures of the Paphian court,
Where on thy bosom he supinely lies
And greedily drinks love at both his eyes,
Till quite o'ercome, snatching an eager kiss,
He hastily goes on to greater bliss.
Then, midst his warm embraces, clasp thy arms
About his neck, and call forth all thy charms,
Caress with all thy subtle arts, become
A flatterer, and beg a peace for Rome.

For midst rough wars how can verse smoothly flow?
Or in such storms the learned laurel grow?
How can my Memmius have time to read,
Who, by his ancestors' famed glory led

* Translated by Thomas Creech, London, 1682. Revised by the editors.

To noble actions, must espouse the cause
Of his dear country's liberties and laws?

Appeal to
Memmius

And you, my Memmius, free from other cares,
Receive right reason's voice with well-purged ears,
Lest what I write and send you for your good,
Be scorned, and damned, before well understood.

The subject
of the poem

    For I shall treat of the immortal gods,
The vast and steady motions of the sky,
The rise of things—how nature joins
The various seed, and in one mass combines
The jarring principles; what new supplies
Bring nourishment and strength; how she unties
The Gordian knot, and the poor compound dies . . .
    Men long had lain oppressed with slavish fear.

Epicurus'
conquest of
religion

Religion's tyranny did domineer,
And being placed on high looked proudly down,
And frightened abject spirits with her frown.
At last a mighty man of Greece began
To claim the natural liberty of man,
By senseless terrors and vain fancies led
To slavery—straight the phantom fled!
No fables told about the deities,
Nor all the thunder of the threatening skies,
Could stop his valiant soul; through all he passed,
The strongest bonds that powerful nature cast.
The lively power of his mind prevailed,
He scaled the flaming ramparts of the world,
And crossed the endless universe in thought, to see
How things begin, what can, what cannot be,
How all must die, all yield to fatal force,
What steady limits bound their natural course.
Thus by his conquest we our right regain—
Religion he subdued, and we now reign.

The evils of
religion

    Lest you should start at these bold truths, and fly
These lines, as maxims of impiety,
Consider that religion did, and will,
Contrive, promote, and act the greatest ill;
Recall that by Diana's altar flowed

An innocent and royal virgin's blood—
Unhappy maid! with sacred ribbons bound,
Religion's pride! and holy garlands crowned
To meet an undeserved, untimely fate.
She saw her father by, whose tears did flow
In streams—the only pity he could show.
She saw the crafty priest conceal the knife
From him, blessed and prepared against her life
She saw her citizens with weeping eyes
Unwillingly attend the sacrifice,
Then, dumb with grief, her tears did pity crave;
But 'twas beyond her father's power to save . . .
She fell, though now grown ripe for bridal joy,
To bribe the gods, and buy a wind for Troy.
So died this innocent, this royal maid:
Such evil deeds religion could persuade!

The fear
of death
But still some frightful tales, some furious threats,
By poets formed, those grave and holy cheats,
May bias thee. And even I could find
A thousand stories to distract thy mind,
Invent new fears, whose horrid looks should fright,
And damp thy thoughts when eager on delight—
And reason good—but if it once appear
That after death there's neither hope nor fear,
Then men might freely triumph, then disdain
The poets' tales, and scorn their fancied pain.
But now we must submit, since pains we fear
Eternal after death, we know not where.
We know not yet the soul, how 'tis produced,
Whether with body born, or else infused,
Whether, in death breathed out into the air,
She mix confusedly with it, and perish there;
Or through vast shades and horrid silence go
To visit brimstone caves, and pools below . . .

The cure
Therefore I'll sing, to cure these needless fears,
Why sun and moon mete out the circling years,
How bodies first began, but chiefly this,
Whence comes the soul, and what her nature is,

What frights her thoughts, what cheats her eyes
When, sleeping, or diseased, she thinks she spies
Thin ghosts in various shapes about her bed
And seems to hear the voices of the dead . . .

These fears, that darkness, which o'erspreads our
souls,
The gleaming shafts of day cannot disperse—
But only insight into nature's laws.

*The first
principle:
Even the
gods can
make
nothing out
of nothing*

And now let this as the first rule be laid:
No thing was by the gods of nothing made.
From hence proceeds all our distrust and fear,
That many things in heaven and earth appear,
Whose causes far remote and hidden lie
Beyond the ken of vulgar reason's eye—
And therefore men ascribe them to the gods.
But this once proved, it gives an open way
To nature's secrets, and we walk in day.
How things are made, and how preserved we'll prove,
Without invoking any powers above.

If things can come to be from nought,
Why do not things of every kind proceed
From every thing? What use of similar seed?
Why do not birds, why fish not rise from earth?
And men and trees from water take their birth?
Why do not herds and flocks drop down from air?
Wild creatures and untamed spring everywhere?
The same tree would not rise from the same root,
The cherry would not blush in the same fruit;
Nought fixed and constant be; but every year
Whole nature change, and all things all things bear . . .
But this is false—each mean observer sees,
Things grow from certain seeds by just degrees,
And growing keep their kind. And hence we know
That things from proper matter rise and grow;
By proper matter fed, and nourished too . . .

What's more, as nothing nature can create
From nothing, so can she not annihilate,
But only into elements dissolve.

*The second
principle:
Nothing can
be reduced
to nothing*

    For could the parts of bodies die,
They suddenly would vanish from our eye,
And without force dissolving, perish all.
But now since things from seeds eternal rise
Their parts well joined and fitted, nothing dies—
Unless some force break off the natural ties.

    If all things, over which long years prevail,
Did wholly perish, and their matter fail,
How could the powers of Venus breed
A constant race of creatures to succeed?
Or how the earth eternally supply,
With constant food, each his necessity?
How could the springs and rivers flow so far
And fill a sea? How could the ether feed each star?
For whatsoe'er could into nothing waste,
That infinite space of time already passed
Had quite consumed.
But if those bodies which compose this all,
Could for so many ages past endure,
They are immortal, and from death secure,
And therefore cannot into nothing fall.

    Lastly, when father Ether kindly pours
Onto the lap of mother Earth his showers,
They seem to perish there, but soon bright crops
Arise, and various herbs and trees,
Whose trunks grow strong, and spreading branches
            shoot,
Look fresh, and green, and bend beneath their fruit.
These nourishment to man and beast provide;
Our cities fill with youth, with birds each grove,
Who sit, and sing, and in a numerous throng,
With new-fledged wings, clap, and applaud the song.
These fat our cattle that distended lie
On fertile banks, their lively young ones by,
Reveling on milk, which swollen udders yield,
In merry play they gambol o'er the field.
And therefore bodies can not fall to nought,
Since one thing still is from another brought

By provident nature, who lets nothing rise,
Nor be, except from something else that dies.

The particles   Lest you dissent, because these seeds must lie
are invisible Beyond the vision of the sharpest eye,
Know there are bodies which no eye can see,
Yet, them, from their effects, we grant to be.
For first the winds disturb the seas, and tear
The stoutest ships, and chase the clouds through air,
Sometimes through humble plains their violent course
They bend, and bear down trees with mighty force;
Sometimes they rise so high, their strength so great,
With furious storms they lofty mountains beat,
And tear the woods.
These must be bodies, though unseen they be,
Which thus disturb the earth and air and sea,
Which hardest rocks, and oaks, and all things tear,
And snatch them up in whirlings through the air . . .

The numerous odors too, whose smells delight,
And please the nose, are all too thin for sight.
We view not heat, nor sharpest colds, which wound
The tender nerves, nor can we see a sound.
Yet these are bodies, for they move the sense,
And straight sweet pleasures, or quick pains commence;
They shake the nerves. Now whatsoe'er does touch,
Or can be touched, is body, must be granted such.

Moreover, clothes hung by the surf-struck shore,
Grow damp, but by the sun are dried again;
Yet what eye saw when first the moisture came?
Or when it rose, and fled before the heat?
Therefore we must conclude, the drops have been
Dissolved to parts, too subtle to be seen.

Nay more, 'tis certain every circling year,
The rings, which grace the hands, diminish there;
Drops hollow stones; and, while we plough, the share
Grows less; the streets, from frequent treading, wear.
The brazen statues, that our gates adorn,
Show their right hands diminished much, and worn,
By touch of those that visit or pass by.

'Tis certain from all these some parts must fly,
But when those bodies part, or what they be,
A niggard nature grants not power to see . . .

    Yet bodies do not fill up every place.

Besides the For in addition, there is empty space,
primary par- The void . . .
ticles, there
is the void For were there none, no body could be moved.

Because where'er the pressing motion goes,
It still must meet with stops, still meet with foes—
'Tis natural for bodies to oppose.
So that to move would be in vain to try,
But all would fixed and still and stubborn lie,
Because no yielding body could be found,
Which first should move, and give the other ground.
But everyone now sees that things do move
With various turns, in earth, and heaven above—
Were there no void, this we'd have never seen . . .

    Though free from pores, though solid things appear,
Yet many reasons prove them to be rare.
In caverns underground the moisture creeps
Through hardest rocks, and every stone there weeps . . .
Trees grow, and at due seasons, yield their fruit,
Because the juice, drawn by the laboring root,
Does rise into the trunk, and through the branches
        shoot.
Sounds pass through well-closed rooms, and hardest
        stones,
And rigorous winter's frosts affect our bones.
This could not be, were there no empty space,
Through which these moveables might freely pass.

    Besides, why have not bodies equal weight
With those, whose figure is but just as great?
For every part of matter downwards tends,
By nature heavy, but no void descends.
Wherefore those lighter things, of equal size,
Do less of matter, more of void comprise.
But by the heavier more of seeds enjoyed—
And these convincing reasons prove a void. . . .

*The universe
consist of
matter and
of space—
and nothing
else*

I start again to weave the web of words:
All nature's made of body and of space—
That moves, and this affords the motion place.
That bodies are, we all from sense receive;
Unless we do in this believe,
On what can reason fix, on what rely,
What rule the truth of her deductions try
In greater secrets of philosophy?

Suppose no void, as former reasons prove,
No body could enjoy a place, or move:
Besides these two, there is no third degree,
Distinct from both, nought that has power to be.
For if 'tis tangible, and has a place,
'Tis body; if intangible, 'tis space.

Besides, whatever is, a power must own,
Either to act, or to be acted on;
Or be a place, in which such things are done.
Now only bodies suffer and act; and place
Is the peculiar gift of empty space—
And thus a different third in vain is sought,
And never can be found by sense or thought.

For whatsoever else may seem to be
Is but the accident or property of these.
. . . We call those properties,
Which never part, except the subject dies.
So weight to stones, so moisture to the sea,
So touch to body is, and to be free
From touching is to void. But peace and wealth,
War, concord, slavery, liberty and health,
Whose presence, or whose absence nor prevents,
Nor brings the subjects ruin, are accidents.

Time of itself is nothing, but from thought
Receives its rise, by laboring fancy wrought
From things considered, while we think on some
As present, some as past, and some to come.
No thought can think on time, that's still confessed,
But thinks on things in motion or at rest . . .

The principles of things no force can break;

*The primary
particles are
indestructi-
ble*

They are too solid, and all strokes too weak.
Though such can hardly be believed, for voice,
Or thunder's sound, or every louder noise
Breaks through our walls, which yet remain intact;
So iron glows, and rocks dissolve in fire,
Strong flames divide the stubborn gold, and brass,
And to a liquid substance break the mass.
This sense perceives: you hold a silver cup,
And pour some water gently in at top,
The imprisoned heat, or cold, straight break their bands,
Grow fierce, fly through and warm or chill the hands.
These instances are strong, they seem to show,
That beings, in their vast extent, contain
No perfect solids—creatures of the brain!
But yet attend my muse; she sweetly sings,
And proves that things from perfect solids rose.

Two sorts of beings reason's eye discerned
And proved before, their difference very great—
Body and void, which never could agree
In any one essential property.
For body, as 'tis matter, is from place
Distinct; and void from body, as 'tis space.
Both these distinct subsist. And thus 'tis proved,
That seeds are solid, and from space removed . . .

So grant no void, no spaces unpossessed,
Then all would solid be, and all at rest.
And grant no solids, which fill up the place
That they possess, all would be empty space.
And thus seeds, mixed with void, compose the whole,
Nor is all empty space, nor is all full . . .

These principles no active flame,
No subtle cold can pierce, and break their frame,
Though every compound yields, no powerful blow,
No driving wedge divide, or break in two.
For nothing can be struck, no part destroyed
By powerful blows, or cleft without a void,
And things that hold most void, when strokes do press,
Or subtle wedges enter, yield with ease.

If seeds then solid are, they must endure
Eternally, from force, from stroke secure . . .
   Besides, since things have time for life and growth
Prefixed, and certain terms are set for both,
Since bounds are placed, o'er which they cannot go,
And laws speak what they can and cannot do,
And things change not—so all the kinds that fly,
Are clothed with plumes of the same curious dye—
The matter must be firm, the seeds must be
Unchangeable, from alteration free.
For grant the seeds may change, we could not know,
What things would be produced, or when, or how;
How great their power would rise, how far extend,
How long they'd live, or when their actions end.
Nor should we find the same delights pursued;
Nor parents' natures in their young renewed . . .

The infinity   The all is every way immensely wide,
of the   Or else it would have bounds on every side.
universe   Now what can be a bound, but that which lies
Beyond the body whose extreme it is?
That nought's beyond the all, even common sense
Declares; therefore the all must be immense.
Thus stand in any quarter of the space,
That's nothing—'tis immense from every place.
   But grant it finite—
Suppose a man on the extremest part,
Suppose him stand and strive to throw a dart,
The dart would forward fly, or, hindered stay.
Choose which you will, the reason's good each way,
And firm; for if some farther space admit,
Or some resistance stop its hasty flight,
That's not the end. So place the utmost part
Where'er you will, I'll follow with the dart,
And by this single argument destroy
Those feigned extremes and bounds you set to space . . .
   But to proceed—
Suppose the all had bounds, suppose an end,
Then bodies, which by nature must descend,

And from eternity pursued the race,
Had long ere this time reached the lowest place,
Whence nothing could in decent order rise.
There could not be a glittering sun or skies,
For all the seeds must lie confusedly mixed,
In a vast chaos, immoveable, and fixed.
But now the seeds still move, because the space
Is boundless, and admits no lowest place,
No end, which heavy seeds, by nature pressed
Might seek below, and settle there, and rest . . .
    Again, nature's eternal laws provide,
The sum of things should be immensely wide,
Boundless and infinite, because they place
Body as bound to void, to body space,
By mutual bounding making both immense.
For did they not each other bound, but one
Were infinite, for instance, space alone,
Nor man, nor earth, nor heaven, nor could the sea,
Nor bodies of the gods one moment be.
For seeds of things, their union all destroyed,
Would fly dissolved, and scattered, through the void,
Or rather into things had ne'er combined,
Because once parted, they had never joined.

No design
in the order
of things

    For sure unthinking seeds did ne'er dispose
Themselves by counsel, nor their order chose,
Nor any compacts made how each should move,
But buffeted by blows throughout all time,
Variously moved and turned, until at last,
Most sorts of motion and of union passed,
By chance into that order hurled,
Which frames the beings that compose the world.
And these same seeds, now orderly maintained,
In the convenient motions they have gained,
Is a sufficient cause why fertile earth,
By sun-beams quickened, gives new fruits their birth;
Why rivers still the greedy deep supply,
Why beasts increase, why sun and moon ne'er die.
Which could not be, unless supplies still came

From the vast mass, and propped the sinking frame.
    As beasts, deprived of food, so things must die,
As soon as matter fails of just supply . . .

*The
universe has
no center*
    But scorn their dreams, who fondly can believe,
And teach, that all things to the middle strive,
And by that natural pressure this whole frame
Might be maintained, its order still the same,
Without external impulse; high and low
Would always be as firmly joined as now,
And their own site, their different place possess,
Since all unto one common center press.
They further teach that ponderous weights below
Unto their resting places upwards go,
And as our shadows in smooth streams appear,
So feet to feet some animals walk there,
Yet can no sooner fall into those skies,
That lie beneath, than we to heaven can rise.
When Phoebus climbs their east, the feeble light
Of stars peeps forth, and beautifies our night.

    But this fantastic dream, this fancy springs
From ignorance of the principles of things.
For since the void is infinite, the space
Immense, how can there be a middle place?
Or grant there were—
Why may not bodies end their tedious race,
And stop as well in any other place,
As there? For every part of empty space,
In midst, or not, must equally allow
To ponderous movements easy passage through.
For there's no place, to which by nature pressed,
Seeds lose their force of weight, and freely rest.
Nor empty space can prop the seeds, nor stay
Their motion; 'tis its nature to give way.
In bodies then there lies no fond desire
To seek the midst, which keeps this frame entire . . .

    This learned, 'tis no uneasy task to know
The rest. I'll lead thee on, and clearly show
The pride of nature, and philosophy,

Her greatest works, and please thy curious eye.
The walk is pleasant, 'tis an easy way,
All bright and clear; for things will things betray
By mutual light, and we from one thing known
To hidden truths successfully go on.

Book II

'Tis pleasant, when the seas are rough, to stand
And view another's danger, safe on land;
Not 'cause he's troubled, but 'tis sweet to see
Those cares and fears, from which our selves are free.
'Tis also pleasant to behold from far
How troops engage, secure ourselves from war.
But nothing's sweeter than to dwell serene,
Raised by the teachings of the wise to heights
Whence we may view deep, wondrous deep below,
How poor mistaken mortals wandering go,
Seeking the path to happiness. Some aim
At learning, wit, nobility, or fame.
Others with cares and dangers vex each hour
To reach the top of wealth, and sovereign power.
Blind wretched man! In what dark paths of strife
We walk this little journey of our life!
While frugal nature seeks for only ease,
A body free from pains, a mind at peace.

And little too is needful to maintain
The body sound in health, and free from pain—
Not delicates, but such as may supply
Contended nature's thrifty luxury.
She asks no more. What though no boys of gold
Adorn the walls, and fiery torches hold,
Whose beauteous rays, scattering their gaudy light,
May grace the feasts, and revels of the night.
What though no gold adorns, no music's sound
With doubled sweetness from the roofs rebounds—
Yet underneath a loving myrtle's shade,
Nearby a swirling stream supinely lain,

When spring with fragrant flowers the earth has spread,
And sweetest roses grow around our head,
Envied by wealth and power, with small expense
We may enjoy the sweet delights of sense.
Who ever heard a fever tamer grown
In clothes embroidered o'er and beds of down,
Than in coarse rags? Since then such toys as these

The vanity Contribute nothing to the body's ease,
of wealth As honor, wealth, and nobleness of blood,
and rank 'Tis plain they likewise do the mind no good.

If when thy fierce embattled troops at land
Mock-fights maintain, or when thy navies stand
In graceful ranks, or sweep the yielding seas,
If then before such martial sights as these,
Disperse not all black jealousies and cares,
Vain dread of death, and superstitious fears
Not leave thy mind, but if all this be vain,
If the same cares, and dread, and fears remain,
If traitor-like they seize thee on the throne,
And dance within the circle of a crown,
If noise of arms, nor darts can make them fly,
Nor the gay sparklings of the purple dye,
If they on emperors will rudely seize,
What makes us value all such things as these,
But folly, and dark ignorance of happiness?
For we, as boys at night, by day do fear
Shadows as vain and senseless as those are.
Wherefore that darkness, which o'erspreads our souls,
The gleaming shafts of day cannot disperse
But only insight into nature's laws . . .

Things are 'Tis certain now no seed to seed adheres
always Unmoved, and fixed; for every thing appears
either Worn out, and wasted by devouring years,
growing or Still wasting, still it vanishes away,
decaying And yet the mass of things feels no decay.
For when the bodies part, those things grow less,
And old; but they to which they join
Do flourish and increase.

So things by turns increase, by turns decay,
Like racers, bear the torch of life, and live,
And their race done, their light to others give.

The atoms   But if you think the seeds can rest and make
move   A change by rest, how great is the mistake?
constantly   For since they through the boundless vacuum rove,
By their own weight, or other's stroke they move.
For when they meet and strike, that furious play
Makes each of them rebound a different way,
For both are perfect solids, and nought lies
Behind, to stop their motion as they rise.

But that you may conceive how thus they move,
Consider, that my former reasons prove,
That seeds seek not the midst, and that the space
Is infinite, and knows no lowest place;
And therefore seeds can never end their race,
But always move, and in a various round.

Some, when they meet, and rudely strike, rebound
To a great distance; others, when they jar,
Will part too, and rebound, but not so far
Now these small seeds that are more closely joined,
And tremble, in a little space confined,
Stopped by their mutual twinings, stones compose,
Iron, or steel, or bodies like to those;
But those, that swim in a wide void alone,
And make their quick and large rebounds, or run
Through a large space, compose the air and sun.

Besides these two, there is another kind:
Bodies from union free, and unconfined,
With others ne'er in friendly motion joined.
For look where'er the glittering sunbeams come
Through narrow chinks, into a darkened room.
A thousand little bodies straight appear
In the small streams of light, and wander there,
Forever fight, reject all shows of peace,
Now meet, now part again, and never cease.
Hence we may judge how atoms always toss
Through the vast empty space . . .

The atoms
move faster
than light

And yet how swift the atoms' motions are,
This following instance will in short declare,
For when the morning climbs the eastern skies,
And bright-hued birds salute her early rise,
In every grove and wood with joy appear,
And fill with liquid notes the yielding air,
How swift the beams of the rising sun
Shoot forth! Their race is finished when begun.
From heaven to earth they take their hasty flight,
And gild the distant globe with brilliant light.
But this thin vapor and this glittering ray,
Through a mere void, make not their easy way,
But with much trouble force a passage through
Resisting air, and therefore move more slow.
Nor are they seeds, but little bodies joined,
And adverse motions in small space confined,
And therefore from without resisting force,
And inbred jars must stop their eager course.
But solid seeds, that move through empty space,
And all whose parts do seek one common place,
Whom nothing from without resists, than light
And beams more swift, must make their hasty flight,
And in that time a larger distance fly,
While the sun's lazy beams creep through our sky . . .

The natural
movement
of things is
downward

And this I think a proper place to prove,
That nothing of itself can upward move,
Lest when you see the ambitious flame aspire,
You think its natural force bears up the fire.
For every tree does rear its lofty head,
Each tender ear and shrub does upward spread,
And all draw up their nourishment from below,
But yet all weights by nature downward go.
So when the fire to houses' roofs leaps up
And swift flames waste the upper beams,
'Tis some force drives them up. So from a wound
Our blood shoots forth, and sprinkles all around,
Again who sees not that a quiet stream
Throws back with mighty force the immersed beam?

For when we strive, in deeper streams, to drown,
And scarce with all our force can press it down,
The waves, with double vigor throw it up,
And make it strongly leap above the top.
And yet who doubts all these would downward tend,
When placed in void, and naturally descend?
So rising flames by air are upwards borne,
Although their natural weights press a return.
Besides, we all behold, how every night
The falling meteors draw long trains of light.
Wherever nature yields a passage through,
We see stars fall, and seek them here below . . .

The atoms sometimes swerve slightly— otherwise they would never meet

    Now seeds in downward motion must depart,
At random times and places from their course.
For did they still move straight, they needs must fall,
Like drops of rain, dissolved and scattered all,
For ever tumbling through the mighty space,
And never join to make one single mass.
If anyone believes, the heavier seed
By faster motions can the lighter catch,
Whence things may rise, how great is the mistake!
It's true, when weights descend through yielding air,
Or streams, the swiftness of the fall must bear
Proportion to the weights—and reason good—
Because the fleeting air, and yielding flood
With equal strength resist not every course,
But sooner yield unto the greater force.
But now no void can stop, no space can stay
The seeds, for 'tis its nature to give way.
Therefore through void unequal weights must be
Like swift in motion, all of like degree . . .
    'Tis certain then and plain, that seeds decline,
Though very little from the straightest line.
But not obliquely move—that fond pretense
Would fight all reason, nay, and common sense.
For everybody sees, a falling weight
Makes its descent by lines direct and straight.
    Besides, did all things move in a straight line,

Nor would there be freedom of the will

Did still one motion to another join
In certain order, and no seeds decline,
And make a motion fit to dissipate
The well-wrought chain of causes, and strong fate,
Whence comes this perfect freedom of the mind?
Whence comes the will so free and unconfined,
Above the power of fate, by which we go
Where'er we please, and what we will we do?
In each of us the will moves first, and then
The motion to the limbs will spread.
For look, and see, when first the barrier's down,
The horse, though eager, cannot start so soon
As his own mind requires; his matter must be roused,
And stirred throughout the limbs, then fitly joined,
Obey the eager motions of his mind.
This proves these motions rise within the heart,
Beginning by the will, then run through every part.
    But now it's otherwise, when it's begun
From force. For then our limbs are hurried on
By violent strokes, no power of our own,
Until the will, by her own natural sway,
Shall check, or turn the force another way.
Wherefore it's plain, though force may drive us on,
And make us move our limbs and make us run,
Yet something lies within, that can oppose
The violent stroke, and still resist the blows,
At whose command the mass of matter flies,
And bends through all our limbs, our arms, our thighs—
And checked again, and all the vigor dies . . .

Conservation of motion

    Nor was this mass of matter, the whole frame,
Ever more loosely or more closely packed,
For it can never fail or greater grow.
Wherefore the seeds still move, just as before,
And ever the like motions will maintain . . .
Nor is there any force can change this all,
For there's no place from which strange seeds may fall,
And make disturbance here. No space does lie
Beyond the whole, to which the seeds may fly,

And leave the mighty all to waste and die.

Though
bodies seem
at rest,
their
elements are
in motion

    'Tis nothing strange that every mass
Seems quiet, and at rest, and keeps its place,
Though every little part moves here and there,
For since the principles are too minute
For sight, their motion too must disappear.
Nay, objects fit for sense, which distant lie,
Conceal their motions too, and cheat our eye.
For often on a distant hill the fleecy sheep
O'er flowery pastures graze, wherever grass,
Crowned with fresh dew, may tempt their appetite.
The lambs, their bellies full, with various turns,
Play o'er the field, and try their tender horns.
Yet all these seem confused, at distance seen,
And like a steady white, spread o'er the green.

The variety
of atomic
shapes

    Now learn what manner of things first bodies are,
What different figures, shapes, and forms they bear.
For though the shape to many is the same,
Yet all agree not in one common frame.
Nor is this strange, or to be wondered at.
For since the numbers are so vastly great,
And know no bound, nor end, it cannot be,
That all in the same figures should agree.

    Besides, consider men, or silent fish
That cut the yielding seas, or birds,
That fill with joyous sounds the listening woods.
Consider each particular, you'll find
How different shapes appear in every kind.

    Else how could dams their tender young, or how
The newborn young their distant mothers know,
Which all perform as well as men can do?
For often when a slaughtered heifer dies,
To angry gods a blameless sacrifice,
And on the incense-smoking altars pours
Hot blood in streams from her young breast,
Her dam roams o'er the fields in wild despair,
And wounds with loud laments the tender air.
Now here, now there will run, and still complain,

Now leaves her stall, and then returns again.
Mad for her young, she every field does scan,
With passionate eyes she visits every place.
No streams, no flowers, her former great delight,
Can raise or quicken her dead appetite,
Allay her grief, divert her pining care.
And though the shapes of other calves appear,
She looks on none, or with a slighting eye.
So plain it is, she looks for something known,
And viewed before; she only seeks her own . . .
And therefore seeds, since they from nature came,
Not made by art, after one common frame,
Must not be all alike, their shapes the same.

Phenomena   And hence a reason's seen why lightning flies
explained   With keener force, through stones, through parted
by these   skies,
differences
Than those blunt flames, which from our torches rise.
Because its little parts, more loosely joined,
More minute far, an easy passage find
Through such small pores, as stop the blunter flame,
Which parts of heavy oil, or timber frame.

Through horn the sunbeams pass, and strike our eye,
But water on the surface stays—and why?
Because the parts of light are less than those
That make up water, and dull streams compose.

So through the strainer wines with ease will flow,
But heavy oil stops, or runs more slow.
The reason's this: it is of parts combined,
Far greater, or more hooked and closely twined,
Which therefore cannot be disjoined as soon,
And through each little passage singly run.

And then the taste of honey or of milk
Is pleasant when these liquids touch the tongue.
When rue, or wormwood's touched, flies every grace,
And violent distortions screw the face.
Whence you may easily guess those round and smooth,
That with delightful touch affect the mouth.
But those which we more rough or bitter find,

Are made of parts more hooked and sharp,
That force a passage through the injured skin.
  In short, what things are good for sense, what bad,
Of seeds of different shape and size are made.
Nor must you fancy bodies that compose
The harsher sounds of saws, as smooth as those,
When gentle strokes the sleeping strings awake.
  Those seeds have different figures, form, and size,
That from all rotting carcasses arise,
From those that new-pressed saffron yields, or rear
From incensed altars, sweetening all the air.
  And so in colors too, that bright-hued dye
That pleases and delights the human eye,
A different form, and shape, and figure bears
From that which wounds the sense and forces tears,
Or mean and ugly to the sight appears.
For seeds of all that please the sense are smooth;
Of all that hurt, are rough, or hooked, or both . . .
  Further, what things seem hard and thick, are joined
Of parts more hooked and firm, and closely twined,
As iron, flints, brass, steel, and diamonds,
Gems free from power of stroke, secure from wounds.
But fluids are composed of smooth and round,
For their small parts, by no strong union bound,
Are very easily disjoined, and move
Now here, now there, at every little shove . . .

The atoms   Now further learn, what I with toil and pain,
are   With many a careful thought, and laboring brain,
colorless   Have sought to teach thee, lest thou shouldst mistake,
And think the seeds of black composures, black,
Of white things, white, or other bodies wear
Those different colors that their atoms bear.
For seeds are colorless, without a dye . . .
  Now if you think such seeds are things unfit
To be conceived, how foolish the conceit!
For men born blind, whose natural night
Was never scattered by one beam of light,
Know things by touch—he's foolish that denies

That any notices of things can rise,
Unless from colors, entering at our eyes.
For in the dark we feel, and form from thence
Some images, yet then no colors strike our sense . . .
    But this position stronger reasons show,
For seeds of things ne'er change, though colors do.
For somewhat must survive each change, and be
Essentially immutable and free,
Lest all should sink to nought.
For what is changed from what it was, that dies.
Then either grant seeds colorless,
Or grant annihilation true.
    Though seeds are colorless, and free from dyes,
They're formed of different figures, whence arise
The numerous colors, gay varieties.
And since, as we discoursed before, we find
It matters much with what first seeds are joined,
What figure, what position they maintain,
What motions give, and what receive again,
'Tis straight resolved why things as black as night
Can change so soon, and put on virgin white,
As in the sea, when the mad ocean raves,
And white curls rise upon the foaming waves.
For thus it is, that which seemed black before,
By losing little parts, or taking more,
Their number, motion, order or position
Changed, from black are turned to white.
But if the sea were tinged with natural sky,
What force, what art could make it change the dye?
    Besides, since colors are alone by day,
And owe their beings to the glittering ray,
But seeds of things do not exist alone
By day, 'tis plain that they are tinged with none.
For how can colors be in darkest night,
Since they all change, and vary with the light,
According as the ray's oblique or right.
So plumes that go around the pigeon's head,
Sometimes look brisker, with a deeper red;

And then in different position seen,
Show a gay sky, all intermixed with green . . .
    And since the eyes a different stroke receive
From white, from that which black, or others give,
And since it matters not what color's worn
By things we touch, but what fit shapes are borne,
We easily infer seeds want no dyes.
Those the variety of shapes supplies,
And thence those different sorts of touch may rise . . .
    Again, break anything, we find at last
The less the parts, the more the colors waste.
The rich-hued robe, in pieces torn,
Its color's lost; the parts unheeded lie
Nor with their tempting purple court our eye.
Which shows that bodies are from colors freed,
Before they come to be as small as seed . . .

The atoms are without smell, taste, sound, heat or cold

    Besides, not only color is not found
In seeds, but neither smell, nor taste, nor sound.
They no brisk odors in effluvia send,
Either to please the nose, or to offend . . .
The seeds on compound bodies ne'er bestow
Their sound, their taste or smell—for they have none,
No proper sound, or odor of their own,
Nor heat, nor cold, nor any quality.
For those are subject to all to change, and die . . .

Nor do the seeds have feeling

    Now further, those composures that perceive,
Ennobled all with various sense, derive
Their beings from insensibles, and live . . .
For look what numerous swarms of worms and flies
From putrid and fermenting clods arise,
When rain descends to drench the ground.
    Besides, leaves, water, grass do make up beast,
And man too feeds on beasts, and is increased;
Their flesh is turned to ours; and so again
The birds and beasts increase by eating men.
All these things prove, that any sort of food
Nature can easily turn to flesh and blood . . .
And hence, as we discoursed before, we find

It matters much with what first seeds are joined,
What site, and what position they maintain,
What motions give, and what receive again.
    But what confirms, what prompts thee to believe,
That things, endowed with sense, can ne'er derive
Their beings from insensibles, and live?
Perchance, as common observation shows,
Because earth, stone, wood, various things compose;
And yet there's neither life, nor sense in those.
But here you must consider, neither I,
Nor any master of philosophy
Affirm, that every being may commence
A sensible, and show the acts of sense,
But that those seeds, whence sensibles arise,
Must all have a convenient shape and size,
Position, motion, order. Now not one
Of these appears in earth, or wood, or stone,
Yet these fermented by a timely rain,
Grow fruitful, and produce a numerous train
Of worms, because the little bodies leave
Their former site and union, and receive
New motion, into new position fall,
And order, fit to make an animal . . .

The earth is the mother of all

    Lastly, we all from seed celestial rise,
Which heaven, our common parent, still supplies.
From him the earth receives enlivening rain,
And straight she bears bird, tree, and beast, and man,
And proper food for all, by which they thrive,
Grow strong, and propagate their race, and live;
Thence justly all the name of mother give.
And so each part returns, when bodies die;
What came from earth to earth; what from the sky
Dropped down, ascends again, and mounts on high.
For death does not destroy, but disunites the seeds,
Then makes new combinations, whence arise
In bodies all those great varieties . . .
    Now I have proved before, this mighty space
Is infinite, and knows no lowest place,

Other
worlds
besides ours
must exist

Nor uppermost; no bounds this all control,
For that's against the nature of the whole.
    Through this vast space since seeds then always
        moved
With various turns, from time eternal strove,
Who can imagine there should only rise
Our single earth, our air, and but our skies,
While all the other matter scattered lies?
Especially, since these from chance arose,
When the unthinking seeds, by various blows,
Now this, now that way moved, at last were hurled,
Into the decent order of this world,
And made fit combinations; whence began
The earth, the heaven, sea, and beast, and man.
Thus then it's proved, and certain, that elsewhere,
The busy atoms join, as well as here.
Such earths, such seas, such men, such beasts arise,
All like to those surrounded by our skies.
    When there exists no hindering cause, and place
And seed enough exist—by nature's laws
Things must be made. Now if the seed surmount
The utmost stretch of numbers' vast account,
And the same nature can compose a mass,
As much in this, as any other place,
It plainly follows, that there must arise
Distinct and numerous worlds, earths, men, and skies,
In places distant, and remote from this . . .

Book III

Praise of
Epicurus

    Thee, who hast light from midst thick darkness
        brought,
And first life's benefits and pleasures taught,
Thee, chiefest glory of the Grecian state,
I follow close, willing to imitate,
Not contradict. For how can larks oppose
The vigorous swan? They are unequal foes.
How can unsteady colts, with feeble force,

Contend in racing with the noble horse?
Thou, parent of philosophy, hast shown
The way to truth by precepts of thy own.
For as in flowery glades, the laboring bee
Extracts her precious sweets, great soul!
We on thy golden sentences do feed,
Golden, and fit eternally to live.
For when I hear thy mighty reasons prove,
This world was made without the powers above,
All fears and terrors waste, and fly apace.
Through parted heavens, I see the mighty space,
The rise of things, the gods, their happy seats,
Which storm or violent tempest never beats,
Nor snow invades, but with the purest air,
And brilliant light diffused, look gay and fair.
There bounteous nature makes supplies for ease,
There minds enjoy uninterrupted peace.
But that which senseless we so grossly fear,
No hell, no sulphurous lakes, no pools appear.
And through the earth I can distinctly view,
What underneath the busy atoms do.
From thoughts like these, I mighty pleasure find,
And silently admire thy strength of mind,
By whose one single force, to curious eyes,
All naked and exposed whole nature lies.

Only Epicurean-ism frees men of the fear of death

Since then I've taught what seeds of bodies are,
And how they move, what different shapes they wear,
And how from these all beings first may spring,
Next of the mind, and of the soul I'll sing,
And chase that dread of hell, those idle fears,
That spoil our lives with jealousies and cares,
Disturb our joys with dread of pains beneath,
And sully them with the black fear of death.

For though some say they should less fear to die,
Than live in a disease, or infamy;
That they know well, the soul consists in blood,
And our philosophy can do no good;
Observe, they talk this way from love

Of empty praise, not from conviction.
For these same men, to chains or banishment
Condemned, to galley or to prison sent,
Though infamous by horrid crimes they're grown,
Yet still endure, and patiently live on.
Nay, more, where'er these boasting wretches come,
They sacrifice black sheep on every tomb,
To please the spirits, and of all the mob,
When cares and dangers press, grow most devout.

Therefore, to know men's souls, and what they are,
View them beset with dangers, and with care.
For then their words will with their thoughts agree,
And all the mask pulled off, show what they be.

The mind is   First, then, the mind, in which the reason lies,
a part of   Is part of man, as hands, and feet, and eyes
man   Are parts of animals . . .
. . . our lives not equally depend,
For their first rise, continuance, and end,
On every part, but chiefly heat and air
Make life within us, and preserve it there.
Then both these two are there, but swiftly gone,
And leave our limbs, as treacherous death comes on . . .

The relation   Next, then, I must affirm the soul and mind
of soul and   Make up one single nature, closely joined.
mind   But yet the mind's the head, and ruling part,
Called reason, and is seated in the heart.
For there our passions live, our joy, our fear,
And hope; which proves the mind must needs be there.
But the inferior part, the soul, confined
To all the limbs, obeys the ruling mind,
And moves as that directs. For only that
Can of itself rejoice, or fear, or hate,
Passion and thought belong to that alone,
For soul and limbs are capable of none.
As when the hand, or eye, or head complains,
Not all the body then is vexed with pains,
So often, while the laboring mind, oppressed,
Sinks under cares, the soul enjoys her rest.

But when the mind a violent passion shakes,
Of that disturbance too the soul partakes.
Cold sweats bedew the limbs, the face looks pale,
The tongue begins to falter, speech to fail,
The ears are filled with noise, the eyes grow dim,
And feeble shakings seize on every limb.
And thus, on sudden frights men often swoon,
A strange effect! from which 'tis plainly known,
The mind and soul are joined, and make but one.
For here the mind's force strikes the soul, and so
The stroke goes on, and strikes the body too.

The mind and soul are material   But, to enlarge this instance more, this proves
The mind material too, because it moves
And shakes the limbs, makes them look pale and wan—
In short, directs and governs the whole man.
These things are done by touch, and all that touch
Are bodies; therefore mind and soul are such.

You find the spirit and the body share
Both pain and pleasure by their mutual ties.
For when the weapon's force cuts through our flesh
Though present death does not attend the wound,
Yet chilling damps the sickening soul surround;
Drooping, we falter to the ground,
Doubtful to take our flight, or lag behind.
That soul is kindred with the body's plain,
Since by corporeal blows it suffers pain.

Mind and soul atoms are very small   The mind proved body, I'll go on to find,
What kind of body 'tis, that makes the mind.
First then, it is a very minute sort,
Because no action is so swiftly done,
As what the mind begins. This instance proves,
The mind, than other things, more swiftly moves ...

Now since the nature of the mind is found
So apt to move, of bodies small and round
It must be framed ...
How minute all its parts! How small a space,
If crushed together, it would all take up!
For when the stroke of fate invades the heart,

And the affrighted mind and soul depart,
The weight and bulk remain. Contented death
Leaves all secure, but vital sense and breath.
Therefore the seeds that frame this soul,
Through all our limbs diffused, are thin and small,
Because when that's all gone, each limb retains
The former bulk, the former weight remains.
So when the flavor of the wine is gone,
And perfume's fragrance has combined with air,
The body weighs the same, the same bulk shows,
Because small seeds all taste, all smells compose . . .

The soul is a composite of breath, heat, air and a fourth substance

    The soul's not simple—when life's powers decay,
A thinnish breath, with heat commingled, flies away
This vapor likewise shows that air is there,
All heat has air; for heat, by nature rare,
Must still be intermixed with parts of air.

    Well then, we know the mind and soul comprise
Three things; yet from all these no sense can rise,
No vigorous thought from such a frame as this.
Then we must add a fourth thing to this frame.
And yet that fourth, though something, has no name.
Its parts are smooth, and small, and apt to move
When pressed, or troubled by the weakest shove.
From this comes sense. This the first stroke receives,
And then the impulse to the heat it gives,
Then to the unseen wind, then to the air,
Thence through our limbs 'tis scattered everywhere.
The blood, with troubled motion, strikes the heart,
And a quick sense runs through each inward part,
Then through the marrow, then through every bone . . .

The union of soul and body is the cause of life

    This nature through the limbs spreads everywhere,
And life and health preserves with provident care.
For they are joined, and each on each depends,
And for the least separation death attends . . .
Nor can the soul and body, separate,
Perceive or think in their divided state,
For the first stroke is by the nerves conveyed,
And from their common motions sense is made . . .

. . . The seeds of souls are less than those
Which all the bodies' grosser parts compose,
Neither in number, nor in bulk so great,
And over the limbs in distant spaces set,
As far apart as are the smallest seeds
That sense can start.
For often falling dust we scarce perceive,
Nor dew by night, nor what the spiders weave,
When o'er our limbs the flimsy chains are spread,
Or the decaying web falls over our head . . .

The mind is   The mind's the chiefest part of all the whole.
more   Life more depends on that, than on the soul,
essential to   When that departs, no soul can longer stay,
life than   But servilely attends, and flies away,
the soul   And leaves the limbs in the cold hands of death.
But he still lives, whose mind remains alone,
Though limbs are mangled and the soul is gone.
So let ingenious tyrants' malice strive,
Of many limbs, though not of all, deprive,
And so divide the soul, the man will live . . .

Mind and   And now, my lovely youth, to let thee know,
soul are   That souls and minds are born, and mortal too,
mortal   I'll write such verse, as shall appear to be
By curious labor wrought, and worthy thee.
Do you take both expressed by either name,
Both words in this dispute shall mean the same.
So that, for instance, when the soul you find
Proved mortal, think I likewise mean the mind,
Since both do make but one, two natures joined.

First then, since I have proved the soul consists
Of smaller parts than water, smoke, or mists . . .
And since you see, that when the vessel's broke,
The water runs away, since the thin smoke,
By every tempest scattered through the air,
Will mix with it, and perish there—
Conclude the thin contexture of the mind
An easy prey to every little breeze,
With ease dissolved when from the body gone

'Tis tossed in air, all naked, and alone.
For since the limbs, that vessel of the soul,
Could not contain its parts and keep it whole,
When bruised or drained of blood, how then can air,
A body than our flesh and blood more rare?

    Besides, 'tis plain that souls are born, and grow,
And all by age decay, as bodies do.
To prove this truth—in infants, minds appear
Infirm, and tender as their bodies are;
In man, the mind is strong; when age prevails,
And the quick vigor of each member fails,
The powers of the mind decrease, and waste apace,
And grave and reverend folly takes the place.
'Tis likely then the soul and mind must die,
Like smoke in air, its scattered atoms fly.

    Further, as violent pains, and strong disease
Torment the limbs, and all the body seize,
So grief and trouble mind and soul surprise.
'Tis likely, therefore, that the soul too dies.
Sometimes, when violent fevers vex the brain,
The mind grows mad, and raves with equal pain.
Sometimes, when dull and death-like lethargy,
And lasting sleep sits heavy on the eye,
The soul is lulled; the man nor knows, nor hears
His friends' kind voice, nor sees their falling tears,
While they with pious care about him weep,
And strive to rouse him from his death of sleep.
Since then corporeal disease affects the mind,
That must be mortal too.

    Besides, when wine's quick force has pierced the brain,
And the brisk heat's diffused through every vein,
Why do the members all grow dull and weak?
The eye-balls swim? The legs not firm and straight,
But bend beneath the body's natural weight?
Unmanly quarrels, noise, and sobs deface
The powers of reason, and usurp their place.
How could this be, did not wine's violence
Affect the mind itself, and spoil its use?

Now things that can be thus disturbed
Would die, if but the force, or strokes, increase . . .
    And since our minds as well as bodies feel
The powers of medicines that change or heal,
They must be mortal. For to change the soul,
You either change the order of the whole,
Take off some old, or add some parts anew.
Now what's immortal, common sense has told,
Can gain not one new part, nor lose one old.
For whatsoever suffers change, unties
Its union, is not what it was, but dies.
The mind, then, either by diseases grieved,
Or by the power of medicines relieved,
Shows herself mortal . . .
    And if the soul's immortal, if she lives
Divided from the body, if perceives,
She must enjoy five senses still; for who
Can fancy how the soul can live below,
Unless 'tis thus endowed? Thus painters please,
And poets too, to draw their souls with these.
But as without the soul, nor eye, nor ear,
Nor either hand can touch, or see, or hear,
So neither can this soul, this mind perceive
Without these hands, these eyes, these ears—nor live.
    Besides, our vital sense is spread o'er all;
The whole composure makes one animal.
So that if sudden violent strokes divide
This whole, and cast the parts on either side,
The soul and mind too suffer the same fate,
And part remains in this, and part in that.
Now what can be divided, what can lie,
And waste in several parts, can likewise die.
So chariots armed on every side to wound,
When fiercely driven, bring death to all around.
And yet the wounded man, so quick's the blow,
Is scarce disturbed, scarce seems to feel, or know
His wound; and now but half a body grown,
Still hastes to fight, still eagerly goes on;

Nor misses he his arm, dragged o'er the field,
And by the chariots torn, much less his shield . . .
Others, their legs lopped off, attempt to rise,
While the poor foot lies trembling by and dies . . .
    Were souls immortal, and never begun,
But crept into the limbs to make up man,
Why cannot they remember what was done
In former times? Why all their memory gone?
Now if the mind's frail powers so far can waste,
As to forget those numerous actions past,
'Tis almost dead, and sure can die at last.
Therefore the former soul must needs be dead;
And that, which now informs us, newly made.
    But when the body's made, when we begin
To view the light, if then the soul crept in,
How is it likely it should seem to grow,
Increase, and flourish, as the members do?
No—she would live confined to her close cage,
With powers, as great in infancy, as age.
Again then and again, the soul is born and dies.
For let's suppose it framed without—what ties
Could knit this soul so close? How could this mind,
As sense assures, with every limb be twined?
For now 'tis knit to every nerve, and vein,
To every bone, that even the teeth feel pain . . .

Death should have no terror

    Then what has death to frighten man,
Since souls can die, as well as bodies can?
For as we neither knew, nor felt those harms,
When dreadful Carthage frightened Rome with arms,
And all the world was shook with fierce alarms,
While undecided yet, which part should fall,
Which nation rise the glorious lord of all,
So after death, when we shall be no more,
What though the seas forsake their usual shore,
And rise to heaven? What though the stars desert the
    sky?
How can all this disturb our perished sense? . . .
Nay, grant the scattered ashes of our urn

Be joined again, and life and sense return.
Yet how can that concern us, when 'tis done,
Since all remembrance of past life is gone?
We never joy nor grieve to think that we
Were heretofore, nor what those things shall be,
Which, framed from us, the following age shall see.
When we recall how numerous years have run,
How oft the east beheld the rising sun,
Ere we began, and how the atoms move,
How the unthinking seeds forever strove—
'Tis probable, and reason's laws allow,
These seeds of ours were once combined as now.
Yet now who minds, who knows his former state?
The interim of death, the hand of fate
Has stopped the seeds, or made them all commence
Such motions, as destroyed the former sense.

    He that is miserable must perceive,
While he is so. He then must be and live.
But now since death permits to feel no more
Those cares, those troubles which we felt before,
It follows too, that when we die again,
We need not fear. For he must live, who lives in
        pain . . .

    Now when you hear a man complain, and moan,
And mourn his fate, because, when life is gone,
His limbs must waste, and rot in earth, or feast
The greedy flames, or some devouring beast,
All is not well. He, by strong fancy led,
Imagines sense remains among the dead.
Nor can I think, though he himself denies,
But that some strong conceits he still believes,
Poor fool! that he himself himself survives.
For even while he breathes, and while he lives,
And thinks he must be torn, or burnt, he grieves,
Thinks still his carcass must be he, and thence
His idle fears infer, there must be sense.
And hence he grieves that he was born to die,
Subject to treacherous mortality.

But never thinks, the fool! that when kind death
Shall close his eyes in night, and stop his breath,
Then nothing of this thinking thing remains
To mourn his fate, or feel sharp griefs and pains . . .
    So when the jolly blades, with garlands crowned,
Sit down to drink, while frequent healths go round,
Some, looking grave, this observation make:
"All the delights are short, we men can take;
Now we enjoy, but, gone, we wish in vain,
In vain desire to call them back again."
As if the greatest ill in graves they fear,
Were thirst, or to want wine or garlands there,
Or any other thing they fancy here.
    "Ay, but he now is snatched from all his joys—
No more shall his chaste wife, or prattling boys
Run to their dad with eager haste, and strive
Which first shall have a kiss, as when alive.
Ay, but he now no more from wars shall come,
Bring peace and safety to his friends at home.
O wretched, wretched man! one fatal day
Has snatched the vast delights of life away."
Thus they bewail, but go no farther on,
Nor add that his desires and wants are gone,
Which if they thought, how soon would all give o'er
Their empty causeless fears, and weep no more?
" 'Tis true, thou sleepest in death, and there shalt lie,
Free from all cares, to all eternity,
But we shall mourn thee; still no length of years
Shall overcome our grief, or dry our tears."
Now I would gladly know, come tell me why,
Why dost thou pine with grief, and weep, and sigh?
Why dost thou vex thyself, and beat thy breast,
Because thou once must sleep in death, and rest? . . .
    But now if nature should begin to speak,
And thus with loud complaints our folly check:
"Fond mortal, what's the reason that you sigh?
Why all these fears, because you once must die,
Must once submit to strong mortality?

For if the race you have already run
Was pleasant, if with joy you saw the sun,
If all your pleasures did not pass your mind,
As through a sieve, but left some sweets behind,
Why do you not then, like a thankful guest,
Rise cheerfully from life's abundant feast,
And with a quiet mind go take your rest?
But if all those delights are lost and gone,
Spilled idly all, and life a burden grown,
Then why, fond mortal, do you ask for more,
Why still seek to increase your wretched store,
Not rather free yourself from pains and fear,
And end your life, and necessary care?
My pleasures always in a circle run,
The same returning with the yearly sun—
And thus, though you may still enjoy your prime,
And though your limbs feel not the rage of time,
Yet I can find no new, no fresh delight.
The same dull joys must vex the appetite,
Although you should prolong your wretched breath
For many years, much more, if free from death."
What could we answer, what excuses trust?
We must confess that her reproofs are just.
　　But if an older man, oppressed by fate,
Mourns coming death, and begs a longer date,
Him she more fiercely chides: "Forbear your sighs,
You wretch, cease your complaints, and dry your eyes.
You have enjoyed the mighty store
Of gay delights, and now can taste no more.
But yet because you always strove to have
The absent, and condemned the present sweet,
Death seems unwelcome, and your race half run,
And, unexpected, hasty death destroys,
Before your greedy mind is full of joys.
Yet leave these toys, ill fitted to your age;
New actors now come on—resign the stage" . . .
　　Our life must have an end, in vain we fly
Pursuing fate—and even now we die.

Life adds no new delights to those possessed.
But since the absent pleasures seem the best,
With winged desire and haste we those pursue;
But those enjoyed we loathe, and call for new.
Life, life we wish, still greedy to live on,
And yet what fortune with the following sun
Will rise, what chance will bring, is all unknown.
    What though a thousand years prolong our breath,
How can this shorten the long stage of death?
For though our life should numerous ages fill,
The state of death will be eternal still.
And he that dies today, shall long be dead—
As long as those that perished long before.

Book IV

The poet's mission

    I travel the trackless muses' realms,
Untrodden yet—'Tis sweet to visit first
Untouched and virgin streams, and quench my thirst;
I joy to crop fresh flowers, and get a crown
For new and rare inventions of my own . . .
For, first, I teach great things in lofty strains,
And loose men from religion's grievous chains;
Next, though my subject's dark, my verse is clear,
And sweet, with fancy flowing everywhere.
And this designed. For as physicians will,
In giving children bitter medicine,
To make them take it, tinge the cup with honey sweet,
To cheat the lip—this first they eager meet,
And then drink on, and take the bitter draught,
And so are harmlessly deceived, not caught;
For, by these means, they get their strength, their ease,
Their vigor, health, and baffle the disease—
So, since our method of philosophy
Seems harsh to some, since most our maxims fly,
I thought it was the fittest way to please,
To dress these rigid principles in verse,
With fancy sweetening them, to bribe thy mind

To read my book, and lead it on to find
The nature of the world, the rise of things.
And what vast profit, too, that knowledge brings!

Things give
off images
which cause
visual
sensation

 . . . Now, for 'tis time, my muse declares and sings,
What those are we call images of things,
Which, like thin films, from bodies rise in streams,
Play in the air, and dance upon the beams.
By day these meet and strike our minds; and fright
And show pale ghosts and horrid shapes by night;
These break our sleep, these check our gay delight.
For sure no airy souls get loose, and fly
From hell's dark shades, nor flutter in our sky;
For what remains beyond the greedy urn,
Since soul and body to their seeds return?

A stream of forms from every surface flows,
Which may be called the film or shell of those.
Because they bear the shape, they show the frame,
And figure of the bodies, whence they came.
The dullest may perceive, and know 'tis true.
For bodies, big enough for sense to view,
Do often rise—some more diffused and broke,
Thus fire, thus heated wood still breathe forth smoke;
And some more close and joined. In summer's heat,
Cicadas seem to sweat, and shed their coats . . .
Snakes leave their glittering garb among the thorns,
A fluttering coat each tree, each bush adorns.
This proves, that numerous trains of images
(For why can these, and not more thin than these)
From every surface flow. For first they lie
Unchained, and loose, and ready for our eye.
They soon cast off, and still preserve their frame,
Their ancient form, and tell from whence they came.
Nay more, they're thin, they on the surface play,
Therefore, few chains to break, few stops to stay
Their course, or hinder when they fly away . . .

Touch and
sight have
similar
causes

So feel by night our touch will soon betray
The shape, like that the sight beheld by day.
Thus then the cause, whence touch and sight must rise

Is one, the same affects the hands and eyes.
For thus, if when 'tis dark we feel a square,
The touch informs what shape the thing does bear;
What is it makes us see the like by day,
But the square image riding on the ray?
Therefore these images are cause of sight;
All would be dark without them, and all hid in
        night . . .

The square   Now further, 'tis by sure experience found,
tower and   A square, when seen at distance, seems a round—
other   Because all angles seem, when seen from far,
illusions   Obtuse, or rather not at all appear.
For images that through much air do fly,
Are struck, and blunted in the lower sky,
And so grow weak, and never move the eye.
So, all the angles hid, the things appear
All round, though each may be a perfect square—
Yet not like perfect rounds do, seen from near.
    And shadows seem to move, to turn, and stay,
As bodies do, and servilely obey.
Now how can air, only deprived of light,
(For shadow is no more, a sudden night)
On all the members various motions wait,
And turn, and imitate her body's gait?
But thus it happens, when we walk by day,
Our bodies stop the passage of the ray;
But when we leave the place, rays farther flow,
And their warm kisses on the earth bestow.
And thus the shadow seems to move, to bend,
As bodies do, and all their walk attend;
For still new rays spring from the glorious sun,
The former dying when their race is run.
And therefore earth is soon deprived of light,
And rays as soon come on, and chase the night;
The negro shadow washed becomes a white.

The mind,   And yet here's no deception of the eye,
not the   For 'tis its office only to perceive,
sense, is   In what place light, in what place shadow is.
deceived

It must not pass the narrow bounds of this.
But if the shadows are the same, or no,
Whether they die, or, as the body go,
'Tis not the office of the eye to know.
'Tis reason's office that; for that's designed
The nature of things to find—
Then fix not on the eye the failures of the mind.

Thus ships, though driven by a prosperous gale,
Seem fixed to sailors; those seem under sail,
That lie at anchor safe; and all admire,
As they row by, to see the rocks retire . . .

And porticos of equal width, yet seem to bend,
And grow more narrow at the distant end.
The roof depressed, the sides seem joined in one,
The wearied sight lost in a darksome cone.

Thus ignorants, when placed on steady shores,
Think that maimed ships are rowed with broken oars—
And they are loath to trust their safety there.
Because that part, which lies above the flood,
Seems firm and straight and regular and good;
But that below seems broke and, turning up,
Ascends, so that it nearly floats upon the flood . . .

If any presses underneath his eyes,
Straight all the objects doubled seem to rise—
Two lamps appear, when only one is brought,
His wealth seems doubled, and he's rich in thought.

And lastly, when the eyes with sleep oppressed,
And all the body lies dissolved in rest,
The members seem awake and vigorous still.
Now o'er a plain, now flood, or shady hill,
They seem to move; even in darkest night,
They think they see the sun diffuse his light,
They see him chase the frightened shades away,
And clear a passage for approaching day.
They seem to hear a voice, though all around
Deep silence stands, nor bears the weakest sound.

Ten thousand such appear, ten thousand foes
To certainty of sense, and all oppose.

In vain—not sense, but judgment makes mistakes,
And fancied things for real object takes.

Skepticism   He that says nothing can be known, o'erthrows
His own opinion. For he nothing knows,
So knows not that. What need of long dispute?
These maxims kill themselves, themselves confute.
But grant this might be known, and that he knew—
Yet since he has discovered nothing true,
What mark, or what criterion then can show,
Or tell, what 'tis to know, or not to know?
Or how could he, what truth, what falsehood learn?
How what was doubt, what certainty, discern?

From sense all truth and certainty arise.
In vain some strive to prove that sense can err.
For that which would convince, which would oppose
The senses, must be surer far than those.
Now what is more to be believed than sense?
Is false and erring reason, raised from thence?
Errors in parent sense, can reason show?
Errors, which she from sense alone can know?
If sense be false, then reason too is so.
What, can the ears convict the eyes? Can those
Convict the hand, the palate, or the nose?
Tell them whene'er they err, whene'er they miss,
And give false notions? Foolish fancy this!
For each a proper use, and power enjoys,
A proper object every sense employs.
Thus heat, and cold, and other qualities
Affect the touch, while colors strike the eyes;
Odors the smell, savors the taste; but none
Invades another's right, usurps his throne.
All live at peace, contented with their own.
Therefore, from what the other senses show,
In vain we seek to prove one sense untrue—
Or from itself.
For still we must an equal credit give
To each, and all must equally believe.

'Tis truth, whate'er the senses do declare,

Though reason cannot tell you why a square
Should seem a perfect round, when seen from far.
Better assign a false, than this pretense
Should overthrow the certainty of sense,
Question its truth, rather than that should fall,
On which depends our safety, life, our all.
For now, not only reason is o'erthrown,
Unless we trust our sense, but life is gone.
For how can man avoid the bad, or choose
What's good for life, unless they follow those?
Therefore those pompous reasons some afford
Against our sense are empty and absurd . . .

Nature and origin of love

When Venus' shafts inflict their wounds—now hurled
By a boy with girlish limbs, now by a wench
Whose body breathes hot lust at every pore—
Man tends toward where the wound came from, and tries
To join, to pass his seed into the other's frame.
His mute desire foretells delight.
This is our Venus—this the source of love.
From this that drop of Venus' sweetness first
Drips down into the heart, pursued by freezing care.

And though the pleasing object is removed,
Though we no longer view the one beloved,
Her image is at hand. If we should hear
Her name, love enters with it at the ear.

But it is wise and prudent to remove
And banish all incentives unto love.
And let your age, your vigorous youth, be thrown
On all in common, not reserved for one.
For that breeds cares and fears; that mad disease,
Those raging pains, if nourished, will increase,
Unless you fancy every one you view,
Revel in love, and cure old wounds by new.

Nor do they miss the fruits, who love disdain,
But rather take the sweet without the pain.
Nay, they have purer sweets. When lovers' arms

Embrace their dears, when they possess their charms,
Straight doubts arise, their storm-tossed mind's em-
    ployed,
Which sweets must first be tasted, which enjoyed.
What they desired they hurt, and midst the bliss
Raise pain; and often, with a furious kiss,
They wound the tender lip. This they will do,
Because the joy's not perfect, is not pure.
And still some sting remains, some fierce desire
To hurt whatever 'twas that raised the fire.
But Venus gives us some relief from pain—
The mixed delight does make the hurt the less.
    Perhaps they hope that she that struck, the same
Can heal, that she that raised, can stop the flame:
Such foolishness, this love! We never cease.
The more we know, and have, the more we wish.
    Because the meat and drink are taken in,
Absorbed, the thirst is quenched, the hunger quelled.
But now from beauty, now from forms that please,
What comes, but thin and empty images?
Even such as he enjoys that drinks in dreams,
His thirst increases midst the fancied streams.
So love deludes poor men; their covetous eye,
What long, what frequent sights can satisfy?
What from the tender limbs, with wanton play,
And amorous touch, poor lovers bring away?
    Nay, even in the embrace, while both employ
Their strength, and bodies feel the coming joy,
Though then they twine, and join their watering
        mouths,
Though ardent breathings fire each other's loves;
In vain! Poor fools, they cannot mix their souls,
Although they seem to try, in amorous rolls.
So coupled eagerly, their passion melts.
Then a short pause between, and then returns
The same fierce lust, the same fierce fury burns.
While they both seek to have they know not what.
For this no cure, for this no help is found.

They waste and perish by a secret wound.
 And so they waste their strength, their vigor kill,
And live poor slaves unto another's will.
Debts they contract apace, their money flies;
Their fame, their honor too, grows sick, and dies.
Rich shoes adorn her feet, and jewels set
In gold and richest purple vests are worn.
The wealth their fathers toiled and fought to gain
Now buys a robe, a ribbon, or a crown.
Great shows and sports are made, and royal feasts,
Where choicest meats and wines provoke the guests,
Where bright-hued tapestry and odors spread
O'er all the room, and crowns grace every head.
In vain, for still some bitter thought destroys
His fancied mirth, and poisons all his joys.

 First, guilty conscience does the mirror bring,
Then sharp remorse shoots out her angry sting,
And anxious thoughts, within themselves at strife,
Upbraid the long misspent luxurious life.
Perhaps some doubtful word torments his mind,
Sinks deep, and wounds, and leaves a sting behind.
Perhaps he thinks his mistress' wanton eyes.
Gloat on his friend; perhaps faint smiles he spies.

 Such mischiefs happen even in prosperous love.
But those that crossed and hopeless passion prove,
Those wretched lovers meet ten thousand more,
Ten thousand scarce can measure the vast store,
So obvious all, that with the strictest care
'Tis good to keep my rules, and shun the snare.
'Tis easier to avoid, than break the chain
When once entrapped or be redeemed again;
The nets are strong, and we may strive in vain . . .
 Yet, though securely caught, you may be free
Again, unless you are resolved to be
A trifling slave and from your thoughts remove
The faults in mind and face of her you love.
For often men, quite blind by foolish lust,
First think their loves great beauties, then admire.

Their powerful working fancy still supplies
With borrowed shapes and flattering disguise,
The meaner beauties great necessities.
Hence 'tis that ugly things, in fancy dressed,
Seem gay, look fair to lovers' eyes, and please.
The black seems brown; the nasty, negligent;
Owl-eyed, like Pallas, and my heart's content;
The little dwarf is pretty, grace all o'er;
The vast, surprising, and we must adore;
The stammering lisps, the lover thinks he hears
The broken sounds breathed forth in softest airs;
She's modest if she's dumb, and nought can say;
The fierce and prattling thing is brisk and gay;
She's thin, if scrawny, and but one remove
From death; the meager is my slender love;
The great and swelling breast like Ceres is;
The big and hanging lip, a very kiss.

 Ten thousand such—but grant the sweetest face,
Grant each part lovely, grant each part a grace,
Yet others equal beauties do enjoy;
Yet we have lived before without this toy;
Yet she is base; yet she perfumes, to hide
Her natural smell, her maids on every side
Stand off, and smile, and waggishly deride.

 Nay though a lover, when denied the bliss,
Stands long and waits, and warms with softening kiss
The less obdurate gate, though then he pours
His ointments on, and crowns the gates with flowers,
Yet, when admitted, when, no longer coy,
The miss provokes the eager fool to joy,
Then everything offends, he fancies none,
But seeks some fit excuses to be gone.
Then he forgets the stories he designed,
Nor tells how much her coldness vexed his mind.
Nor sighs "And why, my dear, were you unkind?"
Then grieves he gave to her that awful love,
He only vowed to the great powers above.
 And this our misses know, and strive to hide

Their faults from those whom they would bind in love.
Though foul behind, they look all bright before.
In vain—for you can understand the cheat,
Discover, know her wiles and gross deceit.
And if she's fair, has no designs to vex,
Nor cross your courtship, or your thoughts perplex,
You can ignore the failures of her sex . . .

Book V

The gods
unconcerned
with man

. . . Even the few exalted souls that know
The gods must live at ease, not look below,
Free from all meddling cares, from hate and love,
If they admire, and view the world above,
And wonder how those glorious beings move,
They are entrapped, they bind their slavish chain,
And sink to their religious fears again;
And then the world with heavenly tyrants fill,
Whose force is as unbounded as their will.
Deluded ignorants! who never saw,
By reason's light, what can, what cannot be,
How every thing must yield to fatal force,
What steady bounds confine things' natural course.

The world
will have
an end

But now to prove all this, first cast an eye,
And look at all below, at all on high
The solid earth, the seas, and vaulting sky
One fatal hour, dear youth, must ruin all,
This glorious frame, that stood so long, must fall . . .

The heavens
not the gods'
dwelling
place

We must not think these are the blessed abodes,
The quiet mansions of the happy gods;
Their substance is so thin, so much refined,
Unknown to sense, nay, scarce perceived by mind.
Now since their substance can't be touched by man,
They cannot touch those other things that can;
For whatsoever touches, that must itself be touched.
Therefore the mansions of those happy powers
Must all be far unlike, distinct from ours,
Of subtle nature, suitable to their own.

All which, by long discourse, I'll prove anon.

*The world
not made for
man's sake*

But now to say this spacious world began,
By bounteous gods contrived to pleasure man;
And therefore this vast frame they toiled to raise,
And fit for us, should meet with equal praise,
And be esteemed eternal, all secure
From ruin, and the teeth of time endure;
And that 'tis impious to try to prove,
What was established by the powers above,
And fixed eternal for the man they love,
That this can die, that this to fate can bow,
And, with bold reason, strive to overthrow,
And make that mortal they designed not so—
'Tis folly. What could man return again?
What profit to the gods for all their pain,
That they should work for him? Why break their rest,
In which they lived before, secure and blessed?
What coming joy, what pleasure could they view,
To leave their former life and seek anew?
For they delight in new whose former state
Was made unhappy by some treacherous fate.
But why should they, who lived in perfect ease,
Who never saw a thing that did not please,
Be tickled thus with love of novelties?
　　Besides, what harm had the sun idly run,
Not warmed the mud, nor kindled it to man?
True, those that are in being once, should strive,
As long as pleasure will invite, to live;
But they, who'd never tasted joys, nor seen,
What hurt to them, if they had never been? . . .

*Imperfec-
tions of the
world*

And were I ignorant how beings rise,
How things begin, yet reasons from the skies,
From everything deduced, will plainly prove,
This world never framed by the powers above,
So foolish the design, contrived so ill!
For first, of all the space that heaven overlays
Why beasts in every grove and shady hill?
Vast pools take part, and the impetuous tide,

Whose spreading waves the distant shores divide.
Two parts in three the torrid sun does burn,
Or frost does chill, and all to deserts turn.

And all the other fields, what would they breed,
If let alone, but briars, thorns, and weed?
These are their proper fruits, this nature'd bear,
Did not laborious mortals toil for food,
And bend in sweat to break the ground with hoes.
Did they not turn up fruitful clods with plows,
By frequent torments forcing them to bear,
No tender fruits, none of their own accord
Would rise to feed proud man, their fancied lord.

Nay, often too, when man, with pains and toil,
Has ploughed and overcome the unwilling soil,
When flowers put forth, and budding branches shoot,
Look gay, and promise long-awaited fruit,
The scorching sun, with his too busy beams,
Burns up, or clouds destroy the fruits with streams.
Or, chilled by too much snow, they soon decay,
Or storms blow them, and all our hopes, away.

But further, why should parent nature breed
Such harmful animals? Why cherish, feed
Destructive beasts? Why should such monsters grow,
Did gods so kind dispose of things below?
Why plagues to all the seasons of the year belong?
Why stalks abroad untimely death?

A man, when first he leaves his primitive night,
Breaks from his mother's womb to view the light,
Like a sailor, cast upon the beach by cruel waves,
He lies all naked, speechless and afraid—
An infant, weak and destitute of food.
With rueful cries the pitying air he fills,
An apt prediction of his coming ills.
While beasts are born, and grow with greater ease.
No need of sounding rattles them to please;
No need of prattling nurses' busy care.
They want no change of garments, but can wear
The same at any season of the year.

They need no arms, no garrison, or town,
No stately castles to defend their own.
Nature supplies their wants; whate'er they crave,
She gives them, and preserves the life she gave.

The mortality of the world

But now, since air, and water, earth, and fire
Are bodies all produced, and all expire,
Since these are such, these that compose this frame,
The nature of the whole must be the same.
For those are made, and die, so must the whole . . .
It follows then, for which our proofs contend,
That this vast frame began, and so must end . . .

How the world came to be

Now I will sing, how moving seeds were hurled,
How tossed to order, how they framed the world,
How sun and moon began, what steady force
Marked out their path, what makes them keep their
        course.
For sure unthinking seeds did ne'er dispose
Themselves by counsel, nor their order chose,
Nor any compacts make, how each should move;
But from eternity through vacuum roamed,
Moved by their weight, or by external blows,
All motions tried, all unions too . . .
Thus long they whirled, most sorts of motion past,
Most sorts of union too; they joined at last
In such convenient order, whence began
The sea, the heaven, earth, and beasts and man,
But yet no glittering sun, no twinkling star,
No heaven, no roaring sea, no earth, no air,
Nor anything like these did then appear,
But a vast heap—and from this mighty mass
Each part retired, and took its proper place . . .
Agreeing seeds combined, each atom ray,
And sought his like, and so the frame began . . .
For first the earthy parts, a heavy mass,
And closely twined, possessed the middle place.
Now as these heavy parts combined more close,
Descending still, they vexed with constant blows
The lurking parts of sea, of stars, and skies,

And sun, and squeezed them out, and made them rise,
Because those seeds are tiny, more refined
Than those of earth; and so can freely pass
The minute pores of the descending mass.
And thus the parts of heaven did first retire,
And bore up with them numerous seeds of fire . . .
The tenuous ether, thus combined above,
And vastly wide, and spread o'er every place,
Contains the rest within her greedy grasp.
Thus heaven. Then rose the moon, and stars, and sun,
Which through the sky with constant motions run,
Because their seeds were all too light to lie
In earth, not light enough to rise on high,
And pass the utmost limits of the sky;
But, placed between them both, the midst control,
Certain, but moving portions of the whole . . .

    These things retired, the heavier parts of clay
Sunk further down, and made an easy way
For flowing streams, and caverns for the sea.
And as, by constant blows, the vigorous sun
Did strike the upper parts, and press them down,
More moisture rose, and then did streams increase,
More parts were still squeezed out, and swelled the
        seas.
More ether then, of air more parts did rise,
And borne on high, there thickened into skies.
The mountains raised their heads, the humble field
Sunk low. The stubborn stones refused to yield,
The rocks did proudly still their height maintain,
Nor could all sink into an equal plain.
Thus earth at first was framed, and thus did fall
The lowest, as the sediment of all . . .

The sun and
moon no
larger than
they appear

    But further on—the sun's bright disk does bear
No greater figure, and no less than does appear,
Because that space, through which the rays can fly,
The heat can reach our touch, the light our eye,
Can lessen nothing, nor contract the frame,
Nor make the fire appear a milder flame.

Now since the vigorous rays do freely flow
As far as us, and visit all below,
Their fires, and figures are the same they show;
Nor greater all, nor less. And thus the moon,
Whether with borrowed rays, or with her own,
She view the world, carries no larger size,
No fiercer flames, than those that strike our eyes.
For objects, far removed, at distance seen,
When too much hindering air is placed between,
No certain figure show, no eye can trace
Each line, each figure of the distant face.
But since the moon presents a certain size,
A certain shape, and figure, to our eyes,
'Tis plain, that it appears as great as 'tis . . .

*The origin
of the
species—
earth the
mother of
all*

Now let's descend again to newborn earth,
And find to what she gave the soonest birth,
What sort of beings, which of all the kinds
She first dared venture to the faithless winds.

She, first of all, green herbs, and flowers did yield,
And spread a bright-hued green o'er all the field;
And next the tree, with spreading branches, fights
To rise into the air . . .

So newborn earth with herbs and trees began,
And then by various ways bore beast and man.
For heaven surely did not fashion all,
Then let the various creatures downwards fall,
Nor seas produce an earthly animal.
And therefore parent earth does justly bear
The name of mother, since all rose from her.
She now bears animals, when softening dew
Descends; when sun sends heats, she bears a thousand
    new.
So who can wonder now, that then she bore
Far stronger, bulky animals, and more,
When air and she were young, in nature's pride,
A lusty bridegroom he, and she a buxom bride?
First of all animals, in teeming spring,

The feathered kind peeped forth and clapped their
    wing,
As even now our tender insects strive.
To break their shells, get forth, and eat, and live.
Next beasts, and thoughtful man received their birth,
For then much vital heat in mother earth,
Much moisture lay; and where fit place was found,
There wombs were formed, and fastened to the
    ground;
In these, the yet imperfect embryos lay,
Through these, when grown mature, they forced their
    way,
Broke forth from night and saw the cheerful day.
Then nature fashioned for the infant's use
Small breasts in earth, and filled with milky juice,
Such as in women's breasts she now provides
For future infants; thither nature guides
The chiefest parts of food, and there they meet
Fit ferment, there they grow both white and sweet.
Earth gave the infants food, warm mists were spread
For clothes, the grassy meadows gave a bed.
The earth, when new, produced no raging cold,
No heats, nor storms; these grew, as she grew old.
Thus for a certain time earth bore mankind
And beasts that shake the wood with dreadful roar,
And various kinds of birds . . .

Earth no   But wearied now, and tired by length of time,
longer bears The earth grows old, and weak, as women past their
    prime.
Time changes all, and as with swiftest wings
He passes forward on, he quickly brings
A different face, a different sight of things;
And nature alters. This grows weak, this strong;
This dies, this, newly made, is firm and young.
Thus altering age leads on the world to fate,
The earth is different from her former state.
And what in former times with ease she bore,

Grown feeble now, and weak, she bears no more,
And now does that she could not do before.

    The earth did once produce a numerous train
Of monsters—those her labor wrought in vain.
Some without hands, or feet, or mouth, or eyes,
Some shapeless lumps, nature's absurdities;
Dull, moveless things, and destitute of food,
Which could not fly the bad, nor choose the good.
A thousand such in vain arose from earth,
For nature, frightened at the ugly birth,
Their strength, and life to narrow bounds confined,
Denied them food, or to increase their kind.
For that one power a thousand things requires,
Almost as many as its own desires.
There must be food, and seed, and organs fit
For flowing seed, while all the happy night
The body lies dissolved in soft delight.
That male and female may their powers employ,
They must have organs fit for mutual joy.

    And so the years must many kinds destroy,
They could not all preserve their feeble race.
For those we see remain and bear their young
Craft, strength, or swiftness has preserved so long.
Many their profit, and their use commends—
Those species man preserves, kind man defends.
Wild beasts and lion's race their native rage
Preserves secure, through all-devouring age.
Swiftness preserves the deer, and craft the fox.
The vigilant, faithful dog, the horse, the ox,
They shun wild beasts, they fly the dreadful wood;
They seek for peace, and much, and easy food,
Gotten without their toil. And this we give
For the vast profits we from them receive.
But those to whom their nature gave no force,
No courage, strength, nor swiftness to the course,
Whom neither profit could, nor use commend,
Those man refused to feed, or to defend.

Thus, doomed by chance, they lived an easy prey
To all, and thus their kinds did soon decay . . .

Primitive
man

Then man was hard, as hard as parent-stones,
And built on bigger, and on firmer bones.
The nerves, that joined their limbs, were firm and
      strong;
Their life was healthy, and their age was long.
Returning years still saw them in their prime;
They wearied even the wings of measuring time . . .
Like beasts they lay in every wood and cave,
Gathering the easy food, that nature gave.
No impious ploughman yet had learned to tear
His parent's bowels with the crooked share;
None planted fruitful trees, none dressed the vine,
None pruned decaying boughs, none pressed the wine.
Contented they with meager, easy store,
That sun and earth bestowed, they wished no more.
Soft acorns were their first and chiefest food,
And those red apples that adorn the wood . . .

When thirsty, then did swirling streams invite
To satisfy their eager appetite,
As now, in murmurs loud, the headlong floods,
Invite the thirsty creatures of the woods . . .

They knew no use of fire to dress their food,
No clothes, but wandered naked in the wood.
They lived to shady groves and caves confined,
Mere shelter from the cold, the heat, and wind.

No fixed society, no steady laws,
No public good was sought, no common cause;
But, all at war, each ranged, and sought his food,
By nature taught to seek his private good.

Then to renew frail man's decaying race,
Their mutual lust did prompt them to embrace,
Or else the greater vigor of the male,
Or some few tempting presents did prevail.
Some acorns, apples some, some pears bestowed,
The thing the same, the price was less than now.

Then strong, and swift, they did the beasts pursue;
Their arms were stones, and clubs. And some they
　　　slew,
And some they fled—from those they feared to fight
They ran, and owed their safety to their flight.

When drowsy night came on, they naked lay,
Spread o'er the ground like bears, and rough as they.
Their sleep was sound; they waked not all the night,
Nor wandered here and there, while shades affright,
Nor viewed the east with longing eyes for light.
But all dissolved in sweetest slumbers lay,
Till the bright sun arose, and brought the day.
For since they had beheld, e'er since their birth,
The day and night by turns spread o'er the earth,
They never feared the sun should lose his light,
And all lie buried in eternal night.

The most they dreaded was the furious beast;
For he, in dead of night, did oft molest,
And lengthen into death their slumbering rest . . .

Yet fewer died than now; for singly then,
Each caught within the limits of his den,
While the beast tore the living, trembling food,
And reveled in full draughts of reeking blood,
With dreadful cries he filled each wood and cave,
To see his limbs go down a living grave.
Others, that 'scaped with life, but wounded, groaned,
Holding their hands on the corrupting wound,
Not skilled in herbs, and now grown desperate,
With horrid cries they called on lingering fate,
Till worms increased, and eating through the clay,
Made passage for the soul to fly away.

But then no armies fell en masse, no plain
Grew red, no rivers swelled with thousands slain.
None ploughed the floods, none shipwrecked made
　　　their graves
In seas, none drank cold death among the waves.
But oft the furious ocean raged in vain;
No mischief done, the waves grew mild again.

Then want, not surfeit brought a hasty death;
Our bellies swell so much, they stop our breath.
　　Then poisonous herbs, when plucked by chance did
　　　kill;
Now poison's grown an art, improved by skill.

Beginning of　But when they built their huts, when fire began,
civilization　And skins of murdered beasts gave clothes to man;
When one to one confined, in chaste embrace,
Enjoyed sweet love, and saw a numerous race;
Then man grew soft, the temper of his mind
Was changed from rough to mild, from fierce to kind.
For used to fire, his limbs refused to bear
The piercing sharpness of the open air;
And lust enfeebled him; besides, the child,
Softened by parents' love, grew tame and mild.

　　Then neighbors, by degrees familiar grown,
Made leagues, and bonds, and each secured his own.
And then by signs, and broken words agreed
That they would keep, preserve, defend, and feed
Defenseless infants, and the women too,
As natural pity prompted them to do.
Though this fixed not an universal peace,
Yet many kept their faith, and lived at ease;
Or else, almost as soon as it began,
The race had fallen, this age ne'er seen a man.

　　Kind nature power of framing sounds affords
To man; and then convenience taught us words.
As infants now, for want of words, devise
Expressive signs; they speak with hands and eyes,
Their speaking hand the want of words supplies.
All know their powers, they are by nature shown.
Thus tender calves with naked front will run,
And fiercely butt before their horns are grown . . .
　　To say that one the names of things contrived,
And that from him their knowledge all derived,
Is foolishness. For why should that man tell
The names of things, or lisp a syllable,
And not another have this power too?

Nay more, if others used not words as soon,
How was their use, and how the profit known?
And where did he derive the power to see,
Perceive in mind what he desired to do?
For he, alone, by neither force, nor wit
Could conquer many men, make them submit
To learn his words, and practice what was fit.
How he persuade those so unfit to hear?
Or how could savage they with patience bear
Strange sounds and words still rattling in their ear . . .

The wiser left the field, and kings began
To build them towns, for safety's sake.
Then cattle too was shared, and steady bounds
Marked out to every man his proper grounds.
Each had his proper share, each what was fit,
According to his beauty, strength, or wit.
For beauty then and strength had most command;
Those had the greatest share in beasts and land.
But when once gold was found . . .
Then wit and beauty were esteemed no more,
But wealth enjoyed their honor, seized their place.
The wise and beauteous bow to fortune's ass.

But if men would live up to reason's rules,
They would not scrape and cringe to wealthy fools.
For 'tis the greatest wealth to live content
With little . . .

And so the kings were put to death, were overthrown,
The glory of the scepter and the crown
Decreased. The diadem, that sign of state,
Now wept in drops of blood, the wearer's fate,
Trampled by the rabble's feet, who feared no more.
'Tis sweet to spurn the things we feared before.
Thus monarchy was lost.

That sun once set, a thousand little stars
Gave a dim light to jealousies and wars,
While each among the many sought the throne,
And thought no head, like his, deserved the crown.
This made them seek for laws, this led their choice

To rulers; power was given by public voice.
For men, worn out, and tired by constant strife,
At last began to wish an easy life,
And so submitted of their own accord
To rigid laws, and their elected lord.

   Men had grown weary of continual wars,
Which soured the sweet of life with constant fears;
For violence and wrong entangle all
Who give them birth; nay, oft the wrongs recoil,
With double force on the contrivers fall.
Nor can those men expect to live at ease,
Who violate the common bounds of peace.
Though now it lies concealed from man and god,
They still must fear their secret will come out,
Since some diseased, and some by night betray
The wicked actions they have done by day.

Origin of religion

   Now sing, my muse, for that's my next design,
Why all do bow to something as divine,
Why every nation has its proper shrine,
Why all do temples build, why altars raise,
And why all sacrifice on sacred days,
How this diffused, this lasting fame was spread
Of power above, whence came that awful dread,
That parent of religion through the rout,
Which forces them to bow, and grow devout?
This is an easy task. For newborn man,
Just sprung from earth, when first this frame began,
Divine and glorious forms descending came,
And struck his mind by day—by night the same,
But then increased. Their working fancies showed
Great limbs and strength, and fit to make a god;
Their words were all majestic, as their look.

   Eternal too, because a new supply,
A constant stream, where'er they turned their eye,
Of forms came in, and showed the deity.
Nor could they think such mighty things could fail,
Or powerful blows on so much strength prevail.
And happy too, because no fear destroys,

No dread of sullen death corrupts their joys.
    Besides, in dreams they often seemed to do
A thousand various things, and wonders show.
Yet never weary they, but vigorous still;
Their strength as much unbounded as their will.
    Besides they saw the heavens in order roll
Their various motions round the steady pole.
The seasons of the year by constant laws
Run round, but knowing not the natural cause,
They therefore thought that gods must rule above—
Poor shift!—and all at their instruction move.
In heaven they placed their seat, their stately throne,
For there the sun, the stars, and various moon,
And day, and night, their constant courses run;
And hail and rain and, through a broken cloud,
Swift lightning flies, and thunder roars aloud.
Unhappy man! who taught the gods engage
In these, that they are subject unto rage,
A curse to theirs, to ours, and future age.
What grief they brought themselves, to us what fears?
To poor posterity what sighs, what tears?
Alas! what piety? Alas! 'Tis none,
To bend all covered to a senseless stone,
Lie prostrate, or to visit every shrine,
Or, with spread arms, invoke the powers divine
Before their temples, while the altar flows
With blood of beasts, and we make vows on vows.
    But sure 'tis piety to view the whole,
And search all nature with a quiet soul . . .

SUGGESTED READINGS

See the accounts and sayings of Epicurus in Diogenes Laertius, *Lives of the Philosophers*; in A. E. Taylor, *Epicurus*; and in C. Bailey, *The Greek Atomists and Epicurus*. The complete writings of Epicurus and Lucretius are available in an excellent Random House edition: *The*

Stoic and Epicurean Philosophers, ed. W. J. Oates. A. E. Taylor, *Epicurus,* and W. Wallace, *Epicureanism,* are excellent surveys. See also N. W. DeWitt, *Epicurus and His Philosophy,* and H. D. Sedgwick, *The Art of Happiness.* Very fine is G. Santayana, *Three Philosophical Poets,* ch. i. See also G. E. Woodberry, *The Inspiration of Poetry,* pp. 172-202. A good, fuller account appears in R. D. Hicks, *Stoic and Epicurean,* chs. v, vi, vii.

The classic English work on Lucretius is J. Masson, *Lucretius, Epicurean and Poet.* See also, by the same author, *Atomic Theory of Lucretius.*

The best literary appreciation of Epicureanism is W. Pater, *Marius the Epicurean.* See also G. Murray's sensitive handling of Epicurus in his *Five Stages of Greek Religion.* A sympathetic treatment of Epicureanism, together with a translation of the works of Epicurus and parallel passages from Lucretius, is given by G. K. Strodach in *The Philosophy of Epicurus.*

For an account of the scientific theory of the Epicureans, see F. Kahn, *Design of the Universe,* or L. L. Whyte, *Essay on Atomism: From Democritus to 1960.*

II

STOICISM

INTRODUCTION

Just as Cyrenaicism, claiming to derive its central conception from Socrates, had provided a point of departure for Epicureanism, so Cynicism, similarly claiming intellectual descent from Socrates, first struck the posture which was to come to characterize Stoicism. The earliest known advocate of Cynicism, Antisthenes (440-370 B.C.), had construed the whole Socratic mission as implying that men ought to divorce themselves completely from emotional involvement in that which lay outside their power to control. Profoundly elaborated, and bolstered by an appropriate metaphysic, logic and epistemology, it is precisely this conception which lies at the heart of the Stoic philosophy.

No little significance attaches to the social positions occupied by the founder and the three greatest literary exponents of Stoicism. Zeno of Citium (340-265 B.C.)—traditionally regarded as the originator of the Stoa—was a Semite from the East who finally settled and taught in Athens. Seneca (4 B.C.–65 A.D.) was a rhetorician and tutor to the Emperor Nero; Epictetus (60-120 A.D.), a manumitted slave; and Marcus Aurelius (121-180 A.D.), the last of the great Roman Emperors. Stoicism may thus be seen as possessed of the capacity to bring men from the most diverse levels of society into substantial intellectual and moral agreement. Indeed, in its long history, Stoicism has always been a cosmopolitan force, acting to cut across well-established social and political bounds to unite men into a single community of sympathy and purpose.

Of Zeno's writings, only a few fragments are extant. Unfortunately, most of the writings of the Early and Middle periods of Stoicism are similarly preserved for us only in fragments, or in the writings of other authors. We are more fortunate where the writings of the Late, or Roman period of Stoicism are concerned, for most of these, preserved in their integrity, are yet available to us.

Presented below are three representative samplings drawn from the works of Stoic writers of the Late period. In the first, Seneca attempts to answer the objection which to this day must disturb the adherent of any system which holds to a view of Providence: why, if Providence obtains, do the good suffer? In the second, the slave Epictetus undertakes to deal with the knotty problem of human freedom, and the final selection gives us an intimate glimpse into the heart and mind of one who, in the opinion of many, was truly "the noblest Roman of them all"—the Emperor Marcus Aurelius Antoninus.

SENECA

ON PROVIDENCE*

WHY ANY MISFORTUNES BEFALL GOOD
MEN WHEN A PROVIDENCE EXISTS

You have asked me, Lucilius,
why it is that many evils befall good men if the world is governed by providence. The answer could more conveniently be
supplied in an organized treatise in the course of which we
would demonstrate that providence rules all things and that
god is concerned for our welfare. But since it is your pleasure
to pluck one member from the whole and reconcile a single
objection without impinging on the problem in its totality
I shall acquiesce; the task is not difficult, for it is the gods'
cause I shall be pleading.

For our present purpose it is superfluous to point out that
so mighty a structure does not persist without some caretaker;
that the concourse and dispersal of the heavenly bodies is not
an effect of a fortuitous impulse; that whereas what chance
sets into motion is without direction and is likely to run into
collisions, the course which is guided by the rules of eternal
law moves speedily and without running foul and carries
with it the multitudes of objects on land and sea and of brilliant lights shining forth according to a fixed plan; that this
orderliness is not a property of matter moving at random;
and that fortuitous conglomerations cannot arrange their
balance so skillfully that the earth, which is heaviest in

* Reprinted from *The Stoic Philosophy of Seneca*, translated by Moses
Hadas, by permission of Doubleday & Company, Inc. © Copyright, 1958,
by Moses Hadas.

weight, should abide unmoved and, as spectator, observe the
rapid flight of the surrounding sky, how the seas are distilled
into the valleys to soften the earth, how huge growths bur-
geon from tiny seeds. Even those phenomena which seem
irregular and anarchic—I mean clouds and rain and the flashes
of crashing thunder and flames shot up from riven mountain
peaks and the tremors of quaking earth and the other manifestations of the turbulent workings of nature upon earth—
even these phenomena do not happen without a plan, though
their coming may be unexpected; they have their own causes,
as do those phenomena whose incongruous location gives
them an aspect of the miraculous, as, for example, hot springs
in the midst of the waves or new stretches of island springing
up in the vast ocean. Indeed, if a man observe how the shore
is laid bare when the sea withdraws into itself and is then
flooded again in a short time, he might suppose that it is
some blind turbulence which causes the waves at one time to
contract with an inward motion and at another to burst
forth with a great rush to recover their normal position. In
point of fact, their growth is strictly allotted; at the appropriate day and hour they approach in greater volume or less
according as they are attracted by the lunar orb, at whose
sway the ocean wells up. But such questions as these must be
reserved for their proper occasion, especially since you are
merely complaining of providence, not questioning its existence. I shall reconcile you with the gods, who prove best to
men who are best. Nature never suffers the good to be
harmed by the good; between good men and the gods there
subsists a friendship, with virtue as its bond.

Did I say friendship? It is rather a kinship and a close resemblance, for the only difference between the good man and
god is in the matter of time. Man is god's disciple and emula-
tor and true progeny, whom the glorious parent, who insists
upon virtue, educated very strictly, like a stern father. When
you see men who are good and acceptable to the gods toil
and sweat and climb laboriously upward, therefore, while

the wicked run riot and luxuriate in wantonness, remember that in our sons it is modesty that pleases, whereas pertness pleases us only in home-born slaves; and that our sons we restrain by severe discipline, whereas we encourage the slaves' sauciness. Be sure that god's course is the same. He does not treat the good man like a toy, but tries him, hardens him, and readies him for himself.

[2. "Why do many misfortunes fall to the lot of good men?" It is not possible that any evil can befall a good man. Opposites cannot combine. Just as the influx of so many streams and the downpour of so much rain and the flavor of so many mineral springs do not change the tang of the sea or even so much as dilute it, just so the assaults of adversity do not affect the spirit of a stalwart man. He maintains his poise and assimilates all that falls to his lot to his own complexion, for he is more potent than the world without. I do not maintain that he is insensible to externals, but that he overcomes them; unperturbed and serene, he rises to meet every sally. All adversity he regards as exercise. Is not every upstanding man who is intent upon what is right eager for appropriate exertion and ready for service which involves danger? Does not any diligent man regard idleness as a punishment? In the case of athletes, whose concern is for physical strength, we observe that they employ very strong adversaries in their practice bouts and insist that their trainers use all their strength against them. They submit to blows and bruises, and if they cannot find individuals strong enough to match with them, they take on several at once. Without an antagonist prowess fades away. Its true proportions and capacities come to light only when action proves its endurance. You must know that good men should behave similarly; they must not shrink from hardship and difficulty or complain of fate; they should take whatever befalls in good part and turn it to advantage. The thing that matters is not what you bear but how you bear it.

Observe how differently fathers and mothers show their affection. Fathers make their children get up to attend to their tasks betimes; even on holidays they do not suffer them to be idle but drive them to sweat and sometimes to tears. Mothers want to cuddle them in their laps, keep them in the shade, never let them be disappointed or cry or work hard. God's attitude to good men is a father's; his love for them is a manly love. "Let them be harassed by toil and sorrow and loss," says he, "that so they may acquire true strength." Pampered bodies grow sluggish through sloth; not work but movement and their own weight exhausts them. Prosperity unbruised cannot endure a single blow, but a man who has been at constant feud with misfortunes acquires a skin calloused by suffering; he yields to no evil and even if he stumbles carries the fight on upon his knee.

Do you find it strange that god, who so loves good men that he wishes them to attain pre-eminent goodness, should allot them a fortune on which to exercise themselves? I myself do not find it strange that the gods are sometimes moved to enjoy the spectacle of great men wrestling with some disaster. It gives us pleasure, on occasion, when a young man of steadfast courage meets a wild beast's charge with his hunting spear or faces a rushing lion without flinching, and the spectacle is the more pleasing in the degree that the hero is a man of position. Yet those are not achivements to attract the attention of the gods but the childish amusements of human frivolity. But look you upon this spectacle worthy the attention of a god intent upon his own work, look you upon this bout worthy a god—a stalwart man matched with evil fortune, especially when the man takes the initiative. I cannot see, I declare, what fairer spectacle Jupiter could enjoy on earth, if he should wish to direct his attention there, than Cato still standing upright amidst his country's ruins after his party had repeatedly been crushed. "Though all the world has yielded to one man's sway," says he, "though Caesar's legions guard the dry land and his fleets the sea, though his soldiers beset the city gates, yet does Cato possess a

way of egress; with a single hand he can open a wide path to
freedom. This sword which has remained untainted and
guiltless even in civil war shall at last perform a good and
noble deed; it shall give Cato the freedom it could not give
his country. Take up, my soul, the task you have long studied;
deliver yourself from the world of men. Petreius and Juba
have already run their race, and each lies slain by the hand of
the other. That was a brave and noble compact with fate,
but not seemly for my stature; for Cato it is as ignominious
to beg death of anyone as it is life."

I am sure the gods looked on with great satisfaction when
that man who was so uncompromising in maintaining his own
freedom took measures to secure the safety of others and
arranged the escape of those who were leaving, when he spent
even his last night in study, when he thrust his sword into
his hallowed bosom, when he pulled his vitals apart and with
his own hand released that holy spirit which was too pure to
be defiled by steel. That is why, I should suppose, the
wound was badly aimed and ineffectual: for the immortal
gods it was not enough to look on Cato but once; he was
encored and kept on the stage to exhibit his character in a
more demanding role, for it wants a loftier spirit to seek
death a second time. How could the gods fail to be pleased
when they viewed their charge making his way to freedom
by so glorious and memorable a departure? Death hallows
men whose mode of dying is praised even by those who
dread it.

[3. As my discourse proceeds I shall show that what seem to
be evils are not actually such. For the present, I will say so
much of the eventualities which you style harsh, unfortunate,
and detestable: in the first place, they benefit the individuals
to whose lot they fall, and, in the second place, they benefit
the whole body of mankind, for which the gods are more concerned than they are for individuals; next, good men receive
these eventualities willingly, and deserve ill fortune if they
do not; further, these things are destined, and befall good

men by the same law that makes them good. And finally I shall persuade you never to commiserate a good man; he may be called unhappy, he cannot be unhappy.

Of all these propositions the most difficult, apparently, is the first in the list, that the objects of our dread, and horror are actually advantageous to the persons to whose lot they fall. "Is it for the victim's advantage," you object, "to be driven into exile, to be reduced to poverty, to bury wife and children, to be branded with ignominy, to be made a cipher?" If you find it strange that these things are beneficial, you will find it no less strange that certain maladies are treated by surgery and cautery and by hunger and thirst as well. But if you reflect that for the sake of a cure some persons have their bones scraped or removed, their veins pulled out, or members whose presence would be deleterious to the organism as a whole amputated, you will also allow yourself to be convinced that certain misfortunes work to the advantage of those whom they befall—precisely, by Hercules, as certain things which are praised and sought after work to the disadvantage of those who delight in them; overeating, drunkenness, and other indulgences, for example, kill through giving pleasure. Among the many magnificent sayings of our friend Demetrius is the following, which I have just heard; it still rings and reverberates in my ears. "No one is more unhappy, in my judgment," says he, "than a man who has never met with adversity." He has never had the privilege of testing himself. Everything has come easily to him according to his wish; yet the gods' judgment of him has been unfavorable. He was deemed unworthy of ever vanquishing Fortune, which shuns any cowardly antagonist, as if to say, "Why should I take on that kind of opponent? He will lay his arms down at once, and I will not need to use my full strength against him. A threatening gesture will rout him; he cannot face my grim expression. I must look around for someone else with whom to match my strength; I am ashamed to fight a man who is ready to be beaten." A gladiator counts it a disgrace to be matched with an inferior; he knows that a victory devoid of danger is a victory devoid of glory. Fortune follows the same principle: she searches out stalwart adversaries, and passes some by in disdain. It is the upstanding and inflexible that she challenges, for against them she can exert all her force. She tries Mucius by fire, Fabricius by poverty, Rutilius by exile, Regulus by torture, Socrates by poison, Cato by death. Only misfortune can reveal such outstanding models.

Is Mucius unfortunate because he grasped the enemy's fire with his right hand and himself exacted punishment for his own mistake? Because the hand burned routed the king whom his hand armed could not? Would he have been more fortunate, then, if he had been coddling his hand in his mistress' bosom? Is Fabricius unfortunate because he tilled his own field when he was not engaged in affairs of state? Because he waged war alike against Pyrrhus and against riches? Because, though an old man with a triumph to his credit, he dined by his own fireside upon roots and herbs he himself plucked as he cleared his field? Would he have been more fortunate, then, if he had gorged his belly with fish from a distant shore and fowl imported from abroad? If he had stimulated his jaded and cloyed appetite with sea food from the upper and lower seas? If he had been served prime game, taken at the cost of many hunters' lives, garnished with heaps of fruit? Is Rutilius unfortunate because those who condemned him will have to defend themselves before all posterity? Because he was more indifferent to losing his country than to losing his exile? Because he was the only man to say no to the dictator Sulla, and when he was invited to return all but drew back and went to deeper exile? "That," says he, "is the business of those whom your Happy Reign has caught at Rome. It is for them to look upon the Forum drenched with blood and the heads of senators above the pool of Servilius (it was there that the victims of Sulla's proscriptions were stripped) and bands of assassins roaming through the city, and many thousands of Roman citizens massacred in a single spot after they had received a pledge, indeed by means of that pledge. Those are sights for men who cannot go into exile." Is Sulla happy, then, because his way down to the Forum is cleared by the sword, because he has the hardihood to inspect the heads of consulars which are exhibited to him and pays out blood money from the public exchequer through the treasurer? All these things Sulla did, Sulla who passed the Cornelian Law!

We come now to Regulus. How did Fortune harm him when she made him a model of loyalty, a model of endurance? Nails pierce his skin, and wherever he leans his tormented frame he inflicts a wound; his eyes stare open, forever sleepless. But the greater the torment, the greater shall the glory be. Would you learn how little he regrets the price he set upon virtue? Make him whole again and send him back to the senate: he will urge the same course. Would you count Maecenas more fortunate because, when he was lovesick and bewailing the repulses of his disagreeable wife, he wooed slumber through the strains of music sounding softly in the distance? Though he drug himself with strong wine and divert himself with the rippling of water and beguile his distraught mind with a thousand delights, he will be as sleepless on his bed of down as Regulus upon his cross. But Regulus has consolation: the hardship he endures is for honor's sake, and he looks away from his suffering to its cause; whereas Maecenas, enervated by pleasure and sick with excess of prosperity, suffers greater torment from the cause of his suffering than from the actual suffering. Vice has not taken such complete possession of the human race as to leave any doubt that, if men could choose their destiny, more would prefer to be born a Regulus than a Maecenas. Or if anyone should have the effrontery to declare that he would rather be born a Maecenas than a Regulus, that same man, though he might not admit it, actually prefers to be born a Terentia.

Do you judge that Socrates was badly used because he drained that potion the state compounded as though it were a specific for immortality and discoursed on death until death came? Was he badly dealt with because his blood cooled and, as the chill gradually spread, the pulsing of his veins stopped? How much more enviable is he than are they who are served in jeweled cups, whose drink some catamite trained to every abuse, a creature unsexed or sexless, dilutes with snow dropped from a golden vessel! Such men will measure back in vomit all they have drunk, with the sour taste of their own bile, whereas Socrates quaffs his poison willingly and cheerfully.

Touching Cato, enough has been said; general consensus acknowledges that Nature's choice for her formidable sparring has attained the pinnacle of happiness. "The enmity of men in power is a serious handicap," says Nature. "Cato must face Pompey, Caesar, and Crassus simultaneously. It is a hard thing to be defeated for office by an inferior: Cato must run second to Vatinius. It is a hard thing to be involved in civil war: Cato shall fight for the good cause the whole world over, with as ill success as perserverance. It is a hard thing to do violence to oneself: Cato shall do so. What shall I gain by all this? All men shall know that these things of which I deem Cato worthy are not evils."

[4. Prosperity can come to the vulgar and to ordinary talents, but to triumph over the disasters and terrors of mortal life is the privilege of the great man. To be lucky always and to pass through life without gnawing of the mind is to be ignorant of the half of nature. You are a great man, but how can I know, if Fortune has never given you a chance to display your prowess? You have entered the Olympic games but have no rival; you gain the crown but not the victory. I felicitate you, not as a brave man, but as one who has obtained a consulship or praetorship; your dignity is enhanced. I can say the same of a good man whom no difficult conjuncture has afforded an occasion for displaying the force of his mind. "I account you unfortunate because you have never been unfortunate. You have passed through life without an adversary; no one can know your potentiality, not even you." For self-knowledge, testing is necessary; no one can discover what he can do except by trying. That is why some men have voluntarily exposed themselves to misfortune when it was reluctant, and have sought an opportunity for their prowess, which would otherwise pass into obscurity, to shine forth. Great men, I insist, sometimes rejoice in adversity precisely as brave soldiers rejoice in war. I once heard Triumphus, a gladiator in the days of Caligula, complain of the scarcity of performances. "It was fine in the old days," he said.

Prowess is avid for danger and thinks rather of the goal than of its trials, for these too are part of glory. Soldiers glory in their wounds and gladly vaunt themselves over the blood they were privileged to shed; though those who returned from the fray unhurt may have fought as well, the man who brings back a wound is more respected. To those men he desires shall achieve the highest excellence, god shows his favor whenever he affords them a field for spirited and courageous action, and for this some particular exertion is requisite. You assay a pilot in a storm, a soldier in the battle line. How can I know with what spirit you would confront poverty if you are running over with riches? How can I know with what constancy you will confront disgrace, dishonor, and public contumely if you reach old age amidst acclamations, if you are always attended by an inexpugnable popularity which gravitates in your direction by general inclination? How do I know how serenely you would endure bereavement when all the children you have raised are present to your sight? I have heard you offering condolences to others; I might have glimpsed your true character if you had been consoling yourself, if you had been bidding yourself not to grieve.

Do not, I beseech you, dread the things which the immortal gods apply to our souls like goads; disaster is virtue's opportunity. Those whom an excess of prosperity has rendered sluggish may justly be called unfortunate; a dead calm holds them fast, as it were, on a motionless sea, and whatever befalls them comes as a surprise. Cruelty presses hardest on the inexperienced; the tender neck chafes at the yoke. The recruit pales at the thought of a wound; the veteran can look at his flowing gash with composure, for he knows that he has often won the victory after losing blood. So god hardens and scrutinizes and exercises those he approves and loves; but those he appears to indulge and spare he is only keeping tender for disasters to come. If you suppose that anyone is immune you are mistaken. The man who has long prospered will get his share one day; the man you thought discharged has only been reprieved. Why does god afflict every good man with sickness or grief or other misfortune? Because in the army, too, the most hazardous duties are assigned to the bravest soldiers. It is only the picked men that the general sends to surprise the enemy by a night attack, to reconnoiter the road, or to dislodge a garrison. And no man in such a detachment will say, "The general has treated me badly," but rather, "The general thinks well of me." Similarly, those told off to undergo what cowards and weaklings would weep over should say, "God has judged us fit subjects to try how much human nature can endure."

Avoid luxury, avoid debilitating prosperity which makes men's minds soggy and which, unless something intervenes to remind them of the human condition, renders them comatose as in unending inebriation. If a man has always been protected from the wind by glass windows, if his feet have been kept warm by constant relays of poultices, if the temperature of his dining room has been maintained by hot air circulating under the floor and through the walls, he will be dangerously susceptible to a slight breeze. All excesses are injurious, but immoderate prosperity is the most dangerous of all. It affects the brain, it conjures empty fantasies up in the mind, and it befogs the distinction between true

and false with a confusing cloud. Is it not better to endure
everlasting misfortune, with virtue's help, than to burst with
endless and immoderate prosperity? Death by starvation
comes gently, gluttony makes men explode.

In the case of good men, accordingly, the gods follow the
plan that teachers follow with their pupils: they demand
more effort from those in whom they have confident expectations. Can you imagine that the Lacedaemonians hate their
children because they try their mettle by public flogging?
Their own fathers urge them to bear up under the scourge
and, when they are mangled and half dead, beg them to per-
severe and offer their wounds for further wounding. What
wonder, then, if god tries noble spirits with sternness? The
demonstration of courage can never be gentle. Fortune
scourges and rends us: we must endure it. It is not cruelty but
a contest, and the oftener we submit to it the braver shall
we be. The most robust part of the body is that which is
most frequently put to active use. We must offer ourselves
to Fortune so that we may be inured against her through her
own agency; gradually she will make us her peers, and constant exposure to peril will beget contempt for danger. So
sailors' bodies are hardened by enduring the sea, and farmers
have calloused hands, and soldiers' biceps are powerful for
hurling missiles, and runners have nimble legs; the member
each exercises is the most robust. By suffering misfortune
the mind grows able to belittle suffering.

You will realize how effective this can be in our case if you
observe how profitable labor is to naked tribes whom poverty
makes rugged. Consider all the nations beyond the bounds of
the Roman peace—I mean the Germans and the nomad tribes
that infest the Danube. Endless winter and dismal skies weigh
them down and the barren earth grudges them food. They
keep the rain off with thatch or leaves, they bound over
marshes hardened into ice, they hunt wild animals for their
food. Do you think them wretched? There is no wretchedness
where habit has restored men to nature; what they begin out

of necessity gradually becomes a pleasure. They have no homes and no lodgings except those which weariness appoints for the day. Their victuals are vile and must be obtained by their own hands, their brooding climate is repulsive, their bodies uncovered. What you regard as disastrous is the daily life of many races. Why do you wonder that good men are shaken to make them strong? No tree stands firm and sturdy if it is not buffeted by constant wind; the very stresses cause it to stiffen and fix its roots firmly. Trees that have grown in a sunny vale are fragile. It is therefore to the advantage of good men, and it enables them to live without fear, to be on terms of intimacy with danger and to bear with serenity a fortune that is ill only to him who bears it ill.

[5. Consider further that it is to the common interest for the best men to be soldiers, so to speak, and do our service. It is god's purpose, and the sage's as well, to show that what the crowd desires or fears is neither good nor evil; things will evidently be good if god bestows them upon none but good men, and evil if he inflicts them only upon evil men. Blindness would be execrable if no one lost his eyes except the man who deserved to have them gouged out. That is why Appius and Metellus must be deprived of light. Riches are not a good; that is why the pimp Elius must have riches, so that men who sanctify money in temples may see that it is in the brothel also. God can discredit the objects of our concupiscence in no more effective way than by bestowing them upon vile characters and withholding them from the best. "But," you object, "it is unfair for a good man to become invalid or be pierced or fettered while rogues mince about carefree and dainty and in sound health." Why so? Is it not unfair for brave men to take up arms and spend their nights in camp and stand guard before the rampart with bandaged wounds while perverts and professional profligates loll at ease in the city? Why so? Is it not unfair for the noblest of our maidens to be aroused before daylight to perform the Vestal rites while tainted women enjoy sound sleep? The best men are conscripts of toil. Frequently the senate is in session the live-long day while nobodies are taking their pleasure in the sporting field or lurking in some tavern or passing their time with cronies.

The same thing happens in the commonwealth of the world. Good men toil, spend and are spent, and willingly; they are not dragged along by Fortune but follow her and keep in step. If they knew how, they would have outstripped her. Here is another spirited utterance of that stalwart Demetrius which I remember hearing: "This one complaint I can make of you, immortal gods," said he, "you did not make your will known to me sooner, for I would then myself have long ago reached the state to which I am now called. Do you wish to take my children? It was for you I reared them. Do you want some part of my body? Take it; it is no great boon I grant, for soon I shall leave the whole of it. Do you want the breath of my life? Why not? I shall not balk at your taking back what you have given. Whatever you ask you shall obtain from a willing giver. What then is my complaint? I should have preferred to offer rather than to surrender. What need was there for you to take it when I would have handed it to you? But even now you will not really be taking it, for nothing can be wrested from a man if he does not cling to it."

I am not under duress, I do not submit against my will, I am not god's slave but his follower, and the more willingly because I know that all things proceed according to a law that is fixed and eternally valid. Fate directs us, and the first hour of our birth determines each man's span. Cause is linked with cause, and a long chain of events governs all matters public and private. Everything must therefore be borne with fortitude, because events do not, as we suppose, happen but arrive by appointment. What would make you rejoice and what would make you weep was determined long ago, and though individual lives seem to differ in a wide range, the sum amounts to the same thing: what we receive is perishable and we shall ourselves perish. Why then are we indignant? Why do we complain? It is for this we were born. Nature may use her own bodies as she will; we must be cheerful and steadfast whatever befalls, in the thought that nothing that is ours is lost.

What is the duty of the good man? To offer himself to Fate. It is a great consolation that our rapid course is one with the universe's. Whatever it is that has ordained the mode of our life and the mode of our death has bound the gods, too, by the same necessity. The course that carries human affairs and divine alike is irrevocable. The very founder and ruler of all things has prescribed the fates indeed, but he follows them; he obeys always, he commanded but once. "Yet why was god so unfair in distributing destinies as to allot good men poverty and wounds and painful death?" The artisan cannot transform his material; such is its nature. Certain elements cannot be separated from others; they cohere and are indivisible. Languid constitutions that are prone to sleep or to a wakefulness indistinguishable from sleep are compounded of sluggish elements; it requires more vigorous endowment to produce a man who merits careful study. His path will not be level, he must go uphill and down, he must be wave-tossed and steer his craft through troubled waters, he must maintain his course in the face of Fortune. Much that is hard and rough will befall him, but he will himself soften it and smooth it down. Gold is tried by fire, brave men by misfortune. See how high virtue must mount: you will realize the perils that beset the ascent.

Steep is the way at first, and the steeds in their morning
    freshness
Must strain for the climb. The crest is heaven's center.
Thence to look down upon lands and sea has often terrified
    even me,
And my bosom has quaked with panic.
Sheer downward is the last stretch, and wants a firm rein.

Even Tethys who spreads her waves for my descent
Will often fear for my headlong fall.[1]

When he had heard this plea the spirited young man said:
"I like the road and shall climb it. It is worth a fall to travel
through those regions." Phoebus persisted in his attempt to
cow Phaethon's bold spirit with terrors:

Even if you hold your course and are not pulled astray
Yet must you go through the fierce horns of the Bull,
Through the Archer's bow, the maw of raging Leo.[2]

Whereupon Phaethon said: "Harness the chariot you
promised. The adventures you suppose will frighten me prick
me on. I want to stand where Sun himself trembles." To
stick to safety is the part of the puny and the spiritless;
virtue marches on high.

[6. "Yet why does god allow evil to happen to good men?"
But in fact he does not. From good men he keeps every evil
away—sin and crime and wicked thoughts and greedy
schemes and blind lust and avarice which covets another's
property. The good man himself, god protects and defends;
should anyone expect that god will look after the good man's
baggage also? Good men release god from this care, for they
themselves despise externals. Democritus cast his riches
away in the belief that they were a burden to a good mind.
Then why should you wonder that god allows a good man to
light upon a lot which a good man would sometimes himself choose to light upon? Good men lose their sons: why not,
when they sometimes leave their country of their own accord
never to return? They are slain: why not, when they sometimes lay hands upon themselves? Why do they suffer certain hardships? To teach others to endure them; they were
born to serve as models.

[1] Ovid, *Metamorphoses* 2.63-69. This is the story of Phaethon, whom his
father Phoebus is here attempting to dissuade from driving the chariot of
the Sun.
[2] Ovid, *Metamorphoses* 2.79-81.

Imagine that god speaks as follows: "What grounds do you have to complain of me, you who have opted for righteousness? Other men I have surrounded with spurious goods, I have beguiled their empty minds, as it were, with a long and deceptive dream. I have adorned them with gold and silver and ivory, but there is nothing good inside. The men you look upon as happy, if you could see not their outward appearance but their inward nature, are wretched, squalid, mean, well groomed on the surface, like their own house walls; that is no solid and genuine happiness but only a veneer, and a thin one. And so, as long as they can keep their feet and give the impression they desire, they glitter and carry it off; but when something happens to set them awry and uncover them, then one can see what a mass of genuine foulness their adventitious glitter concealed. But to you I have given goods that are sure and abiding, goods which are better and greater the more one turns them about and scrutinizes them from every side. To you I have granted scorn of terrors and disdain of passions. You do not shine outwardly because all your goods are turned inward. So does our world scorn what lies without and rejoice in the contemplation of itself. Your whole good I have bestowed within yourselves: your good fortune is not to need good fortune.

" 'But,' you object, 'many things which are sad and dreadful and hard to bear do happen.' Because I could not make you evade their assault, I have given your minds armor to withstand them; bear them with fortitude. In this respect you can surpass god: he is exempt from enduring evil, you rise superior to it. Scorn poverty: no one is as poor as he was at birth. Scorn pain: either it will go away or you will. Scorn death: either it finishes you or it transforms you. Scorn Fortune: I have given her no weapon with which to strike your soul. Above all, I have taken pains that nothing should detain you against your will: the way out lies open. If you do not wish to fight you may escape. Of all the things which I deemed necessary for you, therefore, I have made none easier than dying. The soul I have placed on a downgrade, where it is pulled by gravity: only observe and you will see what a short and direct road leads to freedom. I have imposed no such long delays at your egress as at your entry. Otherwise, if a man were as slow in dying as he is in being born, Fortune would have enormous power over you. Let every occasion and every situation teach you how easy it is to renounce Nature and throw her gift in her face. At the very altars and the solemn rites of sacrifice, even as you pray for life, study death. Massive bulls fall by a paltry wound, and the blow of a man's hand fells powerful animals. A thin blade severs the joints of the neck, and when the articulation of head and neck is cut the whole mass collapses. The seat of life is not buried at a great depth and need not be rooted out with steel, the vitals need not be searched out with deep wounds; death is near at hand. For the lethal blow I have appointed no specific spot; whatever way you choose will serve. The process called dying, whereby the soul departs from the body, is so short that its passing is imperceptible. Whether the noose strangles the throat, or water suffocates the breath, or the hard ground which breaks the fall crushes the skull, or fire sucked in blocks respiration—whatever the means, it is swift. Do you not blush at fearing so long a thing that happens so quickly?"

EPICTETUS

ABOUT FREEDOM*

He is free who lives as he wishes to live, who is neither subject to compulsion nor to hindrance, nor to force; whose movements to action are not impeded, whose desires attain

* Reprinted from *The Discourses of Epictetus*, Book IV, Chapter I, translated by G. Long. Bohn's Classical Library edition, London, 1877.

their purpose, and who does not fall into that which he would avoid. Who then chooses to live in error? No man. Who chooses to live deceived, liable to mistake, unjust, unrestrained, discontented, mean? No man. Not one then of the bad lives as he wishes; nor is he then free. And who chooses to live in sorrow, fear, envy, pity, desiring and failing in his desires, attempting to avoid something and falling into it? Not one. Do we then find any of the bad free from sorrow, free from fear, who does not fall into that which he would avoid, and does not obtain that which he wishes? Not one; nor then do we find any bad man free.

If then a man who has been twice consul should hear this, if you add, But you are a wise man; this is nothing to you: he will pardon you. But if you tell him the truth, and say, You differ not at all from those who have been thrice sold as to being yourself not a slave, what else ought you to expect than blows? For he says, What, I a slave, I whose father was free, whose mother was free. I whom no man can purchase: I am also of senatorial rank, and a friend of Caesar, and I have been a consul, and I own many slaves.—In the first place, most excellent senatorial man, perhaps your father also was a slave in the same kind of servitude, and your mother, and your grandfather and all your ancestors in an ascending series. But even if they were as free as it is possible, what is this to you? What if they were of a noble nature, and you of a mean nature; if they were fearless, and you a coward; if they had the power of self-restraint, and you are not able to exercise it?

And what, you may say, has this to do with being a slave? Does it seem to you to be nothing to do a thing unwillingly, with compulsion, with groans, has this nothing to do with being a slave? It is something, you say: but who is able to compel me, except the lord of all, Caesar? Then even you yourself have admitted that you have one master. But that he is the common master of all, as you say, let not this console you at all: but know that you are a slave in a great family. So also the people of Nicopolis are used to exclaim, By the fortune of Caesar, we are free.

However, if you please, let us not speak of Caesar at present. But tell me this: did you never love any person, a young girl, or slave, or free? What then is this with respect to being a slave or free? Were you never commanded by the person beloved to do something which you did not wish to do? have you never flattered your little slave? have you never kissed her feet? And yet if any man compelled you to kiss Caesar's feet, you would think it an insult and excessive tyranny. What else then is slavery? Did you never go out by night to some place whither you did not wish to go, did you not expend what you did not wish to expend, did you not utter words with sighs and groans, did you not submit to abuse and to be excluded? But if you are ashamed to confess your own acts, see what Thrasonides says and does, who having seen so much military service as perhaps not even you have, first of all went out by night, when Geta (a slave) does not venture out, but if he were compelled by his master, would have cried out much and would have gone out lamenting his bitter slavery. Next, what does Thrasonides say? A worthless girl has enslaved me, me whom no enemy ever did. Unhappy man, who are the slave even of a girl, and a worthless girl. Why then do you still call yourself free? and why do you talk of your service in the army? Then he calls for a sword and is angry with him who out of kindness refuses it; and he sends presents to her who hates him, and entreats and weeps, and on the other hand having had a little success he is elated. But even then how? was he free enough neither to desire nor to fear?

Now consider in the case of animals, how we employ the notion of liberty. Men keep tame lions shut up, and feed them, and some take them about; and who will say that this lion is free? Is it not the fact that the more he lives at his ease, so much the more he is in a slavish condition? and who if he had perception and reason would wish to be one of

these lions? Well, these birds when they are caught and are
kept shut up, how much do they suffer in their attempts to
escape? and some of them die of hunger rather than submit
to such a kind of life. And as many of them as live, hardly
live and with suffering pine away; and if they ever find any
opening, they make their escape. So much do they desire their
natural liberty, and to be independent and free from hindrance. And what harm is there to you in this? What do you
say? I am formed by nature to fly where I choose, to live in
the open air, to sing when I choose: you deprive me of all
this, and say, what harm is it to you? For this reason
we shall say that those animals only are free, which cannot
endure capture, but as soon as they are caught, escape
from captivity by death. So Diogenes also somewhere says
that there is only one way to freedom, and that is to die
content: and he writes to the Persian king, You cannot enslave the Athenian state any more than you can enslave
fishes. How is that? cannot I catch them? If you catch them,
says Diogenes, they will immediately leave you, as fishes
do; for if you catch a fish, it dies; and if these men that are
caught shall die, of what use to you is the preparation for
war? These are the words of a free man who had carefully
examined the thing, and, as was natural, had discovered it.
But if you look for it in a different place from where it is,
what wonder if you never find it?

The slave wishes to be set free immediately. Why? Do you
think that he wishes to pay money to the collectors of twen-
tieths? No; but because he imagines that hitherto through
not having obtained this, he is hindered and unfortunate.
If I shall be set free, immediately it is all happiness, I care
for no man, I speak to all as an equal and like to them, I go
where I choose, I come from any place I choose, and go where
I choose. Then he is set free; and forthwith having no
place where he can eat, he looks for some man to flat-
ter, some one with whom he shall sup: then he either works
with his body and endures the most dreadful things; and if

he can obtain a manger, he falls into a slavery much worse than his former slavery; or even if he is become rich, being a man without any knowledge of what is good, he loves some little girl, and in his unhappiness laments and desires to be a slave again. He says, what evil did I suffer in my state of slavery? Another clothed me, another supplied me with shoes, another fed me, another looked after me in sickness; and I did only a few services for him. But now a wretched man, what things I suffer, being a slave to many instead of to one. But however, he says, if I shall acquire rings, then I shall live most prosperously and happily. First, in order to acquire these rings, he submits to that which he is worthy of; then when he has acquired them, it is again all the same. Then he says, If I shall be engaged in military service, I am free from all evils. He obtains military service. He suffers as much as a flogged slave, and nevertheless he asks for a second service and a third. After this when he has put the finishing stroke to his career, and is become a senator, then he becomes a slave by entering into the assembly, then he serves the finer and most splendid slavery—not to be a fool, but to learn what Socrates taught, what is the nature of each thing that exists, and that a man should not rashly adapt preconceptions to the several things which are. For this is the cause to men of all their evils, the not being able to adapt the general preconceptions to the several things. But we have different opinions (about the cause of our evils). One man thinks that he is sick: not so however, but the fact is that he does not adapt his preconceptions right. Another thinks that he is poor; another that he has a severe father or mother; and another again that Caesar is not favorable to him. But all this is one and only one thing, the not knowing how to adapt the preconceptions. For who has not a preconception of that which is bad, that it is hurtful, that it ought to be avoided, that it ought in every way to be guarded against? One preconception is not repugnant to another, only where it comes to the matter of adaptation. What then is this evil, which is both hurtful, and a thing to be avoided? He answers not to be Caesar's friend. —He is gone far from the mark, he has missed the adaptation, he is embarrassed, he seeks the things which are not at all pertinent to the matter; for when he has succeeded in being Caesar's friend, never the less he has failed in finding what he sought. For what is that which every man seeks? To live secure, to be happy, to do every thing as he wishes, not to be hindered, nor compelled. When then he is become the friend of Caesar, is he free from hindrance? free from compulsion, is he tranquil, is he happy? Of whom shall we inquire? What more trustworthy witness have we than this very man who is become Caesar's friend? Come forward and tell us when did you sleep more quietly, now or before you became Caesar's friend? Immediately you hear the answer, Stop, I entreat you, and do not mock me: you know not what miseries I suffer, and sleep does not come to me; but one comes and says, Caesar is already awake, he is now going forth: then come troubles and cares—Well, when did you sup with more pleasure, now or before? Hear what he says about this also. He says that if he is not invited, he is pained: and if he is invited, he sups like a slave with his master, all the while being anxious that he does not say or do any thing foolish. And what do you suppose that he is afraid of; lest he should be lashed like a slave? How can he expect any thing so good? No, but as befits so great a man, Caesar's friend, he is afraid that he may lose his head. And when did you bathe more free from trouble, and take your gymnastic exercise more quietly? In fine, which kind of life did you prefer? Your present or your former life? I can swear that no man is so stupid or so ignorant of truth as not to bewail his own misfortunes the nearer he is in friendship to Caesar.

Since then neither those who are called kings live as they choose, nor the friends of kings, who finally are those who are free? Seek, and you will find; for you have aids from nature for the discovery of truth. But if you are not able yourself by going along these ways only to discover that which follows, listen to those who have made the inquiry. What do they say? Does freedom seem to you a good thing? The greatest good. Is it possible then that he who obtains the greatest good can be unhappy or fare badly? No. Whomsoever then you shall see unhappy, unfortunate, lamenting, confidently declare that they are not free. I do declare it. We have now then got away from buying and selling and from such arrangements about matters of property: for if you have rightly assented to these matters, if the great king (the Persian king) is unhappy, he cannot be free, nor can a little king, nor a man of consular rank, nor one who has been twice consul.—Be it so.

Further then answer me this question also, does freedom seem to you to be something great and noble and valuable?— How should it not seem so? Is it possible then when a man obtains anything so great and valuable and noble to be mean?—It is not possible—When then you see any man subject to another or flattering him contrary to his own opinion, confidently affirm that this man also is not free; and not only if he do this for a bit of supper, but also if he does it for a government or a consulship; and call these men little slaves who for the sake of little matters do these things, and those who do so for the sake of great things call great slaves, as they deserve to be.—This is admitted also— Do you think that freedom is a thing independent and self governing?—Certainly—Whomsoever then it is in the power of another to hinder and compel, declare that he is not free. And do not look, I intreat you, after his grandfathers and great grandfathers, or inquire about his being bought or sold; but if you hear him saying from his heart and with feeling, 'Master,' even if the twelve fasces precede him (as consul), call him a slave. And if you hear him say, 'Wretch that I am, how much I suffer,' call him a slave. If finally you see him lamenting, complaining, unhappy, call him a slave though he wears a praetexta. If then he is doing nothing of this kind, do not yet say that he is free, but learn his opinions, whether they are subject to compulsion, or may produce hindrance, or to bad fortune; and if you find him such, call him a slave who has a holiday in the Saturnalia: say that his master is from home: he will return soon, and you will know what he suffers. Who will return? Whoever has in himself the power over anything which is desired by the man, either to give it to him or to take it away. Thus then have we many masters? We have: for we have circumstances as masters prior to our present masters; and these circumstances are many. Therefore it must of necessity be that those who have the power over any of these circumstances must be our masters. For no man fears Caesar himself, but he fears death, banishment, deprivation of his property, prison, and disgrace. Nor does any man love Caesar, unless Caesar is a person of great merit, but he loves wealth, the office of tribune, praetor or consul. When we love, and hate and fear these things, it must be that those who have the power over them must be our masters. Therefore we adore them even as gods; for we think that what possesses the power of conferring the greatest advantage on us is divine. Then we wrongly assume that a certain person has the power of conferring the greatest advantages; therefore he is something divine. For if we wrongly assume that a certain person has the power of conferring the greatest advantages, it is a necessary consequence that the conclusion from these premises must be false.

What then is that which makes a man free from hindrance and makes him his own master? For wealth does not do it, nor consulship, nor provincial government, nor royal power; but something else must be discovered. What then is that which when we write makes us free from hindrance and unimpeded? The knowledge of the art of writing. What then is it in playing the lute? The science of playing the lute. Therefore in life also it is the science of life. You have then heard in a general way: but examine the thing also in the several parts. Is it possible that he who desires any of the things which depend on others can be free from hindrance? No—Is it possible for him to be unimpeded? No—Therefore he cannot be free. Consider then: whether we have nothing which is in our own power only, or whether we have all things, or whether some things are in our own power, and others in the power of others.—What do you mean?—When you wish the body to be entire (sound), is it in your power or not?—It is not in my power—When you wish it to be healthy?—Neither is this in my power—When you wish it to be handsome? Nor is this—Life or death?—Neither is this in my power.—Your body then is another's, subject to every man who is stronger than yourself?—It is—But your estate, is it in your power to have it when you please, and as long as you please, and such as you please?—No—And your slaves?—No—And your clothes?—No—And your house?—No—And your horses?—Not one of these things—And if you wish by all means your children to live, or your wife, or your brother, or your friends, is it in your power?—This also is not in my power.

Whether then have you nothing which is in your own power, which depends on yourself only and cannot be taken from you, or have you any thing of the kind?—I know not—Look at the thing then thus, and examine it. Is any man able to make you assent to that which is false?—No man—In the matter of assent then you are free from hindrance and obstruction.—Granted—Well; and can a man force you to desire to move towards that to which you do not choose?—He can, for when he threatens me with death or bonds, he compels me to desire to move towards it. If then, you despise death and bonds, do you still pay any regard to him?—No—Is then the despising of death an act of your own or is it not yours?—It is my act—It is your own act then also to desire to move towards a thing: or is it not so?—It is my own act—But to desire to move away from a thing, whose act is that? This also is your act—What then if I have attempted to walk, suppose another should hinder me—What part of you does he hinder? does he hinder the faculty of assent?—No: but my poor body—Yes, as he would do with a stone—Granted; but I no longer walk—And who told you that walking is your own act free from hindrance? for I said that this only was free from hindrance, to desire to move: but where there is need of body and its co-operation, you have heard long ago that nothing is your own.—Granted this also—And who can compel you to desire what you do not wish?—No man—And to propose or intend, or in short to make use of the appearances which present themselves, can any man compel you?—He cannot do this: but he will hinder me when I desire from obtaining what I desire.—If you desire any thing which is your own, and one of the things which cannot be hindered, how will he hinder you?—He cannot in any way—Who then tells you that he who desires the things that belong to another is free from hindrance?

Must I then not desire health? By no means, nor anything else that belongs to another: for what is not in your power to acquire or to keep when you please, this belongs to another. Keep then far from it not only your hands, but more than that, even your desires. If you do not, you have surrendered yourself as a slave; you have subjected your neck, if you admire any thing not your own, to everything that is dependent on the power of others and perishable, to which you have conceived a liking.—Is not my hand my own?—It is a part of your own body; but it is by nature earth, subject to hindrance, compulsion, and the slave of every thing which is stronger. And why do I say your hand? You ought to possess your whole body as a poor ass loaded, as long as it is possible, as long as you are allowed. But if there be a press, and a soldier should lay hold of it, let it go, do not resist, nor murmur; if you do, you will receive blows, and never the less you will also lose the ass. But when you ought to feel thus with respect to the body, consider what remains to be done about all the rest, which is provided for the sake of the body. When the body is an ass, all the other things are bits belonging to the ass, pack-saddles, shoes, barley, fodder. Let these also go: get rid of them quicker and more readily than of the ass.

When you have made this preparation, and have practised this discipline, to distinguish that which belongs to another from that which is your own, the things which are subject to hindrance from those which are not, to consider the things free from hindrance to concern yourself, and those which are not free not to concern yourself, to keep your desire steadily fixed to the things which do concern yourself, and turned from the things which do not concern yourself; do you still fear any man? No one. For about what will you be afraid? about the things which are your own, in which consists the nature of good and evil? and who has power over these things? who can take them away? who can impede them? No man can, no more than he can impede God. But will you be afraid about your body and your possessions, about things which are not yours, about things which in no way concern you? and what else have you been studying from the beginning than to distinguish between your own and not your own, the things which are in your power and not in your power, the things subject to hindrance and not subject? and why have you come to the philosophers? was it that you may never the less be unfortunate and unhappy? You will then in this way, as I have supposed you to have done, be without fear and disturbance. And what is grief to you? for fear comes from what you expect, but grief from that which is present. But what further will you desire? For of the things which are within the power of the will, as being good and present, you have a proper and regulated desire: but of the things which are not in the power of the will you do not desire any one, and so you do not allow any place to that which is irrational, and impatient, and above measure hasty.

When then you are thus affected towards things, what man

can any longer be formidable to you? For what has a man which is formidable to another, either when you see him or speak to him or finally are conversant with him? Not more than one horse has with respect to another, or one dog to another, or one bee to another bee. Things indeed are formidable to every man; and when any man is able to confer these things on another or to take them away, then he too becomes formidable. How then is an acropolis (a stronghold or fortress, the seat of tyranny) demolished? Not by the sword, not by fire, but by opinion. For if we abolish the acropolis which is in the city, can we abolish also that of fever, and that of beautiful women? Can we in a word abolish the acropolis which is in us and cast out the tyrants within us, whom we have daily over us, sometimes the same tyrants, at other times different tyrants? But with this we must begin, and with this we must demolish the acropolis and eject the tyrants, by giving up the body, the parts of it, the faculties of it, the possessions, the reputation, magisterial offices, honors, children, brothers, friends, by considering all these things as belonging to others. And if tyrants have been ejected from us, why do I still shut in the acropolis by a wall of circumvallation, at least on my account; for if it still stands, what does it do to me? why do I still eject (the tyrant's) guards? For where do I perceive them? against others they have their fasces, and their spears and their swords. But I have never been hindered in my will, nor compelled when I did not will. And how is this possible? I have placed my movements towards action in obedience to God. Is it his will that I shall have fever? It is my will also. Is it his will that I should move towards any thing? It is my will also. Is it his will that I should obtain any thing? It is my wish also. Does he not will? I do not wish. Is it his will that I die, is it his will that I be put to the rack? It is my will then to die: it is my will then to be put to the rack. Who then is still able to hinder me contrary to my own judgment, or to compel me? No more than he can hinder or compel Zeus.

Thus the more cautious of travellers also act. A traveller has heard that the road is infested by robbers; he does not venture to enter on it alone, but he waits for the companionship on the road either of an ambassador, or of a quaestor, or of a proconsul, and when he has attached himself to such persons he goes along the road safely. So in the world the wise man acts. There are many companies of robbers, tyrants, storms, difficulties, losses of that which is dearest. Where is there any place of refuge? how shall he pass along without being attacked by robbers? what company shall he wait for that he may pass along in safety? to whom shall he attach himself? To what person generally? to the rich man, to the man of consular rank? and what is the use of that to me? Such a man is stripped himself, groans and laments. But what if the fellow companion himself turns against me and becomes my robber, what shall I do? I will be a friend of Caesar: when I am Caesar's companion no man will wrong me. In the first place, that I may become illustrious, what things must I endure and suffer? how often and by how many must I be robbed? Then, if I become Caesar's friend, he also is mortal. And if Caesar from any circumstance becomes my enemy, where is it best for me to retire? Into a desert? Well, does fever not come there? What shall be done then? Is it not possible to find a safe fellow traveller, a faithful one, strong, secure against all surprises? Thus he considers and perceives that if he attaches himself to God, he will make his journey in safety.

How do you understand "attaching yourself to God"? In this sense, that whatever God wills, a man also shall will; and what God does not will, a man also shall not will. How then shall this be done? In what other way than by examining the movements of God and his administration? What has he given to me as my own and in my own power? what has he reserved to himself? He has given to me the things which are in the power of the will: he has put them in my power free from impediment and hindrance. How was he able to make the earthy body free from hindrance? [He could not], and accordingly he has subjected to the revolution of the whole possessions, household things, house, children, wife. Why then do I fight against God? why do I will what does not depend on the will? why do I will to have absolutely what is not granted to me? But how ought I to will to have things? In the way in which they are given and as long as they are given. But he who has given takes away. Why then do I resist? I do not say that I shall be a fool if I use force to one who is stronger, but I shall first be unjust. For whence had I things when I came into the world?—My father gave them to me—And who gave them to him? and who made the sun? and who made the fruits of the earth? and who the seasons? and who made the connection of men with one another and their fellowship?

Then after receiving everything from another and even yourself, are you angry and do you blame the giver if he takes any thing from you? Who are you, and for what purpose did you come into the world? Did not he (God) introduce you here, did he not show you the light, did he not give you fellow workers, and perceptions and reason? and as whom did he introduce you here? did he not introduce you as subject to death, and as one to live on the earth with a little flesh, and to observe his administration, and to join with him in the spectacle and the festival for a short time? Will you not then, as long as you have been permitted, after seeing the spectacle and the solemnity, when he leads you out, go with adoration of him and thanks for what you have heard and seen?—No; but I would still enjoy the feast.—The initiated too would wish to be longer in the initiation: and perhaps also those at Olympia to see other athletes; but the solemnity is ended: go away like a grateful and modest man; make room for others: others also must be born, as you were, and being born they must have a place, and houses and necessary things. And if the first do not retire, what remains? Why are you insatiable? Why are you not content? why do you contract the world?—Yes, but I would have my little children with me and my wife—What, are they yours? do they not belong to the giver, and to him who made you? then will you not give up what belongs to others? will you not give way to him who is superior?—Why then did he introduce me into the world on these conditions?—And if the conditions do not suit you, depart. He has no need of a spectator who is not satisfied. He wants those who join in the festival, those who take part in the chorus, that they may rather applaud, admire, and celebrate with hymns the solemnity. But those who can bear no trouble, and the cowardly he will not unwillingly see absent from the great assembly; for they did not when they were present behave as they ought to do at a festival nor fill up their place properly, but they lamented, found fault with the deity, fortune, their companions; not seeing both what they had, and their own powers, which they received for contrary purposes, the powers of magnanimity, of a generous mind, manly spirit, and what we are now inquiring about, freedom—For what purpose then have I received these things?—To use them—How long?—So long as he who has lent them chooses.—What if they are necessary to me?—Do not attach yourself to them and they will not be necessary: do not say to yourself that they are necessary, and then they are not necessary.

This study you ought to practise from morning to evening, beginning with the smallest things and those most liable to damage, with an earthen pot, with a cup. Then proceed in this way to a tunic, to a little dog, to a horse, to a small estate in land: then to yourself, to your body, to the parts of your body, to your children, to your wife, to your brothers. Look all round and throw these things from you (which are not yours). Purge your opinions, so that nothing cleave to you of the things which are not your own, that nothing grow to you, that nothing give you pain when it is torn from you; and say, while you are daily exercising yourself as you do there (in the school), not that you are philosophizing, for this is an arrogant (offensive) expression, but that you are presenting an asserter of freedom, for this is really freedom. To this freedom Diogenes was called by Antisthenes, and he said that he could no longer be enslaved by any man. For this reason when he was taken prisoner, how did he behave to the pirates? Did he call any of them master? and I do not speak of the name, for I am not afraid of the word, but of the state of mind, by which the word is produced. How did he reprove them for feeding badly their captives? How was he sold? Did he seek a master? no; but a slave. And when he was sold how did he behave to his master? Immediately he disputed with him and said to his master that he ought not to be dressed as he was, nor shaved in such a manner; and about the children he told them how he ought to bring them up. And what was strange in this? for if his master had bought an exercise master, would he have employed him in the exercises of the palaestra as a servant or as a master? and so if he had bought a physician or an architect. And so in every matter, it is absolutely necessary that he who has skill must be the superior of him who has not. Whoever then generally possesses the science of life, what else must he be than master? For who is master in a ship? The man who governs the helm? Why? Because he who will not obey him suffers for it. But a master can give me stripes. Can he do it then without suffering for it? So I also used to think. But because he cannot do it without suffering for it, for this reason it is not in his power: and no man can do what is unjust without suffering for it. And what is the penalty for him who puts his own slave in chains? what do you think that is? The fact of putting the slave in chains:—and you also will admit this, if you choose to maintain the truth, that man is not a wild beast, but a tame animal. For when is a vine doing badly? When it is in a condition contrary to its nature. When is a cock? Just the same. Therefore a man also is so. What then is a man's nature? To bite, to kick, and to throw into prison and to behead? No; but to do good, to co-operate with others, to wish them well. At that time then he is in a bad condition, whether you choose to admit it or not, when he is acting foolishly.

Socrates then did not fare badly?—No; but his judges and his accusers did—Nor did Helvidius at Rome fare badly?—No; but his murderer did—How do you mean?—The same as you do when you say that a cock has not fared badly when he has gained the victory and been severely wounded; but that the cock has fared badly when he has been defeated and is unhurt: nor do you call a dog fortunate, who neither pursues game nor labors, but when you see him sweating, when you see him in pain and panting violently after running. What paradox do we utter if we say that the evil in every thing is that which is contrary to the nature of the thing? Is this a paradox? for do you not say this in the case of all other things? Why then in the case of man only do you think differently? But because we say that the nature of man is tame (gentle) and social and faithful, you will not say that this is a paradox?—It is not—What then is it a paradox to say that a man is not hurt when he is whipped, or put in chains, or beheaded? does he not, if he suffers nobly, come off even with increased advantage and profit? But is he not hurt, who suffers in a most pitiful and disgraceful way, who in place of a man becomes a wolf, or viper or wasp?

Well then let us recapitulate the things which have been agreed on. The man who is not under restraint is free, to whom things are exactly in that state in which he wishes them to be; but he who can be restrained or compelled or hindered, or thrown into any circumstances against his will, is a slave. But who is free from restraint? He who desires nothing that belongs to (is in the power of) others. And what are the things which belong to others? Those which are not in our power either to have or not to have, or to have of a certain kind or in a certain manner. Therefore the body belongs to another, the parts of the body belong to another, possession (property) belongs to another. If then you are at-

tached to any of these things as your own, you will pay the
penalty which it is proper for him to pay who desires what
belongs to another. This road leads to freedom, this is the
only way of escaping from slavery, to be able to say at last
with all your soul

> Lead me, O Zeus, and thou O destiny,
> The way that I am bid by you to go.

But what do you say, philosopher? The tyrant summons you
to say something which does not become you. Do you say it
or do you not? Answer me—Let me consider—Will you consider now? But when you were in the school, what was it
which you used to consider? Did you not study what are the
things that are good and what are bad, and what things are
neither one nor the other?—I did.—What then was our
opinion?—That just and honorable acts were good; and that
unjust and disgraceful acts were bad.—Is life a good thing?—
No.—Is death a bad thing?—No.—Is prison?—No.—But
what did we think about mean and faithless words and be-
trayal of a friend and flattery of a tyrant?—That they are
bad.—Well then, you are not considering, nor have you considered nor deliberated. For what is the matter for consideration, is it whether it is becoming for me, when I have it in
my power, to secure for myself the greatest of good things,
and not to secure for myself (that is, not to avoid) the
greatest evils?—A fine inquiry indeed, and necessary, and one
that demands much deliberation—Man, why do you mock
us? Such an inquiry is never made. If you really imagined
that base things were bad and honorable things were good,
and that all other things were neither good nor bad, you
would not even have approached this inquiry, nor have come
near it; but immediately you would have been able to distinguish them by the understanding as you would do (in other
cases) by the vision. For when do you inquire if black things
are white, if heavy things are light, and do not comprehend
the manifest evidence of the senses? How then do you now

say that you are considering whether things which are neither good nor bad ought to be avoided more than things
which are bad? But you do not possess these opinions; and
neither do these things seem to you to be neither good nor
bad, but you think that they are the greatest evils; nor do
you think those other things (mean and faithless words, etc.)
to be evils, but matters which do not concern us at all. For
thus from the beginning you have accustomed yourself.
Where am I? In the schools: and are any listening to me? I
am discoursing among philosophers. But I have gone out of
the school. Away with this talk of scholars and fools. Thus a
friend is overpowered by the testimony of a philosopher: thus
a philosopher becomes a parasite; thus he lets himself for
hire for money: thus in the senate a man does not say what
he thinks; in private (in the school) he proclaims his opinions. You are a cold and miserable little opinion, suspended
from idle words as from a hair. But keep yourself strong and
fit for the uses of life and initiated by being exercised in
action. How do you hear (the report)?—I do not say, that
your child is dead—for how could you bear that?—but that
your oil is spilled, your wine drunk up. Do you act in such a
way that one standing by you while you are making a great
noise, may say this only, Philosopher, you say something
different in the school. Why do you deceive us? Why, when
you are only a worm, do you say that you are a man? I
should like to be present when some of the philosophers is
lying with a woman, that I might see how he is exerting himself, and what words he is uttering, and whether he remembers his title of philosopher, and the words which he hears or
says or reads.

And what is this to liberty? Nothing else than this,
whether you who are rich choose or not.—And who is your
evidence for this?—who else than yourselves? who have a
powerful master (Caesar), and who live in obedience to his
nod and motion, and who faint if he only looks at you with a
scowling countenance; you who court old women and old

men, and say, I can't do this: it is not in my power. Why is it not in your power? Did you not lately contend with me and say that you are free? But Aprulla has hindered me? Tell the truth then, slave, and do not run away from your masters, nor deny, nor venture to produce any one to assert your freedom when you have so many evidences of your slavery. And indeed when a man is compelled by love to do something contrary to his opinion (judgment), and at the same time sees the better, but has not the strength to follow it, one might consider him still more worthy of excuse as being held by a certain violent and in a manner a divine power. But who could endure you who are in love with old women and old men, and wipe the old women's noses, and wash them and give them presents, and also wait on them like a slave when they are sick, and at the same time wish them dead, and question the physicians whether they are sick unto death? And again, when in order to obtain these great and much admired magistracies and honors, you kiss the hands of these slaves of others, and so you are not the slave even of free men. Then you walk about before me in stately fashion a praetor or a consul. Do I not know how you became a praetor, by what means you got your consulship, who gave it to you? I would not even choose to live, if I must live by help of Felicion and endure his arrogance and servile insolence: for I know what a slave is, who is fortunate, as he thinks, and puffed up by pride.

You then, a man may say, are you free? I wish, by the Gods, and pray to be free; but I am not yet able to face my masters, I still value my poor body, I value greatly the preservation of it entire, though I do not possess it entire. But I can point out to you a free man, that you may no longer seek an example. Diogenes was free. How was he free?—not because he was born of free parents, but because he was himself free, because he had cast off all the handles of slavery, and it was not possible for any man to approach him, nor had any man the means of laying hold of him to enslave him.

He had everything easily loosed, everything only hanging to him. If you laid hold of his property, he would have rather let it go and be yours, than he would have followed you for it: if you had laid hold of his leg, he would have let go his leg; if of all his body, all his poor body; his intimates, friends, country, just the same. For he knew from whence he had them, and from whom, and on what conditions. His true parents indeed, the Gods, and his real country he would never have deserted, nor would he have yielded to any man in obedience to them and to their orders, nor would any man have died for his country more readily. For he was not used to inquire when he should be considered to have done any-thing on behalf of the whole of things (the universe, or all the world), but he remembered that every thing which is done comes from thence and is done on behalf of that coun-try and is commanded by him who administers it. There-fore see what Diogenes himself says and writes:—"For this reason, he says, Diogenes, it is in your power to speak both with the King of the Persians and with Archidamus the king of the Lacedaemonians, as you please." Was it because he was born of free parents? I suppose all the Athenians and all the Lacedaemonians because they were born of slaves, could not talk with them (these kings) as they wished, but feared and paid court to them. Why then does he say that it is in his power? Because I do not consider the poor body to be my own, because I want nothing, because law is every thing to me, and nothing else is. These were the things which per-mitted him to be free.

And that you may not think that I show you the example of a man who is a solitary person, who has neither wife nor children, nor country, nor friends nor kinsmen, by whom he could be bent and drawn in various directions, take Socrates and observe that he had a wife and children, but he did not consider them as his own; that he had a country, so long as it was fit to have one, and in such a manner as was fit; friends and kinsmen also, but he held all in subjection to law and to the obedience due to it. For this reason he was the first to go out as a soldier, when it was necessary, and in war he exposed himself to danger most unsparingly; and when he was sent by the tyrants to seize Leon, he did not even deliberate about the matter, because he thought that it was a base action, and he knew that he must die (for his refusal), if it so happened. And what difference did that make to him? for he intended to preserve something else, not his poor flesh, but his fidelity, his honorable character. These are things which could not be assailed nor brought into subjection. Then when he was obliged to speak in defence of his life, did he behave like a man who had children, who had a wife? No, but he behaved like a man who has neither. And what did he do when he was (ordered) to drink the poison, and when he had the power of escaping from prison, and when Crito said to him, Escape for the sake of your children, what did Socrates say? did he consider the power of escape as an unexpected gain? By no means: he considered what was fit and proper; but the rest he did not even look at or take into the reckoning. For he did not choose, he said, to save his poor body, but to save that which is increased and saved by doing what is just, and is impaired and destroyed by doing what is unjust. Socrates will not save his life by a base act; he who would not put the Athenians to the vote when they clamored that he should do so, he who refused to obey the tyrants, he who discoursed in such a manner about virtue and right behavior. It is not possible to say such a man's life by base acts, but he is saved by dying, not by running away. For the good actor also preserves his character by stopping when he ought to stop, better than when he goes on acting beyond the proper time. What then shall the children of Socrates do? "If," said Socrates, "I had gone off to Thessaly, would you have taken care of them; and if I depart to the world below, will there be no man to take care of them?" See how he gives to death a gentle name and mocks it. But if you and I had been in his place, we should have immediately answered as philosophers that those who act unjustly must be repaid in the same way, and we should have added, "I shall be useful to many, if my life is saved, and if I die, I shall be useful to no man." For, if it had been necessary, we should have made our escape by slipping through a small hole. And how in that case should we have been useful to any man? for where would they have been then staying? or if we were useful to men while we were alive, should we not have been much more useful to them by dying when we ought to die, and as we ought? And now Socrates being dead, no less useful to men, and even more useful, is the remembrance of that which he did or said when he was alive.

Think of these things, these opinions, these words: look to these examples, if you would be free, if you desire the thing according to its worth. And what is the wonder if you buy so great a thing at the price of things so many and so great? For the sake of this which is called liberty, some hang themselves, others throw themselves down precipices, and sometimes even whole cities have perished: and will you not for the sake of the true and unassailable and secure liberty give back to God when he demands them the things which he has given? Will you not, as Plato says, study not to die only, but also to endure torture, and exile, and scourging and in a word to give up all which is not your own? If you will not, you will be a slave among slaves, even if you be ten thousand times a consul; and if you make your way up to the Palace (Caesar's residence), you will no less be a slave; and you will feel, that perhaps philosophers utter words which are contrary to common opinion, as Cleanthes also said, but not words contrary to reason. For you will know by experience that the words are true, and that there is no profit from the things which are valued and eagerly sought to those who have obtained them; and to those who have not yet obtained them there is an imagination, that when these things are come, all that is good will come with them; then, when they are come, the feverish feeling is the same, the tossing to and

fro is the same, the satiety, the desire of things which are
not present; for freedom is acquired not by the full possession
of the things which are desired, but by removing the desire.
And that you may know that this is true, as you have la-
bored for those things, so transfer your labor to these; be
vigilant for the purpose of acquiring an opinion which will
make you free; pay court to a philosopher instead of to a
rich old man: be seen about a philosopher's doors: you will
not disgrace yourself by being seen; you will not go away
empty nor without profit, if you go to the philosopher as you
ought, and if not (if you do not succeed), try at least: the
trial is not disgraceful.

MARCUS AURELIUS

THE MEDITATIONS OF THE EMPEROR
MARCUS AURELIUS ANTONINUS*

Book IV

That which rules within, when it is according to nature, is
so affected with respect to the events which happen, that it
always easily adapts itself to that which is possible and is
presented to it. For it requires no definite material, but it
moves towards its purpose, under certain conditions however;
and it makes a material for itself out of that which opposes
it, as fire lays hold of what falls into it, by which a small
light would have been extinguished: but when the fire is
strong, it soon appropriates to itself the matter which is
heaped on it, and consumes it, and rises higher by means of
this very material.

* Reprinted from *The Meditations*, translated by George Long. Dolphin
edition, published by Doubleday & Company, Inc.

[2. Let no act be done without a purpose, nor otherwise than according to the perfect principles of art.

[3. Men seek retreats for themselves, houses in the country, sea-shores, and mountains; and thou too art wont to desire such things very much. But this is altogether a mark of the most common sort of men, for it is in thy power whenever thou shalt choose to retire into thyself. For nowhere either with more quiet or more freedom from trouble does a man retire than into his own soul, particularly when he has within him such thoughts that by looking into them he is immediately in perfect tranquility; and I affirm that tranquility is nothing else than the good ordering of the mind. Constantly then give to thyself this retreat, and renew thyself; and let thy principles be brief and fundamental, which, as soon as thou shalt recur to them, will be sufficient to cleanse the soul completely, and to send thee back free from all discontent with the things to which thou returnest. For with what art thou discontented? With the badness of men? Recall to thy mind this conclusion, that rational animals exist for one another, and that to endure is a part of justice, and that men do wrong involuntarily; and consider how many already, after mutual enmity, suspicion, hatred, and fighting, have been stretched dead, reduced to ashes; and be quiet at last.— But perhaps thou art dissatisfied with that which is assigned to thee out of the universe.—Recall to thy recollection this alternative; either there is providence or atoms [fortuitous concurrence of things]; or remember the arguments by which it has been proved that the world is a kind of political community [and be quiet at last].—But perhaps corporeal things will still fasten upon thee.—Consider then further that the mind mingles not with the breath, whether moving gently or violently, when it has once drawn itself apart and discovered its own power, and think also of all that thou hast heard and assented to about pain and pleasure [and be quiet at last].—But perhaps the desire of the thing called fame will torment thee.—See how soon everything is forgotten, and look at the chaos of infinite time on each side of [the present], and the emptiness of applause, and the changeableness and want of judgment in those who pretend to give praise, and the narrowness of the space within which it is circumscribed [and be quiet at last]. For the whole earth is a point, and how small a nook in it is this thy dwelling, and how few are there in it, and what kind of people are they who will praise thee.

This then remains: Remember to retire into this little territory of thy own, and above all do not distract or strain thyself, but be free, and look at things as a man, as a human being, as a citizen, as a mortal. But among the things readiest to thy hand to which thou shalt turn, let there be these, which are two. One is that things do not touch the soul, for they are external and remain immovable; but our perturbations come only from the opinion which is within. The other is that all these things, which thou seest, change immediately and will no longer be; and constantly bear in mind how many of these changes thou hast already witnessed. The universe is transformation: life is opinion.

[4. If our intellectual part is common, the reason also, in respect of which we are rational beings, is common: if this is so, common also is the reason which commands us what to do, and what not to do; if this is so, there is a common law also; if this is so, we are fellow-citizens; if this is so, we are members of some political community; if this is so, the world is in a manner a state. For of what other common political community will any one say that the whole human race are members? And from thence, from this common political community comes also our very intellectual faculty and reasoning faculty and our capacity for law; or whence do they come? For as my earthly part is a portion given to me from certain earth, and that which is watery from another element, and that which is hot and fiery from some peculiar source (for nothing comes out of that which is nothing, as nothing also returns to non-existence), so also the intellectual part comes from some source.

[5. Death is such as generation is, a mystery of nature; composition out of the same elements, and a decomposition into the same; and altogether not a thing of which any man should be ashamed, for it is not contrary to [the nature of] a reasonable animal, and not contrary to the reason of our constitution.

[6. It is natural that these things should be done by such persons, it is a matter of necessity; and if a man will not have it so, he will not allow the fig-tree to have juice. But by all means bear this in mind, that within a very short time both thou and he will be dead; and soon not even your names will be left behind.

[7. Take away thy opinion, and then there is taken away the complaint, "I have been harmed." Take away the complaint, "I have been harmed," and the harm is taken away.

[8. That which does not make a man worse than he was, also does not make his life worse, nor does it harm him either from without or from within.

[9. The nature of that which is [universally] useful has been compelled to do this.

[10. Consider that everything which happens, happens justly, and if thou observest carefully, thou wilt find it to be so. I do not say only with respect to the continuity of the series of things, but with respect to what is just, and as if it were done by one who assigns to each thing its value. Observe then as thou hast begun; and whatever thou doest, do it in conjunction with this, the being good, and in the sense in which a man is properly understood to be good. Keep to this in every action.

[11. Do not have such an opinion of things as he has who does thee wrong, or such as he wishes thee to have, but look at them as they are in truth.

[12. A man should always have these two rules in readiness; the one, to do only whatever the reason of the ruling and legislating faculty may suggest for the use of men; the other, to change thy opinion, if there is any one at hand who sets thee right and moves thee from any opinion. But this change of opinion must proceed only from a certain persuasion, as of what is just or of common advantage, and the like, not because it appears pleasant or brings reputation.

[13. Hast thou reason? I have.—Why then dost not thou use it? For if this does its own work, what else dost thou wish?

[14. Thou hast existed as a part. Thou shalt disappear in that which produced thee; but rather thou shalt be received back into its seminal principle by transmutation.

[15. Many grains of frankincense on the same altar: one falls before, another falls after; but it makes no difference.

[16. Within ten days thou wilt seem a god to those to whom thou art now a beast and an ape, if thou wilt return to thy principles and the worship of reason.

[17. Do not act as if thou wert going to live ten thousand years. Death hangs over thee. While thou livest, while it is in thy power, be good.

[18. How much trouble he avoids who does not look to see what his neighbour says or does or thinks, but only to what he does himself, that it may be just and pure; or as Agathon says, look not round at the depraved morals of others, but run straight along the line without deviating from it.

[19. He who has a vehement desire for posthumous fame does not consider that every one of those who remember him will himself also die very soon; then again also they who have succeeded them, until the whole remembrance shall have been extinguished as it is transmitted through men who foolishly admire and perish. But suppose that those who will remember are even immortal, and that the remembrance will be immortal, what then is this to thee? And I say not what is it to the dead, but what is it to the living. What is praise, except indeed so far as it has a certain utility? For thou now rejectest unseasonably the gift of nature, clinging to something else.

[20. Everything which is in any way beautiful is beautiful in

itself, and terminates in itself, not having praise as part of
itself. Neither worse then nor better is a thing made by
being praised. I affirm this also of the things which are called
beautiful by the vulgar, for example, material things and
works of art. That which is really beautiful has no need of
anything; not more than law, not more than truth, not more
than benevolence or modesty. Which of these things is beautiful because it is praised, or spoiled by being blamed? Is
such a thing as an emerald made worse than it was, if it is
not praised? or gold, ivory, purple, a lyre, a little knife, a
flower, a shrub?

[21. If souls continue to exist, how does the air contain
them from eternity?—But how does the earth contain the
bodies of those who have been buried from time so remote?
For as here the mutation of these bodies after a certain continuance, whatever it may be, and their dissolution make
room for other dead bodies; so the souls which are removed
into the air after subsisting for some time are transmuted
and diffused, and assume a fiery nature by being received
into the seminal intelligence of the universe, and in this way
make room for the fresh souls which come to dwell there.
And this is the answer which a man might give on the hypothesis of souls continuing to exist. But we must not only
think of the number of bodies which are thus buried, but also
of the number of animals which are daily eaten by us and
the other animals. For what a number is consumed, and thus
in a manner buried in the bodies of those who feed on them?
And nevertheless this earth receives them by reason of the
changes [of these bodies] into blood, and the transforma-
tions into the aërial or the fiery element.

What is the investigation into the truth in this matter?
The division into that which is material and that which is
the cause of form [the formal].

[22. Do not be whirled about, but in every movement have
respect to justice, and on the occasion of every impression
maintain the faculty of comprehension [or understanding],

[23. Everything harmonizes with me, which is harmonious to thee, O Universe. Nothing for me is too early nor too late, which is in due time for thee. Everything is fruit to me which thy seasons bring, O Nature: from thee are all things, in thee are all things, to thee all things return. The poet says, Dear city of Cecrops; and wilt not thou say, Dear city of Zeus?

[24. Occupy thyself with few things, says the philosopher, if thou wouldst be tranquil.—But consider if it would not be better to say, Do what is necessary, and whatever the reason of the animal which is naturally social requires, and as it requires. For this brings not only the tranquillity which comes from doing well, but also that which comes from doing few things. For the greatest part of what we say and do being unnecessary, if a man takes this away, he will have more leisure and less uneasiness. Accordingly on every occasion a man should ask himself, Is this one of the unnecessary things? Now a man should take away not only unnecessary acts, but also unnecessary thoughts, for thus superfluous acts will not follow after.

[25. Try how the life of the good man suits thee, the life of him who is satisfied with his portion out of the whole, and satisfied with his own just acts and benevolent disposition.

[26. Hast thou seen those things? Look also at these. Do not disturb thyself. Make thyself all simplicity. Does any one do wrong? It is to himself that he does the wrong. Has anything happened to thee? Well; out of the universe from the beginning everything which happens has been apportioned and spun out to thee. In a word, thy life is short. Thou must turn to profit the present by the aid of reason and justice. Be sober in thy relaxation.

[27. Either it is a well arranged universe or a chaos huddled together, but still a universe. But can a certain order subsist in thee, and disorder in the All? And this too when all things are so separated and diffused and sympathetic.

[28. A black character, a womanish character, a stubborn

character, bestial, childish, animal, stupid, counterfeit, scur-
rilous, fraudulent, tyrannical.

[29. If he is a stranger to the universe who does not know
what is in it, no less is he a stranger who does not know
what is going on in it. He is a runaway, who flies from social
reason; he is blind, who shuts the eyes of the understanding; he is poor, who has need of another, and has not from
himself all things which are useful for life. He is an abcess
on the universe who withdraws and separates himself from
the reason of our common nature through being displeased
with the things which happen, for the same nature produces
this, and has produced thee too: he is a piece rent asunder
from the state, who tears his own soul from that of reasonable
animals, which is one.

[30. The one is a philosopher without a tunic, and the
other without a book; here is another half naked: Bread I
have not, he says, and I abide by reason—And I do not get the
means of living out of my learning, and I abide [by my
reason].

[31. Love the art, poor as it may be, which thou hast
learned, and be content with it; and pass through the rest of
life like one who has intrusted to the gods with his whole
soul all that he has, making thyself neither the tyrant nor
the slave of any man.

[32. Consider, for example, the times of Vespasian. Thou
wilt see all these things, people marrying, bringing up children, sick, dying, warring, feasting, trafficking, cultivating the
ground, flattering, obstinately arrogant, suspecting, plotting,
wishing for some to die, grumbling about the present, loving, heaping up treasure, desiring consulship, kingly power.
Well then, that life of these people no longer exists at all.
Again, remove to the times of Trajan. Again, all is the same.
Their life too is gone. In like manner view also the other
epochs of time and of whole nations, and see how many after
great efforts soon fell and were resolved into the elements.
But chiefly thou shouldst think of those whom thou hast thy-

self known distracting themselves about idle things, neglecting to do what was in accordance with their proper constitution, and to hold firmly to this and to be content with it. And herein it is necessary to remember that the attention given to everything has its proper value and proportion. For thus thou wilt not be dissatisfied, if thou appliest thyself to smaller matters no further than is fit.

[33. The words which were formerly familiar are now antiquated: so also the names of those who were famed of old, are now in a manner antiquated, Camilius, Caeso, Volesus, Leonatus, and a little after also Scipio and Cato, then Augustus, then also Hadrianus and Antoninus. For all things soon pass away and become a mere tale, and complete oblivion soon buries them. And I say this of those, who have shone in a wondrous way. For the rest, as soon as they have breathed out their breath, they are gone, and no man speaks of them. And, to conclude the matter, what is even an eternal remembrance? A mere nothing. What then is that about which we ought to employ our serious pains? This one thing, thoughts just, and acts social, and words which never lie, and a disposition which gladly accepts all that happens, as necessary, as usual, as flowing from a principle and source of the same kind.

[34. Willingly give thyself up to Clotho [one of the fates], allowing her to spin thy thread into whatever things she pleases.

[35. Everything is only for a day, both that which remembers and that which is remembered.

[36. Observe constantly that all things take place by change, and accustom thyself to consider that the nature of the Universe loves nothing so much as to change the things which are and to make new things like them. For everything that exists is in a manner the seed of that which will be. But thou art thinking only of seeds which are cast into the earth or into a womb: but this is a very vulgar notion.

[37. Thou wilt soon die, and thou are not yet simple, nor

free from perturbations, nor without suspicion of being hurt by external things, nor kindly disposed towards all; nor dost thou yet place wisdom only in acting justly.

[38. Examine men's ruling principles, even those of the wise, what kind of things they avoid, and what kind they pursue.

[39. What is evil to thee does not subsist in the ruling principle of another; nor yet in any turning and mutation of thy corporeal covering. Where is it then? It is in that part of thee in which subsists the power of forming opinions about evils. Let this power then not form [such] opinions, and all is well. And if that which is nearest to it, the poor body, is cut, burnt, filled with matter and rottenness, nevertheless let the part which forms opinions about these things be quiet, that is, let it judge that nothing is either bad or good which can happen equally to the bad man and the good. For that which happens equally to him who lives contrary to nature and to him who lives according to nature, is neither according to nature nor contrary to nature.

[40. Constantly regard the universe as one living being, having one substance and one soul; and observe how all things have reference to one perception, the perception of this one living being; and how all things act with one movement; and how all things are the co-operating causes of all things which exist; observe too the continuous spinning of the thread and the contexture of the web.

[41. Thou art a little soul bearing about a corpse, as Epictetus used to say.

[42. It is no evil for things to undergo change, and no good for things to subsist in consequence of change.

[43. Time is like a river made up of the events which happen, and a violent stream; for as soon as a thing has been seen, it is carried away, and another comes in its place, and this will be carried away too.

[44. Everything which happens is as familiar and well known as the rose in spring and the fruit in summer; for such is disease, and death, and calumny, and treachery, and whatever else delights fools or vexes them.

[45. In the series of things those which follow are always aptly fitted to those which have gone before; for this series is not like a mere enumeration of disjointed things, which has only a necessary sequence, but it is a rational connection: and as all existing things are arranged together harmoniously, so the things which come into existence exhibit no mere succession, but a certain wonderful relationship.

[46. Always remember the saying of Heraclitus, that the death of earth is to become water, and the death of water is to become air, and the death of air is to become fire, and reversely. And think too of him who forgets whither the way leads, and that men quarrel with that with which they are most constantly in communion, the reason which governs the universe; and the things which they daily meet with seem to them strange; and consider that we ought not to act and speak as if we were asleep, for even in sleep we seem to act and speak; and that we ought not, like children who learn from their parents, simply to act and speak as we have been taught.

[47. If any god told thee that thou shalt die to-morrow, or certainly on the day after to-morrow, thou wouldst not care much whether it was on the third day or on the morrow, unless thou wast in the highest degree mean-spirited,—for how small is the difference?—so think it no great thing to die after as many years as thou canst name rather than to-morrow.

[48. Think continually how many physicians are dead after often contracting their eyebrows over the sick; and how many astrologers after predicting with great pretensions the deaths of others; and how many philosophers after endless discourses on death or immortality; how many heroes after killing thousands; and how many tyrants who have used their power over men's lives with terrible insolence as if they were immortal;

and how many cities are entirely dead, so to speak, Helice and Pompeii and Herculaneum, and others innumerable. Add to the reckoning all whom thou hast known, one after another. One man after burying another has been laid out dead, and another buries him; and all this in a short time. To conclude, always observe how ephemeral and worthless human things are, and what was yesterday a little mucus, tomorrow will be a mummy or ashes. Pass then through this little space of time conformably to nature, and end thy journey in content, just as an olive falls off when it is ripe, blessing nature who produced it, and thanking the tree on which it grew.

[49. Be like the promontory against which the waves continually break, but it stands firm and tames the fury of the water around it.

Unhappy am I, because this has happened to me—Not so, but Happy am I, though this has happened to me, because I continue free from pain, neither crushed by the present nor fearing the future. For such a thing as this might have happened to every man; but every man would not have continued free from pain on such an occasion. Why then is that rather a misfortune than this a good fortune? And dost thou in all cases call that a man's misfortune, which is not a deviation from man's nature? And does a thing seem to thee to be a deviation from man's nature, when it is not contrary to the will of man's nature? Well, thou knowest the will of nature. Will then this which has happened prevent thee from being just, magnanimous, temperate, prudent, secure against inconsiderate opinions and falsehood; will it prevent thee from having modesty, freedom, and everything else, by the presence of which man's nature obtains all that is its own? Remember too on every occasion which leads thee to vexation to apply this principle: not that this is a misfortune, but that to bear it nobly is good fortune.

[50. It is a vulgar, but still a useful help towards contempt of death, to pass in review those who have tenaciously stuck to life. What more then have they gained than those who have died early? Certainly they lie in their tombs somewhere at last, Cadicianus, Fabius, Julianus, Lepidus, or any one else like them, who have carried out many to be buried, and then were carried out themselves. Altogether the interval is small [between birth and death]; and consider with how much trouble, and in company with what sort of people and in what a feeble body this interval is laboriously passed. Do not then consider life a thing of any value. For look to the immensity of time behind thee, and to the time which is before thee, another boundless space. In this infinity then what is the difference between him who lives three days and him who lives three generations?

[51. Always run to the short way; and the short way is the natural: accordingly say and do everything in conformity with the soundest reason. For such a purpose frees a man from trouble, and warfare, and all artifice and ostentatious display.

Book VI

The substance of the universe is obedient and compliant; and the reason which governs it has in itself no cause for doing evil, for it has no malice, nor does it do evil to anything, nor is anything harmed by it. But all things are made and perfected according to this reason.

[2. Let it make no difference to thee whether thou art cold or warm, if thou art doing thy duty; and whether thou art drowsy or satisfied with sleep; and whether ill-spoken of or praised; and whether dying or doing something else. For it is one of the acts of life, this act by which we die: it is sufficient then in this act also to do well what we have in hand.

[3. Look within. Let neither the peculiar quality of anything nor its value escape thee.

[4. All existing things soon change, and they will either be reduced to vapour, if indeed all substance is one, or they will be dispersed.

[5. The reason which governs knows what its own disposition is and what it does, and on what material it works.

[6. The best way of avenging thyself is not to become like [the wrong doer].

[7. Take pleasure in one thing and rest in it, in passing from one social act to another social act, thinking of God.

[8. The ruling principle is that which rouses and turns itself, and while it makes itself such as it is and such as it wills to be, it also makes everything which happens appear to itself to be such as it wills.

[9. In conformity to the nature of the universe every single thing is accomplished, for certainly it is not in conformity to any other nature that each thing is accomplished, either a nature which externally comprehends this, or a nature which is comprehended within this nature, or a nature external and independent of this.

[10. The universe is either a confusion, and a mutual involution of things, and a dispersion; or it is unity and order and providence. If then it is the former, why do I desire to tarry in a fortuitous combination of things and such a disorder? and why do I care about anything else than how I shall at last become earth? and why am I disturbed, for the dispersion of my elements will happen whatever I do. But if the other supposition is true, I venerate, and I am firm, and I trust in him who governs.

[11. When thou hast been compelled by circumstances to be disturbed in a manner, quickly return to thyself and do not continue out of tune longer than the compulsion lasts; for thou wilt have more mastery over the harmony by continually recurring to it.

[12. If thou hadst a step-mother and a mother at the same time, thou wouldst be dutiful to thy step-mother, but still thou wouldst constantly return to thy mother. Let the court and philosophy now be to thee step-mother and mother: return to philosophy frequently and repose in her, through whom what thou meetest with in the court appears to thee tolerable, and thou appearest tolerable in the court.

[13. When we have meat before us and such eatables, we receive the impression, that this is the dead body of a fish, and this is the dead body of a bird or of a pig; and again, that this Falernian is only a little grape juice, and this purple robe some sheep's wool dyed with the blood of a shell-fish: such then are these impressions, and they reach the things themselves and penetrate them, and so we see what kind of things they are. Just in the same way ought we to act all through life, and where there are things which appear most worthy of our approbation, we ought to lay them bare and look at their worthlessness and strip them of all the words by which they are exalted. For outward show is a wonderful per-verter of the reason, and when thou art most sure that thou art employed about things worth thy pains, it is then that it cheats thee most. Consider then what Crates says of Xenoc-rates himself.

[14. Most of the things which the multitude admire are re-ferred to objects of the most general kind, those which are held together by cohesion or natural organization, such as stones, wood, fig-trees, vines, olives. But those which are ad-mired by men, who are a little more reasonable, are referred to the things which are held together by a living principle, as flocks, herds. Those which are admired by men who are still more instructed are the things which are held together by a rational soul, not however a universal soul, but rational so far as it is a soul skilled in some art, or expert in some other way, or simply rational so far as it possesses a number of slaves. But he who values a rational soul, a soul universal and fitted for political life, regards nothing else except this; and above all things he keeps his soul in a condition and in an activity conformable to reason and social life, and he co-operates to this end with those who are of the same kind as himself.

[15. Some things are hurrying into existence, and others are hurrying out of it; and of that which is coming into existence part is already extinguished. Motions and changes are continually renewing the world, just as the uninterrupted course of time is always renewing the infinite duration of ages. In this flowing stream then, on which there is no abiding, what is there of the things which hurry by on which a man would set a high price? It would be just as if a man should fall in love with one of the sparrows which fly by, but it has already passed out of sight. Something of this kind is the very life of every man, like the exhalation of the blood and the respiration of the air. For such as it is to have once drawn in the air and to have given it back, which we do every moment, just the same is it with the whole respiratory power, which thou didst receive at thy birth yesterday and the day before, to give it back to the element from which thou didst first draw it.

[16. Neither is transpiration, as in plants, a thing to be valued, nor respiration, as in domesticated animals and wild beasts, nor the receiving of impressions by the appearances of things, nor being moved by desires as puppets by strings, nor assembling in herds, nor being nourished by food; for this is just like the act of separating and parting with the useless part of our food. What then is worth being valued? To be received with clapping of hands? No. Neither must we value the clapping of tongues, for the praise which comes from the many is a clapping of tongues. Suppose then that thou hast given up this worthless thing called fame, what remains that is worth valuing? This in my opinion, to move thyself and to restrain thyself in conformity to thy proper constitution, to which end both all employments and arts lead. For every art aims at this, that the thing which has been made should be adapted to the work for which is has been made; and both the vine-planter who looks after the vine, and the horse-breaker, and he who trains the dog, seek this end. But the education and the teaching of youth aim at

something. In this then is the value of the education and
the teaching. And if this is well, thou wilt not seek anything
else. Wilt thou not cease to value many other things too?
Then thou wilt be neither free, nor sufficient for thy own
happiness, nor without passion. For of necessity thou must
be envious, jealous, and suspicious of those who can take
away those things, and plot against those who have that
which is valued by thee. Of necessity a man must be altogether in a state of perturbation who wants any of these
things; and besides, he must often find fault with the gods.
But to reverence and honour thy own mind will make thee
content with thyself, and in harmony with society, and in
agreement with the gods, that is, praising all that they give
and have ordered.

[17. Above, below, all around are the movements of the
elements. But the motion of virtue is in none of these: it is
something more divine, and advancing by a way hardly observed it goes happily on its road.

[18. How strangely men act. They will not praise those who
are living at the same time and living with themselves; but to
be themselves praised by posterity, by those whom they have
never seen or ever will see, this they set much value on. But
this is very much the same as if thou shouldst be grieved because those who have lived before thee did not praise thee.

[19. If a thing is difficult to be accomplished by thyself, do
not think that it is impossible for man; but if anything is
possible for man and conformable to his nature, think that
this can be attained by thyself too.

[20. In the gymnastic exercises suppose that a man has torn
thee with his nails, and by dashing against thy head has in-
flicted a wound. Well, we neither show any signs of vexation,
nor are we offended, nor do we suspect him afterwards as a
treacherous fellow; and yet we are on our guard against him,
not however as an enemy, nor yet with suspicion, but we
quietly get out of his way. Something like this let thy behaviour be in all the other parts of life; let us overlook

many things in those who are like antagonists in the gymnasium. For it is in our power, as I said, to get out of the way, and to have no suspicion nor hatred.

[21. If any man is able to convince me and show me that I do not think or act right, I will gladly change; for I seek the truth by which no man was ever injured. But he is injured who abides in his error and ignorance.

[22. I do my duty: other things trouble me not; for they are either things without life, or things without reason, or things that have rambled and know not the way.

[23. As to the animals which have no reason and generally all things and objects, do thou, since thou hast reason and they have none, make use of them with a generous and liberal spirit. But towards human beings, as they have reason, behave in a social spirit. And on all occasions call on the gods, and do not perplex thyself about the length of time in which thou shalt do this; for even three hours so spent are sufficient.

[24. Alexander the Macedonian and his groom by death were brought to the same state; for either they were received among the same seminal principles of the universe, or they were alike dispersed among the atoms.

[25. Consider how many things in the same indivisible time take place in each of us, things which concern the body and things which concern the soul: and so thou wilt not wonder if many more things, or rather all things which come into existence in that which is the one and all, which we call Cosmos, exist in it at the same time.

[26. If any man should propose to thee the question, how the name Antoninus is written, wouldst thou with a straining of the voice utter each letter? What then if they grow angry, wilt thou be angry too? Wilt thou not go on with composure and number every letter? Just so then in this life also remember that every duty is made up of certain parts. These it is thy duty to observe and without being disturbed or showing anger towards those who are angry with thee to go on thy way and finish that which is set before thee.

[27. How cruel it is not to allow men to strive after the things which appear to them to be suitable to their nature and profitable! And yet in a manner thou dost not allow them to do this, when thou art vexed because they do wrong. For they are certainly moved towards things because they suppose them to be suitable to their nature and profitable to them—But it is not so—Teach them then, and show them without being angry.

[28. Death is a cessation of the impressions through the senses, and of the pulling of the strings which move the appetites, and of the discursive movements of the thoughts, and of the service to the flesh.

[29. It is a shame for the soul to be first to give way in this life, when thy body does not give way.

[30. Take care that thou art not made into a Caesar, that thou art not dyed with this dye; for such things happen. Keep thyself then simple, good, pure, serious, free from affectation, a friend of justice, a worshipper of the gods, kind, affectionate, strenuous in all proper acts. Strive to continue to be such as philosophy wished to make thee. Reverence the gods, and help men. Short is life. There is only one fruit of this terrene life, a pious disposition and social acts. Do everything as a disciple of Antoninus. Remember his constancy in every act which was conformable to reason, and his evenness in all things, and his piety, and the serenity of his countenance, and his sweetness, and his disregard of empty fame, and his efforts to understand things; and how he would never let anything pass without having first most carefully examined it and clearly understood it; and how he bore with those who blamed him unjustly without blaming them in return; how he did nothing in a hurry; and how he listened not to calumnies, and how exact an examiner of manners and actions he was; and not given to reproach people, nor timid, nor suspicious, nor a sophist; and with how little he was satisfied, such as lodging, bed, dress, food, servants; and how laborious and patient; and how he was able on account of his sparing diet to hold out to the evening, not even requiring to relieve himself by any evacuations except at the usual hour; and his firmness and uniformity in his friendships; and how he tolerated freedom of speech in those who opposed his opinions; and the pleasure that he had when any man showed him anything better; and how religious he was without superstition. Imitate all this that thou mayest have as good a conscience, when thy last hour comes, as he had.

[31. Return to thy sober senses and call thyself back; and when thou hast roused thyself from sleep and hast perceived that they were only dreams which troubled thee, now in thy waking hours look at these [the things about thee] as thou didst look at those [the dreams].

[32. I consist of a little body and a soul. Now to this little body all things are indifferent, for it is not able to perceive differences. But to the understanding those things only are indifferent, which are not the works of its own activity. But whatever things are the works of its own activity, all these are in its power. And of these however only those which are done with reference to the present; for as to the future and the past activities of the mind, even these are for the present indifferent.

[33. Neither the labour which the hand does nor that of the foot is contrary to nature, so long as the foot does the foot's work and the hand the hand's. So then neither to a man as a man is his labour contrary to nature, so long as it does the things of a man. But if the labour is not contrary to his nature, neither is it an evil to him.

[34. How many pleasures have been enjoyed by robbers, patricides, tyrants.

[35. Dost thou not see how the handicraftsmen accommodate themselves up to a certain point to those who are not skilled in their craft,—nevertheless they cling to the reason [the principles] of their art and do not endure to depart from it? Is it not strange if the architect and the physician shall have more respect to the reason [the principles] of their own arts than man to his own reason, which is common to him and the gods?

[36. Asia, Europe are corners of the universe: all the sea a drop in the universe; Athos a little clod of the universe: all the present time is a point in eternity. All things are little, changeable, perishable. All things come from thence, from that universal ruling power either directly proceeding or by way of sequence. And accordingly the lion's gaping jaws, and that which is poisonous, and every harmful thing, as a thorn, as mud, are after-products of the grand and beautiful. Do not then imagine that they are of another kind from that which thou dost venerate, but form a just opinion of the source of all.

[37. He who has seen present things has seen all, both everything which has taken place from all eternity and everything which will be for time without end; for all things are of one kin and of one form.

[38. Frequently consider the connection of all things in the universe and their relation to one another. For in a manner all things are implicated with one another, and all in this way are friendly to one another; for one thing comes in order after another, and this is by virtue of the active movement and mutual conspiration and the unity of the substance.

[39. Adapt thyself to the things with which thy lot has been cast: and the men among whom thou hast received thy portion, love them, but do it truly [sincerely].

[40. Every instrument, tool, vessel, if it does that for which it has been made, is well, and yet he who made it is not there. But in the things which are held together by nature there is within and there abides in them the power which made them; wherefore the more is it fit to reverence this

power, and to think, that, if thou dost live and act according
to its will, everything in thee is in conformity to intelligence. And thus also in the universe the things which belong
to it are in conformity to intelligence.

[41. Whatever of the things which are not within thy
power thou shalt suppose to be good for thee or evil, it must
of necessity be that, if such a bad thing befall thee or the
loss of such a good thing, thou wilt blame the gods, and
hate men too, those who are the cause of the misfortune
or the loss, or those who are suspected of being likely to be
the cause; and indeed we do much injustice, because we
make a difference between these things [because we do not
regard these things as indifferent]. But if we judge only
those things which are in our power to be good or bad,
there remains no reason either for finding fault with god or
standing in a hostile attitude to man.

[42. We are all working together to one end, some with
knowledge and design, and others without knowing what they
do; as men also when they are asleep, of whom it is Heraclitus, I think, who says that they are labourers and co-operators
in the things which take place in the universe. But men co-
operate after different fashions: and even those co-operate
abundantly, who find fault with what happens and those who
try to oppose it and to hinder it; for the universe had need
even of such men as these. It remains then for thee to understand among what kind of workmen thou placest thyself; for
he who rules all things will certainly make a right use of thee,
and he will receive thee among some part of the co-operators
and of those whose labours conduce to one end. But be not
thou such a part as the mean and ridiculous verse in the play,
which Chrysippus speaks of.

[43. Does the sun undertake to do the work of the rain, or
Aesculapius the work of the Fruit-bearer [the earth]? And
how is it with respect to each of the stars, are they not different and yet they work together to the same end?

[44. If the gods have determined about me and about the

things which must happen to me, they have determined well, for it is not easy even to imagine a deity without forethought; and as to doing me harm, why should they have any desire towards that? for what advantage would result to them from this or to the whole, which is the special object of their providence? But if they have not determined about me individually, they have certainly determined about the whole at least, and the things which happen by way of sequence in this general arrangement I ought to accept with pleasure and to be content with them. But if they determine about nothing—which it is wicked to believe, or if we do believe it, let us neither sacrifice nor pray nor swear by them nor do anything else which we do as if the gods were present and lived with us—but if however the gods determine about none of the things which concern us, I am able to determine about myself, and I can inquire about that which is useful; and that is useful to every man which is conformable to his own constitution and nature. But my nature is rational and social; and my city and country, so far as I am Antoninus, is Rome, but so far as I am a man, it is the world. The things then which are useful to these cities are alone useful to me.

[45. Whatever happens to every man, this is for the interest of the universal: this might be sufficient. But further thou wilt observe this also as a general truth, if thou dost observe, that whatever is profitable to any man is profitable also to other men. But let the word profitable be taken here in the common sense as said of things of the middle kind [neither good nor bad].

[46. As it happens to thee in the amphitheatre and such places, that the continual sight of the same things and the uniformity make the spectacle wearisome, so it is in the whole of life; for all things above, below, are the same and from the same. How long then?

[47. Think continually that all kinds of men and of all kinds of pursuits and of all nations are dead, so that thy thoughts come down even to Philistion and Phoebus and Origanion. Now turn thy thoughts to the other kinds [of men]. To that place then we must remove, where there are so many great orators, and so many noble philosophers. Heraclitus, Pythagoras, Socrates; so many heroes of former days, and so many generals after them, and tyrants; besides these, Eudoxus, Hipparchus, Archimedes, and other men of acute natural talents, great minds, lovers of labour, versatile, confident, mockers even of the perishable and ephemeral life of man, as Menippus and such as are like him. As to all these consider that they have long been in the dust. What harm then is this to them; and what to those whose names are altogether unknown? One thing here is worth a great deal, to pass thy life in truth and justice, with a benevolent disposition even to liars and unjust men.

[48. When thou wishest to delight thyself, think of the virtues of those who live with thee; for instance, the activity of one, and the modesty of another, and the liberality of a third, and some other good quality of a fourth. For nothing delights so much as the examples of the virtues, when they are exhibited in the morals of those who live with us and present themselves in abundance, as far as is possible. Wherefore we must keep them before us.

[49. Thou art not dissatisfied, I suppose, because thou weighest only so many litrae and not three hundred. Be not dissatisfied then that thou must live only so many years and not more; for as thou art satisfied with the amount of substance which has been assigned to thee, so be content with the time.

[50. Let us try to persuade them [men]. But act even against their will, when the principles of justice lead that way. If however any man by using force stands in thy way, betake thyself to contentment and tranquillity, and at the same time employ the hindrance towards the exercise of some other virtue; and remember that thy attempt was with a reservation [conditionally], that thou didst not desire to do impossibilities. What then didst thou desire?—Some such effort as this—But thou attainest thy object, if the things to which thou wast moved are [not] accomplished.

[51. He who loves fame considers another man's activity to be his own good; and he who loves pleasure, his own sensations; but he who has understanding, considers his own acts to be his own good.

[52. It is in our power to have no opinion about a thing, and not to be disturbed in our soul; for things themselves have no natural power to form our judgments.

[53. Accustom thyself to attend carefully to what is said by another, and as much as it is possible, be in the speaker's mind.

[54. That which is not good for the swarm, neither is it good for the bee.

[55. If sailors abused the helmsman or the sick the doctor, would they listen to anybody else; or how could the helmsman secure the safety of those in the ship or the doctor the health of those whom he attends?

[56. How many together with whom I came into the world are already gone out of it.

[57. To the jaundiced honey tastes bitter, and to those bitten by mad dogs water causes fear; and to little children the ball is a fine thing. Why then am I angry? Dost thou think that a false opinion has less power than the bile in the jaundiced or the poison in him who is bitten by a mad dog?

[58. No man will hinder thee from living according to the reason of thy own nature: nothing will happen to thee contrary to the reason of the universal nature.

[59. What kind of people are those whom men wish to please, and for what objects, and by what kind of acts? How soon will time cover all things, and how many it has covered already.

Book XII

All those things at which thou wishest to arrive by a circuitous road, thou canst have now, if thou dost not refuse them to thyself. And this means, if thou wilt take no notice of all the past, and trust the future to providence, and direct the present only conformably to piety and justice. Conformably to piety, that thou mayst be content with the lot which is assigned to thee, for nature designed it for thee and thee for it. Conformably to justice, that thou mayst always speak the truth freely and without disguise, and do the things which are agreeable to law and according to the worth of each. And let neither another man's wickedness hinder thee, nor opinion nor voice, nor yet the sensations of the poor flesh which has grown about thee; for the passive part will look to this. If then, whatever the time may be when thou shalt be near to thy departure, neglecting everything else thou shalt respect only thy ruling faculty and the divinity within thee, and if thou shalt be afraid not because thou must some time cease to live, but if thou shalt fear never to have begun to live according to nature—then thou wilt be a man worthy of the universe which has produced thee, and thou wilt cease to be a stranger in thy native land, and to wonder at things which happen daily as if they were something unexpected, and to be dependent on this or that.

[2. God sees the minds (ruling principles) of all men bared of the material vesture and rind and impurities. For with his intellectual part alone he touches the intelligence only which has flowed and been derived from himself into these bodies. And if thou also usest thyself to do this, thou wilt rid thyself of thy much trouble. For he who regards not the poor flesh which envelopes him, surely will not trouble himself by looking after raiment and dwelling and fame and such like externals and show.

[3. The things are three of which thou art composed, a little body, a little breath [life], intelligence. Of these the first two are thine, so far as it is thy duty to take care of them; but the third alone is properly thine. Therefore if thou shalt separate from thyself, that is, from thy understanding, whatever others do or say, and whatever thou hast done or said thyself, and whatever future things trouble thee because they may happen, and whatever in the body which envelopes thee or in the breath [life], which is by nature associated with the body, is attached to thee independent of thy will, and whatever the external circumfluent vortex whirls round, so that the intellectual power exempt from the things of fate can live pure and free by itself, doing what is just and accepting what happens and saying the truth; if thou wilt separate, I say, from this ruling faculty the things which are attached to it by the impressions of sense, and the things of time to come and of time that is past, and wilt make thyself like Empedocles' sphere—

All round, and in its joyous rest reposing;

and if thou shalt strive to live only what is really thy life, that is, the present—then thou wilt be able to pass that portion of life which remains for thee up to the time of thy death, free from perturbations, nobly, and obedient to thy own daemon [to the god that is within thee].

[4. I have often wondered how it is that every man loves himself more than all the rest of men, but yet sets less value on his own opinion of himself than on the opinion of others. If then a god or a wise teacher should present himself to man and bid him to think of nothing and to design nothing which he would not express as soon as he conceived it, he could not endure it even for a single day. So much more respect have we to what our neighbours shall think of us than to what we shall think of ourselves.

[5. How can it be that the gods after having arranged all

things well and benevolently for mankind, have overlooked this alone, that some men and very good men, and men who, as we may say, have had most communion with the divinity, and through pious acts and religious observances have been most intimate with the divinity, when they have once died should never exist again, but should be completely extinguished?

But if this is so, be assured that if it ought to have been otherwise, the gods would have done it. For if it were just, it would also be possible; and if it were according to nature, nature would have had it so. But because it is not so, if in fact it is not so, be thou convinced that it ought not to have been so:—for thou seest even of thyself that in this inquiry thou art disputing with the deity; and we should not thus dispute with the gods, unless they were most excellent and most just;—but if this is so, they would not have allowed anything in the ordering of the universe to be neglected unjustly and irrationally.

[6. Practise thyself even in the things which thou despairest of accomplishing. For even the left hand, which is ineffectual for all other things for want of practice, holds the bridle more vigorously than the right hand; for it has been practised in this.

[7. Consider in what condition both in body and soul a man should be when he is overtaken by death; and consider the shortness of life, the boundless abyss of time past and future, the feebleness of all matter.

[8. Contemplate the formative principles [forms] of things bare of their coverings; the purposes of actions; consider what pain is, what pleasure is, and death, and fame; who is to himself the cause of his uneasiness; how no man is hindered by another; that everything is opinion.

[9. In the application of thy principles thou must be like the pancratiast, not like the gladiator; for the gladiator lets fall the sword which he uses and is killed; but the other always has his hand, and needs to do nothing else than use it.

[10. See what things are in themselves, dividing them into matter, form and purpose.

[11. What a power man has to do nothing except what god will approve, and to accept all that god may give him.

[12. With respect to that which happens conformably to nature, we ought to blame neither gods, for they do nothing wrong either voluntarily or involuntarily, nor men, for they do nothing wrong except involuntarily. Consequently we should blame nobody.

[13. How ridiculous and what a stranger he is who is surprised at anything which happens in life.

[14. Either there is a fatal necessity and invincible order, or a kind Providence, or a confusion without a purpose and without a director. If then there is an invincible necessity, why dost thou resist? But if there is a Providence which allows itself to be propitiated, make thyself worthy of the help of the divinity. But if there is a confusion without a governor, be content that in such tempest thou hast in thyself a certain ruling intelligence. And even if the tempest carry thee away, let it carry away the poor flesh, the poor breath, everything else; for the intelligence at least it will not carry away.

[15. Does the light of the lamp shine without losing its splendour until it is extinguished; and shall the truth which is in thee and justice and temperance be extinguished [before thy death]?

[16. When a man has presented the appearance of having done wrong, [say,] How then do I know if this is a wrongful act? And even if he has done wrong, how do I know that he has not condemned himself? and so this is like tearing his own face. Consider that he, who would not have the bad man do wrong, is like the man who would not have the fig-tree to bear juice in the figs and infants to cry and the horse to neigh, and whatever else must of necessity be. For what must a man do who has such a character? If then thou art irritable, cure this man's disposition.

[17. If it is not right, do not do it: if it is not true, do not say it. [For let thy efforts be.—]

[18. In everything always observe what the thing is which produces for thee an appearance, and resolve it by dividing it into the formal, the material, the purpose, and the time within which it must end.

[19. Perceive at last that thou hast in thee something better and more divine than the things which cause the various affects, and as it were pull thee by the strings. What is there now in my mind? is it fear, or suspicion, or desire, or anything of the kind?

[20. First, do nothing inconsiderately, nor without a purpose. Second, make thy acts refer to nothing else than to a social end.

[21. Consider that before long thou wilt be nobody and nowhere, nor will any of the things exist which thou now seest, nor any of those who are now living. For all things are formed by nature to change and be turned and to perish in order that other things in continuous succession may exist.

[22. Consider that everything is opinion, and opinion is in thy power. Take away then, when thou choosest, thy opinion, and like a mariner, who has doubled the promontory, thou wilt find calm, everything stable, and a waveless bay.

[23. Any one activity whatever it may be, when it has ceased at its proper time, suffers no evil because it has ceased; nor he who has done this act, does he suffer any evil for this reason that the act has ceased. In like manner then the whole which consists of all the acts, which is our life, if it cease at its proper time, suffers no evil for this reason that it has ceased; nor he who has terminated this series at the proper time has he been ill dealt with. But the proper time and the limit nature fixes, sometimes as in old age the peculiar nature of man, but always the universal nature, by the

change of whose parts the whole universe continues ever
young and perfect. And everything which is useful to the universal is always good and in season. Therefore the termina-
tion of life for every man is no evil, because neither is it
shameful, since it is both independent of the will and not
opposed to the general interest, but it is good, since it is
seasonable and profitable to and congruent with the universal. For thus too he is moved by the deity who is moved in
the same manner with the deity and moved towards the
same things in his mind.

[24. These three principles thou must have in readiness. In
the things which thou doest do nothing either inconsiderately or otherwise than as justice herself would act; but
with respect to what may happen to thee from without, consider that it happens either by chance or according to Providence, and thou must neither blame chance nor accuse Providence. Second, consider what every being is from the seed to
the time of its receiving a soul, and from the reception of a
soul to the giving back of the same, and of what things every
being is compounded and into what things it is resolved.
Third, if thou shouldst suddenly be raised up above the
earth, and shouldst look down on human things, and observe
the variety of them how great it is, and at the same time
also shouldst see at a glance how great is the number of beings who dwell all around in the air and the aether, consider
that as often as thou shouldst be raised up, thou wouldst see
the same things, sameness of form and shortness of duration.
Are these things to be proud of?

[25. Cast away opinion: thou art saved. Who then hinders
thee from casting it away?

[26. When thou art troubled about anything, thou hast forgotten this, that all things happen according to the universal
nature; and forgotten this, that a man's wrongful act is nothing to thee; and further thou hast forgotten this, that
everything which happens, always happened so and will happen so, and now happens so everywhere; forgotten this

too, how close is the kinship between a man and the whole human race, for it is a community, not of a little blood or seed, but of intelligence. And thou hast forgotten this too, that every man's intelligence is a god, and is an efflux of the deity; and forgotten this, that nothing is a man's own, but that his child and his body and his very soul came from the deity; forgotten this, that everything is opinion; and lastly thou hast forgotten that every man lives the present time only, and loses only this.

[27. Constantly bring to thy recollection those who have complained greatly about anything, those who have been most conspicuous by the greatest fame or misfortunes or enmities or fortunes of any kind: then think where are they all now? Smoke and ash and a tale, or not even a tale. And let there be present to thy mind also everything of this sort, how Fabius Catullinus lived in the country, and Lucius Lupus in his gardens, and Stertinius at Baiae, and Tiberius at Capreae and Velius Rufus [or Rufus at Velia]; and in fine think of the eager pursuit of anything conjoined with pride; and how worthless everything is after which men violently strain; and how much more philosophical it is for a man in the opportunities presented to him to show himself just, temperate, obedient to the gods, and to do this with all simplicity: for the pride which is proud of its want of pride is the most intolerable of all.

[28. To those who ask, Where hast thou seen the gods or how dost thou comprehend that they exist and so worshipest them, I answer, in the first place, they may be seen even with the eyes; in the second place neither have I seen even my own soul and yet I honour it. Thus then with respect to the gods, from what I constantly experience of their power, from this I comprehend that they exist and I venerate them.

[29. The safety of life is this, to examine everything all through, what it is itself, what is its material, what the formal part; with all thy soul to do justice and to say the truth. What remains except to enjoy life by joining one good thing to another so as not to leave even the smallest intervals between?

[30. There is one light of the sun, though it is interrupted by walls, mountains, and other things infinite. There is one common substance, though it is distributed among countless bodies which have their several qualities. There is one soul, though it is distributed among infinite natures and individual circumscriptions [or individuals]. There is one intelligent soul, though it seems to be divided. Now in the things which have been mentioned all the other parts, such as those which are air and matter, are without sensation and have no fellowship: and yet even these parts the intelligent principle holds together and the gravitation towards the same. But intellect in a peculiar manner tends to that which is of the same kin, and combines with it, and the feeling for communion is not interrupted.

[31. What dost thou wish? to continue to exist? Well, dost thou wish to have sensation? movement? growth? and then again to cease to grow? to use thy speech? to think? What is there of all these things which seems to thee worth desiring? But if it is easy to set little value on all these things, turn to that which remains, which is to follow reason and god. But it is inconsistent with honouring reason and god to be troubled because by death a man will be deprived of the other things.

[32. How small a part of the boundless and unfathomable time is assigned to every man? for it is very soon swallowed up in the eternal. And how small a part of the whole substance? and how small a part of the universal soul? and on what a small clod of the whole earth thou creepest? Reflecting on all this consider nothing to be great, except to act as thy nature leads thee, and to endure that which the common nature brings.

[33. How does the ruling faculty make use of itself? for all lies in this. But everything else, whether it is in the power of thy will or not, is only lifeless ashes and smoke.

[34. This reflection is most adapted to move us to contempt of death, that even those who think pleasure to be a good and pain an evil still have despised it.

[35. The man to whom that only is good which comes in due season, and to whom it is the same thing whether he has done more or fewer acts conformable to right reason, and to whom it makes no difference whether he contemplates the world for a longer or a shorter time—for this man neither is death a terrible thing.

[36. Man, thou hast been a citizen in this great state [the world]: what difference does it make to thee whether for five years [or three]? for that which is conformable to the laws is just for all. Where is the hardship then, if no tyrant nor yet an unjust judge sends thee away from the state, but nature who brought thee into it? the same as if a praetor who has employed an actor dismisses him from the stage— "But I have not finished the five acts, but only three of them"—Thou sayest well, but in life the three acts are the whole drama; for what shall be a complete drama is determined by him who was once the cause of its composition, and now of its dissolution: but thou art the cause of neither. Depart then satisfied, for he also who releases thee is satisfied.

SUGGESTED READINGS

Fragments of the writings of the Early Stoics are available in R. D. Hicks, *Stoic and Epicurean*, ch. i; see also A. C. Pearson's *Fragments of Zeno and Cleanthes*.

The teachings of Panaetius and Posidonius of the Middle Stoa can be found in Cicero's *The Offices* and *On the Nature of the Gods*. Many translations of Epictetus are available, those by Long, Matheson or Carter being especially recommended. Long's translation of Marcus Aurelius' *Meditations* is still the best, but the Jackson version runs it a close second. Seneca's *Moral Epistles* and *Moral Essays* are translated in the Loeb Classical Library series.

Of the secondary sources, Gilbert Murray's *The Stoic Philosophy* is a masterpiece. E. R. Bevan's *Stoics and Sceptics* is a most readable and lively account. For fuller treatments, see R. D. Hicks, *Stoic and Epicurean*, ch. i-iv; E. V. Arnold, *Roman Stoicism*; W. W. Capes, *Stoicism*; and E. Zeller, *The Stoics, Epicureans and Sceptics*. T. R. Glover's exposition in *Conflict of Religions in the Early Roman Republic*, ch. ii, is worthwhile and stimulating.

For a clear discussion of the Stoic ethic, see H. Baker, *The Image of Man*, ch. v. Don't miss the readable handling of the relation between Cynicism and Stoicism in Gilbert Murray's classic *Five Stages of Greek Religion*.

For a suggestive account of the impact of Stoicism on Christianity, see E. Hatch, *The Influence of Greek Ideas on Christianity*.

For a scholarly treatment of the Stoic logic, see B. Mates, *Stoic Logic*.

W. De Witt Hyde gives a short, personal treatment of Stoicism's value in contemporary society in his *The Five Great Philosophies of Life*, ch. ii.

III

SKEPTICISM

INTRODUCTION

Both the Epicureans and the Stoics sought to attain peace of mind by discovering the truth about the nature of the world in which they lived. The Skeptics sought that peace too, but by a different method. Sextus Empiricus, our principal source for ancient skepticism, compares them to the painter Apelles. As the story goes, Apelles was trying to portray a horse one day. Frustrated in his attempts to represent the foam on the horse's mouth, he flung at the picture the sponge which he had been using to wipe the paints off his brush. And there it was—the mark of the sponge had produced the effect of the horse's foam! The moral is clear. By giving up in the search for truth, by suspending judgment, the Skeptics succeeded where their dogmatic opponents had failed.

Traditionally, two main varieties of ancient skepticism are distinguished: the Pyrrhonian, which goes back to Pyrrho of Elis (360-275 B.C.), and the Academic, which is traced to two of the later heads of the Platonic Academy, Arcesilaus of Pitane (315-241 B.C.) and Carneades of Cyrene (213-129 B.C.). The Pyrrhonians appear to have been more thorough-going in their skepticism—refusing assent even to the fundamental proposition that knowledge is impossible, whereas the Academics "dogmatically" affirmed its impossibility. More-

over, faced with the necessity of providing a guide for action, the Pyrrhonians proposed merely to follow custom, while the Academics suggested that one act on the belief that seemed more reasonable, or probable—a concession to common sense which was only dubiously consistent with the principle of equipollence (cf. Sextus, ch. iv).

None of the writings of these earlier skeptics have survived. Our best first-hand information comes from Sextus Empiricus, who is represented here by portions of his Outlines of Pyrrhonism. *Sextus is a very late figure (160-210 A.D.), a Greek physician who is thought to have lived for some time in Rome. Though mainly a compiler of the arguments of his predecessors, Sextus presents the skeptic's grounds for doubt clearly and forcefully.*

The Greek satirist Lucian, like Lucretius, sweetens the rim of the bitter cup with the honey of his literary skill. By birth a contemporary of Sextus (c. 125-200 A.D.) and by training a rhetorician, Lucian delighted in poking fun at the foibles of his fellow men. The Hermotimus, *a dialogue reminiscent of the early Platonic dialogues, shows him deflating the pretensions of a pompous Stoic to the point where the victim is ready to abandon philosophy.*

SEXTUS EMPIRICUS

OUTLINES OF PYRRHONISM*

Book I

[1. *Of the main difference between philosophic systems:*
The natural result of any investigation is that the investi- *1*
gators either discover the object of search or deny that it is
discoverable and confess it to be inapprehensible or persist
in their search. So, too, with regard to the objects investi- *2*
gated by philosophy, this is probably why some have
claimed to have discovered the truth, others have asserted
that it cannot be apprehended, while others again go on
inquiring. Those who believe they have discovered it are *3*
the "Dogmatists," specially so called—Aristotle, for example, and Epicurus and the Stoics and certain others; Cleitomachus and Carneades and other Academics treat it as
inapprehensible: the Sceptics keep on searching. Hence it *4*
seems reasonable to hold that the main types of philosophy are three—the Dogmatic, the Academic, and the Sceptic. Of the other systems it will best become others to
speak: our task at present is to describe in outline the
Sceptic doctrine,¹ first premising that of none of our future
statements do we positively affirm that the fact is exactly
as we state it, but we simply record each fact, like a chron-
icler, as it appears to us at the moment.

[2. *Of the arguments of Scepticism:* Of the Sceptic phi-

* Reprinted from *Outlines of Pyrrhonism,* vol. 1 (1933), translated by
R. G. Bury, by permission of Harvard University Press and The Loeb
Classical Library.
¹ "Doctrine." "School," "system" or "way" are other possible renderings
of ἀγωγή. "Procedure," "way of thought," "trend," or "line of argument," "leading" (ἄγω⁴) up to a definite goal is rather what it con-
notes.

5 losophy one argument (or branch of exposition) is called
"general," the other "special." In the general argument we
set forth the distinctive features of Scepticism, stating its
purport and principles, its logical methods, criterion, and
end or aim; the "Tropes," also, or "Modes," which lead to
suspension of judgement, and in what sense we adopt the
Sceptic formulae, and the distinction between Scepticism
and the philosophies which stand next to it. In the special
6 argument we state our objections regarding the several
divisions of so-called philosophy.[2] Let us, then, deal first
with the general argument, beginning our description with
the names given to the Sceptic School.

[3. *Of the nomenclature of Scepticism*: The Sceptic
7 School, then, is also called "Zetetic" from its activity in investigation and inquiry, and "Ephectic" or Suspensive from
the state of mind produced in the inquirer after his search,
and "Aporetic" or Dubitative either from its habit of
doubting and seeking, as some say, or from its indecision
as regards assent and denial, and "Pyrrhonean" from the
fact that Pyrrho appears to us to have applied himself to
Scepticism more thoroughly and more conspicuously than
his predecessors.

8 [4. *What Scepticism is*: Scepticism is an ability, or mental attitude, which opposes appearances to judgements in
any way whatsoever, with the result that, owing to the
equipollence of the objects and reasons thus opposed, we
are brought firstly to a state of mental suspense and next
to a state of "unperturbedness" or quietude. Now we call
9 it an "ability" not in any subtle sense, but simply in respect of its "being able." By "appearances" we now mean
the objects of sense-perception, whence we contrast them
with the objects of thought or "judgements." The phrase
"in any way whatsoever" can be connected either with the
word "ability," to make us take the word "ability," as we

2 In Bks. II and III of the *Outlines,* not reprinted here. (Ed.)

said, in its simple sense, or with the phrase "opposing appearances to judgements"; for inasmuch as we oppose these in a variety of ways—appearances to appearances, or judgements to judgements, or *alternando* appearances to judgements,—in order to ensure the inclusion of all these antitheses we employ the phrase "in any way whatsoever." Or, again, we join "in any way whatsoever" to "appearances and judgements" in order that we may not have to inquire how the appearances appear or how the thought-objects are judged, but may take these terms in the simple sense. The phrase "opposed judgements" we do not employ in the sense of negations and affirmations only but simply as equivalent to "conflicting judgements." [3] "Equipollence" we use of equality in respect of probability and improbability, to indicate that no one of the conflicting judgements takes precedence of any other as being more probable. "Suspense" is a state of mental rest owing to which we neither deny nor affirm anything. "Quietude" is an untroubled and tranquil condition of soul. And how quietude enters the soul along with suspension of judgement we shall explain in our chapter (XII) "Concerning the End."

[5. *Of the Sceptic:* In the definition of the Sceptic system there is also implicitly included that of the Pyrrhonean philosopher: he is the man who participates in this "ability."

[6. *Of the principles of Scepticism:* The originating cause of Scepticism is, we say, the hope of attaining quietude. Men of talent, who were perturbed by the contradictions in things and in doubt as to which of the alternatives they ought to accept, were led on to inquire what is true in things and what false, hoping by the settlement of this

[3] I.e., "Opposites." Includes, for the Skeptics, "contraries" (e.g., "All are wise," "None are wise") as well as "contradictories" (e.g., "Some are wise," "None are wise"), whereas the Stoics used it of the latter only.

question to attain quietude. The main basic principle of the Sceptic system is that of opposing to every proposition an equal proposition; for we believe that as a consequence of this we end by ceasing to dogmatize.

13 [7. *Does the Sceptic dogmatize?* When we say that the Sceptic refrains from dogmatizing we do not use the term "dogma," as some do, in the broader sense of "approval of a thing" (for the Sceptic gives assent to the feelings which are the necessary results of sense-impressions, and he would not, for example, say when feeling hot or cold "I believe that I am not hot or cold"); but we say that "he does not dogmatize" using "dogma" in the sense, which some give it, of "assent to one of the non-evident objects of scientific inquiry"; for the Pyrrhonean philosopher as-

14 sents to nothing that is non-evident. Moreover, even in the act of enunciating the Sceptic formulae concerning things non-evident—such as the formula "No more (one thing than another)," or the formula "I determine nothing," or any of the others which we shall presently mention,—he does not dogmatize. For whereas the dogmatizer posits the things about which he is said to be dogmatizing as really existent, the Sceptic does not posit these formulae in any absolute sense; for he conceives that, just as the formula "All things are false" asserts the falsity of itself as well as of everything else, as does the formula "Nothing is true," so also the formula "No more" asserts that itself, like all the rest, is "No more (this than that)," and thus cancels itself along with the rest. And of the other formulae we

15 say the same. If then, while the dogmatizer posits the matter of his dogma as substantial truth, the Sceptic enunciates his formulae so that they are virtually cancelled by themselves, he should not be said to dogmatize in his enunciation of them. And, most important of all, in his enunciation of these formulae he states what appears to himself and announces his own impression in an undogmatic

way, without making any positive assertion regarding the external realities.[4]

[8. *Has the Sceptic a doctrinal rule?* We follow the same [16] lines in replying to the question "Has the Sceptic a doctrinal rule?" For if one defines a "doctrinal rule" as "adherence to a number of dogmas which are dependent both on one another and on appearances," and defines "dogma" as "assent to a non-evident proposition," then we shall say that he has not a doctrinal rule. But if one defines "doctrinal rule" as "procedure which, in accordance with appearance, follows a certain line of reasoning, that reasoning indicating how it is possible to seem to live rightly (the word 'rightly' being taken, not as referring to virtue only, but in a wider sense) and tending to enable one to suspend judgement," then we say that he has a doctrinal rule. For we follow a line of reasoning which, in accordance with appearances, points us to a life conformable to the customs of our country and its laws and institutions, and to our own instinctive feelings.

[9. *Does the Sceptic deal with physics?* We make a similar reply also to the question "Should the Sceptic deal with [18] physical problems?" For while, on the one hand, so far as regards making firm and positive assertions about any of the matters dogmatically treated in physical theory, we do not deal with physics; yet, on the other hand, in respect of our mode of opposing to every proposition an equal proposition and of our theory of quietude we do treat of physics. This, too, is the way in which we approach the logical and ethical branches of so-called "philosophy."

[10. *Do the Sceptics abolish appearances?* Those who say that "the Sceptics abolish appearances," or phenomena, [19] seem to me to be unacquainted with the statements of our School. For, as we said above, we do not overthrow the

---

[4] Literally "underlying things," i.e., the essences or reals which lie behind, and give rise to, sensations or "appearances."

effective sense-impressions[5] which induce our assent involuntarily; and these impressions are "the appearances."
And when we question whether the underlying object is
such as it appears, we grant the fact that it appears, and
our doubt does not concern the appearance itself but the
account given of that appearance,—and that is a different
thing from questioning the appearance itself. For exam-
20 ple, honey appears to us to be sweet (and this we grant,
for we perceive sweetness through the senses), but whether
it is also sweet in its essence is for us a matter of doubt,
since this is not an appearance but a judgement regarding
the appearance. And even if we do actually argue against
the appearances, we do not propound such arguments with
the intention of abolishing appearances, but by way of
pointing out the rashness of the Dogmatists; for if reason
is such a trickster as to all but snatch away the appearances
from under our very eyes, surely we should view it with
suspicion in the case of things non-evident so as not to display rashness by following it.[6]

[11. *Of the criterion of Scepticism:* That we adhere to
21 appearances is plain from what we say about the Criterion
of the Sceptic School. The word "Criterion" is used in
two senses: in the one it means "the standard regulating
belief in reality or unreality," in the other it denotes the
standard of action by conforming to which in the conduct
of life we perform some actions and abstain from others;
22 and it is of the latter that we are now speaking. The criterion, then, of the Sceptic School is, we say, the appearance, giving this name to what is virtually the sense-
presentation. For since this lies in feeling and involuntary
affection, it is not open to question. Consequently, no one,
I suppose, disputes that the underlying object has this or

---

[5] I.e., "impressions" or "presentations" which cause "affections" or
"feelings" ($\pi\acute{a}\theta\eta$), as described in Chap. 7.
[6] I.e., the "reason," or logic, which serves to discredit phenomena may
be used *a fortiori* to discredit ultra-sensible objects. Instead of "abolishing appearances" it really (as the Skeptics contend) abolishes itself.

that appearance; the point in dispute is whether the object is in reality such as it appears to be.

Adhering, then, to appearances we live in accordance ²³
with the normal rules of life, undogmatically, seeing that
we cannot remain wholly inactive. And it would seem that
this regulation of life is fourfold, and that one part of it
lies in the guidance of Nature, another in the constraint
of the passions, another in the tradition of laws and customs, another in the instruction of the arts. Nature's guid- ²⁴
ance is that by which we are naturally capable of sensation
and thought; constraint of the passions is that whereby
hunger drives us to food and thirst to drink; tradition of
customs and laws, that whereby we regard piety in the conduct of life as good, but impiety as evil; instruction of the
arts, that whereby we are not inactive in such arts as we
adopt. But we make all these statements undogmatically.

[12. *What is the end of Scepticism?* Our next subject will
be the End of the Sceptic system. Now an "End" is "that ²⁵
for which all actions or reasonings are undertaken, while
it exists for the sake of none"; or, otherwise, "the ultimate
object of appetency." We assert still that the Sceptic's
End is quietude in respect of matters of opinion and moderate feeling in respect of things unavoidable. For the
Sceptic, having set out to philosophize with the object of ²⁶
passing judgement on the sense-impressions and ascertain-
ing which of them are true and which false, so as to attain
quietude thereby, found himself involved in contradictions
of equal weight, and being unable to decide between them
suspended judgement; and as he was thus in suspense there
followed, as it happened, the state of quietude in respect
of matters of opinion. For the man who opines that any- ²⁷
thing is by nature good or bad is for ever being disquieted:
when he is without the things which he deems good he believes himself to be tormented by things naturally bad
and he pursues after the things which are, as he thinks,
good; which when he has obtained he keeps falling into

still more perturbations because of his irrational and immoderate elation, and in his dread of a change of fortune he uses every endeavour to avoid losing the things which 28 he deems good. On the other hand, the man who determines nothing as to what is naturally good or bad neither shuns nor pursues anything eagerly; and, in consequence, he is unperturbed.

The Sceptic, in fact, had the same experience which is said to have befallen the painter Apelles. Once, they say, when he was painting a horse and wished to represent in the painting the horse's foam, he was so unsuccessful that he gave up the attempt and flung at the picture the sponge on which he used to wipe the paints off his brush, and the 29 mark of the sponge produced the effect of a horse's foam. So, too, the Sceptics were in hopes of gaining quietude by means of a decision regarding the disparity of the objects of sense and of thought, and being unable to effect this they suspended judgement; and they found that quietude, as if by chance, followed upon their suspense, even as a shadow follows its substance. We do not, however, suppose that the Sceptic is wholly untroubled; but we say that he is troubled by things unavoidable; for we grant that he is cold at times and thirsty, and suffers various affections of 30 that kind. But even in these cases, whereas ordinary people are afflicted by two circumstances,—namely, by the affections themselves and, in no less a degree, by the belief that these conditions are evil by nature,—the Sceptic, by his rejection of the added belief in the natural badness of all these conditions, escapes here too with less discomfort. Hence we say that, while in regard to matters of opinion the Sceptic's End is quietude, in regard to things unavoidable it is "moderate affection." But some notable Sceptics[7] have added the further definition "suspension of judgement in investigations."

[13. *Of the general modes leading to suspension of judge-*

---

[7] Viz., Timon and Aenesidemus.

ment: Now that we have been saying that tranquillity fol- 31
lows on suspension of judgement, it will be our next task
to explain how we arrive at this suspension. Speaking generally, one may say that it is the result of setting things in
opposition. We oppose either appearances to appearances
or objects of thought to objects of thought or *alternando*. 32
For instance, we oppose appearances to appearances when
we say "The same tower appears round from a distance,
but square from close at hand"; and thoughts to thoughts,
when in answer to him who argues the existence of Providence from the order of the heavenly bodies we oppose
the fact that often the good fare ill and the bad fare well,
and draw from this the inference that Providence does not 33
exist. And thoughts we oppose to appearances, as when
Anaxagoras countered the notion that snow is white with
the argument, "Snow is frozen water, and water is black;
therefore snow also is black." With a different idea we oppose things present sometimes to things present, as in the
foregoing examples, and sometimes to things past or future, as, for instance, when someone propounds to us a
theory which we are unable to refute, we say to him in re- 34
ply, "Just as, before the birth of the founder of the School
to which you belong, the theory it holds was not as yet apparent as a sound theory, although it was really in existence, so likewise it is possible that the opposite theory to
that which you now propound is already really existent,
though not yet apparent to us, so that we ought not as yet
to yield assent to this theory which at the moment seems
to be valid."

But in order that we may have a more exact understand- 35
ing of these antitheses I will describe the Modes by which
suspension of judgement is brought about, but without
making any positive assertion regarding either their number or their validity; for it is possible that they may be un-
sound or there may be more of them than I shall enumer-
ate.

[14. *Concerning the Ten Modes*: The usual tradition
36 amongst the older Sceptics is that the "modes" by which
"suspension" is supposed to be brought about are ten in
number; and they also give them the synonymous names
of "arguments" and "positions." They are these: the first,
based on the variety in animals; the second, on the differences in human beings; the third, on the different structures of the organs of sense; the fourth, on the circumstan-
tial conditions; the fifth, on positions and intervals and
37 locations; the sixth, on intermixtures; the seventh, on the
quantities and formations of the underlying objects; the
eighth, on the fact of relativity; the ninth, on the frequency
or rarity of occurrence; the tenth, on the disciplines and
customs and laws, the legendary beliefs and the dogmatic
38 convictions. This order, however, we adopt without prejudice.

As superordinate to these there stand three Modes—
that based on the subject who judges, that on the object
judged, and that based on both. The first four of the ten
Modes are subordinate to the Mode based on the subject
(for the subject which judges is either an animal or a man
or a sense, and existent in some condition): the seventh
and tenth Modes are referred to that based on the object
judged: the fifth, sixth, eighth and ninth are referred to
39 the Mode based on both subject and object. Furthermore,
these three Modes are also referred to that of relation, so
that the Mode of relation stands as the highest *genus*, and
the three as *species*, and the ten as subordinate *sub-species*.
We give this as the probable account of their numbers;
and as to their argumentative force what we say is this:

40   The *First* argument (or *Trope*), as we said, is that which
shows that the same impressions are not produced by the
same objects owing to the differences in animals. This we
infer both from the differences in their origins and from
the variety of their bodily structures. Thus, as to origin,
41 some animals are produced without sexual union, others by

coition. And of those produced without coition, some come from fire, like the animalcules which appear in furnaces; others from putrid water, like gnats; others from wine when it turns sour, like ants; others from earth, like grasshoppers; others from marsh, like frogs; others from mud, like worms; others from asses, like beetles; others from greens, like caterpillars; others from fruits, like the gall-insects in wild figs; others from rotting animals, as bees from bulls and wasps from horses. Of the animals gener- *42* ated by coition, some—in fact the majority—come from homogeneous parents, others from heterogeneous parents, as do mules. Again, of animals in general, some are born alive, like men; others are born as eggs, like birds; and yet others as lumps of flesh, like bears. It is natural, then, that *47* these dissimilar and variant modes of birth should produce much contrariety of sense-affection, and that this is a source of its divergent, discordant and conflicting character.

Moreover, the differences found in the most important *44* parts of the body, and especially in those of which the natural function is judging and perceiving, are capable of producing a vast deal of divergence in the sense-impressions [owing to the variety in the animals]. Thus, sufferers from jaundice declare that objects which seem to us white are yellow, while those whose eyes are bloodshot call them blood-red. Since, then, some animals also have eyes which are yellow, others bloodshot, others albino, others of other colours, they probably, I suppose, have different perceptions of colour. Moreover, if we bend down over a book *45* after having gazed long and fixedly at the sun, the letters seem to us to be golden in colour and circling round. Since, then, some animals possess also a natural brilliance in their eyes, and emit from them a fine and mobile stream of light, so that they can even see by night, we seem bound to suppose that they are differently affected from us by external objects. Jugglers, too, by means of smearing lamp- *46* wicks with the rust of copper or with the juice of the cuttle-fish make the bystanders appear now copper-coloured and now black—and that by just a small sprinkling of extra matter. Surely, then, we have much more reason to suppose that when different juices are intermingled in the vision of animals their impressions of the objects will become differ-

47 ent. Again, when we press the eyeball at one side the forms, figures and sizes of the objects appear oblong and narrow. So it is probable that all animals which have the pupil of the eye slanting and elongated—such as goats, cats, and similar animals—have impressions of the objects which are different and unlike the notions formed of them by the ani-

48 mals which have round pupils. Mirrors, too, owing to differences in their construction, represent the external objects[8] at one time as very small—as when the mirror is concave, —at another time as elongated and narrow—as when the mirror is convex. Some mirrors, too, show the head of the figure reflected at the bottom and the feet at the top. Since,

49 then, some organs of sight actually protrude beyond the face owing to their convexity, while others are quite concave, and others again lie in a level plane, on this account also it is probable that their impressions differ, and that the same objects, as seen by dogs, fishes, lions, men and locusts, are neither equal in size nor similar in shape, but vary according to the image of each object created by the particular sight that receives the impression.

50 Of the other sense-organs also the same account holds good. Thus, in respect of touch, how could one maintain that creatures covered with shells, with flesh, with prickles, with feathers, with scales, are all similarly affected? And as for the sense of hearing, how could we say that its perceptions are alike in animals with a very narrow auditory passage and those with a very wide one, or in animals with

8 τὰ ὑποκείμενα is a favorite term with Sextus for the objective realities which "underlie," or lie behind, the subjective impressions of sense (phenomena): they are called ἐκτός, as "outside" of and not dependent on the percipient. I render the term indifferently by "objects," "real objects," or "realities," and "underlying objects."

hairy ears and those with smooth ears? For, as regards this
sense, even we ourselves find our hearing affected in one
way when we have our ears plugged and in another way
when we use them just as they are. Smell also will differ
because of the variety in animals. For if we ourselves are 51
affected in one way when we have a cold and our internal
phlegm is excessive, and in another way when the parts
about our head are filled with an excess of blood, feeling
an aversion to smells which seem sweet to everyone else
and regarding them as noxious, it is reasonable to suppose
that animals too—since some are flaccid by nature and rich
in phlegm, others rich in blood, others marked by a predominant excess of yellow or of black gall—are in each
case impressed in different ways by the objects of smell.
So too with the objects of taste; for some animals have 52
rough and dry tongues, others extremely moist tongues. We
ourselves, too, when our tongues are very dry, in cases of
fever, think the food proffered us to be earthy and ill-
flavoured or bitter—an affection due to the variation in the
predominating juices which we are said to contain. Since,
then, animals also have organs of taste which differ and
which have different juices in excess, in respect of taste also
they will receive different impressions of the real objects.
For just as the same food when digested becomes in one 53
place a vein, in another an artery, in another a bone, in
another a sinew, or some other piece of the body, displaying
a different potency according to the difference in the parts
which receive it;—and just as the same unblended water, 54
when it is absorbed by trees, becomes in one place bark, in
another branch, in another blossom, and so finally fig and
quince and each of the other fruits;—and just as the single
identical breath of a musician breathed into a flute becomes here a shrill note and there a deep note, and the
same pressure of his hand on the lyre produces here a deep
note and there a shrill note;—so likewise it is probable that
the external objects appear different owing to differences

in the structure of the animals which experience the sense-impressions.

55   But one may learn this more clearly from the preferences and aversions of animals. Thus, sweet oil seems very agreeable to men, but intolerable to beetles and bees; and olive oil is beneficial to men, but when poured on wasps and bees it destroys them; and sea-water is a disagreeable and
56   poisonous potion for men, but fish drink and enjoy it. Pigs, too, enjoy wallowing in the most stinking mire rather than in clear and clean water. And whereas some animals eat grass, others eat shrubs, others feed in woods, others live on seeds or flesh or milk; some of them, too, prefer their food high, others like it fresh, and while some prefer it raw, others like it cooked. And so generally, the things which are agreeable to some are to others disagreeable, dis-
57   tasteful and deadly. Thus, quails are fattened by hemlock, and pigs by henbane; and pigs also enjoy eating salamanders, just as deer enjoy poisonous creatures, and swallows gnats. So ants and wood-lice, when swallowed by men, cause distress and gripings, whereas the bear, whenever she falls sick, cures herself by licking them up. The mere touch
58   of an oak-twig paralyses the viper, and that of a plane-leaf the bat. The elephant flees from the ram, the lion from the cock, sea-monsters from the crackle of bursting beans, and the tiger from the sound of a drum. One might, indeed, cite many more examples, but—not to seem unduly prolix—if the same things are displeasing to some but pleasing to others, and pleasure and displeasure depend upon sense-impression, then animals receive different impressions from the underlying objects.

59   But if the same things appear different owing to the variety in animals, we shall, indeed, be able to state our own impressions of the real object, but as to its essential nature we shall suspend judgement. For we cannot ourselves judge between our own impressions and those of the other animals, since we ourselves are involved in the dis-

pute and are, therefore, rather in need of a judge than
competent to pass judgement ourselves. Besides, we are 60
unable, either with or without proof, to prefer our own impressions to those of the irrational animals. For in addition
to the probability that proof is, as we shall show,[9] a non-
entity, the so-called proof itself will be either apparent to
us or non-apparent. If, then, it is non-apparent, we shall
not accept it with confidence; while if it is apparent to us,
inasmuch as what is apparent to animals is the point in
question and the proof is apparent to us who are animals,
it follows that we shall have to question the proof itself as
to whether it is as true as it is apparent. It is, indeed, ab- 61
surd to attempt to establish the matter in question by
means of the matter in question,[10] since in that case the
same thing will be at once believed and disbelieved,—believed in so far as it purports to prove, but disbelieved in
so far as it requires proof,—which is impossible. Consequently we shall not possess a proof which enables us to
give our own sense-impressions the preference over those
of the so-called irrational animals. If, then, owing to the
variety in animals their sense-impressions differ, and it is
impossible to judge between them, we must necessarily
suspend judgement regarding the external underlying objects.

By way of super-addition, too, we draw comparisons be- 62
tween mankind and the so-called irrational animals in respect of their sense-impressions. For, after our solid arguments, we deem it quite proper to poke fun at those

[9] In Book II, Chap. 12, it is argued that logical demonstration or
"proof" is "non-existent." The argument here is that, even if we grant
the existence of "proof" in the abstract we cannot prove anything in
the particular case before us—the question as to the superiority of our
impressions to those of animals. For all proof must be either "apparent"
to us, or "non-apparent"; the latter kind we reject as incomprehensible;
the former, or "apparent," proof is indecisive, its "apparency" being
relative to us, who are a species of animal, and thus involved in the
dispute. Further, as relative to us the "apparent proof" is not absolute,
and therefore not necessarily "true."

[10] This would be the fallacy of *petitio principii*, or "arguing in a circle."

conceited braggarts, the Dogmatists. As a rule, our School
compare the irrational animals in the mass with mankind;
63 but since the Dogmatists captiously assert that the comparison is unequal, we—super-adding yet more—will carry
our ridicule further and base our argument on one animal
only, the dog for instance if you like, which is held to be
the most worthless of animals. For even in this case we
shall find that the animals we are discussing are no wise
inferior to ourselves in respect of the credibility of their
impressions.

64   Now it is allowed by the Dogmatists that this animal,
the dog, excels us in point of sensation: as to smell it is
more sensitive than we are, since by this sense it tracks
beasts that it cannot see; and with its eyes it sees them
65 more quickly than we do; and with its ears it is keen of
perception. Next let us proceed to the reasoning faculty.
Of reason one kind is internal, implanted in the soul, the
other externally expressed.[11] Let us consider first the internal reason. Now according to those Dogmatists who
are, at present, our chief opponents—I mean the Stoics—
internal reason is supposed to be occupied with the following matters: the choice of things congenial and the avoidance of things alien; the knowledge of the arts contributing
thereto; the apprehension of the virtues pertaining to one's
66 proper nature and of those relating to the passions. Now
the dog—the animal upon which, by way of example, we
have decided to base our argument—exercises choice of
the congenial and avoidance of the harmful, in that it
hunts after food and slinks away from a raised whip. Moreover, it possesses an art which supplies what is congenial,
67 namely hunting. Nor is it devoid even of virtue; for certainly if justice consists in rendering to each his due, the
dog, that welcomes and guards its friends and benefactors

---

11 The Stoic theory of λόγος thus distinguished between its two senses,
internal *reason,* or conception, and the enunciation of thought in the
uttered *word.*

but drives off strangers and evil-doers, cannot be lacking in justice. But if he possesses this virtue, then, since the vir- 68 tues are interdependent, he possesses also all the other virtues; and these, say the philosophers,[12] the majority of men do not possess. That the dog is also valiant we see by the way he repels attacks, and intelligent as well, as Homer too testified when he sang how Odysseus went unrecognized by all the people of his own household and was recognized only by the dog Argus, who neither was deceived by the bodily alterations of the hero nor had lost his original apprehensive impression, which indeed he evidently retained better than the men. And according to Chrysip- 69 pus, who shows special interest in irrational animals, the dog even shares in the far-famed "Dialectic." This person, at any rate, declares that the dog makes use of the fifth complex indemonstrable syllogism[13] when, on arriving at a spot where three ways meet, after smelling at the two roads by which the quarry did not pass, he rushes off at once by the third without stopping to smell. For, says the old writer, the dog implicitly reasons thus: "The creature went either by this road, or by that, or by the other: but it did not go by this road or by that: therefore it went by the other." Moreover, the dog is capable of comprehending 70 and assuaging his own sufferings; for when a thorn has got stuck in his foot he hastens to remove it by rubbing his foot on the ground and by using his teeth. And if he has a wound anywhere, because dirty wounds are hard to cure whereas clean ones heal easily, the dog gently licks off the pus that has gathered. Nay more, the dog admirably ob- 71 serves the prescription of Hippocrates: rest being what cures the foot, whenever he gets his foot hurt he lifts it up and keeps it as far as possible free from pressure. And when

---

[12] I.e., the Stoics.
[13] The Stoic logic had five syllogisms which were termed *anapodeictic,* or "indemonstrable," since they required no proof themselves but served to prove others. The "complex" syllogism was of the form: "Either A or B or C exists: but neither A nor B exists: therefore C exists."

distressed by unwholesome humours he eats grass, by the
72 help of which he vomits what is unwholesome and gets well
again. If, then, it has been shown that the animal upon
which, as an example, we have based our argument not
only chooses the wholesome and avoids the noxious, but
also possesses an art capable of supplying what is wholesome, and is capable of comprehending and assuaging its
own sufferings, and is not devoid of virtue, then—these
being the things in which the perfection of internal reason
consists—the dog will be thus far perfect. And that, I suppose, is why certain of the professors of philosophy have
adorned themselves with the title of this animal.[14]

73   Concerning external reason, or speech, it is unnecessary
for the present to inquire; for it has been rejected even by
some of the Dogmatists as being a hindrance to the acquisition of virtue, for which reason they used to practise silence[15] during the period of instruction; and besides, supposing that a man is dumb, no one will therefore call him
irrational. But to pass over these cases, we certainly see
animals—the subject of our argument—uttering quite hu-
74 man cries,—jays, for instance, and others. And, leaving this
point also aside, even if we do not understand the utterances of the so-called irrational animals, still it is not improbable that they converse although we fail to understand
them; for in fact when we listen to the talk of barbarians
75 we do not understand it, and it seems to us a kind of uniform chatter. Moreover, we hear dogs uttering one sound
when they are driving people off, another when they are
howling, and one sound when beaten, and a quite different sound when fawning. And so in general, in the case of
all other animals as well as the dog, whoever examines the
matter carefully will find a great variety of utterance according to the different circumstances, so that, in consequence, the so-called irrational animals may justly be said

14 A sarcastic allusion to the Cynics.
15 The Pythagoreans.

to participate in external reason. But if they neither fall 76
short of mankind in the accuracy of their perceptions, nor
in internal reason, nor yet (to go still further) in external
reason, or speech, then they will deserve no less credence
than ourselves in respect of their sense-impressions. Probably, too, we may reach this conclusion by basing our argu- 77
ment on each single class of irrational animals. Thus, for
example, who would deny that birds excel in quickness of
wit or that they employ external reason? For they understand not only present events but future events as well,
and these they foreshow to such as are able to comprehend
them by means of prophetic cries as well as by other signs.

I have drawn this comparison (as I previously indicated) 78
by way of super-addition, having already sufficiently proved,
as I think, that we cannot prefer our own sense-impressions
to those of the irrational animals. If, however, the irrational
animals are not less worthy of credence than we in regard
to the value of sense-impressions, and their impressions
vary according to the variety of animal,—then, although
I shall be able to say what the nature of each of the underlying objects appears to me to be, I shall be compelled,
for the reasons stated above, to suspend judgement as to
its real nature.

Such, then, is the First of the Modes which induce sus- 79
pense. The *Second Mode* is, as we said, that based on the
differences in men; for even if we grant for the sake of argument that men are more worthy of credence than irrational
animals, we shall find that even our own differences of
themselves lead to suspense. For man, you know, is said
to be compounded of two things, soul and body, and in
both these we differ one from another.

Thus, as regards the *body*, we differ in our figures and
"idiosyncrasies," or constitutional peculiarities. The body
of an Indian differs in shape from that of a Scythian; and 80
it is said that what causes the variation is a difference in
the predominant humours. Owing to this difference in the

predominant humours the sense-impressions also come to differ, as we indicated in our First Argument. So too in respect of choice and avoidance of external objects men exhibit great differences: thus Indians enjoy some things, our people other things, and the enjoyment of different things is an indication that we receive varying impressions

81 from the underlying objects. In respect of our "idiosyncrasies," our differences are such that some of us digest the flesh of oxen more easily than rock-fish, or get diarrhoea from the weak wine of Lesbos. An old wife of Attica, they say, swallowed with impunity thirty drams of hemlock, and Lysis took four drams of poppy-juice without hurt.

82 Demophon, Alexander's butler, used to shiver when he was in the sun or in a hot bath, but felt warm in the shade: Athenagoras the Argive took no hurt from the stings of scorpions and poisonous spiders; and the Psyllaeans, as they are called, are not harmed by bites from snakes and asps,

83 nor are the Tentyritae of Egypt harmed by the crocodile. Further, those Ethiopians who live beyond Lake Meroë on the banks of the river Astapous eat with impunity scorpions, snakes, and the like. Rufinus of Chalcis when he drank hellebore neither vomited nor suffered at all from purging, but swallowed and digested it just like any ordinary drink.

84 Chrysermus of Erophile was liable to get a heart attack if ever he took pepper; and Soterichus the surgeon was seized with diarrhoea whenever he smelled fried sprats. Andron the Argive was so immune from thirst that he actually traversed the waterless country of Libya without needing a drink. Tiberius Caesar could see in the dark; and Aristotle tells of a Thracian who fancied that the image of a man was continually going in front of him.

85 Seeing, then, that men vary so much in body—to content ourselves with but a few instances of the many collected by the Dogmatists,—men probably also differ from one another in respect of the *soul* itself; for the body is a kind of expression of the soul, as in fact is proved by the

science of Physiognomy. But the greatest proof of the vast
and endless differences in men's intelligence is the discrepancy in the statements of the Dogmatists concerning the
right objects of choice and avoidance, as well as other
things. Regarding this the poets, too, have expressed them- 86
selves fittingly. Thus Pindar says:

> The crowns and trophies of his storm-foot steeds
> Give joy to one; yet others find it joy
> To dwell in gorgeous chambers gold-bedeckt;
> Some even take delight in voyaging
> O'er ocean's billows in a speeding barque.

And the poet says: "One thing is pleasing to one man, another thing to another." Tragedy, too, is full of such sayings; for example:

> Were fair and wise the same thing unto all,
> There had been no contentious quarrelling.

And again:

> 'Tis strange that the same thing abhorr'd by some
> Should give delight to others.

Seeing, then, that choice and avoidance depend on pleas- 87
ure and displeasure, while pleasure and displeasure depend
on sensation and sense-impression, whenever some men
choose the very things which are avoided by others, it is
logical for us to conclude that they are also differently
affected by the same things, since otherwise they would
all alike have chosen or avoided the same things. But if
the same objects affect men differently owing to the differences in the men, then, on this ground also, we shall reasonably be led to suspension of judgement. For while we
are, no doubt, able to state what each of the underlying
objects appears to be, relatively to each difference, we are
incapable of explaining what it is in reality. For we shall
have to believe either all men or some. But if we believe 88

all, we shall be attempting the impossible and accepting contradictories; and if some, let us be told whose opinions we are to endorse. For the Platonist will say "Plato's"; the Epicurean, "Epicurus's"; and so on with the rest; and thus by their unsettled disputations they will bring us round
89 again to a state of suspense. Moreover, he who maintains that we ought to assent to the majority is making a childish proposal, since no one is able to visit the whole of mankind and determine what pleases the majority of them; for there may possibly be races of whom we know nothing amongst whom conditions rare with us are common, and conditions common with us rare,—possibly, for instance, most of them feel no pain from the bites of spiders, though a few on rare occasions feel such pain; and so likewise with the rest of the "idiosyncrasies" mentioned above. Necessarily, therefore, the differences in men afford a further reason for bringing in suspension of judgement.

90   When the Dogmatists—a self-loving class of men—assert that in judging things they ought to prefer themselves to other people, we know that their claim is absurd; for they themselves are a party to the controversy; and if, when judging appearances, they have already given the preference to themselves, then, by thus entrusting themselves with the judgement, they are begging the question before
91 the judgement is begun. Nevertheless, in order that we may arrive at suspension of judgement by basing our argument on one person—such as, for example, their visionary "Sage" [16] —we adopt the Mode which comes Third in order.

This *Third Mode* is, we say, based on differences in the senses. That the senses differ from one another is obvious.
92 Thus, to the eye paintings seem to have recesses and projections, but not so to the touch. Honey, too, seems to some pleasant to the tongue but unpleasant to the eyes; so that it is impossible to say whether it is absolutely pleas-

[16] The ideal wise man of the Stoics.

ant or unpleasant. The same is true of sweet oil, for it pleases the sense of smell but displeases the taste. So too with spurge: since it pains the eyes but causes no pain to any other part of the body, we cannot say whether, in its real nature, it is absolutely painful or painless to bodies. Rain-water, too, is beneficial to the eyes but roughens the wind-pipe and the lungs; as also does olive-oil, though it mollifies the epidermis. The cramp-fish, also, when applied to the extremities produces cramp, but it can be applied to the rest of the body without hurt. Consequently we are unable to say what is the real nature of each of these things, although it is possible to say what each thing at the moment appears to be.

A longer list of examples might be given, but to avoid prolixity, in view of the plan of our treatise, we will say just this. Each of the phenomena perceived by the senses seems to be a complex: the apple, for example, seems smooth, odorous, sweet and yellow. But it is non-evident whether it really possesses these qualities only; or whether it has but one quality but appears varied owing to the varying structure of the sense-organs; or whether, again, it has more qualities than are apparent, some of which elude our perception. That the apple has but one quality might be argued from what we said above regarding the food absorbed by bodies, and the water sucked up by trees, and the breath in flutes and pipes and similar instruments; for the apple likewise may be all of one sort but appear different owing to differences in the sense-organs in which perception takes place. And that the apple may possibly possess more qualities than those apparent to us we argue in this way. Let us imagine a man who possesses from birth the senses of touch, taste and smell, but can neither hear nor see. This man, then, will assume that nothing visible or audible has any existence, but only those three kinds of qualities which he is able to apprehend. Possibly, then, we also, having only our five senses, perceive only such of the apple's qualities as we are capable of apprehending; and possibly it may possess other underlying qualities which affect other sense-organs, though we, not being endowed with those organs, fail to apprehend the sense-objects which come through them.

98 "But," it may be objected, "Nature made the senses commensurate with the objects of sense." What kind of "Nature"? we ask, seeing that there exists so much unresolved controversy amongst the Dogmatists concerning the reality which belongs to Nature. For he who decides the question as to the existence of Nature will be discredited by them if he is an ordinary person, while if he is a philosopher he will be a party to the controversy and therefore 99 himself subject to judgement and not a judge. If, however, it is possible that only those qualities which we seem to perceive subsist in the apple, or that a greater number subsist, or, again, that not even the qualities which affect us subsist, then it will be non-evident to us what the nature of the apple really is. And the same argument applies to all the other objects of sense. But if the senses do not apprehend external objects, neither can the mind apprehend them; hence, because of this argument also, we shall be driven, it seems, to suspend judgement regarding the external underlying objects.

100 In order that we may finally reach suspension by basing our argument on each sense singly, or even by disregarding the senses, we further adopt the *Fourth Mode* of suspension. This is the Mode based, as we say, on the "circumstances," meaning by "circumstances" conditions or dispositions. And this Mode, we say, deals with states that are natural or unnatural, with waking or sleeping, with conditions due to age, motion or rest, hatred or love, emptiness or fulness, drunkenness or soberness, predispositions, con- 101 fidence or fear, grief or joy. Thus, according as the mental state is natural or unnatural, objects produce dissimilar impressions, as when men in a frenzy or in a state of ecstasy

believe they hear daemons' voices, while we do not. Similarly they often say that they perceive an odour of storax or
frankincense, or some such scent, and many other things,
though we fail to perceive them. Also, the same water
which feels very hot when poured on inflamed spots seems
lukewarm to us. And the same coat which seems of a bright
yellow colour to men with blood-shot eyes does not appear
so to me. And the same honey seems to me sweet, but bitter
to men with jaundice. Now should anyone say that it is an *102*
intermixture of certain humours which produces in those
who are in an unnatural state improper impressions from
the underlying objects, we have to reply that, since healthy
persons also have mixed humours, these humours too are
capable of causing the external objects—which really are
such as they appear to those who are said to be in an unnatural state—to appear other than they are to healthy
persons. For to ascribe the power of altering the underly- *103*
ing objects to those humours, and not to these, is purely
fanciful; since just as healthy men are in a state that is
natural for the healthy but unnatural for the sick, so also
sick men are in a state that is unnatural for the healthy
but natural for the sick, so that to these last also we must
give credence as being, relatively speaking, in a natural
state.[17]

Sleeping and waking, too, give rise to different impres- *104*
sions, since we do not imagine when awake what we imagine in sleep, nor when asleep what we imagine when awake;
so that the existence or non-existence of our impressions
is not absolute but relative, being in relation to our sleeping or waking condition. Probably, then, in dreams we
see things which to our waking state are unreal, although
not wholly unreal; for they exist in our dreams, just as
waking realities exist although non-existent in dreams.

Age is another cause of difference. For the same air *105*

---

[17] This is aimed against the Stoic view that only the healthy, or normal,
is "natural."

seems chilly to the old but mild to those in their prime; and the same colour appears faint to older men but vivid to those in their prime; and similarly the same sound seems
[106] to the former faint, but to the latter clearly audible. Moreover, those who differ in age are differently moved in respect of choice and avoidance. For whereas children—to take a case—are all eagerness for balls and hoops, men in their prime choose other things, and old men yet others. And from this we conclude that differences in age also cause different impressions to be produced by the same underlying objects.

[107] Another cause why the real objects appear different lies in motion and rest. For those objects which, when we are standing still, we see to be motionless, we imagine to be in motion when we are sailing past them.

[108] Love and hatred are a cause, as when some have an extreme aversion to pork while others greatly enjoy eating it. Hence, too, Menander said:

> Mark now his visage, what a change is there
> Since he has come to this! How bestial!
> 'Tis actions fair that make the fairest face.

Many lovers, too, who have ugly mistresses think them most beautiful.

[109] Hunger and satiety are a cause; for the same food seems agreeable to the hungry but disagreeable to the sated.

Drunkenness and soberness are a cause; since actions which we think shameful when sober do not seem shameful to us when drunk.

[110] Predispositions are a cause; for the same wine which seems sour to those who have previously eaten dates or figs, seems sweet to those who have just consumed nuts or chickpeas; and the vestibule of the bath-house, which warms those entering from outside, chills those coming out of the bath-room if they stop long in it.

[111] Fear and boldness are a cause; as what seems to the cow-

ard fearful and formidable does not seem so in the least to the bold man.

Grief and joy are a cause; since the same affairs are burdensome to those in grief but delightful to those who rejoice.

Seeing then that the dispositions also are the cause of so *112* much disagreement, and that men are differently disposed at different times, although, no doubt, it is easy to say what nature each of the underlying objects appears to each man to possess, we cannot go on to say what its real nature is, since the disagreement admits in itself of no settlement. For the person who tries to settle it is either in one of the afore-mentioned dispositions or in no disposition whatsoever. But to declare that he is in no disposition at all—as, for instance, neither in health nor sickness, neither in motion nor at rest, of no definite age, and devoid of all the other dispositions as well—is the height of absurdity. And if he is to judge the sense-impressions while he is in some one disposition, he will be a party to the disagreement, and, *113* moreover, he will not be an impartial judge of the external underlying objects owing to his being confused by the dispositions in which he is placed. The waking person, for instance, cannot compare the impressions of sleepers with those of men awake, nor the sound person those of the sick with those of the sound; for we assent more readily to things present, which affect us in the present, than to things not present.

In another way, too, the disagreement of such impres- *114* sions is incapable of settlement. For he who prefers one impression to another, or one "circumstance" to another, does so either uncritically and without proof or critically and with proof; but he can do this neither without these means (for then he would be discredited) nor with them. For if he is to pass judgement on the impressions he must certainly judge them by a criterion; this criterion, then, he *115* will declare to be true, or else false. But if false, he will be

discredited; whereas, if he shall declare it to be true, he
will be stating that the criterion is true either without proof
or with proof. But if without proof, he will be discredited;
and if with proof, it will certainly be necessary for the proof
also to be true, to avoid being discredited. Shall he, then,
affirm the truth of the proof adopted to establish the
116 criterion after having judged it or without judging it? If
without judging, he will be discredited; but if after judging, plainly he will say that he has judged it by a criterion;
and of that criterion we shall ask for a proof, and of that
proof again a criterion. For the proof always requires a
criterion to confirm it, and the criterion also a proof to
demonstrate its truth; and neither can a proof be sound
without the previous existence of a true criterion nor can
the criterion be true without the previous confirmation of
117 the proof. So in this way both the criterion and the proof
are involved in the circular process of reasoning, and
thereby both are found to be untrustworthy; for since each
of them is dependent on the credibility of the other, the
one is lacking in credibility just as much as the other. Consequently, if a man can prefer one impression to another
neither without a proof and a criterion nor with them, then
the different impressions due to the differing conditions
will admit of no settlement; so that as a result of this Mode
also we are brought to suspend judgement regarding the
nature of external realities.

118		The *Fifth Argument* (or *Trope*) is that based on posi-
tions, distances, and locations; for owing to each of these
the same objects appear different; for example, the same
porch when viewed from one of its corners appears cur-
tailed, but viewed from the middle symmetrical on all
sides; and the same ship seems at a distance to be small
and stationary, but from close at hand large and in motion;
and the same tower from a distance appears round but from
a near point quadrangular.

These effects are due to distances; among effects due to [119] locations are the following: the light of a lamp appears dim in the sun but bright in the dark; and the same oar bent when in the water but straight when out of the wa- ter; and the egg soft when inside the fowl but hard when in the air; and the jacinth fluid when in the lynx but hard when in the air; and the coral soft when in the sea but hard when in the air; and sound seems to differ in quality ac- cording as it is produced in a pipe, or in a flute, or simply in the air.

Effects due to positions are such as these: the same [120] painting when laid flat appears smooth, but when inclined forward at a certain angle it seems to have recesses and prominences. The necks of doves, also, appear different in hue according to the differences in the angle of inclination.

Since, then, all apparent objects are viewed in a certain [121] place, and from a certain distance, or in a certain position, and each of these conditions produces a great divergency in the sense-impressions, as we mentioned above, we shall be compelled by this Mode also to end up in suspension of judgement. For in fact anyone who purposes to give the preference to any of these impressions will be attempting the impossible. For if he shall deliver his judgement sim- [122] ply and without proof, he will be discredited; and should he, on the other hand, desire to adduce proof, he will con- fute himself if he says that the proof is false, while if he asserts that the proof is true he will be asked for a proof of its truth, and again for a proof of this latter proof, since it also must be true, and so on *ad infinitum*. But to produce proofs to infinity is impossible; so that neither by the use [123] of proofs will he be able to prefer one sense-impression to another. If, then, one cannot hope to pass judgement on the afore-mentioned impressions either with or without proof, the conclusion we are driven to is suspension; for while we can, no doubt, state the nature which each object appears to possess as viewed in a certain position or at a certain distance or in a certain place, what its real nature is we are, for the foregoing reasons, unable to declare.

124 The *Sixth Mode* is that based on admixtures, by which we conclude that, because none of the real objects affects our senses by itself but always in conjunction with something else, though we may possibly be able to state the nature of the resultant mixture formed by the external object and that along with which it is perceived, we shall not be able to say what is the exact nature of the external reality in itself. That none of the external objects affects our senses by itself but always in conjunction with something else, and that, in consequence, it assumes a different ap-
125 pearance, is, I imagine, quite obvious. Thus, our own complexion is of one hue in warm air, of another in cold, and we should not be able to say what our complexion really is, but only what it looks like in conjunction with each of these conditions. And the same sound appears of one sort in conjunction with rare air and of another sort with dense air; and odours are more pungent in a hot bath-room or in the sun than in chilly air; and a body is light when immersed in water but heavy when surrounded by air.

126 But to pass on from the subject of external admixture, —our eyes contain within themselves both membranes and liquids. Since, then, the objects of vision are not perceived apart from these, they will not be apprehended with exactness; for what we perceive is the resultant mixture, and because of this the sufferers from jaundice see everything yellow, and those with blood-shot eyes reddish like blood. And since the same sound seems of one quality in open places, of another in narrow and winding places, and different in clear air and in murky air, it is probable that we do not apprehend the sound in its real purity; for the ears have crooked and narrow passages, which are also befogged by vaporous effluvia which are said to be emitted by the re-
127 gions of the head. Moreover, since there reside substances

in the nostrils and in the organs of taste, we apprehend the objects of taste and of smell in conjunction with these and not in their real purity. So that, because of these admixtures, the senses do not apprehend the exact quality of the external real objects.

Nor yet does the mind apprehend it, since, in the first [128] place, its guides, which are the senses, go wrong; and probably, too, the mind itself adds a certain admixture of its own to the messages conveyed by the senses; for we observe that there are certain humours present in each of the regions which the Dogmatists regard as the seat of the "Ruling Principle"—whether it be the brain or the heart, or in whatever part of the creature one chooses to locate it. Thus, according to this Mode also we see that, owing to our inability to make any statement about the real nature of external objects, we are compelled to suspend judgement.

The *Seventh Mode* is that based, as we said, on the [129] quantity and constitution of the underlying objects, meaning generally by "constitution" the manner of composition. And it is evident that by this Mode also we are compelled to suspend judgement concerning the real nature of the objects. Thus, for example, the filings of a goat's horn appear white when viewed simply by themselves and without combination, but when combined in the substance of the horn they look black. And silver filings appear black when they are by themselves, but when united to the whole mass they are sensed as white. And chips of the marble of Taenarum [130] seem white when planed, but in combination with the whole block they appear yellow. And pebbles when scattered apart appear rough, but when combined in a heap they produce the sensation of softness. And hellebore if applied in a fine and powdery state produces suffocation, but not so when it is coarse. And wine strengthens us when [131] drunk in moderate quantity, but when too much is taken it paralyses the body. So likewise food exhibits different

effects according to the quantity consumed; for instance, it frequently upsets the body with indigestion and attacks of
132 purging because of the large quantity taken. Therefore in these cases, too, we shall be able to describe the nature of the shaving of the horn and of the compound made up of many shavings, and that of the particle of silver and of the compound of many particles, and that of the sliver of Taenarean marble and of the compound of many such small pieces, and the relative natures of the pebbles, the hellebore, the wine and the food,—but when it comes to the independent and real nature of the objects, this we shall be unable to describe because of the divergency in the sense-impressions which is due to the combinations.

133 As a general rule, it seems that wholesome things become harmful when used in immoderate quantities, and things that seem hurtful when taken to excess cause no harm when in minute quantities. What we observe in regard to the effects of medicines is the best evidence in support of our statement; for there the exact blending of the simple drugs makes the compound wholesome, but when the slightest oversight is made in the measuring, as sometimes happens, the compound is not only unwholesome
134 but frequently even most harmful and deleterious. Thus the argument from quantities and compositions causes confusion as to the real nature of the external substances. Probably, therefore, this Mode also will bring us round to suspension of judgement, as we are unable to make any absolute statement concerning the real nature of external objects.

135 The *Eighth Mode* is that based on relativity; and by it we conclude that, since all things are relative, we shall suspend judgement regarding their independent and real essence. But this point we must notice—that here as elsewhere we use the term "are" for the term "appear," and what we virtually mean is "all things appear relative."

And this statement is twofold, implying, firstly, relation to
the thing which judges (for the external object which is
judged appears in relation to that thing), and, in a second
sense, relation to the accompanying percepts, for instance
the right side in relation to the left. Indeed, we have already argued that all things are relative—for example, with [136]
respect to the thing which judges, it is in relation to some
one particular animal or man or sense that each object appears, and in relation to such and such a circumstance; and
with respect to the concomitant percepts, each object appears in relation to some one particular admixture or mode
or combination or quantity or position.

There are also special arguments to prove the relativity [137]
of all things, in this way: Do things which exist "differentially" [18] differ from relative things or not? If they do not
differ, then they too are relative; but if they differ, then,
since everything which differs is relative to something (for
it has its name from its relation to that from which it differs), things which exist differentially are relative. Again, [138]
—of existing things some, according to the Dogmatists, are
summa genera, others *infimae species*, others both genera
and species; and all these are relative; therefore all things
are relative. Further, some existing things are "pre-evi-
dent," as they say, others non-evident; and the apparent
things are significant, but the non-evident signified by the
apparent; for according to them "the things apparent are
the vision of the non-evident." But the significant and the
signified are relative; therefore all things are relative. More- [139]
over, some existent things are similar, others dissimilar,
and some equal, others unequal; and these are relative;
therefore all things are relative. And even he who asserts
that not all things are relative confirms the relativity of all

[18] Or "have a distinct existence of their own," as opposed to a merely
relative existence. This is a technical term for the class of objects which
are "self-existent," "absolute," or "independent."

things, since by his arguments against us he shows that the very statement "not all things are relative" is relative to ourselves, and not universal.

140 When, however, we have thus established that all things are relative, we are plainly left with the conclusion that we shall not be able to state what is the nature of each of the objects in its own real purity, but only what nature it appears to possess in its relative character. Hence it follows that we must suspend judgement concerning the real nature of the objects.

141 The *Mode* which, as we said, comes *Ninth* in order is based on constancy or rarity of occurrence, and we shall explain it as follows. The sun is, of course, much more amazing than a comet; yet because we see the sun constantly but the comet rarely we are so amazed by the comet that we even regard it as a divine portent, while the sun causes no amazement at all. If, however, we were to conceive of the sun as appearing but rarely and setting rarely, and illuminating everything all at once and throwing everything into shadow suddenly, then we should experience much

142 amazement at the sight. An earthquake also does not cause the same alarm in those who experience it for the first time and those who have grown accustomed to such things. How much amazement, also, does the sea excite in the man who sees it for the first time! And indeed the beauty of a human body thrills us more at the first sudden view than when it becomes a customary spectacle. Rare things too we count

143 as precious, but not what is familiar to us and easily got. Thus, if we should suppose water to be rare, how much more precious it would appear to us than all the things which are accounted precious! Or if we should imagine gold to be simply scattered in quantities over the earth like stones, to whom do we suppose it would then be precious and worth hoarding?

144 Since then, owing to the frequency or rarity of their occurrence, the same things seem at one time to be amazing

or precious and at another time nothing of the sort, we infer that though we shall be able perhaps to say what nature appears to belong to each of these things in virtue of its frequent or rare occurrence, we are not able to state what nature absolutely belongs to each of the external objects. So because of this Mode also we suspend judgement regarding them.

There is a *Tenth Mode,* which is mainly concerned with [145] Ethics, being based on rules of conduct, habits, laws, legendary beliefs, and dogmatic conceptions. A rule of conduct is a choice of a way of life, or of a particular action, adopted by one person or many—by Diogenes, for instance, or the Laconians. A law is a written contract amongst the [146] members of a State, the transgressor of which is punished. A habit or custom (the terms are equivalent) is the joint adoption of a certain kind of action by a number of men, the transgressor of which is not actually punished; for example, the law proscribes adultery, and custom with us forbids intercourse with a woman in public. Legendary [147] belief is the acceptance of unhistorical and fictitious events, such as, amongst others, the legends about Cronos; for these stories win credence with many. Dogmatic conception is the acceptance of a fact which seems to be established by analogy or some form of demonstration, as, for example, that atoms are the elements of existing things, or homoeomeries, or *minima,* or something else.

And each of these we oppose now to itself, and now to [148] each of the others. For example, we oppose habit to habit in this way: some of the Ethiopians tattoo their children, but we do not; and while the Persians think it seemly to wear a brightly dyed dress reaching to the feet, we think it unseemly; and whereas the Indians have intercourse with their women in public, most other races regard this as shameful. And law we oppose to law in this way: among [149] the Romans the man who renounces his father's property does not pay his father's debts, but among the Rhodians he always pays them; and among the Scythian Tauri it was a law that strangers should be sacrificed to Artemis, but with us it is forbidden to slay a human being at the altar.

150 And we oppose rule of conduct to rule of conduct, as when we oppose the rule of Diogenes to that of Aristippus or that of the Laconians to that of the Italians. And we oppose legendary belief to legendary belief when we say that whereas in one story the father of men and gods is alleged to be Zeus, in another he is Oceanos—"Ocean sire of the gods, and Tethys the mother that bare them." And we op-

151 pose dogmatic conceptions to one another when we say that some declare that there is one element only, others an infinite number; some that the soul is mortal, others that it is immortal; and some that human affairs are controlled by divine Providence, others without Providence.

152 And we oppose habit to the other things, as for instance to law when we say that amongst the Persians it is the habit to indulge in intercourse with males, but amongst the Romans it is forbidden by law to do so; and that, whereas with us adultery is forbidden, amongst the Massagetae it is traditionally regarded as an indifferent custom, as Eudoxus of Cnidos relates in the first book of his *Travels*; and that, whereas intercourse with a mother is forbidden in our country, in Persia it is the general custom to form such marriages; and also among the Egyptians men marry their

153 sisters, a thing forbidden by law amongst us. And habit is opposed to rule of conduct when, whereas most men have intercourse with their own wives in retirement, Crates did it in public with Hipparchia; and Diogenes went about with one shoulder bare, whereas we dress in the customary

154 manner. It is opposed also to legendary belief, as when the legends say that Cronos devoured his own children, though it is our habit to protect our children; and whereas it is customary with us to revere the gods as being good and immune from evil, they are presented by the poets as suffering

155 wounds and envying one another. And habit is opposed to

dogmatic conception when, whereas it is our habit to pray to the gods for good things, Epicurus declares that the Divinity pays no heed to us; and when Aristippus considers the wearing of feminine attire a matter of indifference, though we consider it a disgraceful thing.

And we oppose rule of conduct to law when, though [156] there is a law which forbids the striking of a free or well-born man, the pancratiasts strike one another because of the rule of life they follow; and when, though homicide is forbidden, gladiators destroy one another for the same reason. And we oppose legendary belief to rule of conduct [157] when we say that the legends relate that Heracles in the house of Omphale "toiled at the spinning of wool, enduring slavery's burden," and did things which no one would have chosen to do even in a moderate degree, whereas the rule of life of Heracles was a noble one. And we oppose rule of conduct to dogmatic conception when, whereas [158] athletes covet glory as something good and for its sake undertake a toilsome rule of life, many of the philosophers dogmatically assert that glory is a worthless thing. And we [159] oppose law to legendary belief when the poets represent the gods as committing adultery and practising intercourse with males, whereas the law with us forbids such actions; and we oppose it to dogmatic conception when Chrysippus says [160] that intercourse with mothers or sisters is a thing indifferent, whereas the law forbids such things. And we oppose [161] legendary belief to dogmatic conception when the poets say that Zeus came down and had intercourse with mortal women, but amongst the Dogmatists it is held that such a thing is impossible; and again, when the poet relates that [162] because of his grief for Sarpedon Zeus "let fall upon the earth great gouts of blood," whereas it is a dogma of the philosophers that the Deity is impassive; and when these same philosophers demolish the legend of the hippocentaurs, and offer us the hippocentaur as a type of unreality.

We might indeed have taken many other examples in [163]

connexion with each of the antitheses above mentioned; but in a concise account like ours, these will be sufficient. Only, since by means of this Mode also so much divergency is shown to exist in objects, we shall not be able to state what character belongs to the object in respect of its real essence, but only what belongs to it in respect of this particular rule of conduct, or law, or habit, and so on with each of the rest. So because of this Mode also we are compelled to suspend judgement regarding the real nature of external objects. And thus by means of all the Ten Modes we are finally led to suspension of judgement.

164 [15. *Of the Five Modes:* The later Sceptics hand down Five Modes leading to suspension, namely these: the first based on discrepancy, the second on regress *ad infinitum*, the third on relativity, the fourth on hypothesis, the fifth 165 on circular reasoning. That based on discrepancy leads us to find that with regard to the object presented there has arisen both amongst ordinary people and amongst the philosophers an interminable conflict because of which we are unable either to choose a thing or reject it, and so fall back 166 on suspension. The Mode based upon regress *ad infinitum* is that whereby we assert that the thing adduced as a proof of the matter proposed needs a further proof, and this again another, and so on *ad infinitum*, so that the consequence is suspension, as we possess no starting-point for 167 our argument. The Mode based upon relativity, as we have already said, is that whereby the object has such or such an appearance in relation to the subject judging and to the concomitant percepts, but as to its real nature we suspend 168 judgement. We have the Mode based on hypothesis when the Dogmatists, being forced to recede *ad infinitum*, take as their starting-point something which they do not establish by argument but claim to assume as granted simply and 169 without demonstration. The Mode of circular reasoning is the form used when the proof itself which ought to establish the matter of inquiry requires confirmation derived

from that matter; in this case, being unable to assume either in order to establish the other, we suspend judgement about both.

That every matter of inquiry admits of being brought under these Modes we shall show briefly in this way. The matter proposed is either a sense-object or a thought-object, [170] but whichever it is, it is an object of controversy; for some say that only sensibles are true, others only intelligibles, others that some sensible and some intelligible objects are true.[19] Will they then assert that the controversy can or cannot be decided? If they say it cannot, we have it granted that we must suspend judgement; for concerning matters of dispute which admit of no decision it is impossible to make an assertion. But if they say that it can be decided, we ask by what is it to be decided. For example, in the case of the [171] sense-object (for we shall base our argument on it first), is it to be decided by a sense-object or a thought-object? For if they say by a sense-object, since we are inquiring about sensibles that object itself also will require another to confirm it; and if that too is to be a sense-object, it likewise will require another for its confirmation, and so on *ad infinitum*. And if the sense-object shall have to be decided [172] by a thought-object, then, since thought-objects also are controverted, this being an object of thought will need examination and confirmation. Whence then will it gain confirmation? If from an intelligible object, it will suffer a similar regress *ad infinitum*; and if from a sensible object, since an intelligible was adduced to establish the sensible and a sensible to establish the intelligible, the Mode of circular reasoning is brought in.

If, however, our disputant, by way of escape from this [173] conclusion, should claim to assume as granted and without demonstration some postulate for the demonstration of the

[19] Of these views the first was maintained, e.g., by Protagoras and Epicurus, the second by Platon and Democritus, and the third by Peripatetics and Stoics.

next steps of his argument, then the Mode of hypothesis will be brought in, which allows no escape. For if the author of the hypothesis is worthy of credence, we shall be no less worthy of credence every time that we make the opposite hypothesis. Moreover, if the author of the hypothesis assumes what is true he causes it to be suspected by assuming it by hypothesis rather than after proof; while if it is false, the foundation of his argument will be rotten.

174 Further, if hypothesis conduces at all to proof, let the subject of inquiry itself be assumed and not some other thing which is merely a means to establish the actual subject of the argument; but if it is absurd to assume the subject of inquiry, it will also be absurd to assume that upon which it depends.[20]

175 It is also plain that all sensibles are relative; for they are relative to those who have the sensations. Therefore it is apparent that whatever sensible object is presented can easily be referred to one of the Five Modes. And concerning the intelligible object we argue similarly. For if it should be said that it is a matter of unsettled controversy, the necessity of our suspending judgement will be granted.

176 And if, on the other hand, the controversy admits of decision, then if the decision rests on an intelligible object we shall be driven to the regress *ad infinitum*, and to circular reasoning if it rests on a sensible; for since the sensible again is controverted and cannot be decided by means of itself because of the regress *ad infinitum*, it will require the intelligible object, just as also the intelligible will require

177 the sensible. For these reasons, again, he who assumes anything by hypothesis will be acting illogically. Moreover, objects of thought, or intelligibles, are relative; for they are so named on account of their relation to the person thinking, and if they had really possessed the nature they are said to possess, there would have been no controversy about them. Thus the intelligible also is referred to the Five Modes, so

[20] I.e., the super-ordinate, or more universal, proposition.

that in all cases we are compelled to suspend judgement
concerning the object presented.

Such then are the Five Modes handed down amongst the
later Sceptics; but they propound these not by way of su-
perseding the Ten Modes but in order to expose the rashness of the Dogmatists with more variety and complete-
ness by means of the Five in conjunction with the Ten.

[16. *Of the Two Modes:* They hand down also *Two* other 178
Modes leading to suspension of judgement. Since every
object of apprehension seems to be apprehended either
through itself or through another object, by showing that
nothing is apprehended either through itself or through
another thing, they introduce doubt, as they suppose, about
everything. That nothing is apprehended through itself is
plain, they say, from the controversy which exists amongst
the physicists regarding, I imagine, all things, both sensibles
and intelligibles; which controversy admits of no settlement
because we can neither employ a sensible nor an intelligible
criterion, since every criterion we may adopt is controverted and therefore discredited. And the reason why they 179
do not allow that anything is apprehended through something else is this: If that through which an object is apprehended must always itself be apprehended through some
other thing, one is involved in a process of circular reasoning or in regress *ad infinitum.* And if, on the other hand,
one should choose to assume that the thing through which
another object is apprehended is itself apprehended
through itself, this is refuted by the fact that, for the reasons already stated, nothing is apprehended through itself.
But as to how what conflicts with itself can possibly be apprehended either through itself or through some other
thing we remain in doubt, so long as the criterion of truth
or of apprehension is not apparent, and signs, even apart
from demonstration, are rejected, as we shall discover in
our next Book.

For the present, however, it will suffice to have said thus

much concerning the Modes leading to suspension of judgement.

[17. *Of the Modes by which the Aetiologists are confuted:*
180 Just as we teach the traditional Modes leading to suspense of judgement, so likewise some Sceptics propound Modes by which we express doubt about the particular "aetiologies," or theories of causation, and thus pull up the Dogmatists because of the special pride they take in these theories. Thus Aenesidemus furnishes us with *Eight Modes* by which, as he thinks, he tests and exposes the unsoundness
181 of every dogmatic theory of causation. Of these the First, he says, is that which shows that, since aetiology as a whole deals with the non-apparent, it is unconfirmed by any agreed evidence derived from appearances. The Second Mode shows how often, when there is ample scope for ascribing the object of investigation to a variety of causes,
182 some of them account for it in one way only. The Third shows how to orderly events they assign causes which exhibit no order. The Fourth shows how, when they have grasped the way in which appearances occur, they assume that they have also apprehended how non-apparent things occur, whereas, though the non-apparent may possibly be realized in a similar way to the appearances, possibly they may not be realized in a similar way but in a peculiar way
183 of their own. In the Fifth Mode it is shown how practically all these theorists assign causes according to their own particular hypotheses about the elements, and not according to any commonly agreed methods. In the Sixth it is shown how they frequently admit only such facts as can be explained by their own theories, and dismiss facts which conflict therewith though possessing equal probability. The
184 Seventh shows how they often assign causes which conflict not only with appearances but also with their own hypotheses. The Eighth shows that often, when there is equal doubt about things seemingly apparent and things under investigation, they base their doctrine about things equally

doubtful upon things equally doubtful. Nor is it impossi- *185* ble, he adds, that the overthrow of some of their theories of causation should be referred to certain mixed Modes which are dependent on the foregoing.

Possibly, too, the Five Modes of suspension may suffice as against the aetiologies. For if a person propounds a cause, it will either be or not be in accord with all the philosophical systems and with Scepticism and with appearances. Probably, however, it is impracticable to propound a cause in accord with all these, since all things, whether apparent or non-evident, are matters of controversy. But if, *186* on the other hand, the cause propounded be not in accord therewith, the theorist will be asked in turn for the cause of this cause, and if he assumes an apparent cause for an apparent, or a non-evident for a non-evident, he will be involved in the regress *ad infinitum*, or reduced to arguing in a circle if he grounds each cause in turn on another. And if at any point he makes a stand, either he will state that the cause is well-grounded so far as relates to the previous admissions, thus introducing relativity and destroying its claim to absolute reality, or he will make some assumption *ex hypothesi* and will be stopped by us. So by these Modes also it is, no doubt, possible to expose the rashness of the Dogmatists in their aetiologies.

[18. *Of the Sceptic expressions or formulae*: And because when we make use of these Modes and those which lead to *187* suspension of judgement we give utterance to certain expressions indicative of our sceptical attitude and tone of mind—such as "Not more," "Nothing must be determined," and others of the kind—it will be our next task to discuss these in order. So let us begin with the expression "Not more."

[19. *Of the expression "Not more"*: This expression, then, *188* we sometimes enunciate in the form I have stated but sometimes in the form "Nowise more." For we do not, as some suppose, adopt the form "Not more" in specific inquiries and "Nowise more" in generic inquiries, but we enunciate both "Not more" and "Nowise more" indifferently, and we shall discuss them now as identical expressions. This expression, then, is elliptical. For just as when we say "a double" we are implicitly saying "a double hearth," and when we say "a square" we are implicitly saying "a square roadway," so when we say "Not more" we are implicitly saying "Not this more than that, up than down."

189 Some of the Sceptics, however, in place of the "Not" adopt the form "(For) what this more than that," taking the "what" to denote, in this case, cause, so that the meaning is "For what reason this more than that?" And it is a common practice to use questions instead of assertions, as for example—"The bride of Zeus, what mortal knows her not?" And also assertions in the place of questions; for instance—"I am inquiring where Dion lives," and "I ask you what reason there is for showing surprise at a poet." And further, the use of "What" instead of "For what reason" is found in Menander, "(For) what was I left behind?" And

190 the expression "Not more this than that" indicates also our feeling, whereby we come to end in equipoise because of the equipollence of the opposed objects; and by "equipollence" we mean equality in respect of what seems probable to us, and by "opposed" we mean in general conflicting, and by "equipoise" refusal of assent to either alternative.

191 Then as to the formula "Nowise more," even though it exhibits the character of a form of assent or of denial, we do not employ it in this way, but we take it in a loose and inexact sense, either in place of a question or in place of the phrase "I know not to which of these things I ought to assent, and to which I ought not." For our aim is to indicate what appears to us; while as to the expression by which we indicate this we are indifferent. This point, too, should be noticed—that we utter the expression "Nowise more" not as positively affirming that it really is true and certain, but as stating in regard to it also what appears to us.

[20. *Of "Aphasia" or non-assertion:* Concerning non- [192] assertion what we say is this. The term "assertion" has two senses, general and special; used in the general sense it indicates affirmation or negation, as for example "It is day," "It is not day"; in its special sense it indicates affirmation only, and in this sense negations are not termed assertions. Non-assertion, then, is avoidance of assertion in the general sense in which it is said to include both affirmation and negation, so that non-assertion is a mental condition of ours because of which we refuse either to affirm or to deny anything. Hence it is plain that we adopt non-assertion also [193] not as though things are in reality of such a kind as wholly to induce non-assertion, but as indicating that we now, at the time of uttering it, are in this condition regarding the problems now before us. It must also be borne in mind that what, as we say, we neither posit nor deny, is some one of the dogmatic statements made about what is non-apparent; for we yield to those things which move us emotionally and drive us compulsorily to assent.

[21. *Of the expressions "Perhaps," "Possibly," and* [194] *"Maybe":* The formulae "perhaps" and "perhaps not," and "possibly" and "possibly not," and "maybe" and "maybe not," we adopt in place of "perhaps it is and perhaps it is not," and "possibly it is and possibly it is not," and "maybe it is and maybe it is not," so that for the sake of conciseness we adopt the phrase "possibly not" instead of "possibly it is not," and "maybe not" instead of "maybe it is not," and "perhaps not" instead of "perhaps it is not." But here again we do not fight about phrases nor do we in- [195] quire whether the phrases indicate realities, but we adopt them, as I said, in a loose sense. Still it is evident, as I think, that these expressions are indicative of non-assertion. Certainly the person who says "perhaps it is" is implicitly affirming also the seemingly contradictory phrase "perhaps it is not" by his refusal to make the positive assertion that "it is." And the same applies to all the other cases.

196 [22. *Of the expression "I suspend judgement"*: The phrase "I suspend judgement" we adopt in place of "I am unable to say which of the objects presented I ought to believe and which I ought to disbelieve," indicating that the objects appear to us equal as regards credibility and incredibility. As to whether they are equal we make no positive assertion; but what we state is what appears to us in regard to them at the time of observation. And the term "suspension" is derived from the fact of the mind being held up or "suspended" so that it neither affirms nor denies anything owing to the equipollence of the matters in question.

197 [23. *Of the expression "I determine nothing"*: Regarding the phrase "I determine nothing" this is what we say. We hold that "to determine" is not simply to state a thing but to put forward something non-evident combined with assent. For in this sense, no doubt, it will be found that the Sceptic determines nothing, not even the very proposition "I determine nothing"; for this is not a dogmatic assumption, that is to say assent to something non-evident, but an expression indicative of our own mental condition. So whenever the Sceptic says "I determine nothing," what he means is "I am now in such a state of mind as neither to affirm dogmatically nor deny any of the matters now in question." And this he says simply by way of announcing undogmatically what appears to himself regarding the matters presented, not making any confident declaration, but just explaining his own state of mind.

198 [24. *Of the expression "All things are undetermined"*: Indetermination is a state of mind in which we neither deny nor affirm any of the matters which are subjects of dogmatic inquiry, that is to say, non-evident. So whenever the Sceptic says "All things are undetermined," he takes the word "are" in the sense of "appear to him," and by "all things" he means not existing things but such of the non-evident matters investigated by the Dogmatists as he has exam-

ined, and by "undetermined" he means not superior in
point of credibility or incredibility to things opposed, or in
any way conflicting. And just as the man who says "(I) *199*
walk about" 21 is potentially saying "I walk about," so he
who says "All are undetermined" conveys also, as we hold,
the meaning "so far as relates to me," or "as appears to
me," so that the statement amounts to this—"All the matters of dogmatic inquiry which I have examined appear to
me to be such that no one of them is preferable to the one
in conflict with it in respect of credibility or incredibility."

[25. *Of the expression "All things are non-apprehensible":*
We adopt a similar attitude when we say "All things are *200*
non-apprehensible." For we give a similar explanation of
the word "all," and we similarly supply the words "to me,"
so that the meaning conveyed is this—"All the non-
apparent matters of dogmatic inquiry which I have investigated appear to me non-apprehensible." And this is the
utterance not of one who is positively asserting that the
matters investigated by the Dogmatists are really of such
a nature as to be non-apprehensible, but of one who is announcing his own state of mind, "wherein," he says, "I conceive that up till now I myself have apprehended nothing
owing to the equipollence of the opposites; and therefore
also nothing that is brought forward to overthrow our position seems to me to have any bearing on what we an-
nounce."

[26. *Of the expressions "I am non-apprehensive and "I
apprehend not":* Both the expressions "I am non- *201*
apprehensive" and "I apprehend not" are indicative of a
personal state of mind, in which the Sceptic, for the time
being, avoids affirming or denying any non-evident matter
of inquiry, as is obvious from what we have said above concerning the other expressions.

[27. *Of the phrase "To every argument an equal argument*

---

21 I.e., the personal pronoun "I" is potentially, or implicitly, expressed
in the ending of the Greek verb (first person, singular).

202 *is opposed*": When we say "To every argument an equal argument is opposed," we mean "to every argument" that has been investigated by us, and the word "argument" we use not in its simple sense, but of that which establishes a point dogmatically (that is to say with reference to what is non-evident) and establishes it by any method, and not necessarily by means of premises and a conclusion.[22] We say "equal" with reference to credibility or incredibility, and we employ the word "opposed" in the general sense of "conflicting"; and we supply therewith in thought the

203 phrase "as appears to me." So whenever I say "To every argument an equal argument is opposed," what I am virtually saying is "To every argument investigated by me which establishes a point dogmatically, it seems to me there is opposed another argument, establishing a point dogmatically, which is equal to the first in respect of credibility and incredibility"; so that the utterance of the phrase is not a piece of dogmatism, but the announcement of a human state of mind which is apparent to the person experiencing it.

204 But some also utter the expression in the form "To every argument an equal argument is to be opposed," intending to give the injunction "To every argument which establishes a point dogmatically let us oppose an argument which investigates dogmatically, equal to the former in respect of credibility and incredibility, and conflicting therewith"; for they mean their words to be addressed to the Sceptic, although they use the infinitive form "to be op-

205 posed" instead of the imperative "let us oppose." And they address this injunction to the Sceptic lest haply, through being misled by the Dogmatist, he may give up the Sceptic search, and through precipitancy miss the "quietude" approved by the Sceptics, which they—as we said above—believe to be dependent on universal suspension of judgement.

22 I.e., by the use of syllogisms.

[28. *Supplementary notes on the Sceptic expressions*: In
a preliminary outline it will be sufficient to have explained [206]
the expressions now set forth, especially since it is possible
to explain the rest by deductions from the foregoing. For,
in regard to all the Sceptic expressions, we must grasp first
the fact that we make no positive assertion respecting their
absolute truth, since we say that they may possibly be confuted by themselves, seeing that they themselves are included in the things to which their doubt applies, just as
aperient drugs do not merely eliminate the humours from
the body, but also expel themselves along with the humours. And we also say that we employ them not by way [207]
of authoritatively explaining the things with reference to
which we adopt them, but without precision and, if you
like, loosely; for it does not become the Sceptic to wrangle
over expressions, and besides it is to our advantage that
even to these expressions no absolute significance should
be ascribed, but one that is relative and relative to the
Sceptics. Besides this we must also remember that we do [208]
not employ them universally about all things, but about
those which are non-evident and are objects of dogmatic
inquiry; and that we state what appears to us and do not
make any positive declarations as to the real nature of external objects; for I think that, as a result of this, every
sophism directed against a Sceptic expression can be refuted.

And now that we have reviewed the idea or purpose of [209]
Scepticism and its divisions, and the criterion and the end,
and the modes, too, of suspension, and have discussed the
Sceptic expressions, and have thus made clear the character
of Scepticism, our next task is, we suppose, to explain
briefly the distinction which exists between it and the philosophic systems which lie next to it, in order that we may
more clearly understand the "suspensive" Way of thought.
Let us begin with the Heracleitean philosophy.

[29. *That the Sceptic Way of thought differs from the* [210]

Heracleitean philosophy: Now that this latter differs from our Way of thought is plain at once; for Heracleitus makes dogmatic statements about many non-evident things, whereas we, as has been said, do not. It is true that Aenesidemus and his followers used to say that the Sceptic Way is a road leading up to the Heracleitean philosophy, since to hold that the same thing is the subject of opposite appearances is a preliminary to holding that it is the subject of opposite realities, and while the Sceptics say that the same thing is the subject of opposite appearances, the Heracleiteans go on from this to assert their reality. But in reply to them we declare that the view about the same thing having opposite appearances is not a dogma of the Sceptics but a fact which is experienced not by the Sceptics alone but also by the rest of philosophers and by all mankind; for certainly no one would venture to say that honey does not taste sweet to people in sound health or that it does not taste bitter to those suffering from jaundice; so that the Heracleiteans start from the general preconception of mankind, just as we also do and probably all the other philosophies. Consequently, if they had derived their theory that the same thing is the subject of opposite realities from one of the Sceptic formulae, such as "All things are non-apprehensible," or "I determine nothing," or some similar expression, probably they would have reached the conclusion they assert; but since their starting-points are impressions experienced not by us only but by all the other philosophers and by ordinary people, why should anyone declare that our Way of thought is a road to the Heracleitean philosophy any more than any of the other philosophies or even than the ordinary view, since we all make use of the same common material?

212   Rather it is the case that the Sceptic Way so far from being an aid to the knowledge of the Heracleitean philosophy is actually an obstacle thereto, seeing that the Sceptic decries all the dogmatic statements of Heracleitus as rash

utterances, contradicting his "Ecpyrosis," [23] and contradicting his view that the same thing is the subject of opposite realities, and in respect of every dogma of Heracleitus scoffing at his dogmatic precipitancy, and constantly repeating, as I said before, his own "I apprehend not" and "I determine nothing," which are in conflict with the Heracleiteans. Now it is absurd to say that a conflicting Way is a road to the system with which it is in conflict; therefore it is absurd to say that the Sceptic Way is a road leading to the Heracleitean philosophy.

[30. *Wherein the Sceptic Way differs from the Democritean philosophy*: But it is also said that the Democritean [213] philosophy has something in common with Scepticism, since it seems to use the same material as we; for from the fact that honey appears sweet to some and bitter to others, Democritus, as they say, infers that it really is neither sweet nor bitter, and pronounces in consequence the formula "Not more," which is a Sceptic formula. The Sceptics, however, and the School of Democritus employ the expression "Not more" in different ways; for while they use it to express the unreality of either alternative, we express by it our ignorance as to whether both or neither of the appearances is real. So that in this respect also we differ, [214] and our difference becomes specially evident when Democritus says "But in verity atoms and void" (for he says "In verity" in place of "In truth"); and that he differs from us when he says that the atoms and the void are in truth subsistent, although he starts out from the incongruity of appearances, it is superfluous, I think, to state.

[31. *Wherein Scepticism differs from Cyrenaicism*: Some assert that the Cyrenaic doctrine is identical with Scepti- [215] cism since it too affirms that only mental states are apprehended. But it differs from Scepticism inasmuch as it says that the End is pleasure and the smooth motion of the

---

[23] I.e., "world-conflagration," by which all things are resolved into the primal Fire.

flesh, whereas we say it is "quietude," which is the opposite of their End; for whether pleasure be present or not
present the man who positively affirms pleasure to be the
End undergoes perturbations, as I have argued in my chapter "Of the End." Further, whereas we suspend judgement,
so far as regards the essence of external objects, the Cyre-
naics declare that those objects possess a real nature which
is inapprehensible.

[32. *Wherein Scepticism differs from the Protagorean doc-*
216 *trine:* Protagoras also holds that "Man is the measure of
all things, of existing things that they exist, and of non-
existing things that they exist not"; and by "measure" he
means the criterion, and by "things" the objects, so that he
is virtually asserting that "Man is the criterion of all objects, of those which exist that they exist, and of those
which exist not that they exist not." And consequently he
posits only what appears to each individual, and thus he
217 introduces relativity. And for this reason he seems also to
have something in common with the Pyrrhoneans. Yet he
differs from them, and we shall perceive the difference
when we have adequately explained the views of Protagoras.

What he states then is this—that matter is in flux, and
as it flows additions are made continuously in the place of
the effluxions, and the senses are transformed and altered
according to the times of life and to all the other conditions
218 of the bodies. He says also that the "reasons" of all the appearances subsist in matter, so that matter, so far as depends on itself, is capable of being all those things which
appear to all.[24] And men, he says, apprehend different
things at different times owing to their differing dispositions; for he who is in a natural state apprehends those
things subsisting in matter which are able to appear to

[24] I.e., in brief, all "appearances" (sensations, opinions, etc.) are due
to inter-action between the matter of the percipient subject and the
matter of the objective world, both of which are in constant flux. Thus
"matter" is potentially the "phenomenon."

those in a natural state, and those who are in a non-natural state the things which can appear to those in a non-natural state. Moreover, precisely the same account applies ²¹⁹ to the variations due to age, and to the sleeping or waking state, and to each several kind of condition. Thus, according to him, Man becomes the criterion of real existences; for all things that appear to men also exist, and things that appear to no man have no existence either.

We see, then, that he dogmatizes about the fluidity of matter and also about the subsistence therein of the "reasons" of all appearances, these being non-evident matters about which we suspend judgement.

[33. *Wherein Scepticism differs from the Academic philosophy:* Some indeed say that the Academic philosophy ²²⁰ is identical with Scepticism; consequently it shall be our next task to discuss this statement.

According to most people there have been three Academies—the first and most ancient that of Plato and his School, the second or middle Academy that of Arcesilaus, the pupil of Polemo, and his School, the third or New Academy that of the School of Carneades and Cleitomachus. Some, however, add as a fourth that of the School of Philo and Charmidas; and some even count the School of Antiochus as a fifth. Beginning, then, with the Old Acad- ²²¹ emy let us consider how the philosophies mentioned differ (from ours).

Plato has been described by some as "dogmatic," by others as "dubitative," and by others again as partly dogmatic and partly dubitative. For in his exercitatory discourses, where Socrates is introduced either as talking playfully with his auditors or as arguing against sophists, he shows, they say, an exercitatory and dubitative character; but a dogmatic character when he is speaking seriously by the mouth either of Socrates or of Timaeus or of some similar personage. Now as regards those who describe him as a ²²² dogmatist, or as partly dogmatic and partly dubitative, it would be superfluous to say anything now; for they themselves acknowledge his difference from us. But the question whether Plato is a genuine Sceptic is one which we discuss more fully in our "Commentaries"; but now, in agreement with Menodotus and Aenesidemus (these being the chief champions of this view), we declare in brief that when Plato makes statements about Ideas or about the reality of Providence or about the virtuous life being preferable to the vicious, he is dogmatizing if he is assenting to these as actual truths, while if he is accepting them as more probable than not, since thereby he gives a preference to one thing over another in point of probability or improbability, he throws off the character of a Sceptic; for that such an attitude is foreign to us is quite plain from what has been said above.

223 And if Plato does really utter some statements in a sceptical way when he is, as they say, "exercising," that will not make him a Sceptic; for the man that dogmatizes about a single thing, or ever prefers one impression to another in point of credibility or incredibility, or makes any assertion about any non-evident object, assumes the dogmatic character, as Timon also shows by his remarks about Xenoph-

224 anes. For after praising him repeatedly, so that he even dedicated to him his *Satires*, he represented him as uttering this lamentation—

> Would that I too had attained a mind compacted of wisdom,
> Both ways casting my eyes; but the treacherous pathway
> deceived me,
> Old that I was, and as yet unversed in the doubts of the
> Sceptic.
> For in whatever direction I turned my mind in its questing
> All was resolved into One and the Same; All ever-existing
> Into one self-same nature returning shaped itself all ways.

So on this account he also calls him "semi-vain," and not perfectly free from vanity, where he says—

Xenophanes semi-vain, derider of Homer's deceptions,
Framed him a God far other than Man, self-equal in all ways,
Safe from shaking or scathe, surpassing thought in his thinking.

He called him "semi-vain" as being in some degree free
from vanity, and "derider of Homer's deceptions" because
he censured the deceit mentioned in Homer. Xenophanes,
contrary to the preconceptions of all other men, asserted [225]
dogmatically that the All is one, and that God is consub-
stantial with all things, and is of spherical form and passionless and unchangeable and rational; and from this it is
easy to show how Xenophanes differs from us. However, it
is plain from what has been said that even if Plato evinces
doubt about some matters, yet he cannot be a Sceptic inasmuch as he shows himself at times either making assertions
about the reality of non-evident objects or preferring one
non-evident thing to another in point of credibility.

The adherents of the New Academy, although they af- [226]
firm that all things are non-apprehensible, yet differ from
the Sceptics even, as seems probable, in respect of this very
statement that all things are non-apprehensible (for they
affirm this positively, whereas the Sceptic regards it as possible that some things may be apprehended); but they
differ from us quite plainly in their judgement of things
good and evil. For the Academicians do not describe a thing
as good or evil in the way we do; for they do so with the
conviction that it is more probable[25] that what they call
good is really good rather than the opposite, and so too in
the case of evil, whereas when we describe a thing as good
or evil we do not add it as our opinion that what we assert
is probable, but simply conform to life undogmatically that
we may not be precluded from activity. And as regards [227]
sense-impressions, we say that they are equal in respect of
probability and improbability, so far as their essence is concerned, whereas they assert that some impressions are probable, others improbable.

25 Carneades was the chief exponent of this "probabilism."

And respecting the probable impressions they make distinctions: some they regard as just simply probable, others as probable and tested, others as probable, tested, and "irreversible." For example, when a rope is lying coiled up in a dark room, to one who enters hurriedly it presents the

228 simply "probable" appearance of being a serpent; but to the man who has looked carefully round and has investigated the conditions—such as its immobility and its colour, and each of its other peculiarities—it appears as a rope, in accordance with an impression that is probable and tested. And the impression that is also "irreversible" or incontrovertible is of this kind. When Alcestis had died, Heracles, it is said, brought her up again from Hades and showed her to Admetus, who received an impression of Alcestis that was probable and tested; since, however, he knew that she was dead his mind recoiled from its assent and reverted to

229 unbelief.[26] So then the philosophers of the New Academy prefer the probable and tested impression to the simply probable, and to both of these the impression that is probable and tested and irreversible.

And although both the Academics and the Sceptics say that they believe some things, yet here too the difference

230 between the two philosophies is quite plain. For the word "believe" has different meanings: it means not to resist but simply to follow without any strong impulse or inclination, as the boy is said to believe his tutor; but sometimes it means to assent to a thing of deliberate choice and with a kind of sympathy due to strong desire, as when the incontinent man believes him who approves of an extravagant mode of life. Since, therefore, the followers of Carneades and Cleitomachus declare that a strong inclination accompanies their credence and the credibility of the object, while we say that our belief is a matter of simple yielding

---

[26] This is a curious example of an "irreversible," or indubitable, impression. If the text is right, it looks as if Sextus was nodding.

without any consent, here too there must be a difference between us and them.

Furthermore, as regards the End (or aim of life) we [231] differ from the New Academy; for whereas the men who profess to conform to its doctrine use probability as the guide of life, we live in an undogmatic way by following the laws, customs, and natural affections. And we might say still more about this distinction had it not been that we are aiming at conciseness.

Arcesilaus, however, who was, as we said, the president [232] and founder of the Middle Academy, certainly seems to me to have shared the doctrines of Pyrrho, so that his Way of thought is almost identical with ours. For we do not find him making any assertion about the reality or unreality of anything, nor does he prefer any one thing to another in point of probability or improbability, but suspends judgement about all. He also says that the End is suspension—which is accompanied, as we have said, by "quietude." He declares, too, that suspension regarding particular objects [233] is good, but assent regarding particulars bad. Only one might say that whereas we make these statements not positively but in accordance with what appears to us, he makes them as statements of real facts, so that he asserts that suspension in itself really is good and assent bad. And if one [234] ought to credit also what is said about him, he appeared at the first glance, they say, to be a Pyrrhonean, but in reality he was a dogmatist; and because he used to test his companions by means of dubitation to see if they were fitted by nature for the reception of the Platonic dogmas, he was thought to be a dubitative philosopher, but he actually passed on to such of his companions as were naturally gifted the dogmas of Plato. And this was why Ariston described him as "Plato the head of him, Pyrrho the tail, in the midst Diodorus"; because he employed the dialectic of Diodorus, although he was actually a Platonist.

235 Philo asserts that objects are inapprehensible so far as concerns the Stoic criterion, that is to say "apprehensive impression," but are apprehensible so far as concerns the real nature of the objects themselves. Moreover, Antiochus actually transferred the Stoa to the Academy, so that it was even said of him that "In the Academy he teaches the Stoic philosophy"; for he tried to show that the dogmas of the Stoics are already present in Plato. So that it is quite plain how the Sceptic "Way" differs from what is called the Fourth Academy and the Fifth.

LUCIAN

HERMOTIMUS, OR THE RIVAL PHILOSOPHIES*

Lycinus. Hermotimus

Ly. Good morning, Hermotimus; I guess by your book and the pace you are going at that you are on your way to lecture, and a little late. You were conning over something as you walked, your lips working and muttering, your hand flung out this way and that as you got a speech into order in your mind; you were doubtless inventing one of your crooked questions, or pondering some tricky problem; never a vacant mind, even in the streets; always on the stretch and in earnest, bent on advancing in your studies.

Her. I admit the impeachment; I was running over the details of what he said in yesterday's lecture. One must lose no chance, you know; the Coan doctor[1] spoke so truly: *ars*

* Reprinted from *The Works of Lucian of Samosata,* Vol. II (1905), translated by H. W. and F. G. Fowler, by permission of Oxford University Press.
[1] Hippocrates.

longa, vita brevis. And what *he* referred to was only physic
—a simpler matter. As to philosophy, not only will you
never attain it, however long you study, unless you are wide
awake all the time, contemplating it with intense eager
gaze; the stake is so tremendous, too,—whether you shall
rot miserably with the vulgar herd, or be counted among
philosophers and reach Happiness.

Ly. A glorious prize, indeed! however, you cannot be far ²
off it now, if one may judge by the time you have given to
philosophy, and the extraordinary vigour of your long pursuit. For twenty years now, I should say, I have watched you
perpetually going to your professors, generally bent over a
book taking notes of past lectures, pale with thought and
emaciated in body. I suspect you find no release even in
your dreams, you are so wrapped up in the thing. With all
this you must surely get hold of Happiness soon, if indeed
you have not found it long ago without telling us.

Her. Alas, Lycinus, I am only just beginning to get an
inkling of the right way. Very far off dwells Virtue, as Hesiod says, and long and steep and rough is the way thither,
and travellers must bedew it with sweat.

Ly. And you have not yet sweated and travelled enough?

Her. Surely not; else should I have been on the summit,
with nothing left between me and bliss; but I am only starting yet, Lycinus.

Ly. Ah, but Hesiod, your own authority, tells us, Well ³
begun is half done; so we may safely call you half-way by
this time.

Her. Not even there yet; that would indeed have been
much.

Ly. Where *shall* we put you, then?

Her. Still on the lower slopes, just making an effort to
get on; but it is slippery and rough, and needs a helping
hand.

Ly. Well, your master can give you that; from his station
on the summit, like Zeus in Homer with his golden cord,

he can let you down his discourse, and therewith haul and heave you up to himself and to the Virtue which he has himself attained this long time.

Her. The very picture of what he is doing; if it depended on him alone, I should have been hauled up long ago; it is my part that is still wanting.

4 *Ly.* You must be of good cheer and keep a stout heart; gaze at the end of your climb and the Happiness at the top, and remember that he is working with you. What prospect does he hold out? when are you to be up? does he think you will be on the top next year—by the Great Mysteries, or the Panathenaea, say?

Her. Too soon, Lycinus.

Ly. By next Olympiad, then?

Her. All too short a time, even that, for habituation to Virtue and attainment of Happiness.

Ly. Say two Olympiads, then, for an outside estimate. You may fairly be found guilty of laziness, if you cannot get it done by then; the time would allow you three return trips from the Pillars of Heracles to India, with a margin for exploring the tribes on the way instead of sailing straight and never stopping. How much higher and more slippery, pray, is the peak on which your Virtue dwells than that Aornos crag which Alexander stormed in a few days?

5 *Her.* There is no resemblance, Lycinus; this is not a thing, as you conceive it, to be compassed and captured quickly, though ten thousand Alexanders were to assault it; in that case, the scalers would have been legion. As it is, a good number begin the climb with great confidence, and do make progress, some very little indeed, others more; but when they get half-way, they find endless difficulties and discomforts, lose heart, and turn back, panting, dripping, and exhausted. But those who endure to the end reach the top, to be blessed thenceforth with wondrous days, looking down from their height upon the ants which are the rest of mankind.

Ly. Dear me, what tiny things you make us out—not so big as the Pygmies even, but positively grovelling on the face of the earth. I quite understand it; your thoughts are up aloft already. And we, the common men that walk the earth, shall mingle you with the Gods in our prayers; for you are translated above the clouds, and gone up whither you have so long striven.

Her. If but that ascent might be, Lycinus! but it is far yet.

Ly. But you have never told me *how* far, in terms of time.   6

Her. No; for I know not precisely myself. My guess is that it will not be more than twenty years; by that time I shall surely be on the summit.

Ly. Mercy upon us, you take long views!

Her. Ay; but, as the toil, so is the reward.

Ly. That may be; but about these twenty years—have you your master's promise that you will live so long? is he prophet as well as philosopher? or is it a soothsayer or Chaldean expert that you trust? such things are known to them, I understand. You would never, of course, if there were any uncertainty of your life's lasting to the Virtue-point, slave and toil night and day like this; why, just as you were close to the top, your fate might come upon you, lay hold of you by the heel, and lug you down with your hopes unfulfilled.

Her. God forbid! these are words of ill omen, Lycinus; may life be granted me, that I may grow wise, and have if it be but one day of Happiness!

Ly. For all these toils will you be content with your one day?

Her. Content? yes, or with the briefest moment of it.

Ly. But is there indeed Happiness up there—and worth   7
all the pains? How can you tell? You have never been up yourself.

Her. I trust my master's word; and he knows well; is he not on the topmost height?

Ly. Oh, do tell me what he says about it; what is Happiness like? wealth, glory, pleasures incomparable?

Her. Hush, friend! all these have nought to do with the Virtuous life.

Ly. Well, if these will not do, what *are* the good things he offers to those who carry their course right through?

Her. Wisdom, courage, true beauty, justice, full and firm knowledge of all things as they are; but wealth and glory and pleasure and all bodily things—these a man strips off and abandons before he mounts up, like Heracles burning on Mount Oeta before deification; he too cast off whatever of the human he had from his mother, and soared up to the Gods with his divine part pure and unalloyed, sifted by the fire. Even so those I speak of are purged by the philosophic fire of all that deluded men count admirable, and reaching the summit have Happiness with never a thought of wealth and glory and pleasure—except to smile at any who count them more than phantoms.

Ly. By Heracles (and his death on Oeta), they quit themselves like men, and have their reward, it seems. But there is one thing I should like to know: are they allowed to come down from their elevation sometimes, and have a taste of what they left behind them? or when they have once got up, must they stay there, conversing with Virtue, and smiling at wealth and glory and pleasure?

Her. The latter, assuredly; more than that, a man once admitted of Virtue's company will never be subject to wrath or fear or desire any more; no, nor can he feel pain, nor any such sensation.

Ly. Well, but—if one might dare to say what one thinks —but no—let me keep a good tongue in my head—it were irreverent to pry into what wise men do.

Her. Nay, nay; let me know your meaning.

Ly. Dear friend, I have not the courage.

Her. Out with it, my good fellow; we are alone.

Ly. Well, then—most of your account I followed and accepted—how they grow wise and brave and just, and the rest—indeed I was quite fascinated by it; but then you went on to say they despised wealth and glory and pleasure; well, just there (quite between ourselves, you know) I was pulled up; I thought of a scene t'other day with—shall I tell you whom? Perhaps we can do without a name?

Her. No, no; we must have that too.

Ly. Your own professor himself, then,—a person to whom all respect is due, surely, not to mention his years.

Her. Well?

Ly. You know the Heracleot, quite an old pupil of his in philosophy by this time—red-haired—likes an argument?

Her. Yes; Dion, he is called.

Ly. Well, I suppose he had not paid up punctually; anyhow the other day the old man haled him before the magistrate, with a halter made of his own coat; he was shouting and fuming, and if some friends had not come up and got the young man out of his hands, he would have bitten off his nose, he was in such a temper.

Her. Ah, *he* is a bad character, always an unconscionable ¹⁰ time paying his debts. There are plenty of others who owe the professor money, and he has never treated any of them so; they pay him his interest punctually.

Ly. Not so fast; what in the world does it matter to him, if they do not pay up? he is purified by philosophy, and has no further need of the cast clothes of Oeta.

Her. Do you suppose his interest in such things is selfish? no, but he has little ones; his care is to save them from indigence.

Ly. Whereas he ought to have brought them up to Virtue too, and let them share his inexpensive Happiness.

Her. Well, I have no time to argue it, Lycinus; I must ¹¹ not be late for lecture, lest in the end I find myself left behind.

Ly. Don't be afraid, my duteous one; to-day is a holiday; I can save you the rest of your walk.

Her. What do you mean?

Ly. You will not find him just now, if the notice is to be trusted; there was a tablet over the door announcing in large print, No meeting this day. I hear he dined yesterday with the great Eucrates, who was keeping his daughter's birthday. He talked a good deal of philosophy over the wine, and lost his temper a little with Euthydemus the Peripatetic; they were debating the old Peripatetic objections to the Porch. His long vocal exertions (for it was midnight before they broke up) gave him a bad headache, with violent perspiration. I fancy he had also drunk a little too much, toasts being the order of the day, and eaten more than an old man should. When he got home, he was very ill, they said, just managed to check and lock up carefully the slices of meat which he had conveyed to his servant at table, and then, giving orders that he was not at home, went to sleep, and has not waked since. I overheard Midas his man telling this to some of his pupils; there were a number of them coming away.

Her. Which had the victory, though, he or Euthydemus —if Midas said anything about that?

Ly. Why, at first, I gathered, it was very even between them; but you Stoics had it in the end, and your master was much too hard for him. Euthydemus did not even get off whole; he had a great cut on his head. He was pretentious, insisted on proving his point, would not give in, and proved a hard nut to crack; so your excellent professor, who had a goblet as big as Nestor's in his hand, brought this down on him as he lay within easy reach, and the victory was his.

Her. Good; so perish all who will not yield to their betters!

Ly. Very reasonable, Hermotimus; what was Euthydemus thinking of, to irritate an old man who is purged of wrath and master of his passions, when he had such a heavy goblet in his hand?

But we have time to spare—you might tell a friend like *13*
me the story of your start in philosophy; then I might perhaps, if it is not too late, begin now and join your school;
you are my friends; you will not be exclusive?

Her. If only you would, Lycinus! you will soon find out
how much you are superior to the rest of men. I do assure
you, you will think them all children, you will be so much
wiser.

Ly. Enough for me, if after twenty years of it I am where
you are now.

Her. Oh, I was about your age when I started on philosophy; I was forty; and you must be about that.

Ly. Just that; so take and lead me on the same way; that
is but right. And first tell me—do you allow learners to
criticize, if they find difficulties in your doctrines, or must
juniors abstain from that?

Her. Why, yes, they must; but *you* shall have leave to ask
questions and criticize; you will learn easier that way.

Ly. I thank you for it, Hermotimus, by your name-God
Hermes.

Now, is there only one road to philosophy—the Stoic *14*
way? they tell me there are a great many other philosophers; is that so?

Her. Certainly—Peripatetics, Epicureans, Platonists, followers of Diogenes, Antisthenes, Pythagoras, and more yet.

Ly. Quite so; numbers of them. Now, are their doctrines
the same, or different?

Her. Entirely different.

Ly. But the truth, I presume, is bound to be in one of
them, and not in all, as they differ?

Her. Certainly.

Ly. Then, as you love me, answer this: when you first *15*
went in pursuit of philosophy, you found many gates wide
open; what induced you to pass the others by, and go in at
the Stoic gate? Why did you assume that that was the
only true one, which would set you on the straight road to

Virtue, while the rest all opened on blind alleys? What was the test you applied *then?* Please abolish your present self, the self which is now instructed, or half-instructed, and better able to distinguish between good and bad than we outsiders, and answer in your then character of a layman, with no advantage over me as I am now.

Her. I cannot tell what you are driving at.

Ly. Oh, there is nothing recondite about it. There are a great many philosophers—let us say Plato, Aristotle, Antisthenes, and your spiritual fathers, Chrysippus, Zeno, and all the rest of them; what was it that induced you, leaving the rest alone, to pick out the school you did from among them all, and pin your philosophic faith to it? Were you favoured like Chaerephon with a revelation from Apollo? Did he tell you the Stoics were the best of men, and send you to their school? I dare say he recommends different philosophers to different persons, according to their individual needs?

Her. Nothing of the kind, Lycinus; I never consulted him upon it.

Ly. Why? was it not a *dignus vindice nodus?* or were you confident in your own unaided discrimination?

Her. Why, yes; I was.

16   *Ly.* Then this must be my first lesson from you—how one can decide out of hand which is the best and the true philosophy to be taken, and the others left.

Her. I will tell you: I observed that it attracted most disciples, and thence inferred that it was superior.

Ly. Give me figures; how many more of them than of Epicureans, Platonists, Peripatetics? Of course you took a sort of show of hands.

Her. Well, no; I didn't count; I just guessed.

Ly. Now, now! you are not teaching, but hoaxing me; judge by guesswork and impression, indeed, on a thing of this importance! You are hiding the truth.

Her. Well, that was not my only way; every one told me

the Epicureans were sensual and self-indulgent, the Peripatetics avaricious and contentious, the Platonists conceited and vain; about the Stoics, on the contrary, many said they had fortitude and an open mind; he who goes their way, I heard, was the true king and millionaire and wise man, alone and all in one.

Ly. And, of course, it was other people who so described them; you would not have taken their own word for their excellences. 17

Her. Certainly not; it was others who said it.

Ly. Not their rivals, I suppose?

Her. Oh, no.

Ly. Laymen, then?

Her. Just so.

Ly. There you are again, cheating me with your irony; you take me for a blockhead, who will believe that an intelligent person like Hermotimus, at the age of forty, would accept the word of laymen about philosophy and philosophers, and make his own selection on the strength of what they said.

Her. But you see, Lycinus, I did not depend on their 18
judgement entirely, but on my own too. I saw the Stoics going about with dignity, decently dressed and groomed, ever with a thoughtful air and a manly countenance, as far from effeminacy as from the utter repulsive negligence of the Cynics, bearing themselves, in fact, like moderate men; and every one admits that moderation is right.

Ly. Did you ever see them behaving like your master, as I described him to you just now? Lending money and clamouring for payment, losing their tempers in philosophic debates, and making other exhibitions of themselves? Or perhaps these are trifles, so long as the dress is decent, the beard long, and the hair close-cropped? We are provided for the future, then, with an infallible rule and balance, guaranteed by Hermotimus? It is by appearance and walk and haircutting that the best men are to be distinguished;

and whosoever has not these marks, and is not solemn and thoughtful, shall be condemned and rejected?

19   Nay, do not play with me like this; you want to see whether I shall catch you at it.

Her. Why do you say that?

Ly. Because, my dear sir, this appearance test is one for statues; *their* decent orderly attire has it easily over the Stoics, because Phidias or Alcamenes or Myron designed them to be graceful. However, granting as much as you like that these are the right tests, what is a blind man to do, if he wants to take up philosophy? how is he to find the man whose principles are right, when he cannot see his appearance or gait?

Her. I am not teaching the blind, Lycinus; I have nothing to do with them.

Ly. Ah, but, my good sir, there ought to have been some universal criterion, in a matter of such great and general use. Still, if you will have it so, let the blind be excluded from philosophy, as they cannot see—though, by the way, they are just the people who most need philosophy to console them for their misfortune; but now, the people who *can* see—give them the utmost possible acuity of vision, and what can they detect of the spiritual qualities from this external shell?

20   What I mean is this: was it not from admiration of their *spirit* that you joined them, expecting to have your own spirit purified?

Her. Assuredly.

Ly. How could you possibly discern the true philosopher from the false, then, by the marks you mentioned? It is not the way of such qualities to come out like that; they are hidden and secret; they are revealed only under long and patient observation, in talk and debate and the conduct they inspire. You have probably heard of Momus's indictment of Hephaestus; if not, you shall have it now. According to the myth, Athene, Posidon, and Hephaestus had a match in inventiveness. Posidon made a bull, Athene planned a house, Hephaestus constructed a man; when they came before Momus, who was to judge, he examined their productions; I need not trouble you with his criticisms of the other two; but his objection to the man, and the fault he found with Hephaestus, was this: he should have made a window in his chest, so that, when it was opened, his thoughts and designs, his truth or falsehood, might have been apparent. Momus must have been bleareyed, to have such ideas about men; but you have sharper eyes than Lynceus, and pierce through the chest to what is inside; all is patent to you, not merely any man's wishes and sentiments, but the comparative merits of any pair.

Her. You trifle, Lycinus. I made a pious choice, and do not repent it; that is enough for me. 21

Ly. And will you yet make a mystery of it to your friend, and let him be lost with the vulgar herd?

Her. Why, you will not accept anything I say.

Ly. On the contrary, my good sir, it is you who will not say anything I can accept. Well, as you refuse me your confidence, and are so jealous of my becoming a philosopher and your equal, I must even do my best to find out the infallible test and learn to choose safely for myself. And you may listen, if you like.

Her. That I will, Lycinus; you will very likely hit on some good idea.

Ly. Then attend, and do not mock me, if my inquiry is quite unscientific; it is all I can do, as you, who know better, will not give me any clearer light.

I conceive Virtue, then, under the figure of a State whose 22 citizens are happy—as your professor, who is one of them, phrases it,—absolutely wise, all of them brave, just, and self-controlled, hardly distinguishable, in fact, from Gods. All sorts of things that go on here, such as robbery, assault, unfair gain, you will never find attempted there, I believe; their relations are all peace and unity; and this is quite natural, seeing that none of the things which elsewhere occasion strife and rivalry, and prompt men to plot against their neighbours, so much as come in their way at all. Gold, pleasures, distinctions, they never regard as objects of dispute; they have banished them long ago as undesirable elements. Their life is serene and blissful, in the enjoyment of legality, equality, liberty, and all other good things.

23 *Her*. Well, Lycinus? Must not all men yearn to belong to a State like that, and never count the toil of getting there, nor lose heart over the time it takes? Enough that one day they will arrive, and be naturalized, and given the franchise.

Ly. In good truth, Hermotimus, we should devote all our efforts to this, and neglect everything else; we need pay little heed to any claims of our earthly country; we should steel our hearts against the clingings and cryings of children or parents, if we have them; it is well if we can induce them to go with us; but, if they will not or cannot, shake them off and march straight for the city of bliss, leaving your coat in their hands, if they lay hold of it to keep you back, in your hurry to get there; what matter for a coat? You will be admitted there without one.

24 I remember hearing a description of it all once before from an old man, who urged me to go there with him. He would show me the way, enroll me when I got there, introduce me to his own circles, and promise me a share in the universal Happiness. But I was stiff-necked, in my youthful folly (it was some fifteen years ago); else might I have been in the outskirts, nay, haply at the very gates, by now. Among the noteworthy things he told me, I seem to remember these: all the citizens are aliens and foreigners, not a native among them; they include numbers of barbarians, slaves, cripples, dwarfs, and poor; in fact any one is admitted; for their law does not associate the franchise with income, with shape, size, or beauty, with old or brilliant ancestry; these things are not considered at all; any one who would be a citizen needs only understanding, zeal

for the right, energy, perseverance, fortitude and resolution
in facing all the trials of the road; whoever proves his possession of these by persisting till he reaches the city is *ipso
facto* a full citizen, regardless of his antecedents. Such distinctions as superior and inferior, noble and common, bond
and free, simply do not exist there, even in name.

Her. There, now; you see I am not wasting my pains on 25
trifles; I yearn to be counted among the citizens of that
fair and happy State.

Ly. Why, your yearning is mine too; there is nothing I
would sooner pray for. If the city had been near at hand
and plain for all to see, be assured I would never have
doubted, nor needed prompting; I would have gone thither
and had my franchise long ago; but as you tell me—you
and your bard Hesiod—that it is set exceeding far off, one
must find out the way to it, and the best guide. You agree?

Her. Of course that is the only thing to do.

Ly. Now, so far as promises and professions go, there is
no lack of guides; there are numbers of them waiting about,
all representing themselves as from there. But instead of
one single road there seem to be many different and inconsistent ones. North and South, East and West, they go; one
leads through meadows and vegetation and shade, and is
well watered and pleasant, with never a stumbling-block or
inequality; another is rough and rocky, threatening heat
and drought and toil. Yet all these are supposed to lead to
the one city, though they take such different directions.

That is where my difficulty lies; whichever of them I try, 26
there is sure to be a most respectable person stationed just
at the entrance, with a welcoming hand and an exhortation
to go his way; each of them says he is the only one who
knows the straight road; his rivals are all mistaken, have
never been themselves, nor learnt the way from competent
guides. I go to his neighbour, and he gives the same assur-
ances about *his* way, abusing the other respectable persons;
and so the next, and the next, and the next. This multi-

plicity and dissimilarity of the roads gives me searchings of heart, and still more the assertiveness and self-satisfaction of the guides; I really cannot tell which turning or whose directions are most likely to bring me to the city.

27   *Her.* Oh, but I can solve that puzzle for you; you cannot go wrong, if you trust those who have been already.

Ly. Which do you mean? those who have been by which road, and under whose guidance? It is the old puzzle in a new form; you have only substituted men for measures.

Her. How do you mean?

Ly. Why, the man who has taken Plato's road and travelled with him will recommend that road; so with Epicurus and the rest; and *you* will recommend your own. How else, Hermotimus? it must be so.

Her. Well, of course.

Ly. So you have not solved my puzzle; I know just as little as before which traveller to trust; I find that each of them, as well as his guide, has tried one only, which he now recommends and will have to be the only one leading to the city. Whether he tells the truth I have no means of knowing; that he has attained *some* end, and seen *some* city, I may perhaps allow; but whether he saw the right one, or whether, Corinth being the real goal, he got to Babylon and thought he had seen Corinth—that is still undecided; for surely every one who has seen a city has not seen Corinth, unless Corinth is the only city there is. But my greatest difficulty of all is the absolute certainty that the true road is one; for Corinth is one, and the other roads lead anywhere but to Corinth, though there may be people deluded enough to suppose that the North road and the South road lead equally to Corinth.

Her. But that is absurd, Lycinus; they go opposite ways, you see.

28   *Ly.* Then, my dear good man, this choice of roads and guides is quite a serious matter; we can by no means just follow our noses; we shall be discovering that we are well

on the way to Babylon or Bactria instead of to Corinth. Nor is it advisable to toss up, either, on the chance that we may hit upon the right way if we start upon any one at a venture. That is no impossibility; it may have come off once and again in a cycle; but I cannot think we ought to gamble recklessly with such high stakes, nor commit our hopes to a frail craft, like the wise men who went to sea in a bowl; we should have no fair complaint against Fortune, if her arrow or dart did not precisely hit the centre; the odds are ten thousand to one against her; just so the archer in Homer—Teucer, I suppose it was—when he meant to hit the dove, only cut the string, which held it; of course it is infinitely more likely that the point of the arrow will find its billet in one of the numberless other places, than just in that particular central one. And as to the perils of blundering into one of the wrong roads instead of the right one, misled by a belief in the discretion of Fortune, here is an illustration:—it is no easy matter to turn back and get safe into port when you have once cast loose your moorings and committed yourself to the breeze; you are at the mercy of the sea, frightened, sick and sorry with your tossing about, most likely. Your mistake was at the beginning: before leaving, you should have gone up to some high point, and observed whether the wind was in the right quarter, and of the right strength for a crossing to Corinth, not neglecting, by the way, to secure the very best pilot obtainable, and a seaworthy craft equal to so high a sea.

Her. Much better so, Lycinus. However, I know that, if [29] you go the whole round, you will find no better guides or more expert pilots than the Stoics; if you mean ever to get to Corinth, you will follow them, in the tracks of Chrysippus and Zeno. It is the only way to do it.

Ly. Ah, many can play at the game of assertion. Plato's fellow traveller, Epicurus's follower, and all the rest, will tell me just what you do, that I shall never get to Corinth except with whichever of them it is. So I must either believe them all, or disbelieve impartially. The latter is much the safest, until we have found out the truth.

30   Put a case, now: just as I am, as uncertain as ever which of the whole number has the truth, I choose your school; I rely on you, who are my friend, but who still know only the Stoic doctrine, and have not travelled any way but that. Now some God brings Plato, Pythagoras, Aristotle, and the rest to life again; they gather round and cross-examine me, or actually sue me in court for constructive defamation; *Good Lycinus*, they say, *what possessed or who induced you to exalt Chrysippus and Zeno at our expense? we are far older established; they are mere creatures of yesterday; yet you never gave us a hearing, nor inquired into our statements at all.* Well, what am I to plead? will it avail me to say I trusted my friend Hermotimus? I feel sure they will say, *We know not this Hermotimus, who he is, nor he us; you had no right to condemn us all, and give judgement by default against us, on the authority of a man who knew only one of the philosophic roads, and even that, perhaps, imperfectly. These are not the instructions issued to juries, Lycinus; they are not to hear one party, and refuse the other permission to say what he deems advisable; they are to hear both sides alike, with a view to the better sifting of truth from falsehood by comparison of the arguments; if they fail in these duties, the law allows an appeal to another court.* That is what we may expect them to say.

31   Then one of them might proceed to question me like this: *Suppose, Lycinus, that an Ethiopian who had never been abroad in his life, nor seen other men like us, were to state categorically in an Ethiopian assembly that there did not exist on earth any white or yellow men—nothing but blacks—, would his statement be accepted? or would some Ethiopian elder remark, How do you know, my confident friend? you have never been in foreign parts, nor had any experience of other nations.* Shall I tell him the old man's question was justified? what do you advise, my counsel?

Her. Say that, certainly; I consider the old man's rebuke quite reasonable.

Ly. So do I. But I am not so sure you will approve what comes next; as for me, I have as little doubt of that as of the other.

Her. What is it?

Ly. The next step will be the application; my questioner 32 will say, *Now Lycinus, let us suppose an analogue, in a person acquainted only with the Stoic doctrine, like your friend Hermotimus; he has never travelled in Plato's country, or to Epicurus, or any other land; now, if he were to state that there was no such beauty or truth in those many countries as there is in the Porch and its teaching, would you not be justified in considering it bold of him to give you his opinion about them all, whereas he knew only one, having never set foot outside the bounds of Ethiopia?* What reply do you advise to that?

Her. The perfectly true one, of course, that it is indeed the Stoic doctrine that we study fully, being minded to sink or swim with that, but still we do know what the others say also; our teacher rehearses the articles of their beliefs to us incidentally, and demolishes them with his comments.

Ly. Do you suppose the Platonists, Pythagoreans, Epicu- 33 reans, and other schools, will let that pass? or will they laugh out loud and say, *What remarkable methods your friend has, Lycinus! he accepts our adversaries' character of us, and gathers our doctrines from the description of people who do not know, or deliberately misrepresent them. If he were to see an athlete getting his muscles in trim by kicking high, or hitting out at empty space as though he were getting a real blow home, would he (in the capacity of umpire) at once proclaim him victor, because he could not help winning? No; he would reflect that these displays are easy and safe, when there is no defence to be reckoned with, and that the real decision must wait till he has beaten and mastered his opponent, and the latter "has*

had enough." Well then, do not let Hermotimus suppose
from his teachers' sparrings with our shadows (for we are
not there) that they have the victory, or that our doctrines
are so easily upset; tell him the business is too like the sand
houses which children, having built them weak, have no
difficulty in overturning, or, to change the figure, like people practising archery; they make a straw target, hang it to
a post, plant it a little way off, and then let fly at it; if they
hit and get through the straw, they burst into a shout, as if
it were a great triumph to have driven through the dry
stuff. That is not the way the Persians take, or those Scythian tribes which use the bow. Generally, when they shoot,
in the first place they are themselves mounted and in motion, and secondly, they like the mark to be moving too; it
is not to be stationary, waiting for the arrival of the arrow,
but passing at full speed; they can usually kill beasts, and
their marksmen hit birds. If it ever happens that they want
to test the actual impact on a target, they set up one of
stout wood, or a shield of raw hide; piercing that, they
reckon that their shafts will go through armour too. So,
Lycinus, tell Hermotimus from us that his teachers pierce
straw targets, and then say they have disposed of armed
men; or paint up figures of us, spar at them, and, after a not
surprising success, think they have beaten us. But we shall
severally quote against them Achilles's words against Hec-
tor:

> They dare not face the nodding of my plume.

34   So say all of them, one after the other.

I suspect that Plato, with his intimate knowledge of
Sicily, will add an anecdote from there. Gelo of Syracuse
had disagreeable breath, but did not find it out himself for
a long time, no one venturing to mention such a circumstance to a tyrant. At last a foreign woman who had a connexion with him dared to tell him; whereupon he went to
his wife and scolded her for never having, with all her op-

portunities of knowing, warned him of it; she put in the
defence that, as she had never been familiar or at close
quarters with any other man, she had supposed all men
were like that. So Hermotimus (Plato will say) after his
exclusive association with Stoics, cannot be expected to
know the savour of other people's mouths. Chrysippus, on
the other hand, might say as much or more if I were to put
him out of court and betake myself to Platonism, in re-
liance upon some one who had conversed with Plato alone.
And in a word, as long as it is uncertain which is the true
philosophic school, I choose none; choice of one is insult
to the rest.

Her. For Heaven's sake, Lycinus, let us leave Plato, 35
Aristotle, Epicurus, and the rest of them alone; to argue
with them is not for me. Why not just hold a private inquiry, you and I, whether philosophy is what I say it is? As
for the Ethiopians and Gelo's wife, what a long way you
have brought them on none of their business!

Ly. Away with them, then, if you find their company
superfluous. And now do you proceed; my expectations are
high.

Her. Well, it seems to me perfectly possible, Lycinus,
after studying the Stoic doctrines alone, to get at the truth
from them, without going through a course of all the others
too. Look at it this way: if any one tells you simply, Twice
two is four, need you go round all the mathematicians to
find out whether there is one who makes it five, or seven; or
would you know at once that the man was right?

Ly. Certainly I should.

Her. Then why should you think it impossible for a man
who finds, without going further, that the Stoics make true
statements, to believe them and dispense with further witness? He knows that four can never be five, though ten
thousand Platos or Pythagorases said it was.

Ly. Not to the point. You compare accepted with dis- 36
puted facts, whereas they are completely different. Tell me,

did you ever meet a man who said twice two was seven or eleven?

Her. Not I; any one who did not make four of it must be mad.

Ly. But on the other hand—try to tell the truth, I adjure you—, did you ever meet a Stoic and an Epicurean who did *not* differ about principles or ends?

Her. No.

Ly. You are an honest man; now ask yourself whether you are trapping a friend with false logic. We are trying to find out with whom philosophic truth lies; and you beg the question and make a present of that same truth to the Stoics; for you say (what is quite unproved) that they are the people who make twice two four; the Epicureans or Platonists would say that *they* bring out that result, whereas you get five or seven. Does it not amount to that, when your school reckon goodness the only end, and the Epicureans pleasure? or again when you say everything is material, and Plato recognizes an immaterial element also in all that exists? As I said, you lay hold of the thing in dispute, as though it were the admitted property of the Stoics, and put it into their hands, though the others claim it and maintain that it is theirs; why, it is the very point at issue. If it is once established that Stoics have the monopoly of making four out of twice two, it is time for the rest to hold their tongues; but as long as they refuse to yield that point, we must hear all alike, or be prepared for people's calling us partial judges.

37   *Her.* It seems to me, Lycinus, you do not understand what I mean.

Ly. Very well, put it plainer, if it is something different from that.

Her. You will see in a minute. Let us suppose two people have gone into the temple of Asclepius or Dionysus, and subsequently one of the sacred cups is missing. Both of

them will have to be searched, to see which has it about
him.

Ly. Clearly.

Her. Of course one of them has it.

Ly. Necessarily, if it is missing.

Her. Then, if you find it on the first, you will not strip
the other; it is clear he has not got it.

Ly. Quite.

Her. And if we fail to find it on the first, the other certainly has it; it is unnecessary to search him that way either.

Ly. Yes, he has it.

Her. So with us; if we find the cup in the possession of
the Stoics, we shall not care to go on and search the others;
we have what we were looking for; why trouble further?

Ly. There is no why, if you really find it, and can be certain it is the missing article, the sacred object being unmis-
takable. But there are some differences in this case, friend;
the temple-visitors are not two, so that if one has not got
the booty the other has, but many; and the identity of the
missing object is also uncertain; it may be cup, or bowl, or
garland; every priest gives a different description of it; they
do not agree even about the material; bronze, say these,
silver, say those—anything from gold to tin. So there is
nothing for it but to strip the visitors, if you want to find
it; even if you discover a gold cup on the first man, you
must go on to the others.

Her. What for?

Ly. Because it is not certain that the thing was a cup.
And even if that is generally admitted, they do not all agree
that it was gold; and if it is well known that a gold cup is
missing, and you find a gold cup on your first man, even so
you are not quit of searching the others; it is not clear that
this is *the* sacred cup; do you suppose there is only one gold
cup in the world?

Her. No, indeed.

Ly. So you will have to go the round, and then collect all your finds together and decide which of them is most likely to be divine property.

39   For the source of all the difficulty is this: every one who is stripped has something or other on him, one a bowl, one a cup, one a garland, which again may be bronze, gold, or silver; but whether the one he has is the sacred one, is not yet clear. It is absolutely impossible to know which man to accuse of sacrilege; even if all the objects were similar, it would be uncertain who had robbed the God; for such things may be private property too. Our perplexity, of course, is simply due to the fact that the missing cup—assume it to be a cup—has no inscription; if either the God's or the donor's name had been on it, we should not have had all this trouble; when we found the inscribed one, we should have stopped stripping and inconveniencing other visitors. I suppose, Hermotimus, you have often been at athletic meetings?

Her. You suppose right; and in many places too.

Ly. Did you ever have a seat close by the judges?

Her. Dear me, yes; last Olympia, I was on the left of the stewards; Euandridas of Elis had got me a place in the Elean enclosure; I particularly wanted to have a near view of how things are done there.

Ly. So you know how they arrange ties for the wrestling or the pancratium?

Her. Yes.

Ly. Then you will describe it better than I, as you have seen it so close.

40   *Her.* In old days, when Heracles presided, bay leaves——

Ly. No old days, thank you; tell me what you saw with your own eyes.

Her. A consecrated silver urn is produced, and into it are thrown little lots about the size of a bean, with letters on them. Two are marked alpha, two beta, two more gamma, and so on, if the competitors run to more than that—two lots always to each letter. A competitor comes up, makes a prayer to Zeus, dips his hand into the urn, and pulls out one lot; then another does the same; there is a policeman to each drawer, who holds his hand so that he cannot see what letter he has drawn. When all have drawn, the chief police officer, I think it is, or one of the stewards themselves—I cannot quite remember this detail—, goes round and examines the lots while they stand in a circle, and puts together the two alphas for the wrestling or pancratium, and so for the two betas, and the rest. That is the procedure when the number of competitors is even, as eight, four, or twelve. If it is five, seven, nine, or other odd number, an odd letter is marked on one lot, which is put in with the others, not having a duplicate. Whoever draws this is a bye, and waits till the rest have finished their ties; no duplicate turns up for him, you see; and it is a considerable advantage to an athlete, to know that he will come fresh against tired competitors.

Ly. Stop there; that is just what I wanted. There are nine [41] of them, we will say, and they have all drawn, and the lots are in their hands. You go round—for I promote you from spectator to steward—examining the letters; and I suppose you will not know who is the bye till you have been to them all and paired them.

Her. How do you mean?

Ly. It is impossible for you to hit straight upon the letter which indicates the bye; at least, you may hit upon the letter, but you will not know about the bye; it was not announced beforehand that kappa or mu or iota had the appointment in its gift; when you find alpha, you look for the holder of the other alpha, whom finding, you pair the two. Again finding beta, you inquire into the whereabouts of the second beta which matches it; and so all through, till there is no one left but the holder of the single unpaired letter.

42   *Her.* But suppose you come upon it first or second, what will you do then?

Ly. Never mind me; I want to know what *you* will do, Mr. Steward. Will you say at once, Here is the bye? or will you have to go round to all, and see whether there is a duplicate to be found, it being impossible to know the bye till you have seen all the lots?

Her. Why, Lycinus, I shall know quite easily; nine being the number, if I find the epsilon first or second, I know the holder of it for the bye.

Ly. But how?

Her. How? Why, two of them must have alpha, two beta, and of the next two pairs one has certainly drawn gammas and the other deltas, so that four letters have been used up over eight competitors. Obviously, then, the next letter, which is epsilon, is the only one that can be odd, and the drawer of it is the bye.

Ly. Shall I extol your intelligence, or would you rather I explained to you my own poor idea, which differs?

Her. The latter, of course, though I cannot conceive how you can reasonably differ.

43   *Ly.* You have gone on the assumption that the letters are taken in alphabetical order, until at a particular one the number of competitors runs short; and I grant you it may be done so at Olympia. But suppose we were to pick out five letters at random, say, chi, sigma, zeta, kappa, theta, and duplicate the other four on the lots for eight competitors, but put a single zeta on the ninth, which we meant to indicate the bye—what then would you do if you came on the zeta first? How can you tell that its holder is the bye till you have been all round and found no counterpart to it? for you could not tell by the alphabetical order, as at Olympia.

Her. A difficult question.

44   *Ly.* Look at the same thing another way. Suppose we put

no letters at all on the lots, but, instead of them, signs and marks such as the Egyptians use for letters, men with dogs' or lions' heads. Or no, those are rather too strange; let us avoid hybrids, and put down simple forms, as well as our draughtsmanship will allow—men on two lots, horses on two, a pair of cocks, a pair of dogs, and let a lion be the mark of the ninth. Now, if you hit upon the lion at the first try, how can you tell that this is the bye-maker, until you have gone all round and seen whether any one else has a lion to match?

Her. Your question is too much for me.

Ly. No wonder; there is no plausible answer. Conse- 45
quently, if we mean to find either the man who has the sacred cup, or the bye, or our best guide to the famous city of Corinth, we must absolutely go to and examine them all, trying them carefully, stripping and comparing them; the truth will be hard enough to find, even so. If I am to take any one's advice upon the right philosophy to choose, I insist upon his knowing what they all say; every one else I disqualify; I will not trust him while there is one philosophy he is unacquainted with; that one may possibly be the best of all. If some one were to produce a handsome man, and state that he was the handsomest of mankind, we should not accept that, unless we knew he had seen all men; very likely his man is handsome, but whether the handsomest, he has no means of knowing without seeing all. Now we are looking not simply for beauty, but for the greatest beauty, and if we miss that, we shall account ourselves no further than we were; we shall not be content with chancing upon some sort of beauty; we are in search of a definite thing, the supreme beauty, which must necessarily be *one.*

Her. True. 46

Ly. Well then, can you name me a man who has tried every road in philosophy? one who, knowing the doctrine of Pythagoras, Plato, Aristotle, Chrysippus, Epicurus, and the rest, has ended by selecting one out of all these roads, because he has proved it genuine, and had found it by experience to be the only one that led straight to Happiness? If we can meet with such a man, we are at the end of our troubles.

Her. Alas, that is no easy matter.

47   *Ly.* What shall we do, then? I do not think we ought to despair, in the momentary absence of such a guide. Perhaps the best and safest plan of all is to set to work oneself, go through every system, and carefully examine the various doctrines.

Her. That is what seems to be indicated. I am afraid, though, there is an obstacle in what you said just now: it is not easy, when you have committed yourself with a spread of canvas to the wind, to get home again. How can a man try all the roads, when, as you said, he will be unable to escape from the first of them?

Ly. My notion is to copy Theseus, get dame Ariadne to give us a skein, and go into one labyrinth after another, with the certainty of getting out by winding it up.

Her. Who is to be our Ariadne? Where shall we find the skein?

Ly. Never despair; I fancy I have found something to hold on to and escape.

Her. And what is that?

Ly. It is not original; I borrow it from one of the wise men: "Be sober and doubt all things," says he. If we do not believe everything we are told, but behave like jurymen who suspend judgement till they have heard the other side, we may have no difficulty in getting out of the labyrinths.

Her. A good plan; let us try it.

48   *Ly.* Very well, which shall we start with? However, that will make no difference; we may begin with whomsoever we fancy, Pythagoras, say; how long shall we allow for learning the whole of Pythagoreanism? and do not omit the five

years of silence; including those, I suppose thirty altogether
will do; or, if you do not like that, still we cannot put it
lower than twenty.

Her. Put it at that.

Ly. Plato will come next with as many more, and then
Aristotle cannot do with less.

Her. No.

Ly. As to Chrysippus, I need not ask you; you have told
me already that forty is barely enough.

Her. That is so.

Ly. And we have still Epicurus and the others. I am not
taking high figures, either, as you will see if you reflect
upon the number of octogenarian Stoics, Epicureans, and
Platonists who confess that they have not yet completely
mastered their own systems. Or, if they did not confess it,
at any rate Chrysippus, Aristotle, and Plato would for
them; still more Socrates, who is as good as they; he used to
proclaim to all comers that, so far from knowing all, he
knew nothing whatever, except the one fact of his own ignorance. Well, let us add up. Twenty years we gave Pythagoras, the same to Plato, and so to the others. What
will the total come to, if we assume only ten schools?

Her. Over two hundred years.

Ly. Shall we deduct a quarter of that, and say a hundred
and fifty will do? or can we halve it?

Her. You must decide about that; but I see that, at the ⁴⁹
best, it will be but few who will get through the course,
though they begin philosophy and life together.

Ly. In that case, what are we to do? Must we withdraw
our previous admission, that no one can choose the best
out of many without trying all? We thought selection without experiment a method of inquiry savouring more of divination than of judgement, did we not?

Her. Yes.

Ly. Without such longevity, then, it is absolutely impossible for us to complete the series—experiment, selection,

philosophy, Happiness. Yet anything short of that is a mere game of blindman's-buff; whatever we knock against and get hold of we shall be taking for the thing we want, because the truth is hidden from us. Even if a mere piece of luck brings us straight to it, we shall have no grounded conviction of our success; there are so many similar objects, all claiming to be the real thing.

50   *Her.* Ah, Lycinus, your arguments seem to me more or less logical, but—but—to be frank with you—I hate to hear you going through them and wasting your acuteness. I suspect it was in an evil hour that I came out to-day and met you; my hopes were almost in my grasp; and now here are you plunging me into a slough of despond with your demonstrations; truth is undiscoverable, if the search needs so many years.

    Ly. My dear friend, it would be much fairer to blame your parents, Menecrates and whatever your mother's name may have been—or indeed to go still further back to human nature. Why did not they make you a Tithonus for years and durability? instead of which, they limited you like other men to a century at the outside. As for me, I have only been helping you to deduce results.

51   *Her.* No, no; it is just your way; you want to crow over me; you detest philosophy—I cannot tell why—and poke fun at philosophers.

    Ly. Hermotimus, I cannot show what truth is, so well as wise people like you and your professor; but one thing I do know about it, and that is that it is not pleasant to the ear; falsehood is far more esteemed; it is prettier, and therefore pleasanter; while Truth, conscious of its purity, blurts out downright remarks, and offends people. Here is a case of it: even you are offended with me for having discovered (with your assistance) how this matter really stands, and shown that our common object is hard of attainment. Suppose you had been in love with a statue and hoped to win

it, under the impression that it was human, and I had realized that it was only bronze or marble, and given you a
friendly warning that your passion was hopeless—you might
just as well have thought I was your enemy then, because I
would not leave you a prey to extravagant and impracticable delusions.

Her. Well, well; are we to give up philosophy, then, and 52
idle our lives away like the common herd?

Ly. What have I said to justify that? My point is not that
we are to give up philosophy, but this: whereas we are to
pursue philosophy, and whereas there are many roads, each
professing to lead to philosophy and Virtue, and whereas
it is uncertain which of these is the true road, therefore the
selection shall be made with care. Now we resolved that it
was impossible out of many offers to choose the best, unless a man should try all in turn; and then the process of
trial was found to be long. What do *you* propose?—It is
the old question again. To follow and join philosophic
forces with whomsoever you first fall in with, and let him
thank Fortune for his proselyte?

Her. What is the good of answering your questions? You 53
say no one can judge for himself, unless he can devote the
life of a phoenix to going round experimenting; and on
the other hand you refuse to trust either previous experience or the multitude of favourable testimony.

Ly. Where is your multitude, with knowledge and experience *of all?* Never mind the multitude; one man who
answers the description will do for me. But if you mean
the people who do *not* know, their mere numbers will
never persuade me, as long as they pronounce upon all
from knowledge of, at the most, one.

Her. Are you the only man who has found the truth, and
are all the people who go in for philosophy fools?

Ly. You wrong me, Hermotimus, when you imply that I
put myself above other people, or rank myself at all with

those who know; you forget what I said; I never claimed to know the truth better than others, only confessed that I was as ignorant of it as every one else.

54   *Her.* Well, but, Lycinus, it may be all very well to insist on going the round, testing the various statements, and eschewing any other method of choice; but it is ridiculous to spend so many years on each experiment, as though there were no such thing as judging from samples. That device seems to me quite simple, and economical of time. There is a story that some sculptor, Phidias, I think, seeing a single claw, calculated from it the size of the lion, if it were modelled proportionally. So, if some one were to let you see a man's hand, keeping the rest of his body concealed, you would know at once that what was behind was a man, without seeing his whole body. Well, it is easy to find out in a few hours the essential points of the various doctrines, and, for selecting the best, these will suffice, without any of your scrupulous exacting investigation.

55   *Ly.* Upon my word, how confident you are in your faculty of divining the whole from the parts! and yet I remember being told just the opposite—that knowledge of the whole includes that of the parts, but not vice versa. Well, but tell me; when Phidias saw the claw, would he ever have known it for a lion's, if he had never seen a lion? Could you have said the hand was a man's, if you had never known or seen a man? Why are you dumb? Let me make the only possible answer for you—that you could *not*; I am afraid Phidias has modelled his lion all for nothing; for it proves to be neither here nor there. What resemblance is there? What enabled you and Phidias to recognize the parts was just your knowledge of the wholes—the lion and the man. But in philosophy—the Stoic, for instance—how will the part reveal the other parts to you, or how can you conclude that they are beautiful? You do not know the whole to which the parts belong.

Then you say it is easy to hear in a few hours the essen- 56
tials of all philosophy—meaning, I suppose, their principles and ends, their accounts of God and the soul, their
views on the material and the immaterial, their respective
identification of pleasure or goodness with the desirable
and the Happy; well, it is easy—it is quite a trifle—to deliver an opinion after such a hearing; but really to *know*
where the truth lies will be work, I suspect, not for a few
hours, but for a good many days. If not, what can have induced them to enlarge on these rudiments to the tune of a
hundred or a thousand volumes apiece? I imagine they
only wanted to establish the truth of those few points
which you thought so easy and intelligible. If you refuse
to spend your time on a conscientious selection, after personal examination of each and all, in sum and in detail, it
seems to me you will still want your soothsayer to choose
the best for you. It would be a fine short cut, with no
meanderings or wastings of time, if you sent for him, listened to the summaries, and killed a victim at the end of
each; by indicating in its liver which is the philosophy for
you, the God would save you a pack of troubles.

Or, if you like, I can suggest a still simpler way; you need 57
not shed all this blood in sacrifice to any God, nor employ
an expensive priest; put into an urn a set of tablets, each
marked with a philosopher's name, and tell a boy (he must
be quite young, and his parents both be living) to go to the
urn and pick out whichever tablet his hand first touches;
and live a philosopher ever after, of the school which then
comes out triumphant.

Her. This is buffoonery, Lycinus; I should not have ex- 58
pected it of you. Now tell me, did you ever buy wine? in
person, I mean.

Ly. Many a time.

Her. Well, did you go to every wine vault in town, one
after another, tasting and comparing?

Ly. Certainly not.

Her. No; as soon as you find good sound stuff, you have only to get it sent home.

Ly. To be sure.

Her. And from that little taste you could have answered for the quality of the whole?

Ly. Yes.

Her. Now suppose you had gone to all the wine-merchants and said: I want to buy a pint of wine; I must ask you, gentlemen, to let me drink the whole of the cask which each of you has on tap; after that exhaustive sampling, I shall know which of you keeps the best wine, and is the man for my money. If you had talked like that, they might have laughed at you, and, if you persisted in worrying them, have tried how you liked water.

Ly. Yes; it would be no more than my deserts.

Her. Apply this to philosophy. What need to drink the whole cask, when you can judge the quality of the whole from one little taste?

59 *Ly.* What an adept at evasion you are, Hermotimus! How you slip through one's fingers! However, it is all the better this time; you fancied yourself out, but you have flopped into the net again.

Her. What do you mean?

Ly. You take a thing whose nature is self-evident and universally admitted, like wine, and argue from it to perfectly unlike things, whose nature is obscure and generally debated. In fact I cannot tell what analogy you find between philosophy and wine; there *is* just one, indeed: philosophers and wine-merchants both sell their wares, mostly resorting to adulteration, fraud, and false measures, in the process. But let us look into your real meaning. You say all the wine in a cask is of the same quality—which is perfectly reasonable; further, that any one who draws and tastes quite a small quantity will know at once the quality of the whole—of which the same may be said; I should never have thought of objecting. But mark what comes now: do philosophy and its professors (your own, for instance) give you every day the same remarks on the same subjects, or do they vary them? They vary them a great deal, friend; you would never have stuck to your master through your twenty years' wandering—quite a philosophic Odyssey—if he had always said the same thing; one hearing would have been enough.

Her. So it would. 60

Ly. How could you have known the whole of his doctrines from the first taste, then? They were not homogeneous, like the wine; novelty to-day, and novelty to-morrow on the top of it. Consequently, dear friend, short of drinking the whole cask, you might soak to no purpose; Providence seems to me to have hidden the philosophic Good right at the bottom, underneath the lees. So you will have to drain it dry, or you will never get to that nectar for which I know you have so long thirsted. According to your idea, it has such virtue that, could you once taste it and swallow the very least drop, you would straightway have perfect wisdom; so they say the Delphian prophetess is inspired by one draught of the sacred spring with answers for those who consult the oracle. But it seems not to be so; you have drunk more than half the cask; yet you told me you were only beginning yet.

Now see whether this is not a better analogy. You shall 61 keep your merchant, and your cask; but the contents of the latter are not to be wine, but assorted seeds. On the top is wheat, next beans, then barley, below that lentils, then peas —and other kinds yet. You go to buy seeds, and he takes some wheat out of that layer, and puts it in your hand as a sample; now, could you tell by looking at that whether the peas were sound, the lentils tender, and the beans full?

Her. Impossible.

Ly. No more can you tell the quality of a philosophy from the first statements of its professor; it is not uniform, like the wine to which you compared it, claiming that it must resemble the sample glass; it is heterogeneous, and it had better not be cursorily tested. If you buy bad wine, the loss is limited to a few pence; but to rot with the common herd (in your own words) is not so light a loss. Moreover, your man who wants to drink up the cask as a preliminary to buying a pint will injure the merchant, with his dubious sampling; but philosophy knows no such danger; you may drink your fill, but this cask grows no emptier, and its owner suffers no loss. It is cut and come again here; we have the converse of the Danaids' cask; that would not hold what was put into it; it ran straight through; but here, the more you take away, the more remains.

62   And I have another similar remark to make about these specimen drops of philosophy. Do not fancy I am libelling it, if I say it is like hemlock, aconite, or other deadly poison. Those too, though they have death in them, will not kill if a man scrapes off the tiniest particle with the edge of his nail and tastes it; if they are not taken in the right quantity, the right manner, and the right vehicle, the taker will not die; you were wrong in claiming that the least possible quantity is enough to base a generalization on.

63   *Her.* Oh, have it your own way, Lycinus. Well then, we have got to live a hundred years, and go through all this trouble? There is no other road to philosophy?

Ly. No, none; and we need not complain; as you very truly said, *ars longa, vita brevis*. But I do not know what has come over you; you now make a grievance of it, if you cannot before set of sun develop into a Chrysippus, a Plato, a Pythagoras.

Her. You trap me, and drive me into a corner, Lycinus; yet I never provoked you; it is all envy, I know, because I have made some progress in my studies, whereas you have neglected yourself, when you were old enough to know better.

Ly. Seest, then, thy true course? never mind me, but

leave me as a lunatic to my follies, and you go on your way and accomplish what you have intended all this time.

Her. But you are so masterful, you will not let me make a choice, till I have proved all.

Ly. Why, I confess, you will never get me to budge from that. But when you call me masterful, it seems to me you blame the blameless, as the poet says; for I am myself being dragged along by reason, until you bring up some other reason to release me from durance. And here is reason about to talk more masterfully still, you will see; but I suppose you will exonerate it, and blame me.

Her. What can it be? I am surprised to hear it still has anything in reserve.

Ly. It says that seeing and going through all philosophies 64 will not suffice, if you want to choose the best of them; the most important qualification is still missing.

Her. Indeed? Which?

Ly. Why (bear with me), a critical investigating faculty, mental acumen, intellectual precision and independence equal to the occasion; without this, the completest inspection will be useless. Reason insists that the owner of it must further be allowed ample time; he will collect the rival candidates together, and make his choice with long, lingering, repeated deliberation; he will give no heed to the candidate's age, appearance, or repute for wisdom, but perform his functions like the Areopagites, who judge in the darkness of night, so that they must regard not the pleaders, but the pleadings. Then and not till then will you be able to make a sound choice and live a philosopher.

Her. Live? an after life, then. No mortal span will meet your demands; let me see: go the whole round, examine each with care, on that examination form a judgement, on that judgement make a choice, on that choice be a philosopher; so and no otherwise you say the truth may be found.

Ly. I hardly dare tell you—even that is not exhaustive; 65

I am afraid, after all, the solid basis we thought we had found was imaginary. You know how fishermen often let down their nets, feel a weight, and pull them up expecting a great haul; when they have got them up with much toil, behold, a stone, or an old pot full of sand. I fear our catch is one of those.

Her. I don't know what this particular net may be; your nets are all round me, anyhow.

Ly. Well, try and get through; providentially, you are as good a swimmer as can be. Now, this is it: granted that we go all round experimenting, and get it done at last, too, I do not believe we shall have solved the elementary question, whether *any* of them has the much-desired; perhaps they are all wrong together.

Her. Oh, come now! not one of *them* right either?

Ly. I cannot tell. Do you think it impossible they may all be deluded, and the truth be something which none of them has yet found?

66 *Her.* How can it possibly be?

Ly. This way: take a correct number, twenty; suppose, I mean, a man has twenty beans in his closed hand, and asks ten different persons to guess the number; they guess seven, five, thirty, ten, fifteen—various numbers, in short. It is possible, I suppose, that one may be right?

Her. Yes.

Ly. It is not impossible, however, that they may all guess different incorrect numbers, and not one of them suggest twenty beans. What say you?

Her. It is not impossible.

Ly. In the same way, all philosophers are investigating the nature of Happiness; they get different answers, one Pleasure, another Goodness, and so through the list. It is probable that Happiness *is* one of these; but it is also not improbable that it is something else altogether. We seem to have reversed the proper procedure, and hurried on to the end before we had found the beginning. I suppose we

ought first to have ascertained that the truth has actually
been discovered, and that some philosopher or other has it,
and only then to have gone on to the next question, *which*
of them is to be believed.

Her. So that, even if we go all through all philosophy, we
shall have no certainty of finding the truth even then; that
is what you say.

Ly. Please, please do not ask *me*; once more, apply to reason itself. Its answer will perhaps be that there can be no
certainty yet—as long as we cannot be sure that it is one or
other of the things they say it is.

Her. Then, according to you, we shall never finish our 67
quest nor be philosophers, but have to give it up and live
the life of laymen. What you say amounts to that: philosophy is impossible and inaccessible to a mere mortal; for
you expect the aspirant first to choose the best philosophy;
and you considered that the only guarantee of such choice's
being correct was to go through all philosophy before choosing the truest. Then in reckoning the number of years required by each you spurned all limits, extended the thing
to several generations, and made out the quest of truth too
long for the individual life; and now you crown all by proving success doubtful even apart from all that; you say it is
uncertain whether the philosophers have ever found truth
at all.

Ly. Could you state on oath that they have?

Her. Not on oath, no.

Ly. And yet there is much that I have intentionally
spared you, though it merits careful examination too.

Her. For instance? 68

Ly. Is it not said that, among the professed Stoics, Platonists, and Epicureans, some do know their respective doctrines, and some do not (without prejudice to their general respectability)?

Her. That is true.

Ly. Well, don't you think it will be a troublesome busi-

ness to distinguish the first, and know them from the ignorant professors?

Her. Very.

Ly. So, if you are to recognize the best of the Stoics, you
will have to go to most, if not all, of them, make trial, and
appoint the best your teacher, first going through a course
of training to provide you with the appropriate critical
faculty; otherwise you might mistakenly prefer the wrong
one. Now reflect on the additional time this will mean; I
purposely left it out of account, because I was afraid you
might be angry; all the same, it is the most important and
necessary thing of all in questions like this—so uncertain
and dubious, I mean. For the discovery of truth, your one
and only sure or well-founded hope is the possession of this
power: you *must* be able to judge and sift truth from falsehood; you must have the assayer's sense for sound and true
or forged coin; if you could have come to your examination
of doctrines equipped with a technical skill like that, I
should have nothing to say; but without it there is nothing
to prevent their severally leading you by the nose; you will
follow a dangled bunch of carrots like a donkey; or, better
still, you will be water spilt on a table, trained whichever way one chooses with a finger-tip; or again, a reed growing on a river's bank, bending to every breath, however
gentle the breeze that shakes it in its passage.

If you could find a teacher, now, who understood demonstration and controversial method, and would impart his
knowledge to you, you would be quit of your troubles; the
best and the true would straightway be revealed to you, at
the bidding of this art of demonstration, while falsehood
would stand convicted; you would make your choice with
confidence; judgement would be followed by philosophy;
you would reach your long-desired Happiness, and live in
its company, which sums up all good things.

Her. Thank you, Lycinus; that is a much better hearing;
there is more than a glimpse of hope in that. We must

surely look for a man of that sort, to give us discernment,
judgement, and, above all, the power of demonstration;
then all will be easy and clear, and not too long. I am grateful to you already for thinking of this short and excellent
plan.

Ly. Ah, no, I cannot fairly claim gratitude yet. I have not
discovered or revealed anything that will bring you nearer
your hope; on the contrary, we are further off than ever; it
is a case of much cry and little wool.

Her. Bird of ill omen, pessimist, explain yourself.

Ly. Why, my friend, even if we find some one who claims 7•
to know this art of demonstration, and is willing to impart
it, we shall surely not take his word for it straight off; we
shall look about for another man to resolve us whether the
first is telling the truth. Finding number two, we shall still
be uncertain whether our guarantor really knows the difference between a good judge and a bad, and shall need a
number three to guarantee number two; for how can we
possibly know ourselves how to select the best judge? You
see how far this must go; the thing is unending; its nature does not allow us to draw the line and put a stop to it;
for you will observe that all the demonstrations that can
possibly be thought of are themselves unfounded and
open to dispute; most of them struggle to establish their
certainty by appealing to facts as questionable as themselves; and the rest produce certain truisms with which
they compare, quite illegitimately, the most speculative
theories, and then say they have demonstrated the latter:
our eyes tell us there are altars to the Gods; therefore
there must be Gods; that is the sort of thing.

Her. How unkindly you treat me, Lycinus, turning my 71
treasure into ashes; I suppose all these years are to have
been lost labour.

Ly. At least your chagrin will be considerably lessened
by the thought that you are not alone in your disappoint-
ment; practically all who pursue philosophy do no more

than disquiet themselves in vain. Who could conceivably go through all the stages I have rehearsed? you admit the impossibility yourself. As to your present mood, it is that of the man who cries and curses his luck because he cannot climb the sky, or plunge into the depths of the sea at Sicily and come up at Cyprus, or soar on wings and fly within the day from Greece to India; what is responsible for his discontent is his basing of hopes on a dream-vision or his own wild fancy, without ever asking whether his aspirations were realizable or consistent with humanity. You too, my friend, have been having a long and marvellous dream; and now reason has stuck a pin into you and startled you out of your sleep; your eyes are only half open yet, you are reluctant to shake off a sleep which has shown you such fair visions, and so you scold. It is just the condition of the day-dreamer; he is rolling in gold, digging up treasure, sitting on his throne, or somehow at the summit of bliss; for dame *How-I-wish* is a lavish facile Goddess, that will never turn a deaf ear to her votary, though he have a mind to fly, or change statures with Colossus, or strike a gold-reef; well, in the middle of all this, in comes his servant with some every-day question, wanting to know where he is to get bread, or what he shall say to the landlord, tired of waiting for his rent; and then he flies into a temper, as though the intrusive questioner had robbed him of all his bliss, and is ready to bite the poor fellow's nose off.

72   As you love me, do not treat me like that. I see you digging up treasure, spreading your wings, nursing extravagant ideas, indulging impossible hopes; and I love you too well to leave you to the company of a life-long dream—a pleasant one, if you will, but yet a dream; I beseech you to get up and take to some every-day business, such as may direct the rest of your life's course by common sense. Your acts and your thoughts up to now have been no more than Centaurs, Chimeras, Gorgons, or what else is figured by dreams and poets and painters, chartered libertines all,

who reck not of what has been or may be. Yet the common
folk believe them, bewitched by tale and picture just because they are strange and monstrous.

I fancy you hearing from some teller of tales how there 73
is a certain lady of perfect beauty, beyond the Graces
themselves or the Heavenly Aphrodite, and then, without
ever an inquiry whether his tale is true, and such a person
to be found on earth, falling straight in love with her, like
Medea in the story enamoured of a dream-Jason. And
what most drew you on to love, you and the others who
worship the same phantom, was, if I am not mistaken, the
consistent way in which the inventor of the lady added to
his picture, when once he had got your ear. That was the
only thing you all looked to, with that he turned you about
as he would, having got his first hold upon you, averring
that he was leading you the straight way to your beloved.
After the first step, you see, all was easy; none of you ever
looked round when he came to the entrance, and inquired
whether it was the right one, or whether he had acciden-
tally taken the wrong; no, you all followed in your predecessors' footsteps, like sheep after the bell-wether, whereas
the right thing was to decide at the entrance whether you
should go in.

Perhaps an illustration will make my meaning clearer: 74
when one of those audacious poets affirms that there was
once a three-headed and six-handed man, if you accept
that quietly without questioning its possibility, he will proceed to fill in the picture consistently—six eyes and ears,
three voices talking at once, three mouths eating, and thirty
fingers instead of our poor ten all told; if he has to fight,
three of his hands will have a buckler, wicker targe, or shield
apiece, while of the other three one swings an axe, another
hurls a spear, and the third wields a sword. It is too late to
carp at these details, when they come; they are consistent
with the beginning; it was about that that the question
ought to have been raised whether it was to be accepted

and passed as true. Once grant that, and the rest comes flooding in, irresistible, hardly now susceptible of doubt, because it is consistent and accordant with your initial admissions. That is just your case; your love-yearning would not allow you to look into the facts at each entrance, and so you are dragged on by consistency; it never occurs to you that a thing may be self-consistent and yet false; if a man says twice five is seven, and you take his word for it without checking the sum, he will naturally deduce that four times five is fourteen, and so on *ad libitum*. This is the way that weird geometry proceeds: it sets before beginners certain strange assumptions, and insists on their granting the existence of inconceivable things, such as points having no parts, lines without breadth, and so on, builds on these rotten foundations a superstructure equally rotten, and pretends to go on to a demonstration which is true, though it starts from premises which are false.

75   Just so you, when you have granted the principles of any school, believe in the deductions from them, and take their consistency, false as it is, for a guarantee of truth. Then with some of you, hope travels through, and you die before you have seen the truth and detected your deceivers, while the rest, disillusioned too late, will not turn back for shame: what, confess at their years that they have been abused with toys all this time? so they hold on desperately, putting the best face upon it and making all the converts they can, to have the consolation of good company in their deception; they are well aware that to speak out is to sacrifice the respect and superiority and honour they are accustomed to; so they will not do it if it may be helped, knowing the height from which they will fall to the common level. Just a few are found with the courage to say they were deluded, and warn other aspirants. Meeting such a one, call him a good man, a true and honest; nay, call him philosopher, if you will; to my mind, the name is his or no one's; the rest either have no knowledge of the truth, though they

think they have, or else have knowledge and hide it, shame-faced cowards clinging to reputation.

But now for goodness' sake let us drop all this, cover it 76
up with an amnesty, and let it be as if it had not been said; let us assume that the Stoic philosophy, and no other, is correct; then we can examine whether it is practicable and possible, or its disciples wasting their pains; it makes wonderful promises, I am told, about the Happiness in store for those who reach the summit; for none but they shall enter into full possession of the true God. The next point you must help me with—whether you have ever met such a Stoic, such a pattern of Stoicism, as to be uncon-scious of pain, untempted by pleasure, free from wrath, superior to envy, contemptuous of wealth, and, in one word, Happy; such should the example and model of the Virtuous life be; for any one who falls short in the slightest degree, even though he is better than other men at all points, is not complete, and in that case not yet Happy.

Her. I never saw such a man.   77

Ly. I am glad you do not palter with the truth. But what are your hopes in pursuing philosophy, then? You see that neither your own teacher, nor his, nor his again, and so on to the tenth generation, has been absolutely wise and so at-tained Happiness. It will not serve you to say that it is enough to get near Happiness; that is no good; a person on the doorstep is just as much outside and in the air as an-other a long way off, though with the difference that the former is tantalized by a nearer view. So it is to get into the neighbourhood of Happiness—I will grant you so much—that you toil like this, wearing yourself away, letting this great portion of your life slip from you, while you are sunk in dullness and wakeful weariness; and you are to go on with it for twenty more years at the least, you tell me, to take your place when you are eighty—always assuming some one to assure you that length of days—in the ranks of the not yet Happy. Or perhaps you reckon on being the exception; you are to crown your pursuit by attaining what many a good man before you, swifter far, has pursued and never overtaken.

78   Well, overtake it, if that is your plan, grasp it and have it whole, this something, mysterious to me, of which the possession is sufficient reward for such toils; this something which I wonder how long you will have the enjoyment of, old man that you will be, past all pleasure, with one foot in the grave; ah, but perhaps, like a brave soul, you are getting ready for another life, that you may spend it the better when you come to it, having learned how to live: as though one should take so long preparing and elaborating a superlative dinner that he fainted with hunger and exhaustion!

79   However, there is another thing I do not think you have observed: Virtue is manifested, of course, in action, in doing what is just and wise and manly; but you—and when I say you, I mean the most advanced philosophers—you do not seek these things and ensue them, but spend the greater part of your life conning over miserable sentences and demonstrations and problems; it is the man who does best at these that you hail a glorious victor. And I believe that is why you admire this experienced old professor of yours: he nonplusses his associates, knows how to put crafty questions and inveigle you into pitfalls; so you pay no attention to the fruit—which consists in action—, but are extremely busy with the husks, and smother each other with the leaves in your debates; come now, Hermotimus, what else are you about from morning to night?

    Her. Nothing; that is what it comes to.

    Ly. Is it wronging you to say that you hunt the shadow or the snake's dead slough, and neglect the solid body or the creeping thing itself? You are no better than a man pouring water into a mortar and braying it with an iron pestle; he thinks he is doing a necessary useful job, whereas, let him

bray till all's blue (excuse the slang), the water is as much
water as ever it was.

And here let me ask you whether, putting aside his dis- *80*
course, you would choose to resemble your master, and be
as passionate, as sordid, as quarrelsome, ay, and as addicted
to pleasure (though that trait of his is not generally
known). Why no answer, Hermotimus? Shall I tell you a
plea for philosophy which I lately heard? It was from the
mouth of an old, old man, who has quite a company of
young disciples. He was angrily demanding his fees from
one of these; they were long overdue, he said; the day stated
in the agreement was the first of the month, and it was now
the fifteenth.

The youth's uncle was there, a rustic person without any *81*
notion of your refinements; and by way of stilling the
storm, *Come, come, sir, says he, you need not make such a
fuss because we have bought words of you and not yet settled the bill. As to what you have sold us, you have got it
still; your stock of learning is none the less; and in what I
really sent the boy to you for, you have not improved him a
bit; he has carried off and seduced neighbour Echecrates's
daughter, and there would have been an action for assault,
only Echecrates is a poor man; but the prank cost me a
couple of hundred. And the other day he struck his mother;
she had tried to stop him when he was smuggling wine out
of the house, for one of his club-dinners, I suppose. As to
temper and conceit and impudence and brass and lying, he
was not half so bad twelve months ago as he is now. That is
where I should have liked him to profit by your teaching;
and we could have done without his knowing the stuff he
reels off at table every day: "a crocodile seized hold of a
baby," says he, "and promised to give it back if its father
could answer"—the Lord knows what; or how, "day being,
night cannot be"; and sometimes his worship twists round
what we say somehow or other, till there we are with horns*

on our heads! We just laugh at it—most of all when he
stuffs up his ears and repeats to himself what he calls tem-
peraments and conditions and conceptions and impressions, and a lot more like that. And he tells us God is not in
heaven, but goes about in everything, wood and stone and
animals—the meanest of them, too; and if his mother asks
him why he talks such stuff, he laughs at her and says if
once he gets the "stuff" pat off, there will be nothing to
prevent him from being the only rich man, the only king,
and counting every one else slaves and offscourings.[2]

82   When he had finished, mark the reverend philosopher's
answer. You should consider, he said, that if he had never
come to me, he would have behaved far worse—very possibly have come to the gallows. As it is, philosophy and the
respect he has for it have been a check upon him, so that
you find he keeps within bounds and is not quite unbeara-
ble; the philosophic system and name tutor him with their
presence, and the thought of disgracing them shames him.
I should be quite justified in taking your money, if not for
any positive improvement I have effected, yet for the ab-
stentions due to his respect for philosophy; the very nurses
will tell you as much: children should go to school, because, even if they are not old enough to learn, they will at

[2] Lucian is never tired of ridiculing the verbal quibbles in which the
philosophers of his time indulged. He attributes them especially to the
Stoics, whose insistence on reason, as opposed to emotion, for the guide
of life, resulted in much attention to logic, including its paradoxical
forms. Among these logical puzzles are the following: (1) Sorites, the
heap trick. Suppose a heap of corn. Is it a heap? Yes. Take a grain
away. Is it a heap? Yes. And so on until only one grain is left. The
drawing of the line is impossible. (2) The Horns. If you have not lost a
thing, you still have it? Certainly. Have you lost your horns? No. Then
you are horned. (3) The Crocodile. A child is caught by a crocodile; the
father asks it to give him back. I will, says the crocodile, on condition
that you tell me correctly whether I shall do so or not. The dilemma is
obvious. (4) The Day and Night. This appears to be a proof that there
is no such thing as night, through the ambiguity in "Day being, Night
cannot be," which in Greek, though not in English, is equally natural
in the sense of, Since it is day, it cannot be night, and, if day exists,
night cannot.

*least be out of mischief there. My conscience is quite easy
about him; if you like to select any of your friends who is
acquainted with Stoicism and bring him here to-morrow,
you shall see how the boy can question and answer, how
much he has learnt, how many books he has read on axi-
oms, syllogisms, conceptions, duty, and all sorts of subjects.
As for his hitting his mother or seducing girls, what have I
to do with that? am I his keeper?*

A dignified defence of philosophy for an old man! Per- *83*
haps *you* will say too that it is a good enough reason for
pursuing it, if it will keep us from worse employments.
Were our original expectations from philosophy at all of a
different nature, by the way? did they contemplate anything beyond a more decent behaviour than the average?
Why this obstinate silence?

Her. Oh, why but that I could cry like a baby? It cuts me
to the heart, it is all so true; it is too much for me, when I
think of my wretched, wasted years—paying all that money
for my own labour, too! I am sober again after a debauch. I
see what the object of my maudlin affection is like, and
what it has brought upon me.

Ly. No need for tears, dear fellow; that is a very sensible *84*
fable of Aesop's. A man sat on the shore and counted the
waves breaking; missing count, he was excessively annoyed.
But the fox came up and said to him: "Why vex yourself,
good sir, over the past ones? you should let them go, and
begin counting afresh." So you, since this is your mind, had
better reconcile yourself now to living like an ordinary man;
you will give up your extravagant haughty hopes and put
yourself on a level with the commonalty; if you are sensible,
you will not be ashamed to unlearn in your old age, and
change your course for a better.

Now I beg you not to fancy that I have said all this as an *85*
anti-Stoic, moved by any special dislike of your school; my
arguments hold against all schools. I should have said just

the same if you had chosen Plato or Aristotle, and condemned the others unheard. But, as Stoicism was your choice, the argument has seemed to be aimed at that, though it had no such special application.

86　*Her.* You are quite right. And now I will be off to metamorphose myself. When we next meet, there will be no long, shaggy beard, no artificial composure; I shall be natural, as a gentleman should. I may go as far as a fashionable coat, by way of publishing my renunciation of nonsense. I only wish there were an emetic that would purge out every doctrine they have instilled into me; I assure you, if I could reverse Chrysippus's plan with the hellebore, and drink forgetfulness, not of the world but of Stoicism, I would not think twice about it. Well, Lycinus, I owe you a debt indeed; I was being swept along in a rough turbid torrent, unresisting, drifting with the stream; when lo, you stood there and fished me out, a true *deus ex machina.* I have good enough reason, I think, to shave my head like the people who get clear off from a wreck; for I am to make votive offerings to-day for the dispersion of that thick cloud which was over my eyes. Henceforth, if I meet a philosopher on my walks (and it will not be with my will), I shall turn aside and avoid him as I would a mad dog.

SUGGESTED READINGS

Sextus Empiricus' *Outlines of Pyrrhonism* is the one surviving document of ancient Skepticism. See also Cicero's version of Greek Skepticism in his *Academica* and *On the Nature of the Gods.*

There is a suggestive introduction in E. Bevan, *Stoics and Sceptics,* ch. iv, and a clear summary in R. D. Hicks, *Stoic and Epicurean,* ch. viii, ix, and x. See also E. Zeller, *The Stoics, Epicureans and Sceptics.* Fuller accounts appear in N. Nicoll, *The Greek Sceptics* and M. M. Patrick, *The Greek Sceptics.*

Lucian is the most attractive literary representative of Skepticism, and Fowler has done a complete translation of his works. A suggestive introduction to his work and thought is J. Chapman, *Plato and Lucian*. St. Augustine's *Contra Academicos* is an interesting response to the skepticism of the Academy.

For the impact of ancient skepticism on modern philosophy, see Richard Popkin's *The History of Scepticism from Erasmus to Descartes*.

IV

NEOPLATONISM

INTRODUCTION

"Neoplatonism" is the name by which historians have come to designate the philosophy set forth in the writings of Plotinus (205-270 A.D.). Paradoxically, it was never Plotinus' intention to found a philosophy. He saw himself as doing nothing more in his writings than restating the philosophy of Plato: a program which he conceived and executed in the belief that the genuine ideas of Plato had suffered corruption and misrepresentation at the hands of the Hellenistic thinkers. In the process of restatement, however, Plotinus set forth a system which appears to be quite different from anything ever intended by Plato. Hence, the writings, embodying what Plotinus himself thought of as a Platonism purged of exotic accretions, have come to be recognized by later observers as actually embodying a rich but wholly novel interpretation of Plato: a "neo" Platonism, indeed.

Despite this unpretentious origin, the Neoplatonic philosophy has played a profoundly significant role in the history of thought. Together with the philosophy of Aristotle it shares the distinction of being one of the two major forms in which the philosophy of Plato has been developed and fed into the Western intellectual tradition. For, in one form or another, the Plotinian vision of a supra-sensible realm which is but *poorly shadowed forth in the visible world has inspired and served centuries of philosophers, mystics, religious thinkers and poets.*

Plotinus, born in Egypt, studied in Alexandria under the famed Ammonius Sacca, and finally settled in Rome around the year 244. Here he quickly attracted a band of adoring disciples, among them personages no less great than the Emperor Gallienus and his empress. It was here in Rome, among his closely knit and reverent coterie, that Plotinus composed the essays which comprise the definitive statement of Neoplatonism. Most of the writings were entrusted by Plotinus to his beloved disciple and biographer, Porphyry, who then edited them carefully and arranged them in six groups, each containing nine essays. Thus, it is owing to Porphyry's arrangement that Plotinus' writings go under the title Enneads, or "sets of nine."

The Enneads are quite difficult to read. The student should not become lost in the technical terminology, but should seek to follow Plotinus' main course along the upward path of knowledge to the supreme Principle of Intelligibility, and the downward path of the generation of values. The portions of the Enneads which follow can best be understood if read in the order presented.

PLOTINUS

THE FIRST ENNEAD*

Sixth Tractate

Beauty

[1. Beauty addresses itself chiefly to sight; but there is a beauty for the hearing too, as in certain combinations of words and in all kinds of music, for melodies and cadences are beautiful; and minds that lift themselves above the realm of sense to a higher order are aware of beauty in the conduct of life, in actions, in character, in the pursuits of the intellect; and there is the beauty of the virtues. What loftier beauty there may be, yet, our argument will bring to light.

What, then, is it that gives comeliness to material forms and draws the ear to the sweetness perceived in sounds, and what is the secret of the beauty there is in all that derives from Soul?

Is there some One Principle from which all take their grace, or is there a beauty peculiar to the embodied and another for the bodiless? Finally, one or many, what would such a Principle be?

Consider that some things, material shapes for instance, are gracious not by anything inherent but by something communicated, while others are lovely of themselves, as, for example, Virtue.

The same bodies appear sometimes beautiful, sometimes not; so that there is a good deal between being body and being beautiful.

What, then, is this something that shows itself in certain

---

* Reprinted from *The Enneads,* Second Edition, translated by Stephen MacKenna, by permission of Pantheon Books (a division of Random House, Inc.). All rights reserved.

material forms? This is the natural beginning of our inquiry.

What is it that attracts the eyes of those to whom a beautiful object is presented, and calls them, lures them, towards it, and fills them with joy at the sight? If we possess ourselves of this, we have at once a standpoint for the wider survey.

Almost everyone declares that the symmetry of parts towards each other and towards a whole, with, besides, a certain charm of colour, constitutes the beauty recognized by the eye, that in visible things, as indeed in all else, universally, the beautiful thing is essentially symmetrical, patterned.

But think what this means.

Only a compound can be beautiful, never anything devoid of parts; and only a whole; the several parts will have beauty, not in themselves, but only as working together to give a comely total. Yet beauty in an aggregate demands beauty in details: it cannot be constructed out of ugliness; its law must run throughout.

All the loveliness of colour and even the light of the sun, being devoid of parts and so not beautiful by symmetry, must be ruled out of the realm of beauty. And how comes gold to be a beautiful thing? And lightning by night, and the stars, why are these so fair?

In sounds also the simple must be proscribed, though often in a whole noble composition each several tone is delicious in itself.

Again since the one face, constant in symmetry, appears sometimes fair and sometimes not, can we doubt that beauty is something more than symmetry, that symmetry itself owes its beauty to a remoter principle?

Turn to what is attractive in methods of life or in the expression of thought; are we to call in symmetry here? What symmetry is to be found in noble conduct, or excellent laws, in any form of mental pursuit?

What symmetry can there be in points of abstract thought?

The symmetry of being accordant with each other? But there may be accordance or entire identity where there is nothing but ugliness: the proposition that honesty is merely a generous artlessness chimes in the most perfect harmony with the proposition that morality means weakness of will; the accordance is complete.

Then again, all the virtues are a beauty of the Soul, a beauty authentic beyond any of these others; but how does symmetry enter here? The Soul, it is true, is not a simple unity, but still its virtue cannot have the symmetry of size or of number: what standard of measurement could preside over the compromise or the coalescence of the Soul's faculties or purposes?

Finally, how by this theory would there be beauty in the Intellectual-Principle, essentially the solitary?

[2. Let us, then, go back to the source, and indicate at once the Principle that bestows beauty on material things.

Undoubtedly this Principle exists; it is something that is perceived at the first glance, something which the Soul names as from an ancient knowledge and, recognizing, welcomes it, enters into unison with it.

But let the Soul fall in with the Ugly and at once it shrinks within itself, denies the thing, turns away from it, not accordant, resenting it.

Our interpretation is that the Soul—by the very truth of its nature, by its affiliation to the noblest Existents in the hierarchy of Being—when it sees anything of that kin, or any trace of that kinship, thrills with an immediate delight, takes its own to itself, and thus stirs anew to the sense of its nature and of all its affinity.

But, is there any such likeness between the loveliness of this world and the splendours in the Supreme? Such a likeness in the particulars would make the two orders alike: but what is there in common between beauty here and beauty There?

We hold that all the loveliness of this world comes by communion in Ideal-Form.

All shapelessness whose kind admits of pattern and form,

as long as it remains outside of Reason and Idea, is ugly by that very isolation from the Divine-Thought. And this is the Absolute Ugly: an ugly thing is something that has not been entirely mastered by pattern, that is by Reason, the Matter not yielding at all points and in all respects to Ideal-Form.

But where the Ideal-Form has entered, it has grouped and co-ordinated what from a diversity of parts was to become a unity: it has rallied confusion into co-operation: it has made the sum one harmonious coherence: for the Idea is a unity and what it moulds must come to unity as far as multiplicity may.

And on what has thus been compacted to unity, Beauty enthrones itself, giving itself to the parts as to the sum: when it lights on some natural unity, a thing of like parts, then it gives itself to that whole. Thus, for an illustration, there is the beauty, conferred by craftsmanship, of all a house with all its parts, and the beauty which some natural quality may give to a single stone.

This, then, is how the material thing becomes beautiful— by communicating in the thought (Reason, Logos) that flows from the Divine.

[3. And the Soul includes a faculty peculiarly addressed to Beauty—one incomparably sure in the appreciation of its own, when Soul entire is enlisted to support its judgement.

Or perhaps the Soul itself acts immediately, affirming the Beautiful where it finds something accordant with the Ideal-Form within itself, using this Idea as a canon of accuracy in its decision.

But what accordance is there between the material and that which antedates all Matter?

On what principle does the architect, when he finds the house standing before him correspondent with his inner ideal of a house, pronounce it beautiful? Is it not that the house before him, the stones apart, is the inner idea stamped upon the mass of exterior matter, the indivisible exhibited in diversity?

So with the perceptive faculty: discerning in certain objects the Ideal-Form which has bound and controlled shapeless matter, opposed in nature to Idea, seeing further stamped upon the common shapes some shape excellent above the common, it gathers into unity what still remains fragmentary, catches it up and carries it within, no longer a thing of parts, and presents it to the Ideal-Principle as something concordant and congenial, a natural friend: the joy here is like that of a good man who discerns in a youth the early signs of a virtue consonant with the achieved perfection within his own soul.

The beauty of colour is also the outcome of a unification: it derives from shape, from the conquest of the darkness inherent in Matter by the pouring-in of light, the unembodied, which is a Rational-Principle and an Ideal-Form.

Hence it is that Fire itself is splendid beyond all material bodies, holding the rank of Ideal-Principle to the other elements, making ever upwards, the subtlest and sprightliest of all bodies, as very near to the unembodied; itself alone admitting no other, all the others penetrated by it: for they take warmth but this is never cold; it has colour primally; they receive the Form of colour from it: hence the splendour of its light, the splendour that belongs to the Idea. And all that has resisted and is but uncertainly held by its light remains outside of beauty, as not having absorbed the plenitude of the Form of colour.

And harmonies unheard in sound create the harmonies we hear and wake the Soul to the consciousness of beauty, showing it the one essence in another kind: for the measures of our sensible music are not arbitrary but are determined by the Principle whose labour is to dominate Matter and bring pattern into being.

Thus far of the beauties of the realm of sense, images and shadow-pictures, fugitives that have entered into Matter—to adorn, and to ravish, where they are seen.

[4. But there are earlier and loftier beauties than these. In the sense-bound life we are no longer granted to know them, but the Soul, taking no help from the organs, sees and proclaims them. To the vision of these we must mount, leaving sense to its own low place.

As it is not for those to speak of the graceful forms of the material world who have never seen them or known their grace—men born blind, let us suppose—in the same way those must be silent upon the beauty of noble conduct and of learning and all that order who have never cared for such things, nor may those tell of the splendour of virtue who have never known the face of Justice and of Moral-Wisdom beautiful beyond the beauty of Evening and of Dawn.

Such vision is for those only who see with the Soul's sight —and at the vision, they will rejoice, and awe will fall upon them and a trouble deeper than all the rest could ever stir, for now they are moving in the realm of Truth.

This is the spirit that Beauty must ever induce, wonderment and a delicious trouble, longing and love and a trembling that is all delight. For the unseen all this may be felt as for the seen; and this the Souls feel for it, every Soul in some degree, but those the more deeply that are the more truly apt to this higher love—just as all take delight in the beauty of the body but all are not stung as sharply, and those only that feel the keener wound are known as Lovers.

[5. These Lovers, then, lovers of the beauty outside of sense, must be made to declare themselves.

What do you feel in presence of the grace you discern in actions, in manners, in sound morality, in all the works and fruits of virtue, in the beauty of Souls? When you see that you yourselves are beautiful within, what do you feel? What is this Dionysiac exultation that thrills through your being, this straining upwards of all your soul, this longing to break away from the body and live sunken within the veritable self?

These are no other than the emotions of Souls under the spell of love.

But what is it that awakens all this passion? No shape, no colour, no grandeur of mass: all is for a Soul, something whose beauty rests upon no colour, for the moral wisdom the Soul enshrines and all the other hueless splendour of the virtues. It is that you find in yourself, or admire in another, loftiness of spirit; righteousness of life; disciplined purity; courage of the majestic face; gravity, modesty that goes fearless and tranquil and passionless; and, shining down upon all, the light of god-like Intellection.

All these noble qualities are to be reverenced and loved, no doubt, but what entitles them to be called beautiful?

They exist: they manifest themselves to us: anyone that sees them must admit that they have reality of Being; and is not Real-Being really beautiful?

But we have not yet shown by what property in them they have wrought the Soul to loveliness: what is this grace, this splendour as of Light, resting upon all the virtues?

Let us take the contrary, the ugliness of the Soul, and set that against its beauty: to understand, at once, what this ugliness is and how it comes to appear in the Soul will certainly open our way before us.

Let us then suppose an ugly Soul, dissolute, unrighteous: teeming with all the lusts; torn by internal discord; beset by the fears of its cowardice and the envies of its pettiness; thinking, in the little thought it has, only of the perishable and the base; perverse in all its impulses; the friend of unclean pleasures; living the life of abandonment to bodily sensation and delighting in its deformity.

What must we think but that all this shame is something that has gathered about the Soul, some foreign bane outraging it, soiling it, so that, encumbered with all manner of turpitude, it has no longer a clean activity or a clean sensation, but commands only a life smouldering dully under the crust of evil; that, sunk in manifold death, it no longer sees what a Soul should see, may no longer rest in its own being, dragged ever as it is towards the outer, the lower, the dark?

An unclean thing, I dare to say; flickering hither and thither at the call of objects of sense, deeply infected with the taint of body, occupied always in Matter, and absorbing Matter into itself; in its commerce with the Ignoble it has trafficked away for an alien nature its own essential Idea.

If a man has been immersed in filth or daubed with mud, his native comeliness disappears and all that is seen is the foul stuff besmearing him: his ugly condition is due to alien matter that has encrusted him, and if he is to win back his grace it must be his business to scour and purify himself and make himself what he was.

So, we may justly say, a Soul becomes ugly—by something foisted upon it, by sinking itself into the alien, by a fall, a descent into body, into Matter. The dishonour of the Soul is in its ceasing to be clean and apart. Gold is degraded when it is mixed with earthy particles; if these be worked out, the gold is left and is beautiful, isolated from all that is foreign, gold with gold alone. And so the Soul; let it be but cleared of the desires that come by its too intimate converse with the body, emancipated from all the passions, purged of all that embodiment has thrust upon it, withdrawn, a solitary, to itself again—in that moment the ugliness that came only from the alien is stripped away.

[6. For, as the ancient teaching was, moral-discipline and courage and every virtue, not even excepting Wisdom itself, all is purification.

Hence the Mysteries with good reason adumbrate the immersion of the unpurified in filth, even in the Nether-World, since the unclean loves filth for its very filthiness, and swine foul of body find their joy in foulness.

What else is Sophrosyny, rightly so-called, but to take no part in the pleasures of the body, to break away from them as unclean and unworthy of the clean? So too, Courage is but being fearless of the death which is but the parting of the Soul from the body, an event which no one can dread whose delight is to be his unmingled self. And Magnanimity is but disregard for the lure of things here. And Wisdom is but the Act of the Intellectual-Principle withdrawn from the lower places and leading the Soul to the Above.

The Soul thus cleansed is all Idea and Reason, wholly free of body, intellective, entirely of that divine order from which the wellspring of Beauty rises and all the race of Beauty.

Hence the Soul heightened to the Intellectual-Principle is beautiful to all its power. For Intellection and all that proceeds from Intellection are the Soul's beauty, a graciousness native to it and not foreign, for only with these is it truly Soul. And it is just to say that in the Soul's becoming a good and beautiful thing is its becoming like to God, for from the Divine comes all the Beauty and all the Good in beings.

We may even say that Beauty *is* the Authentic-Existents and Ugliness is the Principle contrary to Existence: and the Ugly is also the primal evil; therefore its contrary is at once good and beautiful, or is Good and Beauty: and hence the one method will discover to us the Beauty-Good and the Ugliness-Evil.

And Beauty, this Beauty which is also The Good, must be posed as The First: directly deriving from this First is the Intellectual-Principle which is pre-eminently the manifestation of Beauty; through the Intellectual-Principle Soul is beautiful. The beauty in things of a lower order—actions and pursuits for instance—comes by operation of the shaping Soul which is also the author of the beauty found in the world of sense. For the Soul, a divine thing, a fragment as it were of the Primal Beauty, makes beautiful to the fullness of their capacity all things whatsoever that it grasps and moulds.

[7. Therefore we must ascend again towards the Good, the desired of every Soul. Anyone that has seen This, knows what I intend when I say that it is beautiful. Even the desire of it is to be desired as a Good. To attain it is for those that will take the upward path, who will set all their forces towards it, who will divest themselves of all that we have put on in our descent: so, to those that approach the Holy Celebrations of the Mysteries, there are appointed purifications and the laying aside of the garments worn before, and the entry in nakedness—until, passing, on the upward way, all that is other than the God, each in the solitude of himself shall behold that solitary-dwelling Existence, the Apart, the Unmingled, the Pure, that from Which all things depend, for Which all look and live and act and know, the Source of Life and of Intellection and of Being.

And one that shall know this vision—with what passion of love shall he not be seized, with what pang of desire, what longing to be molten into one with This, what wondering delight! If he that has never seen this Being must hunger for It as for all his welfare, he that has known must love and reverence It as the very Beauty; he will be flooded with awe and gladness, stricken by a salutary terror; he loves with a veritable love, with sharp desire; all other loves than this he must despise, and disdain all that once seemed fair.

This, indeed, is the mood even of those who, having witnessed the manifestation of Gods or Supernals, can never again feel the old delight in the comeliness of material forms: what then are we to think of one that contemplates Absolute Beauty in Its essential integrity, no accumulation of flesh and matter, no dweller on earth or in the heavens—so perfect Its purity—far above all such things in that they are non-essential, composite, not primal but descending from This?

Beholding this Being—the Choragus of all Existence, the Self-Intent that ever gives forth and never takes—resting, rapt, in the vision and possession of so lofty a loveliness, growing to Its likeness, what Beauty can the Soul yet lack? For This, the Beauty supreme, the absolute, and the primal, fashions Its lovers to Beauty and makes them also worthy of love.

And for This, the sternest and the uttermost combat is set before the Souls; all our labour is for This, lest we be left without part in this noblest vision, which to attain is to be blessed in the blissful sight, which to fail of is to fail utterly.

For not he that has failed of the joy that is in colour or in visible forms, not he that has failed of power or of honours or of kingdom has failed, but only he that has failed of only This, for Whose winning he should renounce kingdoms and command over earth and ocean and sky, if only, spurning the world of sense from beneath his feet, and straining to This, he may see.

[8. But what must we do? How lies the path? How come to vision of the inaccessible Beauty, dwelling as if in consecrated precincts, apart from the common ways where all may see, even the profane?

He that has the strength, let him arise and withdraw into himself, foregoing all that is known by the eyes, turning away for ever from the material beauty that once made his joy. When he perceives those shapes of grace that show in body, let him not pursue: he must know them for copies, vestiges, shadows, and hasten away towards That they tell of. For if anyone follow what is like a beautiful shape playing over water—is there not a myth telling in symbol of such a dupe, how he sank into the depths of the current and was swept away to nothingness? So too, one that is held by material beauty and will not break free shall be precipitated, not in body but in Soul, down to the dark depths loathed of the Intellective-Being, where, blind even in the Lower-World, he shall have commerce only with shadows, there as here.

"Let us flee then to the beloved Fatherland": this is the soundest counsel. But what is this flight? How are we to gain the open sea? For Odysseus is surely a parable to us when he commands the flight from the sorceries of Circe or Calypso—not content to linger for all the pleasure offered to his eyes and all the delight of sense filling his days.

The Fatherland to us is There whence we have come, and There is The Father.

What then is our course, what the manner of our flight?

This is not a journey for the feet; the feet bring us only from land to land; nor need you think of coach or ship to carry you away; all this order of things you must set aside and refuse to see: you must close the eyes and call instead upon another vision which is to be waked within you, a vision, the birth-right of all, which few turn to use.

[9. And this inner vision, what is its operation?

Newly awakened it is all too feeble to bear the ultimate splendour. Therefore the Soul must be trained—to the habit of remarking, first, all noble pursuits, then the works of beauty produced not by the labour of the arts but by the virtue of men known for their goodness: lastly, you must search the souls of those that have shaped these beautiful forms.

But how are you to see into a virtuous Soul and know its loveliness?

Withdraw into yourself and look. And if you do not find yourself beautiful yet, act as does the creator of a statue that is to be made beautiful: he cuts away here, he smoothes there, he makes this line lighter, this other purer, until a lovely face has grown upon his work. So do you also: cut away all that is excessive, straighten all that is crooked, bring light to all that is overcast, labour to make all one glow of beauty and never cease chiselling your statue, until there shall shine out on you from it the godlike splendour of virtue, until you shall see the perfect goodness surely established in the stainless shrine.

When you know that you have become this perfect work, when you are self-gathered in the purity of your being, nothing now remaining that can shatter that inner unity, nothing from without clinging to the authentic man, when you find yourself wholly true to your essential nature, wholly that only veritable Light which is not measured by space, not narrowed to any circumscribed form nor again diffused as a thing void of term, but ever unmeasurable as something greater than all measure and more than all quantity—when you perceive that you have grown to this, you are now become very vision: now call up all your confidence, strike forward yet a step—you need a guide no longer—strain, and see.

This is the only eye that sees the mighty Beauty. If the eye that adventures the vision be dimmed by vice, impure, or weak, and unable in its cowardly blenching to see the uttermost brightness, then it sees nothing even though another point to what lies plain to sight before it. To any vision must be brought an eye adapted to what is to be seen, and having some likeness to it. Never did eye see the sun unless it had first become sunlike, and never can the Soul have vision of the First Beauty unless itself be beautiful.

Therefore, first let each become godlike and each beautiful who cares to see God and Beauty. So, mounting, the Soul will come first to the Intellectual-Principle and survey all the beautiful Ideas in the Supreme and will avow that this is Beauty, that the Ideas are Beauty. For by their efficacy comes all Beauty else, by the offspring and essence of the Intellectual-Being. What is beyond the Intellectual-Principle we affirm to be the nature of Good radiating Beauty before it. So that, treating the Intellectual-Cosmos as one, the first is the Beautiful: if we make distinction there, the Realm of Ideas constitutes the Beauty of the Intellectual Sphere; and The Good, which lies beyond, is the Fountain at once and Principle of Beauty: the Primal Good and the Primal Beauty have the one dwelling-place and, thus, always, Beauty's seat is There.

THE FOURTH ENNEAD

Eighth Tractate

The Soul's Descent Into Body

[1. Many times it has happened: lifted out of the body into myself; becoming external to all other things and self-encentred; beholding a marvellous beauty; then, more than ever, assured of community with the loftiest order; enacting the noblest life, acquiring identity with the divine; stationing within It by having attained that activity; poised above whatsoever within the Intellectual is less than the Supreme; yet there comes the moment of descent from intellection to reasoning, and after that sojourn in the divine, I ask myself how it happens that I can now be descending, and how did the Soul ever enter into my body, the Soul which, even within the body, is the high thing it has shown itself to be.

Heraclitus, who urges the examination of this matter, tells of 'compulsory alternation from contrary to contrary,' speaks of ascent and descent, says that 'change reposes,' and that 'it is weariness to keep toiling at the same things and to be always overcome by them'; but he seems to teach by metaphor, not concerning himself about making his doctrine clear to us, probably with the idea that it is for us to seek within ourselves as he sought for himself and found.

Empedocles—where he says that it is law for faulty souls to descend to this sphere, and that he himself was here because he turned 'a deserter, wandered from God, in slavery to a raving discord'—reveals neither more nor less than Pythagoras and his school seem to me to convey on this as on many other matters; but in his case, versification has some part in the obscurity.

We have to fall back on the illustrious Plato, who uttered many noble sayings about the Soul, and has in many places dwelt upon its entry into body, so that we may well hope to get some light from him.

What do we learn from this philosopher?

We will not find him so consistent throughout that it is easy to discover his mind.

Everywhere, no doubt, he expresses contempt for all that is of sense, blames the commerce of soul with body as an enchainment, an entombment, and upholds as a great truth the saying of the Mysteries that the Soul is here a prisoner. In the Cavern of Plato and in the Cave of Empedocles, I discern this universe, where the 'breaking of the fetters' and the

'ascent' from the depths are figures of the wayfaring towards the Intellectual Realm.

In the Phaedrus he makes a failing of the wings the cause
of the entry to this realm: and there are Periods which send
back the Soul after it has risen; there are judgements and lots
and fates and necessities driving other souls down to this
order.

In all these explanations he finds guilt in the arrival of the
Soul at body. But treating, in the Timaeus, of our universe
he exalts the Cosmos and entitles it 'a blessed god,' and holds
that the Soul was given by the goodness of the Creator to the
end that the total of things might be possessed of intellect,
for thus intellectual it was planned to be, and thus it cannot
be except through soul. There is a reason, then, why the Soul
of this All should be sent into it from God: in the same way
the Soul of each single one of us is sent, that the universe
may be complete; it was necessary that all beings of the Intellectual should be tallied by just so many forms of living
creatures here in the realm of sense.

[2. Inquiring, then, of Plato as to our own soul, we find ourselves forced to inquire into the nature of soul in general—to
discover what there can be in its character to bring it into
partnership with body, and, again, what this Cosmos must be
in which, willing, unwilling or in any way at all, soul has its
activity.

We have to face also the question as to whether the Creator has planned well, or whether the World-Soul, it may be,
resembles our human souls which, in governing their inferior,
the body, must sink deeper and deeper into it if they are to
control it.

No doubt the individual body—though in all cases ap-
propriately placed within the universe—is of itself in a state
of dissolution, always on the way to its natural terminus, demanding much irksome forethought to save it from every
kind of outside assailant, always gripped by need, requiring
every help against constant difficulty: but the body inhabited

by the World-Soul—complete, competent, self-sufficing, exposed to nothing contrary to its nature—this needs no more than a brief word of command, while the governing soul is undeviatingly what its nature makes it wish to be, and, amenable neither to loss nor to addition, knows neither desire nor distress.

This is how we come to read that our soul, entering into association with that complete soul and itself thus made perfect, 'walks the lofty ranges, administering the entire Cosmos,' and that as long as it does not secede and is neither inbound to body nor held in any sort of servitude, so long it tranquilly bears its part in the governance of the All, exactly like the World-Soul itself; for in fact it suffers no hurt whatever by furnishing body with the power to existence, since not every form of care for the inferior need wrest the providing soul from its own sure standing in the highest.

The Soul's care for the universe takes two forms: there is the supervising of the entire system, brought to order by deedless command in a kingly presidence, and there is that over the individual, implying direct action, the hand to the task, one might say, in immediate contact: in the second kind of care the agent absorbs much of the nature of its object.

Now in its comprehensive government of the heavenly system, the Soul's method is that of an unbroken transcendence in its highest phases, with penetration by its lower power: at this, God can no longer be charged with lowering the All-Soul, which has not been deprived of its natural standing and from eternity possesses and will unchangeably possess that rank and habit which could never have been intruded upon it against the course of nature but must be its characteristic quality, neither failing ever nor ever beginning.

Where we read that the souls of stars stand to their bodily forms as the All-Soul to the body of the All—for these starry bodies are declared to be members of the Soul's circuit—we are given to understand that the star-souls also enjoy the blissful condition of transcendence and immunity that becomes them.

And so we might expect: commerce with the body is repudiated for two only reasons, as hindering the Soul's intellective act and as filling it with pleasure, desire, pain; but neither of these misfortunes can befall a soul which has never deeply penetrated into the body, is not a slave but a sovereign ruling a body of such an order as to have no need and no shortcoming and therefore to give ground for neither desire nor fear.

There is no reason why it should be expectant of evil with regard to such a body nor is there any such preoccupied concern, bringing about a veritable descent, as to withdraw it from its noblest and most blessed vision; it remains always intent upon the Supreme, and its governance of this universe is effected by a power not calling upon act.

[3. The Human Soul, next:

Everywhere we hear of it as in bitter and miserable durance in body, a victim to troubles and desires and fears and all forms of evil, the body its prison or its tomb, the Cosmos its cave or cavern.

Now this does not clash with the first theory (that of the impassivity of soul as in the All); for the descent of the human Soul has not been due to the same causes (as that of the All-Soul).

All that is Intellectual-Principle has its being—whole and all—in the place of Intellection, what we call the Intellectual Cosmos: but there exist, too, the intellective powers included in its being, and the separate intelligences—for the Intellectual-Principle is not merely one; it is one and many. In the same way there must be both many souls and one, the one being the source of the differing many just as from one genus there rise various species, better and worse, some of the more intellectual order, others less effectively so.

In the Intellectual-Principle a distinction is to be made:

there is the Intellectual-Principle itself, which like some huge living organism contains potentially all the other forms; and there are the forms thus potentially included now realized as individuals. We may think of it as a city which itself has soul and life, and includes, also, other forms of life; the living city is the more perfect and powerful, but those lesser forms, in spite of all, share in the one same living quality: or, another illustration, from fire, the universal, proceed both the great fire and the minor fires; yet all have the one common essence, that of fire the universal, or, more exactly, participate in that from which the essence of the universal fire proceeds.

No doubt the task of the Soul, in its more emphatically reasoning phase, is intellection: but it must have another as well, or it would be undistinguishable from the Intellectual-Principle. To its quality of being intellective it adds the quality by which it attains its particular manner of being: it ceases to be an Intellectual-Principle, and has thenceforth its own task, as everything must that exists in the Intellectual Realm.

It looks towards its higher and has intellection; towards itself and orders, administers, governs its lower.

The total of things could not have remained stationary in the Intellectual Cosmos, once there was the possibility of continuous variety, of beings inferior but as necessarily existent as their superiors.

[4. So it is with the individual souls; the appetite for the divine Intellect urges them to return to their source, but they have, too, a power apt to administration in this lower sphere; they may be compared to the light attached upwards to the sun, but not grudging its bounty to what lies beneath it. In the Intellectual, then, they remain with the All-Soul, and are immune from care and trouble; in the heavenly sphere, inseparable from the All-Soul, they are administrators with it just as kings, associated with the supreme ruler and governing with him, do not descend from their kingly stations: the souls indeed are thus far in the one place; but there comes a

stage at which they descend from the universal to become
partial and self-centred; in a weary desire of standing apart
they find their way, each to a place of its very own. This state
long maintained, the Soul is a deserter from the totality; its
differentiation has severed it; its vision is no longer set in the
Intellectual; it is a partial thing, isolated, weakened, full of
care, intent upon the fragment; severed from the whole, it
nestles in one form of being; for this it abandons all else,
entering into and caring for only the one, for a thing buffeted
about by a worldful of things: thus it has drifted away from
the universal and, by an actual presence, it administers the
particular; it is caught into contact now, and tends to the
outer to which it has become present and into whose inner
depths it henceforth sinks far.

With this comes what is known as the casting of the wings,
the enchaining in body: the Soul has lost that innocency of
conducting the higher which it knew when it stood with the
All-Soul, that earlier state to which all its interest would bid
it hasten back.

It has fallen: it is at the chain: debarred from expressing
itself now through its intellectual phase, it operates through
sense; it is a captive; this is the burial, the encavernment, of
the Soul.

But in spite of all it has, for ever, something transcendent:
by a conversion towards the intellective act, it is loosed from
the shackles and soars—when only it makes its memories the
starting-point of a new vision of essential being. Souls that
take this way have place in both spheres, living of necessity
the life there and the life here by turns, the upper life reigning in those able to consort more continuously with the divine Intellect, the lower dominant where character or circumstances are less favourable.

All this is indicated by Plato, without emphasis, where he
distinguishes those of the second mixing-bowl, describes them
as 'parts,' and goes on to say that, having in this way become
partial, they must of necessity experience birth.

Of course, where he speaks of God sowing them, he is to be understood as when he tells of God speaking and delivering orations; what is rooted in the nature of the All is figuratively treated as coming into being by generation and creation: stage and sequence are transferred, for clarity of exposition, to things whose being and definite form are eternal.

[5. It is possible to reconcile all these apparent contradictions—the divine sowing to birth, as opposed to a voluntary descent aiming at the completion of the universe; the judgement and the cave; necessity and free choice—in fact the necessity includes the choice; embodiment as an evil; the Empedoclean teaching of a flight from God, a wandering away, a sin bringing its punishment; the 'solace by flight' of Heraclitus; in a word, a voluntary descent which is also involuntary.

All degeneration is no doubt involuntary, yet when it has been brought about by an inherent tendency, that submission to the inferior may be described as the penalty of an act.

On the other hand these experiences and actions are determined by an eternal law of nature, and they are due to the movement of a being which in abandoning its superior is running out to serve the needs of another: hence there is no inconsistency or untruth in saying that the Soul is sent down by God; final results are always to be referred to the starting-point even across many intervening stages.

Still there is a twofold flaw: the first lies in the motive of the Soul's descent (its audacity, its Tolma), and the second in the evil it does when actually here: the first is punished by what the Soul has suffered by its descent: for the faults committed here, the lesser penalty is to enter into body after body—and soon to return—by judgement according to desert, the word judgement indicating a divine ordinance; but any outrageous form of ill-doing incurs a proportionately greater punishment administered under the surveillance of chastising daimons.

Thus, in sum, the Soul, a divine being and a dweller in the loftier realms, has entered body: it is a god, a later phase of the divine: but, under stress of its powers and of its tendency to bring order to its next lower, it penetrates to this sphere in a voluntary plunge: if it turns back quickly all is well; it will have taken no hurt by acquiring the knowledge of evil and coming to understand what sin is, by bringing its forces into manifest play, by exhibiting those activities and productions which, remaining merely potential in the unembodied, might as well never have been even there, if destined never to come into actuality, so that the Soul itself would never have known that suppressed and inhibited total.

The act reveals the power, a power hidden, and we might almost say obliterated or non-existent, unless at some moment it became effective: in the world as it is, the richness of the outer stirs us all to the wonder of the inner whose greatness is displayed in acts so splendid.

[6. Something besides a unity there must be or all would be indiscernibly buried, shapeless within that unbroken whole: none of the real beings (of the Intellectual Cosmos) would exist if that unity remained at halt within itself: the plurality of these beings, offspring of the unity, could not exist without their own nexts taking the outward path; these are the beings holding the rank of souls.

In the same way the outgoing process could not end with the souls, their issue stifled: every Kind must produce its next; it must unfold from some concentrated central principle as from a seed, and so advance to its term in the varied forms of sense. The prior in its being will remain unalterably in the native seat; but there is the lower phase, begotten to it by an ineffable faculty of its being, native to soul as it exists in the Supreme.

To this power we cannot impute any halt, any limit of jealous grudging; it must move for ever outward until the universe stands accomplished to the ultimate possibility. All, thus, is produced by an inexhaustible power giving its gift to the universe, no part of which it can endure to see without some share in its being.

There is, besides, no principle that can prevent anything from partaking, to the extent of its own individual receptivity, in the nature of Good. If, therefore, Matter has always existed, that existence is enough to ensure its participation in the being which, according to each receptivity, communicates the supreme Good universally: if on the contrary, Matter has come into being as a necessary sequence of the causes preceding it, that origin would similarly prevent it standing apart from the scheme as though it were out of reach of the principle to whose grace it owes its existence.

In sum: the loveliness that is in the sense-realm is an index of the nobleness of the Intellectual sphere, displaying its power and its goodness alike: and all things are for ever linked; the one order Intellectual in its being, the other of sense; one self-existent, the other eternally taking its being by participation in that first, and to the full of its power reproducing the Intellectual nature.

[7. The Kind, then, with which we are dealing is twofold, the Intellectual against the sensible: better for the Soul to dwell in the Intellectual, but, given its proper nature, it is under compulsion to participate in the sense-realm also. There is no grievance in its not being, through and through, the highest; it holds mid-rank among the authentic existences, being of divine station but at the lowest extreme of the Intellectual and skirting the sense-known nature; thus, while it communicates to this realm something of its own store, it absorbs in turn whenever—instead of employing in its government only its safeguarded phase—it plunges in an excessive zeal to the very midst of its chosen sphere; then it abandons its status as whole soul with whole soul, though even thus it is always able to recover itself by turning to account the experience of what it has seen and suffered here, learning, so, the greatness of rest in that Supreme, and more clearly discerning the finer things by comparison with what is almost their direct antithesis. Where the faculty is incapable of knowing without contact, the experience of evil brings the clearer perception of Good.

The outgoing that takes place in the Intellectual-Principle is a descent to its own downward ultimate: it cannot be a movement to the transcendent; operating necessarily outwards from itself, wherein it may not stay inclosed, the need and law of Nature bring it to its extreme term, to soul—to which it entrusts all the later stages of being while itself turns back on its course.

The Soul's operation is similar: its next lower act is this universe: its immediate higher is the contemplation of the Authentic Existences. To individual souls such divine operation takes place only at one of their phases and by a temporal process when from the lower in which they reside they turn towards the noblest; but that soul, which we know as the All-Soul, has never entered the lower activity, but, immune from evil, has the property of knowing its lower by inspection, while it still cleaves continuously to the beings above itself; thus its double task becomes possible; it takes hence and, since as soul it cannot escape touching this sphere, it gives hither.

[8. And—if it is desirable to venture the more definite statement of a personal conviction clashing with the general view —even our human Soul has not sunk entire; something of it is continuously in the Intellectual Realm, though if that part, which is in this sphere of sense, hold the mastery, or rather be mastered here and troubled, it keeps us blind to what the upper phase holds in contemplation.

The object of the Intellectual Act comes within our ken only when it reaches downward to the level of sensation: for not all that occurs at any part of the Soul is immediately known to us; a thing must, for that knowledge, be present to the total soul; thus desire locked up within the desiring faculty remains unknown except when we make it fully ours by the central faculty of perception, or by deliberate choice, or by both at once. Once more, every soul has something of the lower on the body side and something of the higher on the side of the Intellectual-Principle.

The Soul of the All, as an entirety, governs the universe through that part of it which leans to the body side, but since it does not exercise a will based on calculation as we do—but proceeds by purely intellectual act as in the execution of an artistic conception—its ministrance is that of a labourless overpoising, only its lowest phase being active upon the universe it embellishes.

The souls that have gone into division and become appropriated to some thing partial have also their transcendent phase, but are pre-occupied by sensation, and in the mere fact of exercising perception they take in much that clashes with their nature and brings distress and trouble since the object of their concern is partial, deficient, exposed to many alien influences, filled with desires of its own and taking its pleasure, that pleasure which is its lure.

But there is always the other (the transcendent phase of soul), that which finds no savour in passing pleasure, but holds its own even way.

THE FIFTH ENNEAD

First Tractate

The Three Initial Hypostases

[1. What can it be that has brought the souls to forget the father, God, and, though members of the Divine and entirely of that world, to ignore at once themselves and It?

The evil that has overtaken them has its source in self-will, in the entry into the sphere of process, and in the primal differentiation with the desire for self-ownership. They conceived a pleasure in this freedom and largely indulged their own motion; thus they were hurried down the wrong path, and in the end, drifting further and further, they came to lose even the thought of their origin in the Divine. A child wrenched young from home and brought up during many years at a distance will fail in knowledge of its father and of itself: the souls, in the same way, no longer discern either the divinity or their own nature; ignorance of their rank brings self-depreciation; they misplace their respect, honouring everything more than themselves; all their awe and admiration is for the alien, and, clinging to this, they have broken apart, as far as a soul may, and they make light of what they have deserted; their regard for the mundane and their disregard of themselves bring about their utter ignoring of the Divine.

Admiring pursuit of the external is a confession of inferiority; and nothing thus holding itself inferior to things that rise and perish, nothing counting itself less honourable and less enduring than all else it admires could ever form any notion of either the nature or the power of God.

A double discipline must be applied if human beings in this pass are to be reclaimed, and brought back to their origins, lifted once more towards the Supreme and One and First.

There is the method, which we amply exhibit elsewhere, declaring the dishonour of the objects which the Soul holds here in honour; the second teaches or recalls to the Soul its race and worth; this latter is the leading truth, and, clearly brought out, is the evidence of the other.

It must occupy us now, for it bears closely upon our inquiry (as to the Divine Hypostases) to which it is the natural preliminary: the seeker is soul and it must start from a true notion of the nature and quality by which soul may undertake the search; it must study itself in order to learn whether it has the faculty for the inquiry, the eye for the object proposed, whether in fact we ought to seek; for if the

object is alien the search must be futile, while if there is relationship the solution of our problem is at once desirable
and possible.

[2. Let every soul recall, then, at the outset the truth that
soul is the author of all living things, that it has breathed the
life into them all, whatever is nourished by earth and sea, all
the creatures of the air, the divine stars in the sky; it is the
maker of the sun; itself formed and ordered this vast heaven
and conducts all that rhythmic motion: and it is a principle
distinct from all these to which it gives law and movement
and life, and it must of necessity be more honourable than
they, for they gather or dissolve as soul brings them life or
abandons them, but soul, since it never can abandon itself, is
of eternal being.

How life was purveyed to the universe of things and to the
separate beings in it may be thus conceived:

That great soul must stand pictured before another soul,
one not mean, a soul that has become worthy to look, emancipate from the lure, from all that binds its fellows in bewitch-
ment, holding itself in quietude. Let not merely the envelop-
ing body be at peace, body's turmoil stilled, but all that lies
around, earth at peace, and sea at peace, and air and the very
heavens. Into that heaven, all at rest, let the great soul be
conceived to roll inward at every point, penetrating, permeat-
ing, from all sides pouring in its light. As the rays of the sun
throwing their brilliance upon a louring cloud make it gleam
all gold, so the soul entering the material expanse of the
heavens has given life, has given immortality: what was abject it has lifted up; and the heavenly system, moved now in
endless motion by the soul that leads it in wisdom, has become a living and a blessed thing; the soul domiciled within,
it takes worth where, before the soul, it was stark body—clay
and water—or, rather, the blankness of Matter, the absence
of Being, and, as an author says, 'the execration of the Gods.'

The Soul's nature and power will be brought out more
clearly, more brilliantly, if we consider next how it envelops

the heavenly system and guides all to its purposes: for it has bestowed itself upon all that huge expanse so that every interval, small and great alike, all has been ensouled.

The material body is made up of parts, each holding its own place, some in mutual opposition and others variously separated; the Soul is in no such condition; it is not whittled down so that life tells of a part of the Soul and springs where some such separate portion impinges; each separate life lives by the Soul entire, omnipresent in the likeness of the engendering father, entire in unity and entire in diffused variety. By the power of the Soul the manifold and diverse heavenly system is a unit: through soul this universe is a God: and the sun is a God because it is ensouled; so too the stars: and whatsoever we ourselves may be, it is all in virtue of soul; for 'dead is viler than dung.'

This, by which the gods are divine, must be the oldest God of them all: and our own soul is of that same Ideal nature, so that to consider it, purified, freed from all accruement, is to recognize in ourselves that same value which we have found soul to be, honourable above all that is bodily. For what is body but earth, and even if it be fire (as Stoics think), what (but soul) is its burning power? So it is with all the compounds of earth and fire, even with water and air added to them.

If, then, it is the presence of soul that brings worth, how can a man slight himself and run after other things? You honour the Soul elsewhere; honour then yourself.

[3. The Soul once seen to be thus precious, thus divine, you may hold the faith that by its possession you are already nearing God: in the strength of this power make upwards towards Him: at no great distance you must attain: there is not much between.

But over this divine, there is a still diviner: grasp the upward neighbour of the Soul, its prior and source.

Soul, for all the worth we have shown to belong to it, is yet a secondary, an image of the Intellectual-Principle: reason uttered is an image of the reason stored within the Soul, and in the same way soul is an utterance of the Intellectual-Principle: it is even the total of its activity, the entire stream of life sent forth by that Principle to the production of further being; it is the forthgoing heat of a fire which has also heat essentially inherent. But within the Supreme we must see energy not as an overflow but in the double aspect of integral inherence with the establishment of a new being. Sprung, in other words, from the Intellectual-Principle, soul is intellective, but with an intellection operating by the method of reasonings: for its perfecting it must look to that Divine Mind, which may be thought of as a father watching over the development of his child born imperfect in comparison with himself.

Thus its substantial existence comes from the Intellectual-Principle; and the Reason within it becomes Act in virtue of its contemplation of that prior; for its thought and act are its own intimate possession when it looks to the Supreme Intelligence; those only are soul-acts which are of this intellective nature and are determined by its own character; all that is less noble is foreign (traceable to Matter) and is accidental to the Soul in the course of its peculiar task.

In two ways, then, the Intellectual-Principle enhances the divine quality of the Soul, as father and as immanent presence; nothing separates them but the fact that they are not one and the same, that there is succession, that over against a recipient there stands the Ideal-Form received; but this recipient, Matter to the Supreme Intelligence, is also noble as being at once informed by divine intellect and uncompounded.

What the Intellectual-Principle must be is carried in the single word that Soul, itself so great, is still inferior.

[4. But there is yet another way to this knowledge:

Admiring the world of sense as we look out upon its vastness and beauty and the order of its eternal march, thinking of the gods within it, seen and hidden, and the celestial spirits and all the life of animal and plant, let us mount to its archetype, to the yet more authentic sphere: there we are to contemplate all things as members of the Intellectual—eternal in their own right, vested with a self-springing consciousness and life—and, presiding over all these, the unsoiled Intelligence and the unapproachable wisdom.

That archetypal world is the true Golden Age, age of Kronos, whose very name suggests (in Greek) Abundance (κόρος) and Intellect (νοῦς). For here is contained all that is immortal: nothing here but is Divine Mind; all is God; this is the place of every soul. Here is rest unbroken: for how can that seek change, in which all is well; what need that reach to, which holds all within itself; what increase can that desire, which stands utterly achieved? All its content, thus, is perfect, that itself may be perfect throughout, as holding nothing that is less than the divine, nothing that is less than intellective. Its knowing is not by search but by possession, its blessedness inherent, not acquired; for all belongs to it eternally and it holds the authentic Eternity imitated by Time which, circling round the Soul, makes towards the new thing and passes by the old. Soul deals with thing after thing—now Socrates; now a horse: always some one entity from among beings—but the Intellectual-Principle is all and therefore its entire content is simultaneously present in that identity: this is pure being in eternal actuality; nowhere is there any future, for every then is a now; nor is there any past, for nothing there has ever ceased to be; everything has taken its stand for ever, an identity well pleased, we might say, to be as it is; and everything, in that entire content, is Intellectual-Principle and Authentic-Existence; and the total of all is Intellectual-Principle entire and Being entire. Intellectual-Principle by its intellective act establishes Being, which in turn, as the object of intellection, becomes the cause of intellection and of existence to the Intellectual-Principle—

though, of course, there is another cause of intellection which is also a cause to Being, both rising in a source distinct from either.

Now while these two are coalescents, having their existence in common, and are never apart, still the unity they form is two-sided; there is Intellectual-Principle as against Being, the intellectual agent as against the object of intellection; we consider the intellective act and we have the Intellectual-Principle; we think of the object of that act and we have Being.

Such difference there must be if there is to be any intellection; but similarly there must also be identity (since, in perfect knowing, subject and object are identical).

This the Primals (the first "Categories") are seen to be: Intellectual-Principle; Existence; Difference; Identity: we must include also Motion and Rest: Motion provides for the intellectual act, Rest preserves identity as Difference gives at once a Knower and a Known, for, failing this, all is one, and silent.

So too the objects of intellection (the ideal content of the Divine Mind)—identical in virtue of the self-concentration of the principle which is their common ground—must still be distinct each from another; this distinction constitutes Difference.

The Intellectual Cosmos thus a manifold, Number and Quantity arise: Quality is the specific character of each of these Ideas which stand as the principles from which all else derives.

[5. As a manifold, then, this God, the Intellectual-Principle, exists above the Soul here, the Soul which once for all stands linked a member of the divine, unless by a deliberate apostasy.

Bringing itself close to the divine Intellect, becoming, as it were, one with this, it seeks still further: what Being, now, has engendered this God, what is the Simplex preceding this multiple; what the cause at once of its existence and of its existing as a manifold; what the source of this Number, this Quantity?

Number, Quantity, is not primal: obviously before even duality, there must stand the unity.

The Dyad is a secondary; deriving from unity, it finds in unity the determinant needed by its native indetermination: once there is any determination, there is Number, in the sense, of course, of the real (the archetypal) Number. And the Soul is such a number or quantity. For the Primals are not masses or magnitudes; all of that gross order is later, real only to the sense-thought; even in seed the effective reality is not the moist substance but the unseen—that is to say Number (as the determinant of individual being) and the Reason-Principle (of the product to be).

Thus by what we call the Number and the Dyad of that higher realm, we mean Reason Principles and the Intellectual-Principle: but while the Dyad is undetermined—representing, as it were, the underlie (or Matter) of the Intellectual World—the number which rises from the Dyad and The One is always a Form-Idea: thus the Intellectual-Principle is, so to speak, shaped by the Ideas rising within it—or rather, it is shaped in a certain sense by The One and in another sense by itself, since its potential vision becomes actual and intellection is, precisely, an act of vision in which subject and object are identical.

[6. But how and what does the Intellectual-Principle see and, especially, how has it sprung from that which is to become the object of its vision?

The mind demands the existence of these Beings, but it is still in trouble over the problem endlessly debated by the most ancient philosophers: from such a unity as we have declared The One to be, how does anything at all come into substantial existence, any multiplicity, dyad, or number? Why has the Primal not remained self-gathered so that there be none of this profusion of the manifold which we observe in existence and yet are compelled to trace to that absolute unity?

In venturing an answer, we first invoke God Himself, not in loud word but in that way of prayer which is always within our power, leaning in soul towards Him by aspiration, alone towards the alone. But if we seek the vision of that great Being within the Inner Sanctuary—self-gathered, tranquilly remote above all else—we begin by considering the images stationed at the outer precincts, or, more exactly to the moment, the first image that appears. How the Divine Mind comes into being must be explained:

Everything moving has necessarily an object towards which it advances; but since the Supreme can have no such object, we may not ascribe motion to it: anything that comes into being after it can be produced only as a consequence of its unfailing self-intention; and, of course, we dare not talk of generation in time, dealing as we are with eternal Beings: where we speak of origin in such reference, it is in the sense, merely, of cause and subordination: origin from the Supreme must not be taken to imply any movement in it: that would make the Being resulting from the movement not a second principle but a third: the Movement would be the second hypostasis.

Given this immobility in the Supreme, it can neither have yielded assent nor uttered decree nor stirred in any way towards the existence of a secondary.

What happened, then? What are we to conceive as rising in the neighbourhood of that immobility?

It must be a circumradiation—produced from the Supreme but from the Supreme unaltering—and may be compared to the brilliant light encircling the sun and ceaselessly generated from that unchanging substance.

All existences, as long as they retain their character, produce—about themselves, from their essence, in virtue of the power which must be in them—some necessary, outward-

facing hypostasis continuously attached to them and representing in image the engendering archetypes: thus fire gives
out its heat; snow is cold not merely to itself; fragrant substances are a notable instance; for, as long as they last, something is diffused from them and perceived wherever they are
present. . . .

Again, all that is fully achieved engenders: therefore the
eternally achieved engenders eternally an eternal being. At
the same time, the offspring is always minor: what then are
we to think of the All-Perfect but that it can produce nothing
less than the very greatest that is later than itself? This greatest, later than the divine unity, must be the Divine Mind,
and it must be the second of all existence, for it is that
which sees The One on which alone it leans while the First
has no need whatever of it. The offspring of the prior to
Divine Mind can be no other than that Mind itself and thus
is the loftiest being in the universe, all else following upon it
—the Soul, for example, being an utterance and act of the
Intellectual-Principle as that is an utterance and act of The
One. But in soul the utterance is obscured, for soul is an
image and must look to its own original: that Principle, on
the contrary, looks to the First without mediation—thus becoming what it is—and has that vision not as from a distance
but as the immediate next with nothing intervening, close to
the One as Soul to it.

The offspring must seek and love the begetter; and especially so when begetter and begotten are alone in their sphere;
when, in addition, the begetter is the highest Good, the offspring (inevitably seeking its good) is attached by a bond of
sheer necessity, separated only in being distinct.

[7. We must be more explicit:

The Intellectual-Principle stands as the image of The One,
firstly because there is a certain necessity that the first
should have its offspring, carrying onward much of its quality, in other words that there be something in its likeness as
the sun's rays tell of the sun. Yet The One is not an Intel-

lectual-Principle; how then does it engender an Intellectual-Principle?

Simply by the fact that in its self-quest it has vision: this very seeing is the Intellectual-Principle. Any perception of the external indicates either sensation or intellection, sensation symbolized by a line, intellection by a circle . . . [corrupt passage].

Of course the divisibility belonging to the circle does not apply to The One; here, to be sure, is a unity, but there the Unity which is the potentiality of all existence.

The items of this potentiality the divine intellection brings out, so to speak, from the unity and knows them in detail, as it must if it is to be an intellectual principle.

It has besides a consciousness, as it were, within itself of this same potentiality; it knows that it can of itself beget an hypostasis and can determine its own Being by the virtue emanating from its prior; it knows that its nature is in some sense a definite part of the content of that First; that it thence derives its essence, that its strength lies there, and that its Being takes perfection as a derivative and a recipient from the First. It sees that, as a member in some sense of the realm of division and part, it receives life and intellection and all else it has and is, from the undivided and partless, since that First is no member of existence, but can be the source of all on condition only of being held down by no one distinctive shape but remaining the undeflected unity.

To be all in itself would place it in the realm of Being. And so the First is not a thing among the things contained by the Intellectual-Principle though the source of all. In virtue of this source things of the later order are essential beings; for from that fact there is determination; each has its form: what has being cannot be envisaged as outside of limit; the nature must be held fast by boundary and fixity; though to the Intellectual Beings this fixity is no more than determination and form, the foundations of their substantial existence.

A being of this quality, like the Intellectual-Principle, must be felt to be worthy of the all-pure: it could not derive from any other than from the first principle of all; as it comes into existence, all other beings must be simultaneously engendered—all the beauty of the Ideas, all the Gods of the Intellectual realm. And it still remains pregnant with this offspring; for it has, so to speak, drawn all within itself again, holding them lest they fall away towards Matter to be brought up in the House of Rhea (in the realm of flux). This is the meaning hidden in the Mysteries, and in the Myths of the gods: Kronos, as the wisest, exists before Zeus; he must absorb his offspring that, full within himself, he may be also an Intellectual-Principle manifest in some product of his plenty; afterwards, the myth proceeds, Kronos engenders Zeus, who already exists as the (necessary and eternal) outcome of the plenty there; in other words the offspring of the Divine Intellect, perfect within itself, is Soul (the life-principle carrying forward the Ideas in the Divine Mind). The perfection entails the offspring; a power so vast could not remain unfruitful.

Now, even in the Divine the engendered could not be the very highest; it must be a lesser, an image; it will be undetermined, as its progenitor was, but will receive determination, and, so to speak, its shaping idea, from the progenitor.

Yet the offspring of the Intellectual-Principle must be a Reason-Principle, that is to say, a substantial existence (hypostasis) identified with the principle of deliberative thought (in the Timaeus): such then is that (higher Soul) which circles about the Divine Mind, its light, its image inseparably attached to it: on the upper level united with it, filled from it, enjoying it, participant in its nature, intellective with it, but on the lower level in contact with the realm beneath itself, or, rather, generating in turn an offspring which must lie beneath; of this lower we will treat later; so far we deal still with the Divine.

[8. This is the explanation of Plato's Triplicity, in the passage where he names as the Primals the Beings gathered about the King of All and establishes a Secondary containing the Secondaries and a Third containing the Tertiaries.

He teaches, also, that there is an author of the Cause, that is of the Intellectual-Principle, which to him is the Creator who made the Soul, as he tells us, in the famous mixing bowl. This author of the causing principle, of the divine mind, is to him the Good, that which transcends the Intellectual-Principle and transcends Being: often too he uses the term 'The Idea' to indicate Being and the Divine Mind. Thus Plato knows the order of generation—from the Good, the Intellectual-Principle; from the Intellectual-Principle, the Soul. These teachings are, therefore, no novelties, no inventions of today, but long since stated, if not stressed; our doctrine here is the explanation of an earlier and can show the antiquity of these opinions on the testimony of Plato himself.

Earlier, Parmenides made some approach to the doctrine in identifying Being with Intellectual-Principle while separating Real Being from the realm of sense.

'Knowing and Being are one thing,' he says, and this unity is to him motionless in spite of the intellection he attributes to it: to preserve its unchanging identity he excludes all bodily movement from it; and he compares it to a huge sphere in that it holds and envelopes all existence and that its intellection is not an outgoing act but internal. Still, with all his affirmation of unity, his own writings lay him open to the reproach that his unity turns out to be a multiplicity.

The Platonic Parmenides is more exact; the distinction is made between the Primal One, a strictly pure Unity, and a secondary One which is a One-Many and a third which is a One-and-Many; thus he too is in accordance with our thesis of the Three Kinds.

[9. Anaxagoras, again, in his assertion of a Mind pure and unmixed, affirms a simplex First and a sundered One, though writing long ago he failed in precision.

Heraclitus, with his sense of bodily forms as things of

ceaseless process and passage, knows the One as eternal and intellectual.

In Empedocles, similarly, we have a dividing principle, "Strife," set against "Friendship"—which is The One and is to him bodiless, while the elements represent Matter.

Later there is Aristotle; he begins by making the First transcendent and intellective but cancels that primacy by supposing it to have self-intellection. Further, he affirms a multitude of other intellective beings—as many indeed as there are orbs in the heavens; one such principle as mover to every orb—and thus his account of the Intellectual Realm differs from Plato's and, failing necessity, he brings in probability; though it is doubtful whether he has even probability on his side; since it would be more probable that all the spheres, as contributory to one system, should look to a unity, to the First.

We are obliged also to ask whether to Aristotle's mind all these Intellectual Beings spring from one, and that one their First; or whether the Principles in the Intellectual are many.

If from one, then clearly the Intellectual system will be analogous to that of the universe of sense—sphere encircling sphere, with one, the outermost, dominating all: the First (in the Intellectual) will envelop the entire scheme and will be an Intellectual (or Archetypal) Cosmos; and as in our universe the spheres are not empty but the first sphere is thick with stars and none without them, so, in the Intellectual Cosmos, those principles of Movement will envelop a multitude of Beings, and that world will be the realm of the greater reality.

If on the contrary each is a principle, then the effective powers become a matter of chance; under what compulsion are they to hold together and act with one mind towards that work of unity, the harmony of the entire heavenly system? Again what can make it necessary that the material bodies of the heavenly system be equal in number to the Intellectual moving principles, and how can these incorporeal Beings be numerically many when there is no Matter to serve as the basis of difference?

For these reasons the ancient philosophers that ranged themselves most closely to the school of Pythagoras and of his later followers and to that of Pherecydes, have insisted upon this Nature, some developing the subject in their writings while others treated of it merely in unwritten discourses, some no doubt ignoring it entirely.

[10. We have shown the inevitability of certain convictions as to the scheme of things:

There exists a Principle which transcends Being; this is The One, whose nature we have sought to establish in so far as such matters lend themselves to proof. Upon The One follows immediately the Principle which is at once Being and the Intellectual-Principle. Third comes the Principle, Soul.

Now just as these three exist for the system of Nature, so, we must hold, they exist for ourselves. I am not speaking of the material order—all that is separable—but of what lies beyond the sense realm in the same way as the Primals are beyond all the heavens; I mean the corresponding aspect of man, what Plato calls the Interior Man.

Thus our soul, too, is a divine thing, belonging to another order than sense; such is all that holds the rank of soul, but (above the life-principle) there is the Soul perfected as containing Intellectual-Principle with its double phase, reasoning and giving the power to reason. The reasoning phase of the Soul, needing no bodily organ for its thinking but maintaining, in purity, its distinctive Act that its thought may be uncontaminated—this we cannot err in placing, separate and not mingled into body, within the first Intellectual. We may not seek any point of space in which to seat it; it must be set outside of all space: its distinct quality, its separateness, its immateriality, demand that it be a thing alone, untouched by all of the bodily order. That is why we read of the universe, that the Demiurge cast the Soul around it from without—understand that phase of soul which is permanently seated in the Intellectual—and of ourselves that the charioteer's head reaches upwards towards the heights.

The admonition to sever soul from body is not, of course, to be understood spatially—that separation stands made in Nature—the reference is to holding our rank, to use of our thinking, to an attitude of alienation from the body in the effort to lead up and attach to the over-world, equally with the other, that phase of soul seated here and, alone, having to do with body, creating, moulding, spending its care upon it.

[11. Since there is a Soul which reasons upon the right and good—for reasoning is an inquiry into the rightness and goodness of this rather than that—there must exist some permanent Right, the source and foundation of this reasoning in our soul; how, else, could any such discussion be held? Further, since the Soul's attention to these matters is intermittent, there must be within us an Intellectual-Principle acquainted with that Right not by momentary act but in permanent possession. Similarly there must be also the principle of this principle, its cause, God. This Highest cannot be divided and allotted, must remain intangible but not bound to space, it may be present at many points, wheresoever there is anything capable of accepting one of its manifestations: thus a centre is an independent unity; everything within the circle has its term at the centre; and to the centre the radii bring each their own. Within our nature is such a centre by which we grasp and are linked and held; and those of us are firmly in the Supreme whose being is concentrated There.

[12. Possessed of such powers, how does it happen that we do not lay hold of them, but for the most part, let these high activities go idle—some, even, of us never bringing them in any degree to effect?

The answer is that all the Divine Beings are unceasingly about their own act, the Intellectual-Principle and its Prior always self-intent; and so, too, the Soul maintains its unfailing movement; for not all that passes in the Soul is, by that fact, perceptible; we know just as much as impinges upon the faculty of sense. Any activity not transmitted to the sensitive faculty has not traversed the entire Soul: we remain unaware because the human being includes sense-perception; man is not merely a part (the higher part) of the Soul but the total.

None the less every being of the order of soul is in continuous activity as long as life holds, continuously executing to itself its characteristic act: knowledge of the act depends upon transmission and perception. If there is to be perception of what is thus present, we must turn the perceptive faculty inward and hold it to attention there. Hoping to hear a desired voice we let all others pass and are alert for the coming at last of that most welcome of sounds: so here, we must let the hearings of sense go by, save for sheer necessity, and keep the Soul's perception bright and quick to the sounds from above.

THE FIFTH ENNEAD

Fourth Tractate

How the Secondaries Rise from The First: and on The One

1. Anything existing after The First must necessarily arise from that First, whether immediately or as tracing back to it through intervenients; there must be an order of secondaries and tertiaries, in which any second is to be referred to The First, any third to the second.

Standing before all things, there must exist a Simplex, differing from all its sequel, self-gathered not interblended with the forms that rise from it, and yet able in some mode of its own to be present to those others; it must be authentically a unity, not merely something elaborated into unity and so in reality no more than unity's counterfeit; it will debar all telling and knowing except that it may be described as transcending Being—for if there were nothing outside all alliance and compromise, nothing authentically one, there would be no Source. Untouched by multiplicity, it will be wholly self-sufficing, an absolute First, whereas any not-first demands its earlier, and any non-simplex needs the simplicities within itself as the very foundations of its composite existence.

There can be only one such being: if there were another, the two (as indiscernible) would resolve into one, for we are not dealing with two corporal entities.

Our One-First is not a body; nothing simplex can be a body and, as a thing of process cannot be a First, the Source cannot be a thing of generation: only a principle outside of body, and utterly untouched by multiplicity, could be The First.

Any unity, then, later than The First must be no longer simplex; it can be no more than a unity in diversity.

Whence must such a sequent arise?

It must be an offspring of The First; for suppose it the product of chance, that First ceases to be the Principle of All.

But how does it arise from The First?

If The First is perfect, utterly perfect above all, and is the beginning of all power, it must be the most powerful of all that is, and all other powers must act in some partial imitation of it. Now other beings, coming to perfection, are observed to generate; they are unable to remain self-closed; they produce: and this is true not merely of beings endowed with will, but of growing things where there is no will; even lifeless objects impart something of themselves, as far as they may; fire warms, snow chills, drugs have their own outgoing efficacy; all things to the utmost of their power imitate the Source in some operation tending to eternity and to service. How then could the most perfect remain self-set—the

First Good, the Power towards all, how could it grudge or be powerless to give of itself, and how at that would it still be the Source?

If things other than itself are to exist, things dependent upon it for their reality, it must produce since there is no other source. And, further, this engendering principle must be the very highest in worth; and its immediate offspring, its secondary, must be the best of all that follows.

[2. If the Intellectual-Principle were the engendering Source, then the engendered secondary, while less perfect than the Intellectual-Principle, would be close to it and similar to it: but since the engendering Source is above the Intellectual-Principle, the secondary can only be that principle.

But why is the Intellectual-Principle not the generating source?

Because (it is not a self-sufficing simplex): the Act of the Intellectual-Principle is intellection, which means that, seeing the intellectual object towards which it has turned, it is consummated, so to speak, by that object, being in itself indeterminate like sight (a vague readiness for any and every vision) and determined by the intellectual object. This is why it has been said that 'out of the indeterminate Dyad and The One arise the Ideas and the numbers': for the Ideas and the numbers constitute the Intellectual-Principle.

Thus it is not a simplex; it is manifold; it exhibits a certain composite quality—within the Intellectual or divine order, of course—as the principle that sees the manifold. It is, further, itself simultaneously object and agent of intellection and is on that count also a duality: and it possesses, besides, another object of intellection in the order following upon The First.

But how can the Intellectual-Principle be a product of the Intellectual Object?

In this way: the intellectual object is self-gathered (self-compact) and is not deficient as the seeing and knowing principle must be—deficient, I mean, as needing an object

—it is therefore no unconscious thing: all its content and accompaniment are its possession; it is self-distinguishing throughout; it is the seat of life as of all things; it is, itself, that self-intellection which takes place in eternal repose, that is to say, in a mode other than that of the Intellectual-Principle.

But if something arises from an entity which in no way looks outside itself, it must arise when that entity is in the fullness of its being: stable in its identity, it produces; but the product is that of an unchanged being: the producer is unchangeably the intellectual object, the product is produced as the Intellectual Act, an Act taking intellection of its source —the only object that exists for it—and so becoming Intellectual-Principle, that is to say, becoming another intellectual being, resembling its source, a reproduction and image of that.

But how from amid perfect rest can an Act arise?

There is in everything the Act of the Essence and the Act going out from the Essence: the first Act is the thing itself in its realized identity, the second Act is an inevitably following outgo from the first, an emanation distinct from the thing itself.

Thus even in fire there is the warmth comported by its essential nature and there is the warmth going instantaneously outward from that characterizing heat by the fact that the fire, remaining unchangeably fire, utters the Act native to its essential reality.

So it is in the divine also: or rather we have there the earlier form of the double act: the divine remains in its own unchanging being, but from its perfection and from the Act included in its nature there emanates the secondary or issuing Act which—as the output of a mighty power, the mightiest there is—attains to Real Being as second to that which stands above all Being. That transcendent was the potentiality of the All; this secondary is the All made actual.

And if this is all things, that must be above and outside of

all, and, so, must transcend real being. And again, if that
secondary is all things, and if above its multiplicity there is a
unity not ranking among those things, once more this unity
transcends Real Being and therefore transcends the Intellectual-Principle as well. There is thus something transcending
Intellectual-Principle, for we must remember that real being is no corpse, the negation of life and of intellection, but
is in fact identical with the Intellectual-Principle. The Intellectual-Principle is not something taking cognizance of things
as sensation deals with sense objects existing independently of
sense: on the contrary, it actually is the things it knows: it
does not merely possess their images or representations: whence
could it have taken them? No: it resides with its objects, identical with them, making a unity with them; knowledge of the
immaterial is universally identical with its objects.

THE SIXTH ENNEAD

Ninth Tractate

On The Good, or The One

[1. It is in virtue of unity that beings are beings.

This is equally true of things whose existence is primal
and of all that are in any degree to be numbered among
beings. What could exist at all except as one thing? Deprived of unity, a thing ceases to be what it is called: no
army unless as a unity: a chorus, a flock, must be one thing.
Even house and ship demand unity, one house, one ship;
unity gone, neither remains: thus even continuous magnitudes could not exist without an inherent unity; break them
apart and their very being is altered in the measure of the
breach of unity.

Take plant and animal; the material form stands a unity;
fallen from that into a litter of fragments, the things have
lost their being; what was is no longer there; it is re-

placed by quite other things—as many others, precisely, as possess unity.

Health, similarly, is the condition of a body acting as a co-ordinate unity. Beauty appears when limbs and features are controlled by this principle, unity. Moral excellence is of a soul acting as a concordant total, brought to unity.

Come thus to soul—which brings all to unity, making, moulding, shaping, ranging to order—there is a temptation to say, 'Soul is the bestower of unity; soul therefore is the unity.' But soul bestows other characteristics upon material things and yet remains distinct from its gift: shape, Ideal-Form, and the rest are all distinct from the giving soul: so, clearly, with this gift of unity; soul to make things unities looks out upon the unity just as it makes man by looking upon Man, realizing in the man the unity belonging to Man.

Anything that can be described as a unity is so in the precise degree in which it holds a characteristic being; the less or more the degree of the being, the less or more the unity. Soul, while distinct from unity's very self, is a thing of the greater unity in proportion as it is of the greater, the authentic, being. Absolute unity it is not: it is soul and one soul, the unity in some sense a concomitant; there are two things, soul and soul's unity, as there is body with body's unity. The looser aggregates such as a choir are furthest from unity, the more compact are the nearer; soul is nearer yet but still a participant.

Is soul to be identified with unity on the ground that unless it were one thing it could not be soul? No; unity is equally necessary to every other thing, yet unity stands distinct from them; body and unity are not identical; body, too, is a participant.

Besides, the soul, even the individual soul, is a manifold, though not composed of parts: it has diverse powers—reasoning, desiring, perceiving—all held together by this chain of unity. Itself a unity, soul confers unity, but also accepts it. [2. It may be suggested that, while in the unities of the partial order the essence and the unity are distinct, yet in collective existence, in Real Being, they are identical, so that when we have grasped Being we hold unity; Real Being would coincide with Unity. Thus, if Essential Being is the Intellectual-Principle, Unity also is the Intellectual-Principle which is at once Primal Being and Pure Unity, purveying, accordingly, to the rest of things something of Being and something, in proportion, of the unity which is itself.

There is nothing (we may be told) with which the unity would be more plausibly identified than with Being; either it is the same as Being—a man and one man are identical—or it will correspond to the Number which rules in the realm of the particular; it will be a number applying to a certain unique thing as the number two applies to others.

Now if Number is a thing among things, then clearly so this unity must be; we would have to discover what thing of things it is. If Number is not a thing but an operation of the mind moving out to reckon, then the unity will not be a thing.

We found that anything losing unity loses its being; we are therefore obliged to inquire whether the unity in particulars is identical with the being, and Unity Absolute identical with Collective Being.

Now the being of the particular is a manifold; unity cannot be a manifold; there must therefore be a distinction between Being and Unity. Thus a man is at once a reasoning living being and a total of parts; his variety is held together by his unity; man therefore and unity are different— man a thing of parts against unity partless. Much more must Collective Being, as container of all existence, be a manifold and therefore distinct from the unity in which it is but participant.

Again, Collective Being contains life and intelligence—it is no dead thing—and so, once more, is a manifold.

If Being is identical with Intellectual-Principle, even at

that it is a manifold; all the more so when count is taken of the Ideal-Forms in it; for the Idea, particular or collective, is, after all, a numerable agglomeration whose unity is that of a cosmos.

Above all, unity is The First: but Intellectual-Principle, Ideas, and Being, cannot be so; for any member of the realm of Forms is an aggregation, a compound, and therefore—since components must precede their compound—is a later.

Other considerations also go to show that the Intellectual-Principle cannot be the First. Intellect must be about the Intellectual Act: at least in its higher phase, that not concerned with the outer universe, it must be intent upon its Prior; its introversion is a conversion upon the Principle.

Considered as at once Thinker and Object of its Thought, it is dual, not simplex, not The Unity: considered as looking beyond itself, it must look to a better, to a prior: looking simultaneously upon itself and upon its Transcendent, it is, once more, not a First.

There is no other way of stating Intellectual-Principle than as that which, holding itself in the presence of The Good and First and looking towards That, is self-present also, self-knowing and knowing itself as All-Being: thus manifold, it is far from being The Unity.

In sum: The Unity cannot be the total of beings for so its oneness is annulled; it cannot be the Intellectual-Principle, for so it would be that total which the Intellectual-Principle is; nor is it Being, for Being is the total of things.

[3. What then must The Unity be, what nature is left for it?

No wonder that to state it is not easy; even Being and Form are not easy, though we have a way, an approach through the Ideas.

The soul or mind reaching towards the formless finds itself incompetent to grasp where nothing bounds it or to take impression where the impinging reality is diffuse; in sheer dread of holding to nothingness, it slips away. The state is painful; often it seeks relief by retreating from all this vagueness to the region of sense, there to rest as on solid ground, just as the sight distressed by the minute rests with pleasure on the bold.

Soul must see in its own way; this is by coalescence, unification; but in seeking thus to know the Unity it is prevented by that very unification from recognizing that it has found; it cannot distinguish itself from the object of this intuition. None the less, this is our one resource if our philosophy is to give us knowledge of The Unity.

We are in search of unity; we are to come to know the principle of all, the Good and First; therefore we may not stand away from the realm of Firsts and lie prostrate among the lasts: we must strike for those Firsts, rising from things of sense which are the lasts. Cleared of all evil in our intention towards The Good, we must ascend to the Principle within ourselves; from many, we must become one; only so do we attain to knowledge of that which is Principle and Unity. We shape ourselves into Intellectual-Principle; we make over our soul in trust to Intellectual-Principle and set it firmly in That; thus what That sees the soul will waken to see: it is through the Intellectual-Principle that we have this vision of The Unity; it must be our care to bring over nothing whatever from sense, to allow nothing from that source to enter into Intellectual-Principle: with Intellect pure, and with the summit of Intellect, we are to see the All-Pure.

If the quester has the impression of extension or shape or mass attaching to That Nature he has not been led by Intellectual-Principle which is not of the order to see such things; the activity has been of sense and of the judgment following upon sense; only Intellectual-Principle can inform us of the things of its scope; its competence is upon its priors, its content, and its issue: but even its content is outside of sense; and still purer, still less touched by multiplicity, are its priors, or rather its Prior.

The Unity, then, is not Intellectual-Principle but something higher still: Intellectual-Principle is still a being but that First is no being but precedent to all Being: it cannot be a being, for a being has what we may call the shape of its reality but The Unity is without shape, even shape Intellectual.

Generative of all, The Unity is none of all; neither thing nor quantity nor quality nor intellect nor soul; not in motion, not at rest, not in place, not in time: it is the self-defined, unique in form or, better, formless, existing before Form was, or Movement or Rest, all of which are attachments of Being and make Being the manifold it is.

But how, if not in movement, can it be otherwise than at rest?

The answer is that movement and rest are states pertaining to Being, which necessarily has one or the other or both. Besides, anything at rest must be so in virtue of Rest as something distinct: Unity at rest becomes the ground of an attribute and at once ceases to be a simplex.

Note, similarly, that when we speak of this First as Cause we are affirming something happening not to it but to us, the fact that we take from this Self-Enclosed: strictly we should put neither a This nor a That to it; we hover, as it were, about it, seeking the statement of an experience of our own, sometimes nearing this Reality, sometimes baffled by the enigma in which it dwells.

[4. The main source of the difficulty is that awareness of this Principle comes neither by knowing nor by the Intellection that discovers the Intellectual Beings but by a presence overpassing all knowledge. In knowing, soul or mind abandons its unity; it cannot remain a simplex: knowing is taking account of things; that accounting is multiple; the mind thus plunging into number and multiplicity departs from unity.

Our way then takes us beyond knowing; there may be no wandering from unity; knowing and knowable must all be left aside; every object of thought, even the highest, we must pass by, for all that is good is later than This and derives from This as from the sun all the light of the day.

'Not to be told; not to be written': in our writing and telling we are but urging towards it: out of discussion we call to vision: to those desiring to see, we point the path; our teaching is of the road and the travelling; the seeing must be the very act of one that has made this choice.

There are those that have not attained to see. The soul has not come to know the splendour There; it has not felt and clutched to itself that love-passion of vision known to the lover come to rest where he loves. Or struck perhaps by that authentic light, all the soul lit by the nearness gained, we have gone weighted from beneath; the vision is frustrate; we should go without burden and we go carrying that which can but keep us back; we are not yet made over into unity.

From none is that Principle absent and yet from all: present, it remains absent save to those fit to receive, disciplined into some accordance, able to touch it closely by their likeness and by that kindred power within themselves through which, remaining as it was when it came to them from the Supreme, they are enabled to see in so far as God may at all be seen.

Failure to attain may be due to such impediment or to lack of the guiding thought that establishes trust; impediment we must charge against ourselves and strive by entire renunciation to become emancipate; where there is distrust for lack of convincing reason, further considerations may be applied:

[5. Those to whom existence comes about by chance and automatic action and is held together by material forces have drifted far from God and from the concept of unity; we are not here addressing them but only such as accept another nature than body and have some conception of soul.

Soul must be sounded to the depths, understood as an emanation from Intellectual-Principle and as holding its value by a Reason-Principle thence infused. Next, this Intellect must be apprehended, an Intellect other than the reasoning faculty known as the rational principle; with reasoning we are already in the region of separation and movement: our sciences are Reason-Principles lodged in soul or mind, having manifestly acquired their character by the presence in the soul of Intellectual-Principle, source of all knowing.

Thus we come to see Intellectual-Principle almost as an object of sense: it is perceptible as standing above soul, father to soul, and it is one with the Intellectual Cosmos; we must think of it as a quiet, unwavering motion; containing all things and being all things, it is a multiple but at once indivisible and comporting difference. It is not discriminate as are the Reason-Principles, which can in fact be known one by one: yet its content is not a confusion; every item stands forth distinctly, just as in a science the entire content holds as an indivisible and yet each item is a self-standing verity.

Now a plurality thus concentrated like the Intellectual Cosmos is close upon The First—and reason certifies its existence as surely as that of soul—yet, though of higher sovranty than soul, it is not The First since it is not a unity, not simplex as unity, principle over all multiplicity, must be.

Before it there is That which must transcend the noblest of the things of Being: there must be a prior to this Principle which aiming towards unity is yet not unity but a thing in unity's likeness. From this highest it is not sundered; it too is self-present: so close to the unity, it cannot be articulated: and yet it is a principle which in some measure has dared secession.

That awesome Prior, The Unity, is not a being, for so its unity would be vested in something else: strictly no name is apt to it, but since name it we must there is a certain rough fitness in designating it as unity with the understanding that it is not the unity of some other thing.

Thus it eludes our knowledge, so that the nearer approach to it is through its offspring, Being: we know it as cause of existence to Intellectual-Principle, as fount of all that is best, as the efficacy which, self-perduring and undiminishing, generates all beings and is not to be counted among these its derivatives to all of which it must be prior.

This we can but name The Unity, indicating it to each other by a designation that points to the concept of its partlessness while we are in reality striving to bring our own minds to unity. We are not to think of such unity and partlessness as belong to point or monad; the veritable unity is the source of all such quantity which could not exist unless first there existed Being and Being's Prior: we are not, then, to think in the order of point and monad but to use these—in their simplicity and their rejection of magnitude and partition—as symbols for the higher concept.

[6. In what sense, then, do we assert this Unity and how is it to be adjusted to our mental processes?

Its oneness must not be belittled to that of monad and point: for these the mind abstracts extension and numerical quantity and rests upon the very minutest possible, ending no doubt in the partless but still in something that began as a partible and is always lodged in something other than itself. The Unity was never in any other and never belonged to the partible: nor is its impartibility that of extreme minuteness; on the contrary it is great beyond anything, great not in extension but in power, sizeless by its very greatness as even its immediate sequents are impartible not in mass but in might. We must therefore take the Unity as infinite not in measureless extension or numerable quantity but in fathomless depths of power.

Think of The One as Mind or as God, you think too meanly; use all the resources of understanding to conceive this Unity and, again, it is more authentically one than God, even though you reach for God's unity beyond the unity the most perfect you can conceive. For This is utterly a selfexistent, with no concomitant whatever. This self-sufficing is the essence of its unity. Something there must be supremely adequate, autonomous, all-transcending, most utterly without need.

Any manifold, anything beneath The Unity, is dependent: combined from various constituents, its essential nature goes in need of unity; but unity cannot need itself; it stands unity accomplished. Again, a manifold depends upon all its factors; and furthermore each of those factors in turn—as necessarily inbound with the rest and not self-standing—sets up a similar need both to its associates and to the total so constituted.

The sovranly self-sufficing principle will be Unity-Absolute, for only in this unity is there a nature above all need whether within itself or in regard to the rest of things. Unity seeks nothing towards its being or its well-being or its safehold upon existence; cause to all, how can it acquire its character outside of itself or know any good outside? The good of its being can be no borrowing: This is The Good. Nor has it station; it needs no standing-ground as if inadequate to its own sustaining; what calls for such underpropping is the soulless, some material mass that must be based or fall. This is base to all, cause of universal existence and of ordered station. All that demands place is in need; a First cannot go in need of its sequents: all need is effort towards a first principle; the First, principle to all, must be utterly without need. If the Unity be seeking, it must inevitably be seeking to be something other than itself; it is seeking its own destroyer. Whatever may be said to be in need is needing a good, a preserver; nothing can be a good to The Unity, therefore.

Neither can it have will to anything; it is a Beyond-Good, not even to itself a good but to such beings only as may be of quality to have part with it. Nor has it Intellection; that would comport diversity: nor Movement; it is prior to Movement as to Intellection.

To what could its Intellection be directed? To itself? But that would imply a previous ignorance; it would be dependent upon that Intellection in order to knowledge of itself; but it is the self-sufficing. Yet this absence of self-knowing, of self-intellection, does not comport ignorance; ignorance is of something outside—a knower ignorant of a knowable—but in the Solitary there is neither knowing nor anything unknown. Unity, self-present, it has no need of self-intellection: indeed this 'self-presence' were better left out, the more surely to preserve the unity; we must eliminate all knowing and all association, all intellection whether internal or external. It is not to be thought of as having but as being Intellection; Intellection does not itself perform the intellective act but is the cause of the act in something else and cause is not to be identified with caused: most assuredly the cause of all is not a thing within that all.

This Principle is not, therefore, to be identified with the good of which it is the source; it is good in the unique mode of being The Good above all that is good.

[7. If the mind reels before something thus alien to all we know, we must take our stand on the things of this realm and strive thence to see. But in the looking beware of throwing outward; this Principle does not lie away somewhere leaving the rest void; to those of power to reach, it is present; to the inapt, absent. In our daily affairs we cannot hold an object in mind if we have given ourselves elsewhere, occupied upon some other matter; that very thing, and nothing else, must be before us to be truly the object of observation. So here also; preoccupied by the impress of something else, we are withheld under that pressure from becoming aware of The Unity; a mind gripped and fastened by some definite thing cannot take the print of the very contrary. As Matter, it is agreed, must be void of quality in order to accept the types of the universe, so and much more must the soul be kept formless if there is to be no infixed impediment to prevent it being brimmed and lit by the Primal Principle.

In sum, we must withdraw from all the extern, pointed wholly inwards; no leaning to the outer; the total of things ignored, first in their relation to us and later in the very idea;

the self put out of mind in the contemplation of the Supreme; all the commerce so closely There that, if report were possible, one might become to others reporter of that communion.

Such converse, we may suppose, was that of Minos, thence known as the Familiar of Zeus; and in that memory he established the laws which report it, enlarged to that task by his vision There. Some, on the other hand, there will be to disdain such citizen service, choosing to remain in the higher: these will be those that have seen much.

God—we read—is outside of none, present unperceived to all; we break way from Him, or rather from ourselves; what we turn from we cannot reach; astray ourselves, we cannot go in search of another; a child distraught will not recognize its father; to find ourselves is to know our source.

[8. Every soul that knows its history is aware, also, that its movement, unthwarted, is not that of an outgoing line; its natural course may be likened to that in which a circle turns not upon some external but on its own centre, the point to which it owes its rise. The soul's movement will be about its source; to this it will hold, poised intent towards that unity to which all souls should move and the divine souls always move, divine in virtue of that movement; for to be a god is to be integral with the Supreme; what stands away is man still multiple, or beast.

Is then this 'centre' of our souls the Principle for which we are seeking?

We must look yet further: we must admit a Principle in which all these centres coincide: it will be a centre by analogy with the centre of the circle we know. The soul is not a circle in the sense of the geometric figure but in that its primal nature (wholeness) is within it and about it, that it owes its origin to what is whole, and that it will be still more entire when severed from body.

In our present state—part of our being weighed down by the body, as one might have the feet under water with all the rest untouched—we bear ourselves aloft by that intact part and, in that, hold through our own centre to the centre of all the centres, just as the centres of the great circles of a sphere coincide with that of the sphere to which all belong. Thus we are secure.

If these circles were material and not spiritual, the link with the centres would be local; they would lie round it where it lay at some distant point: since the souls are of the Intellectual, and the Supreme still loftier, we understand that contact is otherwise procured, that is by those powers which connect Intellectual agent with Intellectual object; indeed soul is closer to the Supreme than Intellect to its object—such is its similarity, identity, and the sure link of kindred. Material mass cannot blend into other material mass: unbodied beings are not under this bodily limitation; their separation is solely that of otherness, of differentiation; in the absence of otherness, it is similars mutually present.

Thus the Supreme as containing no otherness is ever present with us; we with it when we put otherness away. It is not that the Supreme reaches out to us seeking our communion: we reach towards the Supreme; it is we that become present. We are always before it: but we do not always look: thus a choir, singing set in due order about the conductor, may turn away from that centre to which all should attend; let it but face aright and it sings with beauty, present effectively. We are ever before the Supreme—cut off is utter dissolution; we can no longer be—but we do not always attend: when we look, our Term is attained; this is rest; this is the end of singing ill; effectively before him, we lift a choral song full of God.

[9. In this choiring, the soul looks upon the wellspring of Life, wellspring also of Intellect, beginning of Being, fount of Good, root of Soul. It is not that these are poured out from the Supreme, lessening it as if it were a thing of mass. At that the emanants would be perishable; but they are eternal; they spring from an eternal principle, which produces them not by its fragmentation but in virtue of its intact identity: therefore they too hold firm; so long as the sun shines, so long there will be light.

We have not been cut away; we are not separate, what though the the body-nature has closed about us to press us to itself; we breathe and hold our ground because the Supreme does not give and pass but gives on for ever, so long as it remains what it is.

Our being is the fuller for our turning Thither; this is our prosperity; to hold aloof is loneliness and lessening. Here is the soul's peace, outside of evil, refuge taken in the place clean of wrong; here it has its Act, its true knowing; here it is immune. Here is living, the true; that of today, all living apart from Him, is but a shadow, a mimicry. Life in the Supreme is the native activity of Intellect; in virtue of that silent converse it brings forth gods, brings forth beauty, brings forth righteousness, brings forth all moral good; for of all these the soul is pregnant when it has been filled with God. This state is its first and its final, because from God it comes, its good lies There, and, once turned to God again, it is what it was. Life here, with the things of earth, is a sinking, a defeat, a failing of the wing.

That our good is There is shown by the very love inborn with the soul; hence the constant linking of the Love-God with the Psyches in story and picture; the soul, other than God but sprung of Him, must needs love. So long as it is There, it holds the heavenly love; here its love is the baser; There the soul is Aphrodite of the heavens; here, turned harlot, Aphrodite of the public ways: yet the soul is always an Aphrodite. This is the intention of the myth which tells of Aphrodite's birth and Eros born with her.

The soul in its nature loves God and longs to be at one with Him in the noble love of a daughter for a noble father; but coming to human birth and lured by the courtships of this sphere, she takes up with another love, a mortal, leaves her father and falls.

But one day coming to hate her shame, she puts away the evil of earth, once more seeks the father, and finds her peace.

Those to whom all this experience is strange may understand by way of our earthly longings and the joy we have in winning to what we most desire—remembering always that here what we love is perishable, hurtful, that our loving is of mimicries and turns awry because all was a mistake, our good was not here, this was not what we sought; There only is our veritable love and There we may unite with it, not holding it in some fleshly embrace but possessing it in all its verity. Any that have seen know what I have in mind: the soul takes another life as it draws nearer and nearer to God and gains participation in Him; thus restored it feels that the dispenser of true life is There to see, that now we have nothing to look for but, far otherwise, that we must put aside all else and rest in This alone, This become, This alone, all the earthly environment done away, in haste to be free, impatient of any bond holding us to the baser, so that with our being entire we may cling about This, no part in us remaining but through it we have touch with God.

Thus we have all the vision that may be of Him and of ourselves; but it is of a self wrought to splendour, brimmed with the Intellectual light, become that very light, pure, buoyant, unburdened, raised to Godhood or, better, knowing its Godhood, all aflame then—but crushed out once more if it should take up the discarded burden.

[10. But how comes the soul not to keep that ground?

Because it has not yet escaped wholly: but there will be the time of vision unbroken, the self hindered no longer by any hindrance of body. Not that those hindrances beset that in us which has veritably seen; it is the other phase of the soul that suffers, and that only when we withdraw from vision and take to knowing by proof, by evidence, by the reasoning processes of the mental habit. Such logic is not to be confounded with that act of ours in the vision; it is not our reason that has seen; it is something greater than reason, reason's Prior, as far above reason as the very object of that thought must be.

In our self-seeing There, the self is seen as belonging to that order, or rather we are merged into that self in us which has the quality of that order. It is a knowing of the self restored to its purity. No doubt we should not speak of seeing; but we cannot help talking in dualities, seen and seer, instead of, boldly, the achievement of unity. In this seeing, we neither hold an object nor trace distinction; there is no two. The man is changed, no longer himself nor self-belonging; he is merged with the Supreme, sunken into it, one with it: centre coincides with centre, for centres of circles, even here below, are one when they unite, and two when they separate; and it is in this sense that we now (after the vision) speak of the Supreme as separate. This is why the vision baffles telling; we cannot detach the Supreme to state it; if we have seen something thus detached we have failed of the Supreme which is to be known only as one with ourselves.

[11. This is the purport of that rule of our Mysteries: 'Nothing Divulged to the Uninitiate': the Supreme is not to be made a common story, the holy things may not be uncovered to the stranger, to any that has not himself attained to see. There were not two; beholder was one with beheld; it was not a vision compassed but a unity apprehended. The man formed by this mingling with the Supreme must—if he only remember—carry its image impressed upon him: he is become the Unity, nothing within him or without inducing any diversity; no movement now, no passion, no outlooking desire, once this ascent is achieved; reasoning is in abeyance and all Intellection and even, to dare the word, the very self: caught away, filled with God, he has in perfect stillness attained isolation; all the being calmed, he turns neither to this side nor to that, not even inwards to himself; utterly resting he has become very rest. He belongs no longer to the order of the beautiful; he has risen beyond beauty; he has overpassed even the choir of the virtues; he is like one who, having penetrated the inner sanctuary, leaves the temple images behind him—though these become once more first objects of regard when he leaves the holies; for There his converse was not with image, not with trace, but with the very Truth in the view of which all the rest is but of secondary concern.

There, indeed, it was scarcely vision, unless of a mode unknown; it was a going forth from the self, a simplifying, a renunciation, a reach towards contact and at the same time a repose, a meditation towards adjustment. This is the only seeing of what lies within the holies: to look otherwise is to fail.

Things here are signs; they show therefore to the wiser teachers how the supreme God is known; the instructed priest reading the sign may enter the holy place and make real the vision of the inaccessible.

Even those that have never found entry must admit the existence of that invisible; they will know their source and Principle since by principle they see principle and are linked with it, by like they have contact with like and so they grasp all of the divine that lies within the scope of mind. Until the seeing comes they are still craving something, that which only the vision can give; this Term, attained only by those that have overpassed all, is the All-Transcending.

It is not in the soul's nature to touch utter nothingness; the lowest descent is into evil and, so far, into non-being: but to utter nothing, never. When the soul begins again to mount, it comes not to something alien but to its very self; thus detached, it is in nothing but itself; self-gathered it is no longer in the order of being; it is in the Supreme.

There is thus a converse in virtue of which the essential man outgrows Being, becomes identical with the Transcendent of Being. The self thus lifted, we are in the likeness of the Supreme: if from that heightened self we pass still higher—image to archetype—we have won the Term of all our journeying. Fallen back again, we waken the virtue within until we know ourselves all order once more; once more we are lightened of the burden and move by virtue towards Intellectual-Principle and through the Wisdom in That to the Supreme.

This is the life of gods and of the godlike and blessed among men, liberation from the alien that besets us here, a life taking no pleasure in the things of earth, the passing of solitary to solitary.

THE FIRST ENNEAD

Second Tractate

The Virtues

[1. Since Evil is here, 'haunting this world by necessary law,' and it is the Soul's design to escape from Evil, we must escape hence.

But what is this escape?

'In attaining Likeness to God,' we read. And this is explained as 'becoming just and holy, living by wisdom,' the entire nature grounded in Virtue.

But does not Likeness by way of Virtue imply Likeness to some being that has Virtue? To what Divine Being, then, would our Likeness be? To the Being—must we not think?— in Which, above all, such excellence seems to inhere, that is to the Soul of the Cosmos and to the Principle ruling within it, the Principle endowed with a wisdom most wonderful. What could be more fitting than that we, living in this world, should become Like to its ruler?

But, at the beginning, we are met by the doubt whether even in this Divine-Being all the virtues find place—Moral-Balance (Sophrosyny), for example; or Fortitude where there can be no danger since nothing is alien; where there can be nothing alluring whose lack could induce the desire of possession.

If, indeed, that aspiration towards the Intelligible which is in our nature exists also in this Ruling-Power, then we need not look elsewhere for the source of order and of the virtues in ourselves.

But does this Power possess the Virtues?

We cannot expect to find There what are called the Civic Virtues, the Prudence which belongs to the reasoning faculty; the Fortitude which conducts the emotional and passionate nature; the Sophrosyny which consists in a certain pact, in a concord between the passionate faculty and the reason; or Rectitude which is the due application of all the other virtues as each in turn should command or obey.

Is Likeness, then, attained, perhaps, not by these virtues of the social order but by those greater qualities known by the same general name? And if so do the Civic Virtues give us no help at all?

It is against reason utterly to deny Likeness by these while admitting it by the greater: tradition at least recognizes certain men of the civic excellence as divine, and we must believe that these too had in some sort attained Likeness: on both levels there is virtue for us, though not the same virtue.

Now, if it be admitted that Likeness is possible, though by a varying use of different virtues and though the civic virtues do not suffice, there is no reason why we should not, by virtues peculiar to our state, attain Likeness to a model in which virtue has no place.

But is that conceivable?

When warmth comes in to make anything warm, must there needs be something to warm the source of the warmth?

If a fire is to warm something else, must there be a fire to warm that fire?

Against the first illustration it may be retorted that the source of the warmth does already contain warmth, not by an infusion but as an essential phase of its nature, so that, if the analogy is to hold, the argument would make Virtue something communicated to the Soul but an essential constituent of the Principle from which the Soul attaining Likeness absorbs it.

Against the illustration drawn from the fire, it may be urged that the analogy would make that Principle identical with virtue, whereas we hold it to be something higher.

The objection would be valid if what the Soul takes in were one and the same with the source, but in fact virtue is one thing, the source of virtue is quite another. The material house is not identical with the house conceived in the intellect, and yet stands in its likeness: the material house has distribution and order while the pure idea is not constituted by any such elements; distribution, order, symmetry are not parts of an idea.

So with us: it is from the Supreme that we derive order and distribution and harmony, which are virtues in this sphere: the Existences There, having no need of harmony, order, or distribution, have nothing to do with virtue; and, none the less, it is by our possession of virtue that we become like to Them.

Thus much to show that the principle that we attain Likeness by virtue in no way involves the existence of virtue in the Supreme. But we have not merely to make a formal demonstration: we must persuade as well as demonstrate.

[2. First, then, let us examine those good qualities by which we hold Likeness comes, and seek to establish what is this thing which, as we possess it, in transcription, is virtue, but as the Supreme possesses it, is in the nature of an exemplar or archetype and is not virtue.

We must first distinguish two modes of Likeness.

There is the likeness demanding an identical nature in the objects which, further, must draw their likeness from a common principle: and there is the case in which B resembles A, but A is a Primal, not concerned about B and not said to resemble B. In this second case, likeness is understood in a distinct sense: we no longer look for identity of nature, but on the contrary, for divergence, since the likeness has come about by the mode of difference.

What, then, precisely is Virtue, collectively and in the particular? The clearer method will be to begin with the particular, for so the common element by which all the forms hold the general name will readily appear.

The Civic Virtues, on which we have touched above, are a principle of order and beauty in us as long as we remain passing our life here: they ennoble us by setting bound and measure to our desires and to our entire sensibility, and dispelling false judgement—and this by sheer efficacy of the better, by the very setting of the bounds, by the fact that the measured is lifted outside of the sphere of the unmeasured and lawless.

And, further, these Civic Virtues—measured and ordered themselves and acting as a principle of measure to the Soul which is as Matter to their forming—are like to the measure reigning in the over-world, and they carry a trace of that Highest Good in the Supreme; for, while utter measurelessness is brute Matter and wholly outside of Likeness, any participation in Ideal-Form produces some corresponding degree of Likeness to the formless Being There. And participation goes by nearness: the Soul nearer than the body, therefore closer akin, participates more fully and shows a godlike presence, almost cheating us into the delusion that in the Soul we see God entire.

This is the way in which men of the Civic Virtues attain Likeness.

[3. We come now to that other mode of Likeness which, we read, is the fruit of the loftier virtues: discussing this we shall penetrate more deeply into the essence of the Civic Virtue and be able to define the nature of the higher kind whose existence we shall establish beyond doubt.

To Plato, unmistakably, there are two distinct orders of virtue, and the civic does not suffice for Likeness: 'Likeness to God,' he says, 'is a flight from this world's ways and things': in dealing with the qualities of good citizenship he does not use the simple term Virtue but adds the distinguishing word civic: and elsewhere he declares all the virtues without exception to be purifications.

But in what sense can we call the virtues purifications, and how does purification issue in Likeness?

As the Soul is evil by being interfused with the body and by coming to share the body's states and to think the body's thoughts, so it would be good, it would be possessed of virtue, if it threw off the body's moods and devoted itself to its own Act—the state of Intellection and Wisdom—never allowed the passions of the body to affect it—the virtue of Sophrosyny—knew no fear at the parting from the body— the virtue of Fortitude—and if reason and the Intellectual-Principle ruled without opposition—in which state is Righteousness. Such a disposition in the Soul, become thus intellective and immune to passion, it would not be wrong to call Likeness to God; for the Divine, too, is pure and the Divine-Act is such that Likeness to it is Wisdom.

But would not this make virtue a state of the Divine also?

No: the Divine has no states; the state is in the Soul. The Act of Intellection in the Soul is not the same as in the Divine: of things in the Supreme, one (the Intellectual-Principle) has a different mode of intellection (from that of Soul), the other (the Absolute One) has none at all.

Then yet again, the one word, Intellection, covers two distinct Acts?

Rather there is primal Intellection and there is Intellection deriving from the Primal and of other scope.

As speech is the echo of the thought in the Soul, so thought in the Soul is an echo from elsewhere: that is to say, as the uttered thought is an image of the soul-thought, so the soul-thought images a thought above itself and is the interpreter of the higher sphere.

Virtue, in the same way, is a thing of the Soul: it does not belong to the Intellectual-Principle or to the Transcendence.

[4. We come, so, to the question whether Purification is the whole of this human quality, virtue, or merely the forerunner upon which virtue follows? Does virtue imply the achieved state of purification or does the mere process suffice to it, Virtue being something of less perfection than the accomplished pureness which is almost the Term?

To have been purified is to have cleansed away everything alien: but Goodness is something more.

If before the impurity entered there was Goodness, the cleansing suffices; but even so, not the act of cleansing but the cleansed thing that emerges will be The Good. And it remains to establish what (in the case of the cleansed Soul) this emergent is.

It can scarcely prove to be The Good: The Absolute Good cannot be thought to have taken up its abode with Evil. We can think of it only as something of the nature of good but paying a double allegiance and unable to rest in the Authentic Good.

The Soul's true Good is in devotion to the Intellectual-Principle, its kin; evil to the Soul lies in frequenting strangers. There is no other way for it than to purify itself and so enter into relation with its own; the new phase begins by a new orientation.

After the Purification, then, there is still this orientation to be made? No: by the purification the true alignment stands accomplished.

The Soul's virtue, then, is this alignment? No: it is what the alignment brings about within.

And this is . . . ?

That is sees; that, like sight affected by the things seen, the Soul admits the imprint, graven upon it and working within it, of the vision it has come to.

But was not the Soul possessed of all this always, or had it forgotten?

What it now sees, it certainly always possessed, but as lying away in the dark, not as acting within it: to dispel the darkness, and thus come to the knowledge of its inner content, it must thrust towards the light.

Besides, it possessed not the originals but images, pictures; and these it must bring into closer accord with the verities they represent. And, further, if the Intellectual-Principle is said to be a possession of the Soul, this is only in the sense that It is not alien and that the link becomes very close when the Soul's sight is turned towards It: otherwise, ever-present though It be, It remains foreign, just as our knowledge, if it does not determine action, is dead to us.

[5. So we come to the scope of the purification: that understood, the nature of Likeness becomes clear. Likeness to what principle? Identity with what God?

The question is substantially this: how far does purification dispel the two orders of passion—anger, desire, and the like, with grief and its kin—and in what degree the disengagement from the body is possible.

Disengagement means simply that the Soul withdraws to its own place.

It will hold itself above all passions and affections. Necessary pleasures and all the activity of the senses it will employ only for medicament and assuagement lest its work be impeded. Pain it may combat, but, failing the cure, it will bear meekly and ease it by refusing to assent to it. All passionate action it will check: the suppression will be complete if that be possible, but at worst the Soul will never itself take fire but will keep the involuntary and uncontrolled outside its own precincts and rare and weak at that. The Soul has nothing to dread, though no doubt the involuntary has some power here too: fear therefore must cease, except so far as it is purely monitory. What desire there may be can never be for the vile; even the food and drink necessary for restoration will lie outside the Soul's attention, and not less the sexual appetite: or if such desire there must be, it will turn upon the actual needs of the nature and be entirely under control; or if any uncontrolled motion takes place, it will reach no further than the imagination, be no more than a fleeting fancy.

The Soul itself will be inviolately free and will be working to set the irrational part of the nature above all attack, or if that may not be, then at least to preserve it from violent assault, so that any wound it takes may be slight and be healed at once by virtue of the Soul's presence; just as a man living next door to a Proficient would profit by the neighbourhood, either in becoming wise and good himself or, for sheer shame, never venturing any act which the nobler mind would disapprove.

There will no battling in the Soul: the mere intervention of Reason is enough: the lower nature will stand in such awe of Reason that for any slightest movement it has made it will grieve, and censure its own weakness, in not having kept low and still in the presence of its lord.

[6. In all this there is no sin—there is only matter of discipline—but our concern is not merely to be sinless but to be God.

As long as there is any such involuntary action, the nature is twofold, God and Demi-God, or rather God in association with a nature of a lower power: when all the involuntary is suppressed, there is God unmingled, a Divine Being of those that follow upon The First.

For, at this height, the man is the very being that came from the Supreme. The primal excellence restored, the essential man is There: entering this sphere, he has associated himself with a lower phase of his nature but even this he will lead up into likeness with his highest self, as far as it is capable, so that if possible it shall never be inclined to, and at the least never adopt, any course displeasing to its over-lord.

What form, then, does each virtue take in one so lofty?

Wisdom and understanding consist in the contemplation of all that exists in the Intellectual-Principle, and the Intellectual-Principle itself apprehends this all (not by contemplation but) as an immediate presence.

And each of these has two modes according as it exists in the Intellectual-Principle and in the Soul: in the Soul it is Virtue, in the Supreme not Virtue.

In the Supreme, then, what is it?

Its proper Act and Its Essence.

That Act and Essence of the Supreme, manifested in a new form, constitute the virtue of this sphere. For the Ideal-Form of Justice or of any other virtue is not itself a virtue, but, so to speak, an exemplar, the source of what in the Soul becomes virtue: for virtue is dependent, seated in something not itself; the Ideal-Form is self-standing, independent.

But taking Rectitude to be the due ordering of faculty, does it not always imply the existence of diverse parts?

No: there is a Rectitude of Diversity appropriate to what has parts, but there is another, not less Rectitude than the former though it resides in a Unity. And the authentic Absolute-Rectitude is the Act of a Unity upon itself, of a Unity in which there is no this and that and the other.

On this principle, the supreme Rectitude of the Soul is that it direct its Act towards the Intellectual-Principle: its Restraint (Sophrosyny) is its inward bending towards the Intellectual-Principle; its Fortitude is its being impassive in the likeness of That towards Which its gaze is set. Whose nature comports an impassivity which the Soul acquires by virtue and must acquire if it is not to be at the mercy of every state arising in its less noble companion.

[7. The virtues in the Soul run in a sequence correspondent to that existing in the over-world, that is among their exemplars in the Intellectual-Principle.

In the Supreme, Intellection constitutes Knowledge and Wisdom; self-concentration is Sophrosyny; Its proper Act is Its Dutifulness; Its Immateriality, by which It remains inviolate within Itself, is the equivalent of Fortitude.

In the Soul, the direction of vision towards the Intellectual-Principle is Wisdom and Prudence, soul-virtues not appropriate to the Supreme where Thinker and Thought are identical. All the other virtues have similar correspondences.

And if the term of purification is the production of a pure being, then the purification of the Soul must produce all the virtues; if any are lacking, then not one of them is perfect.

And to possess the greater is potentially to possess the minor, though the minor need not carry the greater with them.

Thus we have indicated the dominant note in the life of a Proficient; but whether his possession of the minor virtues be actual as well as potential, whether even the greater are in Act in him or yield to qualities higher still, must be decided afresh in each several case.

Take, for example, Contemplative-Wisdom. If other guides of conduct must be called in to meet a given need, can this virtue hold its ground even in mere potentiality?

And what happens when the virtues in their very nature differ in scope and province? Where, for example, Sophrosyny would allow certain acts or emotions under due restraint and another virtue would cut them off altogether? And is it not clear that all may have to yield, once Contemplative-Wisdom comes into action?

The solution is in understanding the virtues and what each has to give: thus the man will learn to work with this or that as every several need demands. And as he reaches to loftier principles and other standards these in turn will define his conduct: for example, Restraint in its earlier form will no longer satisfy him; he will work for the final Disengagement; he will live, no longer, the human life of the good man—such as Civic Virtue commends—but, leaving this beneath him, will take up instead another life, that of the Gods.

For it is to the Gods, not to the good, that our Likeness must look: to model ourselves upon good men is to produce an image of an image: we have to fix our gaze above the image and attain Likeness to the Supreme Exemplar.

Third Tractate

Dialectic

[1. What art is there, what method, what discipline to bring us there where we must go?

The Term at which we must arrive we may take as agreed: we have established elsewhere, by many considerations, that our journey is to the Good, to the Primal-Principle; and, indeed, the very reasoning which discovered the Term was itself something like an initiation.

But what order of beings will attain the Term?

Surely, as we read, those that have already seen all or most things, those who at their first birth have entered into the life-germ from which is to spring a metaphysician, a musician, or a born lover, the metaphysician taking to the path by instinct, the musician and the nature peculiarly susceptible to love needing outside guidance.

But how lies the course? Is it alike for all, or is there a distinct method for each class of temperament?

For all there are two stages of the path, as they are making upwards or have already gained the upper sphere.

The first degree is the conversion from the lower life; the second—held by those that have already made their way to the sphere of the Intelligibles, have set as it were a footprint there but must still advance within the realm—lasts until they reach the extreme hold of the place, the Term attained when the topmost peak of the Intellectual realm is won.

But this highest degree must bide its time: let us first try to speak of the initial process of conversion.

We must begin by distinguishing the three types. Let us take the musician first and indicate his temperamental equipment for the task.

The musician we may think of as being exceedingly quick

to beauty, drawn in a very rapture to it: somewhat slow to stir of his own impulse, he answers at once to the outer stimulus: as the timid are sensitive to noise so he to tones and the beauty they convey; all that offends against unison or harmony in melodies or rhythms repels him; he longs for measure and shapely pattern.

This natural tendency must be made the starting-point to such a man; he must be drawn by the tone, rhythm, and design in things of sense: he must learn to distinguish the material forms from the Authentic-Existent which is the source of all these correspondences and of the entire reasoned scheme in the work of art: he must be led to the Beauty that manifests itself through these forms; he must be shown that what ravished him was no other than the Harmony of the Intellectual world and the Beauty in that sphere, not some one shape of beauty but the All-Beauty, the Absolute Beauty; and the truths of philosophy must be implanted in him to lead him to faith in that which, unknowing it, he possesses within himself. What these truths are we will show later.

[2. The born lover, to whose degree the musician also may attain—and then either come to a stand or pass beyond—has a certain memory of beauty but, severed from it now, he no longer comprehends it: spellbound by visible loveliness he clings amazed about that. His lesson must be to fall down no longer in bewildered delight before some one embodied form; he must be led, under a system of mental discipline, to beauty everywhere and made to discern the One Principle underlying all, a Principle apart from the material forms, springing from another source, and elsewhere more truly present. The beauty, for example, in a noble course of life and in an admirably organized social system may be pointed out to him—a first training this in the loveliness of the immaterial—he must learn to recognize the beauty in the arts, sciences, virtues; then these severed and particular forms must be brought under the one principle by the explanation of their origin. From the virtues he is to be led to the Intellectual-Principle, to the Authentic-Existent; thence onward, he treads the upward way.

[3. The metaphysician, equipped by that very character, winged already and not, like those others, in need of disengagement, stirring of himself towards the supernal but doubting of the way, needs only a guide. He must be shown, then, and instructed, a willing wayfarer by his very temperament, all but self-directed.

Mathematics, which as a student by nature he will take very easily, will be prescribed to train him to abstract thought and to faith in the unembodied; a moral being by native disposition, he must be led to make his virtue perfect; after the Mathematics he must be put through a course in Dialectic and made an adept in the science.

[4. But this science, this Dialectic essential to all the three classes alike, what, in sum, is it?

It is the Method, or Discipline, that brings with it the power of pronouncing with final truth upon the nature and relation of things—what each is, how it differs from others, what common quality all have, to what Kind each belongs and in what rank each stands in its Kind and whether its Being is Real-Being, and how many Beings there are, and how many non-Beings to be distinguished from Beings.

Dialectic treats also of the Good and the not-Good, and of the particulars that fall under each, and of what is the Eternal and what the not-Eternal—and of these, it must be understood, not by seeming-knowledge ('sense-knowledge') but with authentic science.

All this accomplished, it gives up its touring of the realm of sense and settles down in the Intellectual Cosmos and there plies its own peculiar Act: it has abandoned all the realm of deceit and falsity, and pastures the Soul in the "Meadows of Truth": it employs the Platonic division to the discernment of the Ideal-Forms, of the Authentic-Existence, and of the First-Kinds (or Categories of Being): it establishes, in the light of Intellection, the affiliations of all that issues from these Firsts, until it has traversed the entire Intellectual Realm: then, by means of analysis, it takes the opposite path and returns once more to the First Principle.

Now it rests: instructed and satisfied as to the Being in that sphere, it is no longer busy about many things: it has arrived at Unity and it contemplates: it leaves to another science all that coil of premises and conclusions called the art of reasoning, much as it leaves the art of writing: some of the matter of logic, no doubt, it considers necessary—to clear the ground—but it makes itself the judge, here as in everything else; where it sees use, it uses; anything it finds superfluous, it leaves to whatever department of learning or practice may turn that matter to account.

[5. But whence does this science derive its own initial laws?

The Intellectual-Principle furnishes standards, the most certain for any soul that is able to apply them. What else is necessary Dialectic puts together for itself, combining and dividing, until it has reached perfect Intellection. 'For,' we read, 'it is the purest (perfection) of Intellection and Contemplative-Wisdom.' And, being the noblest method and science that exists it must needs deal with Authentic-Existence, The Highest there is: as Contemplative-Wisdom (or true-knowing) it deals with Being, as Intellection with what transcends Being.

What, then, is Philosophy?

Philosophy is the supremely precious.

Is Dialectic, then, the same as Philosophy?

It is the precious part of Philosophy. We must not think of it as the mere tool of the metaphysician: Dialectic does not consist of bare theories and rules: it deals with verities; Existences are, as it were, Matter to it, or at least it proceeds methodically towards Existences, and possesses itself, at the one step, of the notions and of the realities.

Untruth and sophism it knows, not directly, not of its own nature, but merely as something produced outside itself, something which it recognizes to be foreign to the verities laid up in itself; in the falsity presented to it, it perceives a clash with its own canon of truth. Dialectic, that is to say, has no knowledge of propositions—collections of words—but it knows the truth and, in that knowledge, knows what the schools call their propositions: it knows above all the operation of the Soul, and, by virtue of this knowing, it knows, too, what is affirmed and what is denied, whether the denial is of what was asserted or of something else, and whether propositions agree or differ; all that is submitted to it, it attacks with the directness of sense-perception and it leaves petty precisions of process to what other science may care for such exercises.

[6. Philosophy has other provinces, but Dialectic is its precious part: in its study of the laws of the universe, Philosophy draws on Dialectic much as other studies and crafts use Arithmetic, though, of course, the alliance between Philosophy and Dialectic is closer.

And in morals, too, Philosophy uses Dialectic: by Dialectic it comes to contemplation, though it originates of itself the moral state or rather the discipline from which the moral state develops.

Our reasoning faculties employ the data of Dialectic almost as their proper possession, for their use of these data commonly involves Matter as well as Form.

And while the other virtues bring the reason to bear upon particular experiences and acts, the virtue of Wisdom (i.e. the virtue peculiarly induced by Dialectic) is a certain super-reasoning much closer to the Universal; for it deals with (such abstract ideas as) correspondence and sequence, the choice of time for action and inaction, the adoption of this course, the rejection of that other: Wisdom and Dialectic have the task of presenting all things as Universals and stripped of matter for treatment by the Understanding.

But can these inferior kinds of virtue exist without Dialectic and philosophy?

Yes—but imperfectly, inadequately.

And is it possible to be a Proficient, a Master in Dialectic, without these lower virtues?

It would not happen: the lower will spring either before or together with the higher. And it is likely that everyone normally possesses the natural virtues from which, when Wisdom steps in, the perfected virtue develops. After the natural virtues, then, Wisdom, and so the perfecting of the moral nature. Once the natural virtues exist, both orders, the natural and the higher, ripen side by side to their final excellence: or as the one advances it carries forward the other towards perfection.

But, ever, the natural virtue is imperfect in vision and in strength—and to both orders of virtue the essential matter is from what principles we derive them.

THE FIFTH ENNEAD

The Ninth Tractate

The Intellectual-Principle, the Ideas, and the Authentic Existence

[1. All human beings from birth onward live to the realm of sense more than to the Intellectual.

Forced of necessity to attend first to the material, some of them elect to abide by that order and, their life throughout, make its concerns their first and their last; the sweet and the bitter of sense are their good and evil; they feel they have done all if they live along pursuing the one and barring the doors to the other. And those of them that pretend to reasoning have adopted this as their philosophy; they are like the heavier birds which have incorporated much from the earth and are so weighted down that they cannot fly high for all the wings Nature has given them.

Others do indeed lift themselves a little above the earth; the better in their soul urges them from the pleasant to the nobler, but they are not of power to see the highest and so, in despair of any surer ground, they fall back, in virtue's name, upon those actions and options of the lower from which they sought to escape.

But there is a third order—those godlike men who, in their mightier power, in the keenness of their sight, have clear vision of the splendour above and rise to it from among the cloud and fog of earth and hold firmly to that other world, looking beyond all here, delighted in the place of reality, their native land, like a man returning after long wanderings to the pleasant ways of his own country.

[2. What is this other place and how is it accessible?

It is to be reached by those who, born with the nature of the lover, are also authentically philosophic by inherent temper; in pain of love towards beauty but not held by material loveliness, taking refuge from that in things whose beauty is of the soul—such things as virtue, knowledge, institutions, law and custom—and thence, rising still a step, reach to the source of this loveliness of the Soul, thence to whatever be above that again, until the uttermost is reached, The First, the Principle whose beauty is self-springing: this attained, there is an end to the pain inassuageable before.

But how is the ascent to be begun? Whence comes the power? In what thought is this love to find its guide?

The guiding thought is this: that the beauty perceived on material things is borrowed.

The pattern giving beauty to the corporeal rests upon it as Idea to its Matter and the substrate may change and from being pleasant become distasteful, a sign, in all reason, that the beauty comes by participation.

Now, what is this that gives grace to the corporeal?

Two causes in their degree: the participation in beauty and the power of Soul, the maker, which has imprinted that form.

We ask then: Is soul, of itself, a thing of beauty? We find

it is not since differences are manifest, one soul wise and lovely, another foolish and ugly: soul-beauty is constituted by wisdom.

The question thus becomes, What principle is the giver of wisdom to the soul? and the only answer is 'The Intellectual-Principle,' the veritably intellectual, wise without intermission and therefore beautiful of itself.

But does even this suffice for our First?

No; we must look still inward beyond the Intellectual, which, from our point of approach, stands before the Supreme Beginning, in whose forecourt, as it were, it announces in its own being the entire content of the Good, that prior of all, locked in unity, of which this is the expression already touched by multiplicity.

[3. We will have to examine this Nature, the Intellectual, which our reasoning identifies as the authentically existent and the veritable essential: but first we must take another path and make certain that such a principle does necessarily exist.

Perhaps it is ridiculous to set out inquiring whether an Intellectual-Principle has place in the total of being: but there may be some to hesitate even as to this and certainly there will be the question whether it is as we describe it, whether it is a separate existence, whether it actually is the real beings, whether it is the seat of the Ideas; to this we now address ourselves.

All that we see, and describe as having existence, we know to be compound; hand-wrought or compacted by nature, nothing is simplex. Now the hand-wrought, with its metal or stone or wood, is not realized out of these materials until the appropriate craft has produced statue, house, or bed, by imparting the particular Idea from its own content. Similarly with natural forms of being; those including several constituents, compound bodies as we call them, may be analysed into the materials and the Idea imposed upon the total; the human being, for example, into soul and body; and the hu-

man body into the four elements. Finding everything to be a
compound of Matter and shaping principle—since the Matter of the elements is of itself shapeless—you will inquire
whence this forming Idea comes; and you will ask whether in
the Soul we recognize a simplex or whether this also has constituents, something representing Matter and something else
representing Form, namely, the Intellectual-Principle within
it, this corresponding both to the shape on the statue and to
the artist giving the shape.

Applying the same method to the total of things, here too
we discover the Intellectual-Principle and this we set down as
veritably the maker and creator of the All. The underlie has
adopted, we see, certain shapes by which it becomes fire,
water, air, earth; and these shapes have been imposed upon
it by something else. This other is Soul which, hovering over
the Four (the elements), imparts the pattern of the Cosmos,
the Ideas for which it has itself received from the Intellectual-
Principle as the soul or mind of the craftsman draws upon his
craft for the plan of his work.

The Intellectual-Principle is in one phase the Form of the
Soul, its shape; in another phase it is the giver of the shape—
the sculptor, possessing inherently what is given—imparting
to Soul nearly the authentic reality while what body receives
is but image and imitation.

[4. But, Soul reached, why need we look higher; why not
make this The First?

A main reason is that the Intellectual-Principle is at once
something other and something more powerful than Soul and
that the more powerful is in the nature of things the prior.
For it is certainly not true, as people imagine, that the Soul,
brought to perfection, produces Intellect. How could that
potentiality come to actuality unless there be, first, an effective principle to induce the actualization which, left to
chance, might never occur?

The Firsts must be supposed to exist in actuality, looking
to nothing else, self-complete. Anything incomplete must be

sequent upon these, and take its completion from the principles engendering it which, like fathers, labour in the improvement of an offspring born imperfect: the produced is as Matter to the producing principle and is worked over by it into a shapely perfection.

And if, further, Soul is passible while something impassible there must be or by the mere passage of time all wears away, here too we are led to something above Soul.

Again there must be something prior to Soul because Soul is in the world and there must be something outside a world in which, all being corporeal and material, nothing has enduring reality: failing such a prior, neither man nor the Ideas would be eternal or have true identity.

These and many other considerations establish the necessary existence of an Intellectual-Principle prior to Soul.

[5. This Intellectual-Principle, if the term is to convey the truth, must be understood to be not a principle merely potential and not one maturing from unintelligence to intelligence —that would simply send us seeking, once more, a necessary prior—but a principle which is intelligence in actuality and in eternity.

Now a principle whose wisdom is not borrowed must derive from itself any intellection it may make; and anything it may possess within itself it can hold only from itself: it follows that, intellective by its own resource and upon its own content, it is itself the very things on which its intellection acts.

For supposing its essence to be separable from its intellection and the objects of its intellection to be not-itself, then its essence would be unintellectual; and it would be intellectual not actually but potentially. The intellection and its object must then be inseparable—however the habit induced by our conditions may tempt us to distinguish, There too, the thinker from the thought.

What then is its characteristic Act and what the intellection which makes knower and known here identical?

Clearly, as authentic Intellection, it has authentic intellection of the authentically existent, and establishes their existence. Therefore it is the Authentic Beings.

Consider: it must perceive them either somewhere else or within itself as its very self: the somewhere else is impossible —where could that be?—they are therefore itself and the content of itself.

Its objects certainly cannot be the things of sense, as people think: no First could be of the sense-known order; for in things of sense the Idea (Form) is but an image of the authentic, an image thrown upon Matter, and every Idea thus derivative and exiled traces back to that original and is no more than an image of it.

Further, if the Intellectual-Principle is to be the maker of this All, it cannot make by looking outside itself to what does not yet exist. The Authentic Beings must, then, exist before this All, no copies made on a model but themselves archetypes, primals, and the essence of the Intellectual-Principle.

We may be told that Reason-Principles suffice (to the subsistence of the All): but then these, clearly, must be eternal; and if eternal, if immune, then they must exist in an Intellectual-Principle such as we have indicated, a principle earlier than condition, than nature, than soul, than anything whose existence is potential (or contingent).

The Intellectual-Principle, therefore, is itself the authentic existences, not a knower knowing them in some sphere foreign to it. The Authentic Beings, thus, exist neither before nor after it: it is the primal legislator to Being or, rather, is itself the law of Being. Thus it is true that 'Intellection and Being are identical'; in the immaterial the knowledge of the thing is the thing. And this is the meaning of the dictum 'I sought myself,' namely, as one of the Beings: it also bears on reminiscence.

For none of the Beings is outside the Intellectual-Principle or in space; they remain for ever in themselves, accepting no change, no decay, and by that are the authentically existent.

Things that arise and fall away draw on real being as something to borrow from; they are not of the real; the true being is that on which they draw.

It is by participation that the sense-known has the being we ascribe to it; the underlying nature has taken its shape from elsewhere; thus bronze and wood are shaped into what we see by means of an image introduced by sculpture or carpentry; the craft permeates the materials while remaining integrally apart from the material and containing in itself the reality of statue or couch. And it is so, of course, with all corporeal things.

This universe, characteristically participant in images, shows how the image differs from the authentic beings: against the variability of the one order, there stands the unchanging quality of the other, self-situate, not needing space because having no magnitude, holding an existence intellective and self-sufficing. The body-kind seeks its endurance in another kind; the Intellectual-Principle, sustaining by its marvellous Being the things which of themselves must fall, does not itself need to look for a staying ground.

[6. We take it, then, that the Intellectual-Principle is the authentic existences and contains them all—not as in a place but as possessing itself and being one thing with this its content. All are one There and yet are distinct: similarly the mind holds many branches and items of knowledge simultaneously, yet none of them merged into any other, each acting its own part at call quite independently, every conception coming out from the inner total and working singly. It is after this way, though in a closer unity, that the Intellectual-Principle is all Being in one total—and yet not in one, since each of these beings is a distinct power which, however, the total Intellectual-Principle includes as the species in a genus, as the parts in a whole. This relation may be illustrated by the powers in seed; all lies undistinguished in the unit, the formative ideas gathered as in one kernel; yet in that unit there is eye-principle, and there is hand-principle, each of which is re-

vealed as a separate power by its distinct material product.
Thus each of the powers in the seed is a Reason-Principle one
and complete yet including all the parts over which it presides: there will be something bodily, the liquid for example,
carrying mere Matter; but the principle itself is Idea and
nothing else, Idea identical with the generative Idea belonging to the lower soul, image of a higher. This power is sometimes designated as Nature in the seed-life; its origin is in the
divine; and, outgoing from its priors as light from fire, it converts and shapes the matter of things, not by push and pull
and the lever work of which we hear so much, but by be-
stowal of the Ideas.

[7. Knowledge in the reasoning soul is on the one side concerned with objects of sense, though indeed this can scarcely
be called knowledge and is better indicated as opinion or sur-
face-knowing; it is of later origin than the objects since it
is a reflection from them: but on the other hand there is
the knowledge handling the intellectual objects and this is the
authentic knowledge; it enters the reasoning soul from the
Intellectual-Principle and has no dealing with anything in
sense. Being true knowledge it actually is everything of which
it takes cognizance; it carries as its own content the intellectual act and the intellectual object since it carries the Intellectual-Principle which actually is the primals and is always self-present and is in its nature an Act, never by any
want forced to seek, never acquiring or traversing the remote
—for all such experience belongs to soul—but always self-
gathered, the very Being of the collective total, not an extern
creating things by the act of knowing them.

Not by its thinking God does God come to be; not by its
thinking Movement does Movement arise. Hence it is an error to call the Ideas intellections in the sense that, upon an
intellectual act in this Principle, one such Idea or another is
made to exist or exists. No: the object of this intellection
must exist before the intellective act (must be the very content not the creation of the Intellectual-Principle). How else

could that Principle come to know it? Certainly not (as an external) by luck or by haphazard search.

[8. If, then, the Intellection is an act upon the inner content (of the Intellectual-Principle), that content is the Form, and the Form is the Idea.

What, then, is that content?

An Intellectual-Principle and an Intellective Essence, no Idea distinguishable from the Intellectual-Principle, each actually being that Principle. The Intellectual-Principle entire is the total of the Ideas, and each of them is the (entire) Intellectual-Principle in a special form. Thus a science entire is the total of the relevant considerations each of which, again, is a member of the entire science, a member not distinct in space yet having its individual efficacy in a total.

This Intellectual-Principle, therefore, is a unity while by that possession of itself it is, tranquilly, the eternal abundance.

If the Intellectual-Principle were envisaged as preceding Being, it would at once become a principle whose expression, its intellectual Act, achieves and engenders the Beings: but, since we are compelled to think of existence as preceding that which knows it, we can but think that the Beings are the actual content of the knowing principle and that the very act, the intellection, is inherent to the Beings, as fire stands equipped from the beginning with fire-act; in this conception, the Beings contain the Intellectual-Principle as one and the same with themselves, as their own activity. But Being is itself an activity: there is one activity, then, in both or, rather, both are one thing.

Being, therefore, and the Intellectual-Principle are one Nature: the Beings, and the Act of that which is, and the Intellectual-Principle thus constituted, all are one: and the resultant Intellections are the Idea of Being and its shape and its act.

It is our separating habit that sets the one order before the other: for there is a separating intellect, of another order than the true, distinct from the Intellect, inseparable and unseparating, which is Being and the universe of things.

[9. What, then, is the content—inevitably separated by our minds—of this one Intellectual-Principle? For there is no resource but to represent the items in accessible form just as we study the various articles constituting one science.

This universal is a living thing capable of including every form of life; but its Being and its modes are derived from elsewhere; that source is traced back to the Intellectual-Principle: it follows that the all-embracing archetype is in the Intellectual-Principle, which, therefore, must be an intellectual Cosmos, that indicated by Plato in the phrase 'The living existent.'

Given the Reason-Principle (the outgoing divine Idea) of a certain living thing and the Matter to harbour this seed-principle, the living thing must come into being: in the same way once there exists an intellective Nature, all powerful, and with nothing to check it—since nothing intervenes between it and that which is of a nature to receive it—inevitably the higher imprints the Cosmic form and the lower accepts it. The recipient holds the Idea in division, here man, there sun, while in the giver all remains in unity.

[10. All, then, that is present in the sense realm as Idea comes from the Supreme. But what is not present as Idea, does not. Thus of things conflicting with nature, none is There: the inartistic is not contained in the arts; lameness is not in the seed; for a lame leg is either inborn through some thwarting of the Reason-Principle or is a marring of the achieved form by accident. To that Intellectual Cosmos belong qualities, accordant with Nature, and quantities; number and mass; origins and conditions; all actions and experiences not against nature; movement and repose, both the universals and the particulars: but There time is replaced by eternity and space by its intellectual equivalent, mutual inclusiveness.

In that Intellectual Cosmos, where all is one total, every entity that can be singled out is an intellective essence and a participant in life: it is identity and difference, movement and rest, the object moving and the object at rest, essence and quality. All There is pure essence; for every real being must be in actuality, not merely in potentiality, and therefore quality is never separated from essence.

This suggests the question whether the Intellectual Cosmos contains the form only of the things of sense or of other existents as well. But first we will consider how it stands with artistic creations: there is no question of an ideal archetype of evil: the evil of this world is begotten of need, privation, deficiency, and is a condition peculiar to Matter distressed and to what has come into likeness with Matter.

[11. Now as to the arts and crafts and their productions:

The imitative arts—painting, sculpture, dancing, pantomimic gesturing—are, largely, earth-based; they follow models found in sense, since they copy forms and movements and reproduce seen symmetries; they cannot therefore be referred to that higher sphere except indirectly, through the Reason-Principle in humanity.

On the other hand any skill which, beginning with the observation of the symmetry of living things, grows to the symmetry of all life, will be a portion of the Power There which observes and meditates the symmetry reigning among all beings in the Intellectual Cosmos. Thus all music—since its thought is upon melody and rhythm—must be the earthly representation of the music there is in the rhythm of the Ideal Realm.

The crafts such as building and carpentry which give us Matter in wrought forms, may be said, in that they draw on pattern, to take their principles from that realm and from the thinking There: but in that they bring these down into contact with the sense-order, they are not wholly in the Intellectual, except as contained in the Idea of man. So agriculture, dealing with material growths; so medicine watching over physical health; so the art which aims at corporeal strength and well-being: power and well-being mean something else There, the fearlessness and self-sufficing quality of all that lives.

Oratory and generalship, administration and sovereignty—under any forms in which their activities are associated with Good and when they look to that—possess something derived thence and building up their knowledge from the knowledge There.

Geometry, as a science of the Intellectual entities, holds place There: so, too, philosophy, whose high concern is Being.

For the arts and products of art, these observations may suffice.

[12. It should, however, be added that if the Idea of man exists in the Supreme, there must exist the Idea of reasoning man and of man with his arts and crafts; such arts as are the offspring of intellect must be There.

It must be observed that the Ideas will be of universals; not of Socrates but of Man: though as to man we may inquire whether the individual may not also have place There. Ideas of individual men may be justified by the fact that the same feature varies from man to man, the simian type, for example, and the aquiline: the aquiline and the simian must be taken to be differences in the Idea of Man as there are different types of the animal: but Matter also has its effect in bringing about the degree of aquilinity. Similarly with difference of complexion, determined partly by the Reason-Principle, partly by Matter and by diversity of place.

[13. It remains to decide whether only what is known in sense exists There or whether on the contrary, as Absolute-Man differs from individual man, so there is in the Supreme an Absolute-Soul differing from Soul and an Absolute-Intellect differing from Intellectual-Principle.

It must be stated at the outset that we cannot take all that is here to be image of archetype, or Soul to be an image of Absolute-Soul: one soul, doubtless, ranks higher than another, but here too, though perhaps not as identified with this realm, is the Absolute-Soul.

Every soul, authentically a soul, has some form of rightness and moral wisdom; in the souls within ourselves there is true knowing: and these attributes are no images or copies from the Supreme, as in the sense-world, but actually are those very originals in a mode peculiar to this sphere. For those Beings are not set apart in some defined place; wherever there is a soul that has risen from body, there too these are: the world of sense is one-where, the Intellectual Cosmos is everywhere. Whatever the freed soul attains to here, that it is There.

Thus, if by the content of the sense-world we mean simply the visible objects, then the Supreme contains not only what is in the realm of sense but more: if in the content of the Cosmos we mean to include Soul and the Soul-things, then all is here that is There.

[14. There is, thus, a Nature comprehending in the Intellectual all that exists, and this Principle must be the source of all. But how, seeing that the veritable source must be a unity, simplex utterly?

The mode by which from the unity arises the multiple, how all this universe comes to be, why the Intellectual-Principle is all and whence it springs, these matters demand another approach.

But on the question as to whether the repulsive and the products of putridity have also their Idea—whether there is an Idea of filth and mud—it is to be observed that all that the Intellectual-Principle derived from The First is of the noblest; in those Ideas the base is not included: these repulsive things point not to the Intellectual-Principle but to the Soul which, drawing upon the Intellectual-Principle, takes from Matter certain other things, and among them these.

But all this will be more clearly brought out when we turn to the problem of the production of multiplicity from unity. Compounds, we shall see—as owing existence to hazard and not to the Intellectual-Principle, having been fused into objects of sense by their own impulse—are not to be included under Ideas.

The products of putrefaction are to be traced to the Soul's inability to bring some other thing to being—something in the order of nature, which, else, it would—but producing where it may.

In the matter of the arts and crafts, all that are to be traced to the needs of human nature are laid up in the Absolute Man.

And before the particular Soul there is another Soul, a universal, and, before that, an Absolute-Soul, which is the Life existing in the Intellectual-Principle before Soul came to be and therefore rightly called (as the Life in the Divine) the Absolute-Soul.

THE THIRD ENNEAD

Eighth Tractate

Nature, Contemplation, and the One

[1. Supposing we played a little before entering upon our serious concern and maintained that all things are striving after Contemplation, looking to Vision as their one end— and this, not merely beings endowed with reason but even the unreasoning animals, the Principle that rules in growing things, and the Earth that produces these—and that all achieve their purpose in the measure possible to their kind, each attaining Vision and possessing itself of the End in its own way and degree, some things in entire reality, others in mimicry and in image—we would scarcely find anyone to endure so strange a thesis. But in a discussion entirely among ourselves there is no risk in a light handling of our own ideas.

Well—in the play of this very moment am I engaged in the act of Contemplation?

Yes; I and all that enter this play are in Contemplation:

our play aims at Vision; and there is every reason to believe that child or man, in sport or earnest, is playing or working only towards Vision, that every act is an effort towards Vision; the compulsory act, which tends rather to bring the Vision down to outward things, and the act thought of as voluntary, less concerned with the outer, originate alike in the effort towards Vision.

The case of Man will be treated later on: let us speak, first, of the earth and of the trees and vegetation in general, asking ourselves what is the nature of Contemplation in them, how we relate to any Contemplative activity the labour and productiveness of the earth, how Nature, held to be devoid of reason and even of conscious representation, can either harbour Contemplation or produce by means of the Contemplation which it does not possess.

[2. There is, obviously, no question here of hands or feet, of any implement borrowed or inherent: Nature needs simply the Matter which it is to work upon and bring under Form; its productivity cannot depend upon mechanical operation. What driving or hoisting goes to produce all that variety of colour and pattern?

The wax-workers, whose methods have been cited as parallel to the creative act of Nature, are unable to make colours; all they can do is to impose upon their handicraft colours taken from elsewhere. None the less there is a parallel which demands attention: in the case of workers in such arts there must be something locked up within themselves, an efficacy not going out from them and yet guiding their hands in all their creation; and this observation should have indicated a similar phenomenon in Nature; it should be clear that this indwelling efficacy, which makes without hands, must exist in Nature, no less than in the craftsman—but, there, as a thing completely inbound. Nature need possess no outgoing force as against that remaining within; the only moved thing is Matter; there can be no moved phase in this Nature-Principle; any such moved phase could not be the primal

mover; this Nature-Principle is no such moved entity; it is
the unmoved Principle operating in the Cosmos.

We may be answered that the Reason-Principle is, no
doubt, unmoved, but that the Nature-Principle, another being, operates by motion.

But, if Nature entire is in question here, it is identical
with the Reason-Principle; and any part of it that is unmoved
is the Reason-Principle. The Nature-Principle must be an
Ideal-Form, not a compound of Form and Matter; there is no
need for it to possess (such a changeable element as) Matter,
hot and cold: the Matter that underlies it, on which it exercises its creative act, brings all that with it, or, natively
without quality, becomes hot and cold, and all the rest, when
brought under Reason: Matter, to become fire, demands the
approach not of fire but of a Reason-Principle.

This is no slight evidence that in the animal and vegetable
realms the Reason-Principles are the makers and that Nature
is a Reason-Principle producing a second Reason-Principle, its
offspring, which, in turn, while itself, still, remaining intact,
communicates something to the underlie, Matter.

The Reason-Principle presiding over visible Shape is the
very ultimate of its order, a dead thing unable to produce
further: that which produces in the created realm is the
living Reason-Principle—brother, no doubt, to that which
gives mere shape, but having life-giving power.

[3. But if this Reason-Principle (Nature) is in act—and
produces by the process indicated—how can it have any part
in Contemplation?

To begin with, since in all its production it is stationary
and intact, a Reason-Principle self-indwelling, it is in its own
nature a Contemplative act. All doing must be guided by an
Idea, and will therefore be distinct from that Idea: the Reason-Principle then, as accompanying and guiding the work,
will be distinct from the work; not being action but Reason-
Principle it is, necessarily, Contemplation. Taking the Reason-Principle, the Logos, in all its phases, the lowest and last

springs from a mental act (in the higher Logos) and is itself a contemplation, though only in the sense of being contemplated (i.e., of being object and not subject), but above it stands the total Logos with its two distinguishable phases, first, that identified not as Nature but as All-Soul and, next, that operating in Nature and being itself the Nature-Principle.

And does this Reason-Principle, Nature, spring from a contemplation?

Wholly and solely.

From self-contemplation, then? Or what are we to think? It derives from a Contemplation and some contemplating Being; how are we to suppose it to have Contemplation itself?

The Contemplation springing from the reasoning faculty —that, I mean, of planning its own content—it does not possess.

But why not, since it is a phase of Life, a Reason-Principle, and a creative Power?

Because to plan for a thing is to lack it: Nature does not lack; it creates because it possesses. Its creative act is simply its possession of its own characteristic Essence; now its Essence, since it is a Reason-Principle, is to be at once an act of contemplation and an object of contemplation. In other words, the Nature-Principle produces by virtue of being an act of contemplation, an object of contemplation, and a Reason-Principle; on this triple character depends its creative efficacy.

Thus the act of production is seen to be in Nature an act of contemplation, for creation is the outcome of a contemplation which never becomes anything else, which never does anything else, but creates by simply being a contemplation.

[4. And Nature, asked why it brings forth its works, might answer if it cared to listen and to speak:

It would have been more becoming to put no question but to learn in silence just as I myself am silent and make no habit of talking. And what is your lesson? This; that whatsoever comes into being is my vision, seen in my silence, the vision that belongs to my character who, sprung from vision, am vision-loving and create vision by the vision-seeing faculty within me. The mathematicians from their vision draw their figures: but I draw nothing: I gaze and the figures of the material world take being as if they fell from my contemplation. As with my Mother (the All-Soul) and the Beings that begot me so it is with me: they are born of a Contemplation and my birth is from them, not by their Act but by their Being; they are the loftier Reason-Principles, they contemplate themselves and I am born.'

Now what does this tell us?

It tells: that what we know as Nature is a Soul, offspring of a yet earlier Soul of more powerful life; that it possesses, therefore, in its repose, a vision within itself; that it has no tendency upward nor even downward but is at peace, steadfast, in its own Essence; that, in this immutability accompanied by what may be called Self-Consciousness, it possesses—within the measure of its possibility—a knowledge of the realm of subsequent things perceived in virtue of that understanding and consciousness; and, achieving thus a resplenddent and delicious spectacle, has no further aim.

Of course, while it may be convenient to speak of 'understanding' or 'perception' in the Nature-Principle, this is not in the full sense applicable to other beings; we are applying to sleep a word borrowed from the wake.

For the Vision on which Nature broods, inactive, is a self-intuition, a spectacle laid before it by virtue of its unaccompanied self-concentration and by the fact that in itself it belongs to the order of intuition. It is a Vision silent but somewhat blurred, for there exists another, a clearer, of which Nature is the image: hence all that Nature produces is weak; the weaker act of intuition produces the weaker object.

In the same way, human beings, when weak on the side of contemplation, find in action their trace of vision and of reason: their spiritual feebleness unfits them for contemplation; they are left with a void, because they cannot adequately seize the vision; yet they long for it; they are hurried into action as their way to the vision which they cannot attain by intellection. They act from the desire of seeing their action, and of making it visible and sensible to others when the result shall prove fairly well equal to the plan. Everywhere, doing and making will be found to be either an attenuation or a complement of vision—attenuation if the doer was aiming only at the thing done; complement if he is to possess something nobler to gaze upon than the mere work produced.

Given the power to contemplate the Authentic, who would run, of choice, after its image?

The relation of action to contemplation is indicated in the way duller children, inapt to study and speculation, take to crafts and manual labour.

[5. This discussion of Nature has shown us how the origin of things is a Contemplation: we may now take the matter up to the higher Soul; we find that the Contemplation pursued by this, its instinct towards knowing and inquiring, the birth pangs set up by the knowledge it attains, its teeming fullness, have caused it—in itself all one object of Vision—to produce another Vision (that of the Cosmos): it is just as a given science, complete in itself, becomes the source and cause of what might be called a minor science in the student who attains to some partial knowledge of all its divisions. But the visible objects and the objects of intellectual contemplation of this later creation are dim and helpless by the side of the content of the Soul.

The primal phase of the Soul—inhabitant of the Supreme and, by its participation in the Supreme, filled and illuminated—remains unchangeably There; but in virtue of that first participation, that of the primal participant, a secondary phase also participates in the Supreme, and this secondary goes forth ceaselessly as Life streaming from Life; for energy runs through the Universe and there is no extremity at which it dwindles out. But, travel as far as it may, it never draws that first part of itself from the place whence the outgoing began: for if it abandoned its prior (the Intellectual-Principle), it would no longer be everywhere (its continuous Being would be broken and) it would be present at the end, only, of its course.

None the less that which goes forth cannot be equal to that which remains.

In sum, then:

The Soul is to extend throughout the Universe, no spot void of its energy: but, a prior is always different from its secondary, and energy is a secondary, rising as it must from contemplation or act; act, however, is not at this stage existent since it depends upon contemplation: therefore the Soul while its phases differ must, in all of them, remain a contemplation, and what seems to be an act done under contemplation must be in reality that weakened contemplation of which we have spoken: the engendered must respect the Kind, but in weaker form, dwindled in the descent.

All goes softly since nothing here demands the parade of thought or act upon external things: it is a Soul in vision and, by this vision, creating its own subsequent—this Principle (of Nature), itself also contemplative but in the feebler degree since it lies further away and cannot reproduce the quality or experiences of its prior—a Vision creates the Vision.

(Such creative contemplation is not inexplicable) for no limit exists either to contemplation or to its possible objects, and this explains how the Soul's creation is everywhere: where can this thing fail to be, which is one identical thing in every soul? Vision is not cabined within the bournes of magnitude.

This, of course, does not mean that the Soul is present at the same strength in each and every place and thing—any more than that it is at the same strength in each of its own phases.

The Charioteer (the Leading Principle of the Soul, in the Phaedrus Myth) gives the two horses (its two dissonant faculties) what he has seen and they, taking that gift, showed that they were hungry for what made that vision; there was something lacking to them: if in their desire they acted, their action aimed at what they craved for—and that was vision, and an object of vision.

[6. Action, thus, is set towards contemplation and an object of contemplation, so that even those whose life is in doing have seeing as their object; what they have not been able to achieve by the direct path, they hope to come at by the circuit.

Further: suppose they succeed; they desired a certain thing to come about, not in order to be unaware of it but to know it, to see it present before the mind: their success is the laying up of a vision. We act for the sake of some good; this means not for something to remain outside ourselves, not in order that we may possess nothing but that we may hold the good of the action. And hold it, where? Where but in the mind?

Thus once more, action is brought back to contemplation: for (mind or) Soul is a Reason-Principle and anything that one lays up in the Soul can be no other than a Reason-Principle, a silent thing, the more certainly such a principle as the impression made is the deeper.

This vision achieved, the acting instinct pauses; the mind is satisfied and seeks nothing further; the contemplation, in one so conditioned, remains absorbed within as having acquired certainty to rest upon. The brighter the certainty, the more tranquil is the contemplation as having acquired the more perfect unity; and—for now we come to the serious treatment of the subject—

In proportion to the truth with which the knowing faculty knows, it comes to identification with the object of its knowledge.

As long as duality persists, the two lie apart, parallel as it were to each other; there is a pair in which the two elements remain strange to one another, as when Ideal-Principles laid up in the mind or Soul remain idle.

Hence the Idea must not be left to lie outside but must be made one identical thing with the Soul of the novice so that he finds it really his own.

The Soul, once domiciled within that Idea and brought to likeness with it, becomes productive, active; what it always held by its primary nature it now grasps with knowledge and applies in deed, so becoming, as it were, a new thing and, informed as it now is by the purely intellectual, it sees (in its outgoing act) as a stranger looking upon a strange world. It was, no doubt, essentially a Reason-Principle, even an Intellectual-Principle; but its function is to see a (lower) realm which these do not see.

For, it is not a complete thing: it has a lack; it is incomplete in regard to its Prior; yet it, also, has a tranquil vision of what it produces. What it has once brought into being it produces no more, for all its productiveness is determined by this lack: it produces for the purpose of Contemplation, in the desire of knowing all its content: when there is question of practical things it adapts its content to the outside order.

The Soul has a greater content than Nature has and therefore it is more tranquil; it is more nearly complete and therefore more contemplative. It is, however, not perfect, and is all the more eager to penetrate the object of contemplation, and it seeks the vision that comes by observation. It leaves its native realm and busies itself elsewhere; then it returns, and it possesses its vision by means of that phase of itself from which it had parted. The self-indwelling Soul inclines less to such experiences.

The Sage, then, has gone through a process of reasoning

when he expounds his act to others; but in relation to himself he is Vision: such a man is already set, not merely in regard to exterior things but also within himself, towards what is one and at rest: all his faculty and life are inward-bent.

[7. Certain Principles, then, we may take to be established —some self-evident, others brought out by our treatment above:

All the forms of Authentic Existence spring from vision and are a vision. Everything that springs from these Authentic Existences in their vision is an object of vision—manifest to sensation or to true knowledge or to surface-awareness. All act aims at this knowing; all impulse is towards knowledge, all that springs from vision exists to produce Ideal-Form, that is a fresh object of vision, so that universally, as images of their engendering principles, they all produce objects of vision, Ideal-Forms. In the engendering of these existences, imitations of the Authentic, it is made manifest that the creating powers operate not for the sake of creation and action but in order to produce an object of vision. This same vision is the ultimate purpose of all the acts of the mind and, even further downward, of all sensation, since sensation also is an effort towards knowledge; lower still, Nature, producing similarly its subsequent principle, brings into being the vision and Idea that we know in it. It is certain, also, that as the Firsts exist in vision all other things must be straining towards the same condition; the starting-point is, universally, the goal.

When living things reproduce their kind, it is that the Reason-Principles within stir them; the procreative act is the expression of a contemplation, a travail towards the creation of many forms, many objects of contemplation, so that the universe may be filled full with Reason-Principles and that contemplation may be, as nearly as possible, endless: to bring anything into being is to produce an Idea-Form and that again is to enrich the universe with contemplation: all the failures, alike in being and in doing, are but the swerving of visionaries from the object of vision: in the end the sor-

riest craftsman is still a maker of forms, ungracefully. So
Love, too, is vision with the pursuit of Ideal-Form.

[8. From this basis we proceed:

In the advancing stages of Contemplation rising from that
in Nature, to that in the Soul and thence again to that in the
Intellectual-Principle itself, the object contemplated becomes
progressively a more and more intimate possession of the Contemplating Beings, more and more one thing with them; and
in the advanced Soul the objects of knowledge, well on the
way towards the Intellectual-Principle, are close to identity
with their container.

Hence we may conclude that, in the Intellectual-Principle
itself, there is complete identity of Knower and Known, and
this not by way of domiciliation, as in the case of even the
highest soul, but by Essence, by the fact that, there, no distinction exists between Being and Knowing; we cannot stop at
a principle containing separate parts; there must always be a
yet higher, a principle above all such diversity.

The Supreme must be an entity in which the two are one;
it will, therefore, be a Seeing that lives, not an object of vision like things existing in something other than themselves:
what exists in an outside element owes its life to that element; it is not self-living.

If, therefore, the pure object of Intellection or Contemplation is to have life, it must be Life Absolute and distinct
from the vegetative or sensitive life or any other life determined by Soul.

In a certain sense no doubt all lives are thoughts—but
qualified as thought vegetative, thought sensitive, and thought
psychic.

What, then, makes them thoughts?

The fact that they are Reason-Principles. Every life is
some form of thought, but of a dwindling clearness like the
degrees of life itself. The first and clearest Life and the first
Intelligence are one Being. The First Life, then, is an Intellection and the next form of Life is the next Intellection and

the last form of Life is the last form of Intellection. Thus every Life is of this order; it is an Intellection.

But while men may recognize grades in life they reject grades in thought; to them there are thoughts (full and perfect) and anything else is no thought.

This is simply because they do not seek to establish what Life is.

The essential is to observe that, here again, all reasoning shows that whatever exists is a bye-work of visioning: if, then, the truest Life is such by virtue of an Intellection and is identical with the truest Intellection, then the truest Intellection is a living being; Contemplation and its object constitute a living thing, a Life, two inextricably one.

The duality, thus, is a unity; but how is this unity also a plurality?

The explanation is that in a unity there can be no seeing (a pure unity has no room for vision and an object); and in its Contemplation the One is not acting as a Unity; if it were, the Intellectual-Principle cannot exist. The Highest began as a unity but did not remain as it began; all unknown to itself, it became manifold; it grew, as it were, pregnant: desiring universal possession, it flung itself outward, though it were better had it never known the desire by which a Secondary came into being: it is like a Circle (in the Idea) which in projection becomes a figure, a surface, a circumference, a centre, a system of radii, of upper and lower segments. The Whence is the better; the Whither is less good: the Whither is not of the quality of the Whence-and-Whither, and the Whence-and-Whither is not of the quality of the Whence alone.

The Intellectual-Principle on the other hand was never merely the Principle of an inviolable unity; it was a universal as well and, being so, was the Intellectual-Principle of all things. Being, thus, all things and the Principle of all, it must be such that every part of it is universal, is all things: otherwise, it contains a part which is not Intellectual-Principle; it will be a juxtaposition of non-Intellectuals, a huddled heap waiting to be made over from the mass of things into the Intellectual-Principle!

We conclude that this Being is limitless and that in all the outflow from it there is no lessening, either in its emanation, since this also is the entire universe, nor in itself, the starting point, since it is no assemblage of parts (to be diminished by any outgo).

[9. Clearly a Being of this nature is not the primal existent; there must exist that which transcends it, that Being (the Absolute), to which all our discussion has been leading.

In the first place, Plurality is later than Unity. The Intellectual-Principle is a number (= the expression of a plurality); and number derives from unity: the source of a number such as this must be the authentically One. Further, it is the sum of an Intellectual-Being with the object of its Intellection, so that it is a duality; and, given this duality, we must find what exists before it.

What is this?

The Intellectual-Principle taken separately, perhaps?

No: an Intellect is always inseparable from an intelligible object; eliminate the intelligible, and the Intellectual-Principle disappears with it. If, then, what we are seeking cannot be the Intellectual-Principle but must be something that rejects the duality there present, then the Prior demanded by that duality must be something on the further side of the Intellectual-Principle.

But might it not be the Intelligible object itself?

No: for the Intelligible makes an equally inseparable duality with the Intellectual-Principle.

If, then, neither the Intellectual-Principle nor the Intelligible Object can be the First Existent, what is?

Our answer can only be:

The source of both.

What will This be; under what character can we picture It?

(We will be told that) It must be either Intellective or without Intellection: if Intellective it is the Intellectual-Principle; if not, it will be without even knowledge of itself—and then, what is there so august about it?

If we define it as The Good and the wholly simplex, we will, no doubt, be telling the truth, but we will not be giving any certain and lucid account of it as long as we have in mind no entity in which to lodge the conception by which we define it.

Yet: our knowledge of everything else comes by way of our intelligence; our power is that of knowing the intelligible by means of the intelligence: but this Entity transcends all of the intellectual nature; by what direct intuition, then, can it be brought within our grasp?

To this question the answer is that we can know it only in the degree of human faculty: we indicate it by virtue of what in ourselves is like it.

For in us, also, there is something of that Being; nay, nothing, ripe for that participation, can be void of it.

Wherever you be, you have only to range over against this omnipresent Being that in you which is capable of drawing from It, and you have your share in it: imagine a voice sounding over a vast waste of land, and not only over the emptiness alone but over human beings; wherever you be in that great space you have but to listen and you take the voice entire—entire though yet with a difference.

And what do we take when we thus point the Intelligence?

The Intellectual-Principle in us must mount to its origins: essentially a thing facing two ways, it must deliver itself over to those powers within it which tend upward; if it seeks the vision of that Being, it must become something more than Intellect.

For the Intellectual-Principle is the earliest form of Life: it is the Activity presiding over the outflowing of the universal Order—the outflow, that is, of the first moment, not that of the continuous process.

In its character as Life, as emanation, as containing all things in their precise forms and not merely in the agglomerate mass—for this would be to contain them (against its specific character) imperfectly and inarticulately—it must of necessity derive from some other Being, from one that does not emanate but is the Principle of Emanation, of Life, of Intellect, and of the Universe.

For the Universe is not a Principle and Source: it springs from a source, and that source cannot be the All or anything belonging to the All since it is to generate the All, and must be not a plurality but the Source of plurality since universally a begetting power is less complex than the begotten. Thus the Being that has engendered the Intellectual-Principle must be more simplex than the Intellectual-Principle.

We may be told that this engendering Principle is the One-and-All.

But, at that, it must be either each separate entity from among all or it will be all things in the one mass.

Now if it were the massed total of all, it must be of later origin than any of the things of which it is the sum; if it precedes the total, it differs from the things that make up the total and they from it: if it and the total of things consitute a co-existence, it is not a Source. But what we are probing for must be a Source; it must exist before all, that all may be fashioned as sequel to it.

As for the notion that it may be each separate entity of the All, this would make a self-Identity into a what you like, where you like, indifferently, and would, besides, abolish all distinction in things themselves.

Once more we see that this can be no thing among things but must be prior to all things.

[10. And what will such a Principle essentially be?

The potentiality of the Universe: the potentiality whose non-existence would mean the non-existence of all the Universe and even of the Intellectual-Principle which is the primal Life and all Life.

This Principle on the thither side of Life is the cause of Life—for that Manifestation of Life which is the Universe of things is not the First Activity; it is itself poured forth, so to speak, like water from a spring.

Imagine a spring that has no source outside itself; it gives itself to all the rivers, yet is never exhausted by what they take, but remains always integrally as it was; the tides that proceed from it are at one within it before they run their several ways, yet all, in some sense, know beforehand down what channels they will pour their streams.

Or: think of the Life coursing throughout some mighty tree while yet it is the stationary Principle of the whole, in no sense scattered over all that extent but, as it were, vested in the root: it is the giver of the entire and manifold life of the tree, but remains unmoved itself, not manifold but the Principle of that manifold life.

And this surprises no one: though it is in fact astonishing how all that varied vitality springs from the unvarying, and how that very manifoldness could not be unless before the multiplicity there were something all singleness; for, the Principle is not broken into parts to make the total; on the contrary, such partition would destroy both; nothing would come into being if its cause, thus broken up, changed character.

Thus we are always brought back to The One.

Every particular thing has a One of its own to which it may be traced; the All has its One, its Prior but not yet the Absolute One; through this we reach that Absolute One, where all such reference comes to an end.

Now when we reach a One—the stationary Principle—in the tree, in the animal, in Soul, in the All—we have in every case the most powerful, the precious element: when we come to the One in the Authentically Existent Beings—their Principle and source and potentiality—shall we lose confidence and suspect it of being—nothing?

Certainly this Absolute is none of the things of which it is the source—its nature is that nothing can be affirmed of it—not existence, not essence, not life—since it is That which transcends all these. But possess yourself of it by the very elimination of Being and you hold a marvel. Thrusting forward to This, attaining, and resting in yourself, seek to grasp it more and more—understanding it by that intuitive thrust alone, but knowing its greatness by the Beings that follow upon it and exist by its power.

[11. Another approach:

The Intellectual-Principle is a Seeing, and a Seeing which itself sees; therefore it is a potentiality which has become effective.

This implies the distinction of Matter and Form in it—as there must be in all actual seeing—the Matter in this case being the Intelligibles which the Intellectual-Principle contains and sees. All actual seeing implies duality; before the seeing takes place there is the pure unity (of the power of seeing). That unity (of principle) acquires duality (in the act of seeing), and the duality is (always to be traced back to) a unity.

Now as our sight requires the world of sense for its satisfaction and realization, so the vision in the Intellectual-Principle demands, for its completion, The Good.

It cannot be, itself, The Good, since then it would not need to see or to perform any other Act; for The Good is the centre of all else, and it is by means of The Good that every thing has Act, while The Good is in need of nothing and therefore possesses nothing beyond itself.

Once you have uttered 'The Good,' add no further thought: by any addition, and in proportion to that addition, you introduce a deficiency.

Do not even say that it has Intellection; you would be dividing it; it would become a duality, Intellect and The Good. The Good has no need of the Intellectual-Principle which, on the contrary, needs it, and attaining it, is shaped into Goodness and becomes perfect by it: the Form thus received, sprung from The Good, brings it to likeness with The Good.

Thus the traces of The Good discerned upon it must be taken as indication of the nature of that Archetype: we form a conception of its true character from its image playing upon the Intellectual-Principle. This image of itself it has communicated to the Intellect that contemplates it: thus all the striving is on the side of the Intellect, which is the eternal striver and eternally the attainer. The Being beyond neither strives, since it feels no lack, nor attains, since it has no striving. And this marks it off from the Intellectual-Principle, to which characteristically belongs the striving, the concentrated strain towards its Form.

Yet: The Intellectual-Principle; beautiful; the most beautiful of all; lying lapped in pure light and in clear radiance; circumscribing the Nature of the Authentic Existents; the original of which this beautiful world is a shadow and an image; tranquil in the fullness of glory since in it there is nothing devoid of intellect, nothing dark or out of rule; a living thing in a life of blessedness: this, too, must overwhelm with awe any that has seen it, and penetrated it, to become a unit of its Being.

But: as one that looks up to the heavens and sees the splendour of the stars thinks of the Maker and searches, so whoever has contemplated the Intellectual Universe and known it and wondered for it must search after its Maker too. What Being has raised so noble a fabric? And how? Who has begotten such a child, this Intellectual-Principle, this lovely abundance so abundantly endowed?

The Source of all this cannot be an Intellect; nor can it be an abundant power: it must have been before Intellect and abundance were; these are later and things of lack; abundance had to be made abundant and Intellection needed to know.

These are very near to the un-needing, to that which has no need of knowing, they have abundance and intellection

authentically, as being the first to possess. But, there is That
before them which neither needs nor possesses anything,
since, needing or possessing anything else, it would not be
what it is—The Good.

Eighth Tractate

On the Intellectual Beauty

[1. It is a principle with us that one who has attained to the
vision of the Intellectual Cosmos and grasped the beauty of
the Authentic Intellect will be able also to come to understand the Father and Transcendent of that Divine Being. It
concerns us, then, to try to see and say, for ourselves and as
far as such matters may be told, how the Beauty of the divine Intellect and of the Intellectual Cosmos may be revealed to contemplation.

Let us go to the realm of magnitudes:—suppose two
blocks of stone lying side by side: one is unpatterned, quite
untouched by art; the other has been minutely wrought by
the craftsman's hands into some statue of god or man, a
Grace or a Muse, or if a human being, not a portrait but a
creation in which the sculptor's art has concentrated all loveliness.

Now it must be seen that the stone thus brought under the
artist's hand to the beauty of form is beautiful not as stone—
for so the crude block would be as pleasant—but in virtue of
the Form or Idea introduced by the art. This form is not in
the material; it is in the designer before ever it enters the
stone; and the artificer holds it not by his equipment of eyes
and hands but by his participation in his art. The beauty,
therefore, exists in a far higher state in the art; for it does not
come over integrally into the work; that original beauty is not
transferred; what comes over is a derivative and a minor:

and even that shows itself upon the statue not integrally and with entire realization of intention but only in so far as it has subdued the resistance of the material.

Art, then, creating in the image of its own nature and content, and working by the Idea or Reason-Principle of the beautiful object it is to produce, must itself be beautiful in a far higher and purer degree since it is the seat and source of that beauty, indwelling in the art, which must naturally be more complete than any comeliness of the external. In the degree in which the beauty is diffused by entering into matter, it is so much the weaker than that concentrated in unity; everything that reaches outwards is the less for it, strength less strong, heat less hot, every power less potent, and so beauty less beautiful.

Then again every prime cause must be, within itself, more powerful than its effect can be: the musical does not derive from an unmusical source but from music; and so the art exhibited in the material work derives from an art yet higher.

Still the arts are not to be slighted on the ground that they create by imitation of natural objects; for, to begin with, these natural objects are themselves imitations; then, we must recognize that they give no bare reproduction of the thing seen but go back to the Reason-Principles from which Nature itself derives, and, furthermore, that much of their work is all their own; they are holders of beauty and add where nature is lacking. Thus Pheidias wrought the Zeus upon no model among things of sense but by apprehending what form Zeus must take if he chose to become manifest to sight.

[2. But let us leave the arts and consider those works produced by Nature and admitted to be naturally beautiful which the creations of art are charged with imitating, all reasoning life and unreasoning things alike, but especially the consummate among them, where the moulder and maker has subdued the material and given the form he desired. Now what is the beauty here? It has nothing to do with the blood or the menstrual process: either there is also a colour and form apart from all this or there is nothing unless sheer ugliness or (at best) a bare recipient, as it were the mere Matter of beauty.

Whence shone forth the beauty of Helen, battle-sought; or of all those women like in loveliness to Aphrodite; or of Aphrodite herself; or of any human being that has been perfect in beauty; or of any of these gods manifest to sight, or unseen but carrying what would be beauty if we saw?

In all these is it not the Idea, something of that realm but communicated to the produced from within the producer, just as in works of art, we held, it is communicated from the arts to their creations? Now we can surely not believe that, while the made thing and the Idea thus impressed upon Matter are beautiful, yet the Idea not so alloyed but resting still with the creator—the Idea primal, immaterial, firmly a unity—is not Beauty.

If material extension were in itself the ground of beauty, then the creating principle, being without extension, could not be beautiful: but beauty cannot be made to depend upon magnitude since, whether in a large object or a small, the one Idea equally moves and forms the mind by its inherent power. A further indication is that as long as the object remains outside us we know nothing of it; it affects us by entry; but only as an Idea can it enter through the eyes which are not of scope to take an extended mass: we are, no doubt, simultaneously possessed of the magnitude which, however, we take in not as mass but by an elaboration upon the presented form.

Then again the principle producing the beauty must be, itself, ugly, neutral, or beautiful: ugly, it could not produce the opposite; neutral, why should its product be the one rather than the other? The Nature, then, which creates things so lovely must be itself of a far earlier beauty: we, undisciplined in discernment of the inward, knowing nothing of it, run after the outer, never understanding that it is the inner which stirs us; we are in the case of one who sees his own reflection but not realizing whence it comes goes in pursuit of it.

But that the thing we are pursuing is something different and that the beauty is not in the concrete object is manifest from the beauty there is in matters of study, in conduct and custom; briefly, in soul or mind. And it is precisely here that the greater beauty lies, perceived whenever you look to the wisdom in a man and delight in it, not wasting attention on the face, which may be hideous, but passing all appearance by and catching only at the inner comeliness, the truly personal; if you are still unmoved and cannot acknowledge beauty under such conditions, then looking to your own inner being you will find no beauty to delight you and it will be futile in that state to seek the greater vision, for you will be questing it through the ugly and impure.

This is why such matters are not spoken of to everyone; you, if you are conscious of beauty within, remember.

[3. Thus there is in the Nature-Principle itself an Ideal archetype of the beauty that is found in material forms and, of that archetype again, the still more beautiful archetype in Soul, source of that in Nature. In the proficient soul this is brighter and of more advanced loveliness: adorning the soul and bringing to it a light from that greater light which is Beauty primally, its immediate presence sets the soul reflecting upon the quality of this prior, the archetype which has no such entries, and is present nowhere but remains in itself alone, and thus is not even to be called a Reason-Principle but is the creative source of the very first Reason-Principle which is the Beauty to which Soul serves as Matter.

This prior, then, is the Intellectual-Principle, the veritable, abiding and not fluctuant since not taking intellectual quality from outside itself. By what image, thus, can we represent it? We have nowhere to go but to what is less. Only from itself can we take an image of it; that is, there can be no representation of it, except in the sense that we represent gold by some portion of gold—purified, either actually or mentally, if it be impure—insisting at the same time that this is not the total thing gold, but merely the particular gold of a particular parcel. In the same way we learn in this matter from the purified Intellect in ourselves or, if you like, from the gods and the glory of the Intellect in them.

For assuredly all the gods are august and beautiful in a beauty beyond our speech. And what makes them so? Intellect; and especially Intellect operating within them (the divine sun and stars) to visibility. It is not through the loveliness of their corporeal forms: even those that have body are not gods by that beauty; it is in virtue of Intellect that they, too, are gods, and as gods beautiful. They do not veer between wisdom and folly: in the immunity of Intellect unmoving and pure, they are wise always, all-knowing, taking cognizance not of the human but of their own being and of all that lies within the contemplation of Intellect. Those of them whose dwelling is in the heavens are ever in this meditation—what task prevents them?—and from afar they look, too, into that further heaven by a lifting of the head. The gods belonging to that higher Heaven itself, they whose station is upon it and in it, see and know in virtue of their omnipresence to it. For all There is heaven; earth is heaven, and sea heaven; and animal and plant and man; all is the heavenly content of that heaven: and the gods in it, despising neither men nor anything else that is there where all is of the heavenly order, traverse all that country and all space in peace.

[4. To 'live at ease' is There; and to these divine beings verity is mother and nurse, existence and sustenance; all that is not of process but of authentic being they see, and themselves in all: for all is transparent, nothing dark, nothing resistant; every being is lucid to every other, in breadth and depth; light runs through light. And each of them contains all within itself, and at the same time sees all in every other, so that everywhere there is all, and all is all and each all, and infinite the glory. Each of them is great; the small is great; the sun, There, is all the stars; and every star, again, is all the stars and sun. While some one manner of being is dominant in each, all are mirrored in every other.

Movement There is pure (as self-caused), for the moving principle is not a separate thing to complicate it as it speeds.

So, too, Repose is not troubled, for there is no admixture of the unstable; and the Beauty is all beauty since it is not resident in what is not beautiful. Each There walks upon no alien soil; its place is its essential self; and, as each moves, so to speak, towards what is Above, it is attended by the very ground from which it starts: there is no distinguishing between the Being and the Place; all is Intellect, the Principle and the ground on which it stands, alike. Thus we might think that our visible sky (the ground or place of the stars), lit as it is, produces the light which reaches us from it, though of course this is really produced by the stars (as it were, by the Principles of light alone, not also by the ground as the analogy would require).

In our realm all is part rising from part and nothing can be more than partial; but There each being is an eternal product of a whole and is at once a whole and an individual manifesting as part but, to the keen vision There, known for the whole it is.

The myth of Lynceus seeing into the very deeps of the earth tells us of those eyes in the divine. No weariness overtakes this vision which yet brings no such satiety as would call for its ending; for there never was a void to be filled so that, with the fullness and the attainment of purpose, the sense of sufficiency be induced: nor is there any such incongruity within the divine that one Being There could be repulsive to another: and of course all There are unchangeable. This absence of satisfaction means only a satisfaction leading to no distaste for that which produces it; to see is to look the more, since for them to continue in the contemplation of an

infinite self and of infinite objects is but to acquiesce in the
bidding of their nature.

Life, pure, is never a burden; how then could there be
weariness There where the living is most noble? That very
life is wisdom, not a wisdom built up by reasonings but complete from the beginning, suffering no lack which could set
it inquiring, a wisdom primal, unborrowed, not something
added to the Being, but its very essence. No wisdom, thus, is
greater; this is the authentic knowing, assessor to the divine
Intellect as projected into manifestation simultaneously with
it; thus, in the symbolic saying, Justice is assessor to Zeus.

(Perfect wisdom:) for all the Principles of this order,
dwelling There, are as it were visible images projected from
themselves, so that all becomes an object of contemplation to
contemplators immeasurably blessed. The greatness and
power of the wisdom There we may know from this, that it
embraces all the real Beings, and has made all and all follow
it, and yet that it is itself those beings, which sprang into being with it, so that all is one and the essence There is wisdom.
If we have failed to understand, it is that we have thought of
knowledge as a mass of theorems and an accumulation of
propositions, though that is false even for our sciences of the
sense-realm. But in case this should be questioned, we may
leave our own sciences for the present, and deal with the
knowing in the Supreme at which Plato glances where he
speaks of 'that knowledge which is not a stranger in something strange to it'—though in what sense, he leaves us to
examine and declare, if we boast ourselves worthy of the discussion. This is probably our best starting-point.

[5. All that comes to be, work of nature or of craft, some
wisdom has made: everywhere a wisdom presides at a making.

No doubt the wisdom of the artist may be the guide of the
work; it is sufficient explanation of the wisdom exhibited in
the arts; but the artist himself goes back, after all, to that
wisdom in Nature which is embodied in himself; and this is

not a wisdom built up of theorems but one totality, not a wisdom consisting of manifold detail co-ordinated into a unity but rather a unity working out into detail.

Now, if we could think of this as the primal wisdom, we need look no further, since, at that, we have discovered a principle which is neither a derivative nor a 'stranger in something strange to it.' But if we are told that, while this Reason-Principle is in Nature, yet Nature itself is its source, we ask how Nature came to possess it; and, if Nature derived it from some other source, we ask what that other source may be; if, on the contrary, the principle is self-sprung, we need look no further: but if (as we assume) we are referred to the Intellectual-Principle we must make clear whether the Intellectual-Principle engendered the wisdom: if we learn that it did, we ask whence: if from itself, then inevitably it is itself Wisdom.

The true Wisdom, then (found to be identical with the Intellectual-Principle), is Real Being; and Real Being is Wisdom; it is wisdom that gives value to Real Being; and Being is Real in virtue of its origin in wisdom. It follows that all forms of existence not possessing wisdom are, indeed, Beings in right of the wisdom which went to their forming, but, as not in themselves possessing it, are not Real Beings.

We cannot, therefore, think that the divine Beings of that sphere, or the other supremely blessed There, need look to our apparatus of science: all of that realm (the very Beings themselves), all is noble image, such images as we may conceive to lie within the soul of the wise—but There not as inscription but as authentic existence. The ancients had this in mind when they declared the Ideas (Forms) to be Beings, Essentials.

[6. Similarly, as it seems to me, the wise of Egypt—whether in precise knowledge or by a prompting of nature—indicated the truth where, in their efforts towards philosophical statement, they left aside the writing-forms that take in the detail of words and sentences—those characters that represent sounds and convey the propositions of reasoning—and drew pictures instead, engraving in the temple-inscriptions a separate image for every separate item: thus they exhibited the absence of discursiveness in the Intellectual Realm.

For each manifestation of knowledge and wisdom is a distinct image, an object in itself, an immediate unity, not an aggregate of discursive reasoning and detailed willing. Later from this wisdom in unity there appears, in another form of being, an image, already less compact, which announces the original in terms of discourse and unravels the causes by which things are such that the wonder rises how a generated world can be so excellent.

For, one who knows must declare his wonder that this wisdom, while not itself containing the causes by which Being exists and takes such excellence, yet imparts them to the entities produced according to its canons. This excellence, whose necessity is scarcely or not at all manifest to search, exists, if we could but find it out, before all searching and reasoning.

What I say may be considered in one chief thing, and thence applied to all the particular entities:

[7. Consider the universe: we are agreed that its existence and its nature come to it from beyond itself; are we, now, to imagine that its maker first thought it out in detail—the earth, and its necessary situation in the middle; water and, again, its position as lying upon the earth; all the other elements and objects up to the sky in due place and order; living beings with their appropriate forms as we know them, their inner organs and their outer limbs—and that having thus appointed every item beforehand, he then set about the execution?

Such designing was not even possible; how could the plan for a universe come to one that had never looked outward? Nor could he work on material gathered from elsewhere as our craftsmen do, using hands and tools; feet and hands are of the later order.

One way, only, remains: all things must exist in something else; of that prior—since there is no obstacle, all being continuous within the realm of reality—there has suddenly appeared a sign, an image, whether given forth directly or through the ministry of soul or of some phase of soul matters nothing for the moment: thus the entire aggregate of existence springs from the divine world, in greater beauty There because There unmingled but mingled here.

From the beginning to end all is gripped by the Forms of the Intellectual Realm: Matter itself is held by the Ideas of the elements and to these Ideas are added other Ideas and others again, so that it is hard to work down to crude Matter beneath all that sheathing of Idea. Indeed since Matter itself is, in its degree, an Idea—the lowest—all this universe is Idea and there is nothing that is not Idea as the archetype was. And all is made silently, since nothing had part in the making but Being and Idea—a further reason why creation went without toil. The Exemplar was the Idea of an All and so an All must come into being.

Thus nothing stood in the way of the Idea, and even now it dominates, despite all the clash of things: the creation is not hindered on its way even now; it stands firm in virtue of being All. To me, moreover, it seems that if we ourselves were archetypes, Ideas, veritable Being, and the Idea with which we construct here were our veritable Essence, then our creative power, too, would toillessly effect its purpose: as man now stands, he does not produce in his work a true image of himself: become man, he has ceased to be the All; ceasing to be man—we read—'he soars aloft and administers the Cosmos entire'; restored to the All he is maker of the All.

But—to our immediate purpose—it is possible to give a reason why the earth is set in the midst and why it is round and why the ecliptic runs precisely as it does, but, looking to the creating principle, we cannot say that because this was the way therefore things were so planned: we can say only that because the Exemplar is what it is, therefore the things of this world are good; the causing principle, we might put it, reached the conclusion before all formal reasoning and not from any premises, not by sequence or plan but before either, since all of that order is later, all reason, demonstration, persuasion.

Since there is a Source, all the created must spring from it and in accordance with it; and we are rightly told not to go seeking the causes impelling a Source to produce, especially when this is the perfectly sufficient Source and identical with the Term: a Source which is Source and Term must be the All-Unity, complete in itself.

[8. This then is Beauty primally: it is entire and omnipresent as an entirety; and therefore in none of its parts or members lacking in beauty; beautiful thus beyond denial. Certainly it cannot be anything (be, for example, Beauty) without being wholly that thing; it can be nothing which it is to possess partially or in which it utterly fails (and therefore it must entirely be Beauty entire).

If this principle were not beautiful, what other could be? Its prior does not deign to be beautiful; that which is the first to manifest itself—Form and object of vision to the intellect —cannot but be lovely to see. It is to indicate this that Plato, drawing on something well within our observation, represents the Creator as approving the work he has achieved: the intention is to make us feel the lovable beauty of the archetype and of the Divine Idea; for to admire a representation is to admire the original upon which it was made.

It is not surprising if we fail to recognize what is passing within us: lovers, and those in general that admire beauty here, do not stay to reflect that it is to be traced, as of course it must be, to the Beauty There. That the admiration of the Demiurge is to be referred to the Ideal Exemplar is deliberately made evident by the rest of the passage: 'He admired; and determined to bring the work into still closer likeness with the Exemplar': he makes us feel the magnificent beauty of the Exemplar by telling us that the Beauty sprung from this world is, itself, a copy from That.

And indeed if the divine did not exist, the transcendently beautiful, in a beauty beyond all thought, what could be lovelier than the things we see? Certainly no reproach can rightly be brought against this world save only that it is not That.

[9. Let us, then, make a mental picture of our universe: each member shall remain what it is, distinctly apart; yet all is to form, as far as possible, a complete unity so that whatever comes into view, say the outer orb of the heavens, shall bring immediately with it the vision, on the one plane, of the sun and of all the stars with earth and sea and all living things as if exhibited upon a transparent globe.

Bring this vision actually before your sight, so that there shall be in your mind the gleaming representation of a sphere, a picture holding all the things of the universe moving or in repose or (as in reality) some at rest, some in motion. Keep this sphere before you, and from it imagine another, a sphere stripped of magnitude and of spatial differences; cast out your inborn sense of Matter, taking care not merely to attenuate it: call on God, maker of the sphere whose image you now hold, and pray Him to enter. And may He come bringing His own Universe with all the gods that dwell in it —He who is the one God and all the gods, where each is all, blending into a unity, distinct in powers but all one god in virtue of that one divine power of many facets.

More truly, this is the one God who is all the gods; for, in the coming to be of all those, this, the one, has suffered no diminishing. He and all have one existence, while each again is distinct. It is distinction by state without interval: there is no outward form to set one here and another there and to prevent any from being an entire identity; yet there is no sharing of parts from one to another. Nor is each of those

divine wholes a power in fragment, a power totalling to the
sum of the measurable segments: the divine is one all-power,
reaching out to infinity, powerful to infinity: and so great
is God that his very members are infinites. What place can be
named to which He does not reach?

Great, too, is this firmament of ours and all the powers
constellated within it, but it would be greater still, unspeaka-
bly, but that there is inbound in it something of the petty
power of body; no doubt the powers of fire and other bodily
substances might themselves be thought very great, but in
fact, it is through their failure in the true power that we see
them burning, destroying, wearing things away, and slaving
towards the production of life; they destroy because they are
themselves in process of destruction, and they produce because they belong to the realm of the produced.

The power in that other world has merely Being and
beauty of Being. Beauty without Being could not be, nor Being voided of Beauty: abandoned of Beauty, Being loses
something of its essence. Being is desirable because it is identical with Beauty; and Beauty is loved because it is Being.
How then can we debate which is the cause of the other,
where the nature is one? The very figment of Being needs
some imposed image of Beauty to make it passable, and
even to ensure its existence; it exists to the degree in which it
has taken some share in the beauty of Idea; and the more
deeply it has drawn on this, the less imperfect it is, precisely
because the nature which is essentially the beautiful has
entered into it the more intimately.

[10. This is why Zeus, although the oldest of the gods and
their sovereign, advances first (in the Phaedrus myth) towards that vision, followed by gods and demigods and such
souls as are of strength to see. That Being appears before
them from some unseen place and rising loftily over them
pours its light upon all things, so that all gleams in its
radiance; it upholds some beings, and they see; the lower are

dazzled and turn away, unfit to gaze upon that sun, the trouble falling the more heavily on those most remote.

Of those looking upon that Being and its content, and able to see, all take something but not all the same vision always: intently gazing, one sees the fount and principle of Justice, another is filled with the sight of Moral Wisdom, the original of that quality as found, sometimes at least, among men, copied by them in their degree from the divine virtue which, covering all the expanse, so to speak, of the Intellectual Realm is seen, last attainment of all, by those who have known already many splendid visions.

The gods see, each singly and all as one. So, too, the souls; they see all There in right of being sprung, themselves, of that universe and therefore including all from beginning to end and having their existence There if only by that phase which belongs inherently to the Divine, though often too they are There entire, those of them that have not incurred separation.

This vision Zeus takes and it is for such of us, also, as share his love and appropriate our part in the Beauty There, the final object of all seeing, the entire beauty upon all things; for all There sheds radiance, and floods those that have found their way thither so that they too become beautiful; thus it will often happen that men climbing heights where the soil has taken a yellow glow will themselves appear so, borrowing colour from the place on which they move. The colour flowering on that other height we speak of is Beauty; or rather all There is light and beauty, through and through, for the beauty is no mere bloom upon the surface.

To those that do not see entire, the immediate impression is alone taken into account; but those drunken with this wine, filled with the nectar, all their soul penetrated by this beauty, cannot remain mere gazers: no longer is there a spectator outside gazing on an outside spectacle; the clear-eyed hold the vision within themselves, though, for the most part, they have no idea that it is within but look towards it as to something beyond them and see it as an object of vision caught by a direction of the will.

All that one sees as a spectacle is still external; one must bring the vision within and see no longer in that mode of separation but as we know ourselves; thus a man filled with a god—possessed by Apollo or by one of the Muses—need no longer look outside for his vision of the divine being; it is but finding the strength to see divinity within.

[11. Similarly any one, unable to see himself, but possessed by that God, has but to bring that divine-within before his consciousness and at once he sees an image of himself, himself lifted to a better beauty: now let him ignore that image, lovely though it is, and sink into a perfect self-identity, no such separation remaining; at once he forms a multiple unity with the God silently present; in the degree of his power and will, the two become one; should he turn back to the former duality, still he is pure and remains very near to the God; he has but to look again and the same presence is there.

This conversion brings gain: at the first stage, that of separation, a man is aware of self; but retreating inwards, he becomes possessor of all; he puts sense away behind him in dread of the separated life and becomes one in the Divine; if he plans to see in separation, he sets himself outside.

The novice must hold himself constantly under some image of the Divine Being and seek in the light of a clear conception; knowing thus, in a deep conviction, whither he is going—into what a sublimity he penetrates—he must give himself forthwith to the inner and, radiant with the Divine Intellections (with which he is now one), be no longer the seer, but, as that place has made him, the seen.

Still, we will be told, one cannot be in beauty and yet fail to see it. The very contrary: to see the divine as something external is to be outside of it; to become it is to be most truly in beauty: since sight deals with the external, there can here be no vision unless in the sense of identification with the object.

And this identification amounts to a self-knowing, a self-consciousness, guarded by the fear of losing the self in the desire of a too wide awareness.

It must be remembered that sensations of the ugly and evil impress us more violently than those of what is agreeable and yet leave less knowledge as the residue of the shock: sickness makes the rougher mark, but health, tranquilly present, explains itself better; it takes the first place, it is the natural thing, it belongs to our being; illness is alien, unnatural, and thus makes itself felt by its very incongruity, while the other conditions are native and we take no notice. Such being our nature, we are most completely aware of ourselves when we are most completely identified with the object of our knowledge.

This is why in that other sphere, when we are deepest in that knowledge by intellection, we are aware of none; we are expecting some impression on sense, which has nothing to report since it has seen nothing and never could in that order see anything. The unbelieving element is sense; it is the other, the Intellectual-Principle, that sees; and if this too doubted, it could not even credit its own existence, for it can never stand away and with bodily eyes apprehend itself as a visible object.

[12. We have told how this vision is to be procured, whether by the mode of separation or in identity: now, seen in either way, what does it give to report?

The vision has been of God in travail of a beautiful offspring, God engendering a universe within himself in a painless labour and—rejoiced in what he has brought into being, proud of his children—keeping all closely by Him, for the pleasure He has in his radiance and in theirs.

Of this offspring—all beautiful, but most beautiful those that have remained within—only one has become manifest without; from him (Zeus, sovran over the visible universe), the youngest born, we may gather, as from some image, the greatness of the Father and of the Brothers that remain within the Father's house.

Still the manifested God cannot think that he has come forth in vain from the father; for through him another universe has arisen, beautiful as the image of beauty, and it could not be lawful that Beauty and Being should fail of a beautiful image.

This second Cosmos at every point copies the archetype: it has life and being in copy, and has beauty as springing from that diviner world. In its character of image it holds, too, that divine perpetuity without which it would only at times be truly representative and sometimes fail like a construction of art; for every image whose existence lies in the nature of things must stand during the entire existence of the archetype.

Hence it is false to put an end to the visible sphere as long as the Intellectual endures, or to found it upon a decision taken by its maker at some given moment.

That teaching shirks the penetration of such a making as is here involved: it fails to see that as long as the Supreme is radiant there can be no failing of its sequel but, that existing, all exists. And—since the necessity of conveying our meaning compels such terms—the Supreme has existed for ever and for ever will exist.

[13. The God fettered (as in the Kronos Myth) to an unchanging identity leaves the ordering of this universe to his son (to Zeus), for it could not be in his character to neglect his rule within the divine sphere, and, as though sated with the Authentic-Beauty, seek a lordship too recent and too poor for his might. Ignoring this lower world, Kronos (Intellectual-Principle) claims for himself his own father (Ouranos, the Absolute, or One) with all the upward-tending between them: and he counts all that tends to the inferior, beginning from his son (Zeus, the All-Soul), as ranking beneath him. Thus he holds a mid-position determined on the one side by the differentiation implied in the severance from the very highest and, on the other, by that which keeps him apart from the link between himself and the lower: he stands between a greater father and an inferior son. But since that father is too lofty to be thought of under the name of Beauty, the second God remains the primally beautiful.

Soul also has beauty, but is less beautiful than Intellect as being its image and therefore, though beautiful in nature, taking increase of beauty by looking to that original. Since then the All-Soul—to use the more familiar term—since Aphrodite herself is so beautiful, what name can we give to that other? If Soul is so lovely in its own right, of what quality must that prior be? And since its being is derived, what must that power be from which the Soul takes the double beauty, the borrowed and the inherent?

We ourselves possess beauty when we are true to our own being; our ugliness is in going over to another order; our self-knowledge, that is to say, is our beauty; in self-ignorance we are ugly.

Thus beauty is of the Divine and comes Thence only.

Do these considerations suffice to a clear understanding of the Intellectual Sphere or must we make yet another attempt by another road?

SUGGESTED READINGS

There is a complete English translation of Plotinus' writings by K. S. Guthrie, but the best translation, far and away, is still that of Stephen MacKenna.

The best account of Plotinus is given by Thomas Whittaker in his classic *The Neoplatonists*, ch. iv, v, and vi. An illuminating study is "The Logic of Mysticism in Plotinus," by I. Edman, which has been published in *Columbia Studies in the History of Ideas*, vol. II. W. R. Inge's two-volume work, *The Philosophy of Plotinus*, is interesting and suggestive. B. A. G. Fuller's *The Problem of Evil in*

Plotinus is helpful; and E. Bréhier's little gem of a book, *The Philosophy of Plotinus*, is now available in English in a translation by J. Thomas.

On Neoplatonism in general, Thomas Whittaker's *The Neoplatonists* is about the best work available in English.

There is a brief but suggestive interpretation offered in the appendix on Neoplatonism in vol. I of A. Harnack's *History of Dogma*. Charles Bigg's *Neoplatonism* is short, readable, and valuable. See also J. Katz, *Plotinus' Search for the Good*, an instructive book, well worth reading.

APPENDIX

CICERO

INTRODUCTION

Marcus Tullius Cicero (106-43 B.C.) is one of history's great transmitters of culture. Lawyer, orator, politician, statesman, and reluctant witness to the decay of the Roman Republic, he spent his last two years in an involuntary retirement from public life. But he was not idle. During that brief time he produced nearly all of his many writings on philosophy, including the two works excerpted below. His aim was to make accessible to his Roman countrymen the wisdom of Greece, which lay buried in untranslated—and many said, untranslatable—treatises. To do this he had to create ex nihilo a philosophic vocabulary for the Latin language. His success may be measured by the fact that, whereas the works on which he depended are lost, his have survived, to remain an important influence down to our own generation.

He made no pretension to originality. He proclaimed himself an adherent of the Academy, a Skeptic. But this was an allegiance of the head only, not of the heart. He made use of the freedom which the Academic brand of skepticism gave him to espouse the Stoic doctrines as the more reasonable, or probable. Thus, in his treatise on moral duty, The Offices, he undertakes to explain and defend the ethical views of the Stoic, Panaetius. In his treatise On the Nature of the Gods, he expounds, through the characters of Velleius and Balbus, the theologies of the Epicureans and the Stoics. But though both of these views are subjected to the powerful criticism of the Skeptic Cotta—who seems to emerge victorious—Cicero concludes that the Stoic view strikes him as being more like the truth. Whatever Cicero's own philosophic opinions may have been, however, the former work is nonetheless an important source for our knowledge of Panaetius, and the latter work for our knowledge of Posidonius, who speaks through Balbus, and Carneades, who speaks through Cotta.

CICERO

ON THE NATURE OF THE GODS*

Book I

I propose to lay before you the opinions of various philosophers concerning the nature of the Gods; by which means all men may judge which of them are consistent with truth; and if all agree together, or if any one shall be found to have discovered what may be absolutely called truth, I will then give up the Academy as vain and arrogant. So I may cry out, in the words of Statius, in the Synephebi,—

"Ye gods, I call upon, require, pray, beseech, entreat, and implore the attention of my countrymen all, both young and old"; . . . that they may attend, know, and consider what

* Revision by C. D. Yonge of a translation usually ascribed to Benjamin Franklin.

sentiments they ought to preserve concerning religion, piety, sanctity, ceremonies, faith, oaths, temples, shrines, and solemn sacrifices; what they ought to think of the auspices, . . . for all these have relation to the present question. The manifest disagreement among the most learned on this subject creates doubts in those who imagine they have some certain knowledge of the subject.

Which fact I have often taken notice of elsewhere, and I did so more especially at the discussion that was held at my friend C. Cotta's, concerning the immortal Gods, and which was carried on with the greatest care, accuracy, and precision; for coming to him at the time of the Latin holidays, according to his own invitation and message from him, I found him sitting in his study, and in a discourse with C. Velleius the senator, who was then reputed by the Epicureans the ablest of our countrymen. Q. Lucilius Balbus was likewise there, a great proficient in the doctrine of the Stoics, and esteemed equal to the most eminent of the Greeks in that part of knowledge. As soon as Cotta saw me, he said, You are come very seasonably; for I am having a dispute with Velleius on an important subject, which, considering the nature of your studies, is not improper for you to join in . . . we were discoursing on the nature of the Gods; concerning which, as it is a subject that always appeared very obscure to me, I prevailed on Velleius to give us the sentiments of Epicurus. Therefore, he continued, if it is not troublesome, Velleius, repeat what you have already stated to us. I will, he said; though this new comer will be no advocate for me, but for you; for you have both, he added, with a smile, learned from the same Philo to be certain of nothing. What we have learned from him, replied I, Cotta will discover; but I would not have you think I am come as an assistant to him, but as an auditor, with an impartial and unbiased mind, and not bound by any obligation to defend any particular principle, whether I like or dislike it.

After this Velleius, with the confidence peculiar to his sect, dreading nothing so much as to seem to doubt of anything, began as if he had just then descended from the council of the Gods, and Epicurus's intervals of worlds. Do not attend, he said, to these idle and imaginary tales; nor to the operator and builder of the World, the God of Plato's Timæus; nor to the old prophetic dame, the Πρόνοια of the Stoics, which the Latins call Providence; nor to that round, that burning, revolving deity, the World, endowed with sense and understanding; the prodigies and wonders, not of inquisitive philosophers, but of dreamers!

For with what eyes of the mind was your Plato able to see that workhouse of such stupendous toil, in which he makes the world to be modelled and built by God? What materials, what tools, what bars, what machines, what servants, were employed in so vast a work? How could the air, fire, water, and earth, pay obedience and submit to the will of the architect? . . .

But, what is most remarkable, he gives us a world, which has been not only created, but, if I may so say, in a manner formed with hands, and yet he says it is eternal. Do you conceive him to have the least skill in natural philosophy who is capable of thinking anything to be everlasting that had a beginning? For what can possibly ever have been put together which cannot be dissolved again? Or what is there that had a beginning which will not have an end? If your Providence, Lucilius, is the same as Plato's God, I ask you, as before, who were the assistants, what were the engines, what was the plan and preparation of the whole work? If it is not the same, then why did she make the world mortal, and not everlasting, like Plato's God?

But I would demand of you both, why these world-builders started up so suddenly, and lay dormant for so many ages? For we are not to conclude, that if there was no world there were therefore no ages. I do not now speak of such ages as are finished by a certain number of days and nights in annual courses; for I acknowledge that those could not be without the revolution of the world; but there was a certain eternity from infinite time, not measured by any circumscription of seasons; but how that was in space we cannot understand, because we cannot possibly have even the slightest idea of time before time was. I desire, therefore, to know, Balbus, why this Providence of yours was idle for such an immense space of time? Did she avoid labour? But that could have no effect on the Deity; nor could there be any labour, since all nature, air, fire, earth, and water, would obey the divine essence. What was it that incited the Deity to act the part of an ædile, to illuminate and decorate the world? If it was in order that God might be the better accommodated in his habitation, then he must have been dwelling an infinite length of time before in darkness as in a dungeon. But do we imagine that he was afterwards delighted with that variety with which we see the heaven and earth adorned? What entertainment could that be to the Deity? If it was any, he would not have been without it so long.

Or were these things made, as you almost assert, by God, for the sake of men? Was it for the wise? If so, then this great design was adopted for the sake of a very small number. Or for the sake of fools? First of all, there was no reason why God should consult the advantage of the wicked; and, further, what could be his object in doing so, since all fools are, without doubt, the most miserable of men, chiefly because they are fools? For what can we pronounce more deplorable than folly? Besides, there are many inconveniences in life which the wise can learn to think lightly of, by dwelling rather on the advantages which they receive; but which fools are unable to avoid when they are coming, or to bear when they are come. . . .

Now whoever reflects on the rashness and absurdity of these tenets, must inevitably entertain the highest respect and veneration for Epicurus, and perhaps even rank him in the number of those beings who are the subject of this dispute; for he alone first founded the idea of the existence of the

Gods on the impression which nature herself hath made on the minds of all men. For what nation, what people are there, who have not, without any learning, a natural idea, or prenotion of a Deity? Epicurus calls this πρόληψις; that is, an antecedent conception of the fact in the mind, without which nothing can be understood, inquired after, or discoursed on. . . .

Here, then, you see the foundation of this question clearly laid; for since it is the constant and universal opinion of mankind, independent of education, custom, or law, that there are Gods, it must necessarily follow that this knowledge is implanted in our minds, or rather innate in us. That opinion respecting which there is a general agreement in universal nature, must infallibly be true; therefore it must be allowed that there are Gods; for in this we have the concurrence, not only of almost all philosophers, but likewise of the ignorant and illiterate. . . . On the same principle of reasoning we think that the Gods are happy and immortal; for that nature, which hath assured us that there are Gods, has likewise imprinted in our minds the knowledge of their immortality and felicity; and if so, what Epicurus hath declared in these words, is true: "That which is eternally happy, cannot be burdened with any labour itself, nor can it impose any labour on another; nor can it be influenced by resentment or favour; because things which are liable to such feelings must be weak and frail." We have said enough to prove that we should worship the Gods with piety, and without superstition, if that were the only question.

For the superior and excellent nature of the Gods requires a pious adoration from men, because it is possessed of immortality and the most exalted felicity; for whatever excels has a right to veneration; and all fear of the power and anger of the Gods should be banished; for we must understand that anger and affection are inconsistent with the nature of a happy and immortal being. These apprehensions being removed, no dread of the superior powers remains. . . .

With regard to the Deity's form, we are directed partly by nature, and partly by reason. All men are told by nature that none but a human form can be ascribed to the Gods; for under what other image did it ever appear to any one either sleeping or waking? and without having recourse to our first notions, reason itself declares the same; for as it is easy to conceive that the most excellent nature, either because of its happiness or immortality, should be the most beautiful, what composition of limbs, what conformation of lineaments, what form, what aspect, can be more beautiful than the human? . . . Besides, the Gods are granted to be perfectly happy; and nobody can be happy without virtue, nor can virtue exist where reason is not; and reason can reside in none but the human form; the Gods, therefore, must be acknowledged to be of human form; yet that form is not body, but something like body; nor does it contain any blood, but something like blood. Though these distinctions were more acutely devised and more artfully expressed by Epicurus than any common capacity can comprehend; yet, relying on your understanding, I shall be more brief on the subject than otherwise I should be. Epicurus, who not only discovered and understood the occult and almost hidden secrets of nature, but explained them with ease, teaches that the power and nature of the Gods is not to be discerned by the senses, but by the mind; nor are they to be considered as bodies of any solidity, or reduceable to number, like those things which, because of their firmness, he calls Στερέμνια; but as images, perceived by similitude and transition. As infinite kinds of those images result from innumerable individuals, and centre in the Gods, our minds and understanding are directed towards and fixed with the greatest delight on them, in order to comprehend what that happy and eternal essence is. . . . Your sect, Balbus, frequently ask us how the Gods live, and how they pass their time? Their life is the most happy, and the most abounding with all kinds of blessings, which can be conceived. They do nothing. They are embarrassed with no business; nor do they perform any work. They rejoice in the possession of their own wisdom and virtue. They are satisfied that they shall ever enjoy the fulness of eternal pleasures.

Such a Deity may properly be called happy; but yours is a most laborious God. For let us suppose the world a Deity;— what can be a more uneasy state than, without the least cessation, to be whirled about the axle-tree of heaven with a surprising celerity? But nothing can be happy that is not at ease. Or let us suppose a Deity residing in the world, who directs and governs it, who preserves the courses of the stars, the changes of the seasons, and the vicissitudes and orders of things, surveying the earth and the sea, and accommodating them to the advantage and necessities of man. Truly this Deity is embarrassed with a very troublesome and laborious office. We make a happy life to consist in a tranquillity of mind, a perfect freedom from care, and an exemption from all employment. The philosopher, from whom we received all our knowledge, has taught us that the world was made by nature; that there was no occasion for a work-house to frame it in; and that, though you deny the possibility of such a work without divine skill, it is so easy to her, that she has made, does make, and will make innumerable worlds. But, because you do not conceive that nature is able to produce such effects without some rational aid, you are forced, like the tragic poets, when you cannot wind up your argument in any other way, to have recourse to a Deity, whose assistance you would not seek, if you could view that vast and unbounded magnitude of regions in all parts; where the mind, extending and spreading itself, travels so far and wide that it can find no end, no extremity to stop at. In this immensity of breadth, length, and height, a most boundless company of innumerable atoms are fluttering about, which, notwithstanding the interposition of a void space, meet and cohere, and continue clinging to one another; and by this union these modifications and forms of things arise, which, in your opinions, could not possibly be made without the help of bellows and anvils. Thus you have imposed on us an eternal master, whom we must dread day and night. For who can be free from fear of a Deity, who foresees, regards, and takes notice of everything; one who thinks all things his own: a curious, ever-busy God?

Hence first arose your Εἱμαρμένη, as you call it, your fatal necessity; so that, whatever happens, you affirm that it flows from an eternal chain and continuance of causes. Of what value is this philosophy, which, like old women and illiterate men, attributes everything to fate? Then follows your Μαντική, in Latin called *divinatio*, divination; which, if we would listen to you, would plunge us into such superstition, that we should fall down and worship your inspectors into sacrifices, your augurs, your soothsayers, your prophets, and your fortune-tellers.

Epicurus having freed us from these terrors and restored us to liberty, we have no dread of those beings, whom we have reason to think entirely free from all trouble themselves, and who do not impose any on others. We pay our adoration, indeed, with piety and reverence to that essence, which is above all excellence and perfection. But I fear my zeal for this doctrine has made me too prolix. However, I could not easily leave so eminent and important a subject unfinished, though I must confess I should rather endeavour to hear than speak so long.

Cotta, with his usual courtesy, then began. Velleius, he said, were it not for something which you have advanced, I should have remained silent; for I have often observed, as I did just now upon hearing you, that I cannot so easily conceive why a proposition is true, as why it is false. Should you ask me what I take the nature of the Gods to be, I should perhaps make no answer. But if you should ask whether I think it to be of that nature which you have described, I should answer that I was as far as possible from agreeing with you. . . .

If you should ask me what God is, or what his character

and nature are, I should follow the example of Simonides; who, when Hiero the tyrant proposed the same question to him, desired a day to consider of it. When he required his answer the next day, Simonides begged two days more; and as he kept constantly desiring double the number which he had required before instead of giving his answer, Hiero, with surprise, asked him his meaning in doing so: "Because," he said, "the longer I meditate on it, the more obscure it appears to me." Simonides, who was not only a delightful poet, but reputed a wise and learned man in other branches of knowledge, found, I suppose, so many acute and refined arguments occurring to him, that he was doubtful which was the truest, and therefore despaired of discovering any truth.

But does your Epicurus (for I had rather contend with him than with you,) say anything that is worthy the name of philosophy, or even of common sense?

In the question, concerning the nature of the Gods, his first inquiry is, whether there are Gods or not. It would be dangerous, I believe, to take the negative side before a public auditory; but it is very safe in a discourse of this kind, and in this company. I, who am a priest, and who think that religions and ceremonies ought sacredly to be maintained, am certainly desirous to have the existence of the Gods, which is the principal point in debate, not only fixed in opinion, but proved to a demonstration; for many notions flow into and disturb the mind, which sometimes seem to convince us that there are none. But see how candidly I will behave to you: as I shall not touch upon those tenets you hold in common with other philosophers, consequently I shall not dispute the existence of the Gods, for that doctrine is agreeable to almost all men, and to myself in particular; but I am still at liberty to find fault with the reasons you give for it, which I think are very insufficient.

You have said that the general assent of men of all nations and all degrees, is an argument strong enough to induce us to acknowledge the being of the Gods. This is not only a weak, but a false argument; for, first of all, how do you know the opinions of all nations? I really believe there are many people so savage that they have no thoughts of a Deity. What think you of Diagoras, who was called the atheist; and of Theodorus, after him? Did not they plainly deny the very essence of a Deity? Protagoras, of Abdera, whom you just now mentioned, the greatest sophist of his age, was banished by order of the Athenians from their city and territories, and his books were publicly burnt, because these words were in the beginning of his treatise concerning the Gods, "I am unable to arrive at any knowledge whether there are, or are not, any Gods." This treatment of him, I imagine, restrained many from professing their disbelief of a Deity; since the doubt of it only could not escape punishment. . . . Your reasoning, therefore, to confirm your assertion is not so conclusive as you think it is. But, as this is the manner in which other philosophers have argued on the same subject, I will take no further notice of it at present; I rather choose to proceed to what is properly your own.

I allow that there are Gods. Instruct me, then, concerning their origin; inform me where they are, what sort of body, what mind they have, and what is their course of life; for these I am desirous of knowing. You attribute the most absolute power and efficacy to atoms. Out of them you pretend that everything is made. But there are no atoms, for there is nothing without body;[1] every place is occupied by body, therefore there can be no such thing as a vacuum, or an atom.

I advance these principles of the naturalists, without knowing whether they are true or false; yet they are more like truth than those statements of yours; for they are the absurdities in which Democritus, or before him Leucippus, used to indulge, saying, that there are certain minute corpuscles, some smooth, some rough, some round, some square, some crooked and bent as bows; which by a fortuitous concourse made heaven and earth, without the influence of any natural

---

[1] A portion of Cotta's argument seems to be lost here.

power. . . . But I was forgetting my liberality, which I had promised to exert in your case, and exceeding the bounds which I at first proposed to myself. Granting, then, everything to be made of atoms, what advantage is that to your argument? For we are searching after the nature of the Gods; and allowing them to be made of atoms, they cannot be eternal; because whatever is made of atoms must have had a beginning; if so, there were no Gods till there was this beginning; and if the Gods have had a beginning they must necessarily have an end; as you have before contended when you were discussing Plato's world. Where, then, is your beatitude and immortality, in which two words you say that God is expressed, the endeavour to prove which reduces you to the greatest perplexities? For you said that God had no body, but something like body; and no blood, but something like blood.

It is a frequent practice among you, when you assert anything that has no resemblance to truth, and wish to avoid reprehension, to advance something else which is absolutely and utterly impossible, in order that it may seem to your adversaries better to grant that point which has been a matter of doubt, than to keep on pertinaciously contradicting you on every point: like Epicurus, who, when he found that if his atoms were allowed to descend by their own weight, our actions could not be in our own power, because their motions would be certain and necessary, invented an expedient, which escaped Democritus, to avoid necessity. He says, that when the atoms descend by their own weight and gravity, they move a little obliquely. Surely, to make such an assertion as this is what one ought more to be ashamed of than the acknowledging ourselves unable to defend the proposition. His practice is the same against the logicians, who say that in all alternative propositions, one or the other of the alternatives must be true. He was afraid that if this were granted, then, in such a proposition as "Either Epicurus will be alive tomorrow or he will not be alive tomorrow," either the first or the sec-

ond of the alternatives would be a necessary truth. Therefore, he denied the necessity of alternative propositions. Can
anything show stupidity in a greater degree? Zeno, being
pressed by Arcesilas, who pronounced all things to be false
which are perceived by the senses, said that some things were
false, but not all. Epicurus was afraid that, if any one thing
seen should be false, nothing could be true; and therefore he
asserted all the senses to be infallible directors of truth.
Nothing can be more rash than this; for by endeavouring to
repel a light stroke, he receives a heavy blow. On the subject
of the nature of the Gods, he falls into the same errors.
Whilst he would avoid the concretion of individual bodies,
lest death and dissolution should be the consequence, he denies that the Gods have body, but says they have something
like body; and says they have no blood, but something like
blood. . . .

Now do you understand what is meant by quasi body and
quasi blood? For I not only acknowledge that you are a better
judge of it than I am, but I can bear it without envy. If any
sentiments, indeed, are communicated without obscurity,
what is there that Velleius can understand, and Cotta not? I
know what body is, and what blood is; but I cannot possibly
find out the meaning of quasi body and quasi blood. Not that
you intentionally conceal your principles from me, as Pythagoras did his from those who were not his disciples; or
that you are intentionally obscure like Heraclitus. But the
truth is, (which I may venture to say in this company,) you
do not understand them yourself. . . .

Let me take for granted that which is perfectly unintelligi-
ble; then tell me what are the lineaments and figures of these
sketched out Deities. Here you have plenty of arguments, by
which you would show the Gods to be in human form. The
first is, that our minds are so anticipated and prepossessed,
that whenever we think of a Deity the human shape occurs
to us. The next is, that as the divine nature excels all things,
so it ought to be of the most beautiful form, and there is no

form more beautiful than the human; and the third is, that reason cannot reside in any other shape.

First, let us consider each argument separately. You seem to me to assume a principle, despotically I may say, that has no manner of probability in it. Who was ever so blind, in contemplating these subjects, as not to see that the Gods were represented in human form, either by the particular advice of wise men, who thought by those means the more easily to turn the minds of the ignorant from a depravity of manners, to the worship of the Gods; or through superstition, which was the cause of their believing that when they were paying adoration to these images they were approaching the Gods themselves. These conceits were not a little improved by the poets, painters, and artificers: for it would not have been very easy to represent the Gods planning and executing any work in another form; and perhaps this opinion arose from the idea which mankind have of their own beauty. But do not you, who are so great an adept in physics, see what a soothing flatterer, what a sort of procuress nature is to herself? Do you think there is any creature on the land or in the sea, that is not highly delighted with its own form? . . . Do you suppose, if beasts were endowed with reason, that every one would not give the prize of beauty to his own species? . . .

What if your assertion, Velleius, proves absolutely false, that no form occurs to us, in our contemplations on the Deity, but the human? Will you, notwithstanding that, persist in the defence of such an absurdity? Supposing that form occurs to us, as you say it does, and we know Jupiter, Juno, Minerva, Neptune, Vulcan, Apollo, and the other deities, by the countenance which painters and statuaries have given them . . . yet the Egyptians, the Syrians, and almost all barbarous nations, are without such distinctions. You may see a greater regard paid by them to certain beasts, than by us to the most sacred temples and images of the Gods; for many shrines have been rifled, and images of the deities have been carried from their most sacred places by us; but we

never heard that an Egyptian offered any violence to a crocodile, an ibis, or a cat. What do you think, then? Do not the
Egyptians esteem their sacred bull, their Apis, as a deity?
Yes, by Hercules, as certainly as you do our protectress Juno,
whom you never behold, even in your dreams, without a goat-
skin, a spear, a shield, and broad sandals. . . .

Therefore, ought not a natural philosopher, that is, an inquirer into the secrets of nature, to be ashamed of seeking a
testimony to truth from minds prepossessed by custom. . . .

You indeed, Velleius, have concluded your argument, not
after the manner of your own sect, but of the logicians, to
which your people are utter strangers. You have taken it for
granted that the Gods are happy. I allow it. You say that
without virtue no one can be happy. I willingly concur with
you in this also. You likewise say that virtue cannot reside
where reason is not. That I must necessarily allow. You add,
moreover, that reason cannot exist but in a human form.
Who, do you think, will admit that? If it were true, what occasion was there to come so gradually to it? And to what purpose? You might have answered it on your own authority. I
perceive your gradations from happiness to virtue, and from
virtue to reason; but how do you come from reason to human
form? There, indeed, you do not descend by degrees, but
precipitately. . . .

You have enumerated with so ready a memory, and so
copiously, the opinions of philosophers . . . concerning the
nature of the Gods, that I am surprised to see so much learning in a Roman. But do you think they were all madmen,
who thought that a Deity could by some possibility exist
without hands and feet. Does not even this consideration
have weight with you when you consider what is the use and
advantage of limbs in men, and lead you to admit that the
Gods have no need of them? what necessity can there be of
feet, without walking; or of hands, if there is nothing to be
grasped? . . . Shall the Deity, then, have a tongue, and not
speak; teeth, palate, and jaws, though he will have no use for

them. Shall the members which nature has given to the body for the sake of generation, be useless to the Deity! . . .

You censured those, who, beholding those excellent and stupendous works, the world, and its respective parts; the heaven, the earth, the seas, and the splendour with which they are adorned; who, contemplating the sun, moon, and stars; and who, observing the maturity and changes of the seasons, and vicissitudes of times, inferred from thence that there must be some excellent and eminent essence, that originally made, and still moves, directs, and governs them. Suppose they should mistake in their conjecture, yet I see what they aim at. But what is that great and noble work, which appears to you to be the effect of a divine mind, and from which you conclude that there are Gods? "I have," say you, "a certain information of a Deity imprinted in my mind." Of a bearded Jupiter, I suppose, and a helmeted Minerva.

But do you really imagine them to be such? How much better are the notions of the ignorant vulgar, who not only believe the Deities have members like ours, but that they make use of them; and therefore they assign them a bow and arrows, a spear, a shield, a trident, and lightning; and though they do not behold the actions of the Gods, yet they cannot entertain a thought of a Deity doing nothing. . . . Epicurus truly, like indolent boys, thinks nothing preferable to idleness; yet those very boys, when they have an holiday, entertain themselves in some sportive exercise. But we are to suppose the Deity in such an inactive state, that if he should move, we may justly fear he would be no longer happy. This doctrine divests the Gods of motion and operation; besides, it encourages men to be lazy, as they are by this taught to believe that the least labour is incompatible even with divine felicity.

But let it be as you would have it, that the Deity is in the form and image of a man. . . .

Let us now inquire into his happiness. It is certain, that

without virtue there can be no happiness; but virtue consists in action: now your Deity does nothing; therefore he is void of virtue, and consequently cannot be happy. What sort of life does he lead? He has a constant supply, you say, of good things without any intermixture of bad. What are those good things? Sensual pleasures, no doubt; for you know no delight of the mind, but what arises from the body, and returns to it. I do not suppose, Velleius, that you are like some of the Epicureans, who are ashamed of those expressions of Epicurus, in which he openly avows that he has no idea of any good separate from wanton and obscene pleasures; which, without a blush, he names distinctly. What food, therefore, what drink, what variety of music or flowers, what kind of pleasures of touch, what odours, will you offer to the Gods to fill them with pleasures? The poets indeed provide them with banquets of nectar and ambrosia, and a Hebe or a Ganymede to serve up the cup. But what is it, Epicurus, that you do for them? For I do not see from whence your Deity should have those things, nor how he could use them. Therefore the nature of man is better constituted for a happy life, than the nature of the Gods. . . .

But they are free from pain. Is that sufficient for beings, who are supposed to enjoy all good things and the most supreme felicity? The Deity, they say, is constantly meditating on his own happiness, for he has no other idea which can possibly occupy his mind. Consider a little; reflect what a figure the Deity would make, if he were to be idly thinking of nothing through all eternity but, "it is very well with me, and I am happy"; nor do I see why this happy Deity should not fear being destroyed, since without any intermission he is driven and agitated by an everlasting incursion of atoms, and since images are constantly flowing off from him. Your Deity therefore is neither happy nor eternal. . . .

Epicurus, when he divests the Gods of the power of doing good, extirpates all religion from the minds of men; for though he says the divine nature is the best and the most ex-

cellent of all natures, he will not allow it to be susceptible of
any benevolence; by which he destroys the chief and peculiar
attribute of the most perfect being; for what is better and
more excellent than goodness and beneficence? To refuse
your Gods that quality, is to say that no man is any object of
their favour, and no Gods either; that they neither love nor
esteem any one; in short, that they not only give themselves
no trouble about us, but even look on each other with the
greatest indifference. . . .

But Epicurus, you say, has written a book concerning sanctity. A trifling performance by a man whose wit is not so remarkable in it, as the unrestrained licence of writing which
he has permitted himself; for what sanctity can there be if
the Gods take no care of human affairs? Or how can that nature be called animated, which neither regards nor performs
anything? Therefore our friend Posidonius has well observed,
in his fifth book of the Nature of the Gods, that Epicurus
believed there were no Gods, and that what he had said
about the immortal Gods was only said from a desire to
avoid unpopularity. He could not be so weak as to imagine
that the Deity has only the outward features of a simple
mortal, without any real solidity; that he has all the members
of a man, without the least power to use them; a certain un-
substantial transparent being, neither favourable nor beneficial to any one, neither regarding nor doing anything: there
can be no such being in nature; and as Epicurus said this
plainly, he allows the Gods in words, and destroys them in
fact; and if the Deity is truly such a being that he shows no
favour, no benevolence to mankind, away with him! For why
should I entreat him to be propitious? He can be propitious
to none, since, as you say, all his favour and benevolence are
the effects of imbecility.

Book II

When Cotta had thus concluded, Velleius replied, I certainly was inconsiderate to engage in argument with an Academician who is likewise a rhetorician; I should not have feared an Academician without eloquence, nor a rhetorician without that philosophy, however eloquent he might be; for I am never puzzled by an empty flow of words, nor by the most subtle reasonings delivered without any grace of oratory. But you, Cotta, have excelled in both. You only wanted the assembly and the judges. However, enough of this at present. Now let us hear what Lucilius has to say, if it is agreeable to him.

I had much rather, said Balbus, hear Cotta resume his discourse, and demonstrate the true Gods with the same eloquence which he made use of to explode the false; for on such a subject the loose, unsettled doctrine of the Academy does not become a philosopher, a priest, a Cotta, whose opinions should be, like those we hold, firm and certain. Epicurus has been more than sufficiently refuted; but I would willingly hear your own sentiments, Cotta.

Do you forget, replied Cotta, what I at first said, that it is easier for me, especially on this point, to explain what opinions those are which I do not hold, rather than what those are which I do? Nay, even if I did feel some certainty on any particular point, yet, after having been so diffuse myself already, I would prefer now hearing you speak in your turn. I submit, said Balbus, and will be as brief as I possibly can; for as you have confuted the errors of Epicurus, my part in the dispute will be the shorter. Our sect divide the whole question concerning the immortal Gods into four parts. First, they prove that there are Gods; secondly, of what character and nature they are; thirdly, that the universe is governed by them; and lastly, that they exercise a superintendence over human affairs. . . .

The first point then, I think needs no discourse to prove it; for what can be so plain and evident, when we behold the heavens, and contemplate the celestial bodies, as the existence of some supreme, divine intelligence, by which all these things are governed? Were it otherwise, Ennius would not, with an universal approbation, have said,

> Look up to the refulgent heaven above,
> Which all men call, unanimously, Jove.

This is Jupiter, the governor of the world, who rules all things with his nod, and is, as the same Ennius adds,

> ————of Gods and men the sire,

an omnipresent and omnipotent God. . . . And if the existence of the Gods were not a truth universally impressed on the minds of men, the belief in it would never have been so firm; nor would it have been, as it is, increased by length of years, nor would it have gathered strength and stability through every age. And in truth we see that other opinions, being false and groundless, have already fallen into oblivion by lapse of time. Who now believes in Hippocentaurs and Chimeras? Or what old woman is now to be found so weak and ignorant, as to stand in fear of those infernal monsters which once so terrified mankind? For time destroys the fictions of error and opinion, while it confirms the determinations of nature and of truth. And therefore it is that, both amongst us and amongst other nations, sacred institutions and the divine worship of the Gods have been strengthened and improved from time to time. And this is not to be imputed to chance or folly, but to the frequent appearance of the Gods themselves. In the war with the Latins, when A. Posthumius the dictator attacked Octavius Mamilius the Tusculan at Regillus, Castor and Pollux were seen fighting in our army on horseback; and since that the same offspring of Tyndarus gave notice of the defeat of Perses; for as P. Vatienus, the grandfather of the present young man of that name, was coming in the night to Rome from his government of Reate, two young men on white horses appeared to him, and told him that king Perses was that day taken prisoner. This news he carried to the senate, who immediately threw him into prison for speaking inconsiderately on a state affair; but when it was confirmed by letters from Paullus, he was recompensed by the senate with land and immunities. . . .

What do predictions and foreknowledge of future events indicate, but that such future events are shown, pointed out, portended, and foretold to men? From whence they are called omens, signs, portents, prodigies. But though we should esteem fabulous what is said of Mopsus, Tiresias, Amphiaraus, Calchas, and Helenus, (who would not have been delivered down to us as augurs even in fable, if their art had been despised,) may we not be sufficiently apprised of the power of the Gods by domestic examples? Will not the temerity of P. Claudius, in the first Punic war, affect us? who, when the poultry were let out of the coop and would not feed, ordered them to be thrown into the water, and, joking even upon the Gods, said, with a sneer, Let them drink, since they will not eat; which piece of ridicule, being followed by a victory over his fleet, cost him many tears, and brought great calamity on the Roman people. Did not his colleague Junius, in the same war, lose his fleet in a tempest by disregarding the auspices? Claudius therefore was condemned by the people; and Junius killed himself. . . .

And is not the art of the soothsayers divine? And must not every one who sees what innumerable instances of the same kind there are, confess the existence of the Gods? For they who have interpreters, must certainly exist themselves; now, there are interpreters of the Gods; therefore we must allow there are Gods. But it may be said, perhaps, that all predictions are not accomplished. We may as well conclude there is no art of physic, because all sick persons do not recover. The

Gods show us signs of future events; if we are occasionally deceived in the results it is not to be imputed to the nature of the Gods, but to the conjectures of men. . . .

Chrysippus, indeed, had a very penetrating genius; yet such is the doctrine which he delivers, that he seems rather to have been instructed by nature, than to owe it to any discovery of his own. "If," he said, "there is anything in the universe which no human reason, ability, or power can make, the being who produced it must certainly be preferable to man; now celestial bodies, and all those things which proceed in any eternal order, cannot be made by man; the being who made them is therefore preferable to man. What then is that being but a God? If there be no such thing as a Deity, what is there better than man, since he only is possessed of reason, the most excellent of all things? But it is a foolish piece of vanity in man to think there is nothing preferable to him; there is therefore something preferable, consequently there is certainly a God. . . ."

Yet even from this inferior intelligence of man we may discover the existence of some intelligent agent that is divine, and wiser than ourselves, for, as Socrates says, in Xenophon, from whence had man his portion of understanding? And, indeed, if any one were to push his inquiries about the moisture and heat which is diffused through the human body, and the earthy kind of solidity existing in our entrails, and that soul by which we breathe, and to ask whence we derived them, it would be plain that we have received one thing from the earth, another from liquid, another from fire, and another from that air which we inhale every time that we breathe.

But where did we find that which excels all these things, I mean reason, or (if you please, in other terms) the mind, understanding, thought, prudence? and from whence did we receive it? Shall the world be possessed of every other perfection, and be destitute of this one, which is the most important and valuable of all? But certainly there is nothing better, or more excellent, or more beautiful than the world, and not only there is nothing better, but we cannot even conceive anything superior to it; and if reason and wisdom are the greatest of all perfections, they must necessarily be a part of what we all allow to be the most excellent.

Who is not compelled to admit the truth of what I assert by that agreeable, uniform, and continued agreement of things in the universe? Could the earth at one season be adorned with flowers, at another be covered with snow? Or, if such a number of things regulated their own changes, could the approach and retreat of the sun in the summer and winter solstices be so regularly known and calculated? Could the flux and reflux of the sea and the height of the tides be affected by the increase or wane of the moon? Could the different courses of the stars be preserved by the uniform movement of the whole heaven? Could these things subsist, I say, in such a harmony of all the parts of the universe, without the continued influence of a divine spirit? . . . the arguments which I am enlarging upon are thus briefly laid down by Zeno:—

"That which reasons, is superior to that which does not; nothing is superior to the world; the world, therefore, reasons." By the same rule the world may be proved to be wise, happy, and eternal; for the possession of all these qualities is superior to the want of them; and nothing is superior to the world; the inevitable consequence of which argument is, that the world therefore is a Deity. He goes on, "No part of anything void of sense is capable of perception; some parts of the world have perception; the world therefore has sense." He proceeds, and pursues the argument closely. "Nothing," says he, "that is destitute itself of life and reason, can generate a being possessed of life and reason; but the world does generate beings possessed of life and reason; the world therefore is not itself destitute of life and reason. . . ."

But as I have been insensibly led into a length of discourse beyond my first design, (for I said that as the existence of the Gods was evident to all, there was no need of any long oration to prove it,) I will demonstrate it by reasons deduced from the nature of things. For it is a fact, that all beings which take nourishment and increase, contain in themselves a power of natural heat, without which they could neither be nourished nor increase. For everything which is of a warm and fiery character is agitated and stirred up by its own motion. But that which is nourished and grows is influenced by a certain regular and equable motion. And as long as this motion remains in us, so long does sense and life remain; but the moment that it abates and is extinguished, we ourselves decay and perish.

By arguments like these, Cleanthes shows how great is the power of heat in all bodies. He observes, that there is no food so gross as not to be digested in a night and a day; and that even in the excrement, which nature rejects, there remains a heat. The veins and arteries seem, by their continual quivering, to resemble the agitation of fire; and it has often been observed when the heart of an animal is just plucked from the body, that it palpitates with such visible motion as to resemble the rapidity of fire. Everything, therefore, that has life, whether it be animal or vegetable, owes that life to the heat inherent in it; it is this nature of heat which contains in itself the vital power which extends throughout the whole world. This will appear more clearly on a more close explanation of this fiery quality, which pervades all things.

Every division, then, of the world, (and I shall touch upon the most considerable,) is sustained by heat; and first it may be observed in earthly substances, that fire is produced from stones, by striking or rubbing one against another; that "the warm earth smokes" when just turned up, and that water is drawn warm from well-springs; and this is most especially the case in the winter season, because there is a great quantity of heat contained in the caverns of the earth; and this becomes more dense in the winter, and on that account confines more closely the innate heat which is discoverable in the earth.

It would require a long dissertation, and many reasons

would require to be adduced, to show that all the seeds which the earth conceives, and all those which it contains having been generated from itself, and fixed in roots and trunks, derive all their origin and increase from the temperature and regulation of heat. And that even every liquor has a mixture of heat in it is plainly demonstrated by the effusion of water; for it would not congeal by cold, nor become solid, as ice or snow, and return again to its natural state, if it were not that, when heat is applied to it, it again becomes liquefied and dissolved, and so diffuses itself. Therefore by northern and other cold winds it is frozen and hardened, and in turn it dissolves and melts again by heat. The seas likewise, we find, when agitated by winds, grow warm, so that from this fact we may understand that there is heat included in that vast body of water; for we cannot imagine it to be external and adventitious heat, but such as is stirred up by agitation from the deep recesses of the seas; and the same thing takes place with respect to our bodies, which grow warm with motion and exercise.

And the very air itself, which indeed is the coldest element, is by no means void of heat; for there is a great quantity, arising from the exhalations of water, which appears to be a sort of steam occasioned by its internal heat, like that of boiling liquors. The fourth part of the universe is entirely fire, and is the source of the salutary and vital heat which is found in the rest. From hence we may conclude, that, as all parts of the world are sustained by heat, the world itself also has such a great length of time subsisted from the same cause; and so much the more because we ought to understand that that hot and fiery principle is so diffused over universal nature, that there is contained in it a power and cause of generation and procreation, from which all animate beings and all those creatures of the vegetable world, the roots of which are contained in the earth, must inevitably derive their origin and their increase.

It is nature consequently that continues and preserves the

world; and that, too, a nature which is not destitute of sense and reason; for in every essence that is not simple, but composed of several parts, there must be some predominant quality; as for instance, the mind in man, and in beasts something resembling it; from which arise all the appetites and desires for anything. As for trees, and all the vegetable produce of the earth, it is thought to be in their roots. I call that the predominant quality, which the Greeks call ἡγεμονικόν; which must and ought to be the most excellent quality, wherever it is found. That, therefore, in which the prevailing quality of all nature resides, must be the most excellent of all things and most worthy of the power and preeminence over all things.

Now we see that there is nothing in being that is not a part of the universe, and as there are sense and reason in the parts of it, there must therefore be these qualities, and these too in a more energetic and powerful degree, in that part in which the predominant quality of the world is found. The world, therefore, must necessarily be possessed of wisdom; and that element, which embraces all things, must excel in perfection of reason. The world, therefore, is a God, and the whole power of the world is contained in that divine element.

The heat also of the world is more pure, clear, and lively, and consequently better adapted to move the senses, than the heat allotted to us; and it vivifies and preserves all things within the compass of our knowledge.

It is absurd, therefore, to say that the world, which is endued with a perfect, free, pure, spirituous and active heat, is not sensitive, since by this heat men and beasts are preserved, and move, and think; more especially since this heat of the world is itself the sole principle of agitation, and has no external impulse, but is moved spontaneously; for what can be more powerful than the world, which moves and raises that heat by which it subsists?

For let us listen to Plato, who is regarded as a God amongst philosophers. He says that there are two sorts of motion, one innate and the other external; and that that which is moved spontaneously, is more divine than that which is moved by another power. This self-motion he places in the mind alone, and concludes that the first principle of motion is derived from the mind. Therefore, since all motion arises from the heat of the world, and that heat is not moved by the effect of any external impulse, but of its own accord, it must necessarily be a mind; from whence it follows, that the world is animated. . . .

If we proceed from the first rude unfinished natures, to the most superior and perfect ones, we shall inevitably come at last to the nature of the Gods. For, in the first place, we observe that those vegetables which are produced out of the earth are supported by nature, and she gives them no further supply than is sufficient to preserve them, by nourishing them and making them grow. To beasts she has given sense and motion, and a faculty which directs them to what is wholesome, and prompts them to shun what is noxious to them. On man she has conferred a greater portion of her favour; inasmuch as she has added reason, by which he is enabled to command his passions, to moderate some, and to subdue others.

In the fourth and highest degree are those beings, which are naturally wise and good, who from the first moment of their existence are possessed of right and consistent reason, which we must consider superior to man and deserving to be attributed to a God; that is to say, to the world: in which it is inevitable that that perfect and complete reason should be inherent. Nor is it possible that it should be said with justice, that there is any arrangement of things in which there cannot be something entire and perfect. For as in a vine or in beasts we see that nature, if not prevented by some superior violence, proceeds by her own appropriate path to her destined end; and as in painting, architecture, and the other arts, there is a point of perfection, which is attainable, and occasionally attained; so it is even much more necessary that in universal nature there must be some complete and perfect result arrived at. Many external accidents may happen to all other natures which may impede their progress to perfection, but nothing can hinder universal nature, because she is herself the ruler and governor of all other natures. That therefore must be the fourth and most elevated degree, to which no other power can approach.

But this degree is that on which the nature of all things is placed; and since she is possessed of this, and she presides over all things, and is subject to no possible impediment, the world must necessarily be an intelligent, and even a wise being. . . .

Chrysippus says, very acutely, that as the case is made for the buckler, and the scabbard for the sword, so all things, except the universe, were made for the sake of something else. As for instance, all those crops and fruits which the earth produces were made for the sake of animals, and animals for man; as the horse for carrying, the ox for the plough, the dog for hunting and for a guard. But man himself was born to contemplate and imitate the world; being in nowise perfect, but, if I may so express myself, a particle of perfection; but the world, as it comprehends all, and as nothing exists that is not contained in it, is entirely perfect. In what, therefore, can it be defective, since it is perfect? It cannot want understanding and reason, for they are the most desirable of all qualities. The same Chrysippus observes also, by the use of similitudes, that everything in its kind, when arrived at maturity and perfection, is superior to that which is not; as a horse to a colt, a dog to a puppy, and a man to a boy; so whatever is best in the whole universe must exist in some complete and perfect being. But nothing is more perfect than the world, and nothing better than virtue. Virtue, therefore, is an attribute of the world. But human nature is not perfect, and nevertheless virtue is produced in it: with how much greater reason, then, do we conceive it to be inherent in the world?

Therefore, the world has virtue, and it is also wise, and consequently a Deity.

The divinity of the world being now clearly perceived, we must acknowledge the same divinity to be likewise in the stars, which are formed from the lightest and purest part of the æther, without a mixture of any other matter; and, being altogether hot and transparent, we may justly say they have life, sense, and understanding. . . .

It now remains that we consider what is the character of the Gods. Nothing is more difficult than to divert our thoughts and judgment from the information of our corporeal sight, and the view of objects which our eyes are accustomed to: and it is this difficulty which has had such an influence on the unlearned, and on philosophers also who resembled the unlearned multitude, that they have been unable to form any idea of the immortal Gods except under the clothing of the human figure; the weakness of which opinion Cotta has so well confuted, that I need not add my thoughts upon it. But as the previous idea which we have of the Deity comprehends two things,—first of all, that he is an animated being; secondly, that there is nothing in all nature superior to him,—I do not see what can be more consistent with this idea and preconception, than to attribute a mind and divinity to the world, the most excellent of all beings. . . .

Epicurus may be as merry with this notion as he pleases; a man not the best qualified for a joker, as not having the wit and sense of his country. Let him say that a rotating round Deity is to him incomprehensible; yet he shall never dissuade me from a principle, which he himself approves; for he is of opinion there are Gods, when he allows that there must be a nature most excellently perfect. But it is certain that the world is most excellently perfect: nor is it to be doubted, that whatever has life, sense, reason, and understanding, must excel that which is destitute of these things. It follows then that the world has life, sense, reason, and understanding, and is consequently a Deity. But this shall soon be made more manifest by the operation of these very things which the world causes.

In the meanwhile, Velleius, let me entreat you not to be always saying that we are utterly destitute of every sort of learning. The cone, you say, the cylinder, and the pyramid, are more beautiful to you than the sphere. This is to have different eyes from other men. But suppose they are more beautiful to the sight only, which does not appear to me, for I can see nothing more beautiful than that figure which contains all others, and which has nothing rough in it, nothing offensive, nothing cut into angles, nothing broken, nothing swelling, and nothing hollow; yet as there are two forms most esteemed, the sphere in solids, and the circle in planes; and as they only have an exact similitude of parts, in which every extreme is equally distant from the centre, what can we imagine in nature to be more just and proper? But if you have never raked into this learned dust, to find out these things, surely at all events you natural philosophers must know that equality of motion and invariable order could not be preserved in any other figure. . . .

I am now to show that the world is governed by the providence of the Gods. This is an important point, which you Academics endeavour to confound; and, indeed, the whole contest is with you, Cotta; for your sect, Velleius, know very little of what is said on different subjects by other schools. You read and have a taste only for your own books, and condemn all others without examination. For instance, when you mentioned that prophetic old dame Πρόνοια, Providence, invented by the Stoics, you were led into that error by imagining that Providence was made by them to be a particular Deity that governs the whole universe, whereas it is only spoken in a short manner . . . when we say "the world is governed by providence," we mean "by the providence of the Gods." . . . Be not, therefore, lavish of your railleries, of which your sect has little to spare. It does not become you, it is not your talent, nor is it in your power. This is not applied to you in particular, who have the education and politeness of a Roman, but to all your sect in general, and especially to your leader,—a man unpolished, illiterate, insulting, without wit, without reputation, without elegance.

I assert, then, that the universe, with all its parts, was originally constituted, and has, without any cessation, been ever governed by the providence of the Gods. . . . But, first of all, it is proper to explain precisely what that nature is, in order to come to the more easy understanding of what I would demonstrate. Some think that nature is a certain irrational power exciting in bodies the necessary motions. Others, that it is an intelligent power, acting by order and method, designing some end in every cause, and always aiming at that end; whose works express such skill, as no art, no hand can imitate; for, they say, such is the virtue of its seed, that, however small it is, if it falls into a place proper for its reception, and meets with matter conducive to its nourishment and increase, it forms and produces everything in its respective kind; either vegetables, which receive their nourishment from their roots; or animals, endowed with motion, sense, appetite, and abilities to beget their likeness.

Some apply the word nature to everything; as Epicurus does, who acknowledges no cause, but atoms, a vacuum, and their accidents. But when we say that nature forms and governs the world, we do not mean to liken it to a clod of earth, or piece of stone, or anything of that sort, whose parts have only the necessary cohesion, but to a tree, in which there is not the appearance of chance, but of order, and a resemblance of art . . . if all the parts of the universe are so constituted that nothing could be better for use or beauty, let us consider whether this is the effect of chance, or whether, in such a state, they could possibly cohere, but by the direction of wisdom and divine providence. Nature therefore cannot be void of reason, if art can bring nothing to perfection without it, and if the works of nature exceed those of art. How is it consistent with common sense, that when you view an image or a picture, you imagine it is wrought by art; when you behold afar off a ship under sail, you judge it is steered by reason and art; when you see a dial or water-clock, you believe the hours are shown by art, and not by chance; and yet that you should imagine that the universe, which contains all arts and the artificers, can be void of reason and understanding? . . . In the sky innumerable fiery stars exist, of which the sun is the chief, enlightening all with his refulgent splendour, and being by many degrees larger than the whole earth; and this multitude of vast fires are so far from hurting the earth, and things terrestrial, that they are of benefit to them; whereas, if they were moved from their stations, we should inevitably be burnt, through the want of a proper moderation and temperature of heat.

Is it possible for any man to behold these things, and yet imagine that certain solid and individual bodies move by their natural force and gravitation, and that a world so beautifully adorned was made by their fortuitous concourse? He who believes this, may as well believe, that if a great quantity of the one-and-twenty letters, composed either of gold, or any other matter, were thrown upon the ground, they would fall into such order as legibly to form the Annals of Ennius. I doubt whether fortune could make a single verse of them. How therefore can these people assert that the world was made by the fortuitous concourse of atoms, which have no colour, no quality, which the Greeks call ποιότης, no sense? or that there are innumerable worlds, some rising and some perishing, in every moment of time? But if a concourse of atoms can make a world, why not a porch, a temple, a house, a city, which are works of less labour and difficulty? . . .

Well, then, did Aristotle[2] observe: "If there were men whose habitations had been always under ground, in great and commodious houses, adorned with statues and pictures, furnished with everything which they who are reputed

[2] In a lost dialogue, *De Philosophia*.

happy abound with; and if, without stirring from thence, they should be informed of a certain divine power and majesty, and, after some time, the earth should open, and they should quit their dark abode to come to us; where they should immediately behold the earth, the seas, the heavens; should consider the vast extent of the clouds and force of the winds; should see the sun, and observe his grandeur and beauty, and also his generative power, inasmuch as day is occasioned by the diffusion of his light through the sky; and when night has obscured the earth, they should contemplate the heavens bespangled and adorned with stars; the surprising variety of the moon, in her increase and wane; the rising and setting of all the stars, and the inviolable regularity of their courses; when," says he, "they should see these things, they would undoubtedly conclude that there are Gods, and that these are their mighty works." . . .

Is he worthy to be called a man, who attributes to chance, not to an intelligent cause, the constant motion of the heavens, the regular courses of the stars, the agreeable proportion and connexion of all things, conducted with so much reason, that our intellect itself is unable to estimate it rightly? When we see machines move artificially, as a sphere, a clock, or the like, do we doubt whether they are the productions of reason? And when we behold the heavens moving with a prodigious celerity, and causing an annual succession of the different seasons of the year, which vivify and preserve all things, can we doubt that this world is directed, I will not say only by reason, but by reason most excellent and divine? For without troubling ourselves with too refined a subtlety of discussion, we may use our eyes to contemplate the beauty of those things, which we assert have been arranged by divine providence. . . . What is most wonderful is, that the world is so durable, and so perfectly made for lasting that it is not to be impaired by time; for all its parts tend equally to the centre, and are bound together by a sort of chain, which surrounds the elements; this chain is nature, which being diffused through the universe, and performing all things with judgment and reason, attracts the extremities to the centre.

If, then, the world is round, and if on that account all its parts, being of equal dimensions and relative proportions, mutually support and are supported by one another, it must follow that as all the parts incline to the centre (for that is the lowest place of a globe) there is nothing whatever which can put a stop to that propensity, in the case of such great weights. For the same reason, though the sea is higher than the earth, yet because it has the like tendency, it is collected everywhere, equally concentres, and never overflows, and is never wasted.

The air, which is contiguous, ascends by its lightness, but diffuses itself through the whole; therefore it is by nature joined and united to the sea, and at the same time borne by the same power towards the heaven, by the thinness and heat of which it is so tempered as to be made proper to supply life, and wholesome air for the support of animated beings. This is encompassed by the highest region of the heavens, which is called the sky, which is joined to the extremity of the air, but retains its own heat pure and unmixed.

The stars have their revolutions in the sky, and are continued by the tendency of all parts towards the centre; their duration is perpetuated by their form and figure, for they are round; which form, as I think has been before observed, is the least liable to injury; and, as they are composed of fire, they are fed by the vapours which are exhaled by the sun from the earth, the sea, and other waters; but when these vapours have nourished and refreshed the stars, and the whole sky, they are sent back to be exhaled again; so that very little is lost or consumed by the fire of the stars and the flame of the sky. Hence we Stoics conclude . . . that the whole world at last would be consumed by a general conflagration; when all moisture being exhausted, neither the earth could have any nourishment, nor the air return again, since water, of which it is formed, would then be all consumed; so that only fire would subsist; and from this fire, which is an animating power and a Deity, a new world would arise and be re-established in the same beauty. . . .

Let us proceed from celestial to terrestrial things. What is there in them which does not prove the principle of an intelligent nature? First, as to vegetables; they have roots to sustain their stems, and to draw from the earth a nourishing moisture to support the vital principle which those roots contain. They are clothed with a rind or bark, to secure them more thoroughly from heat and cold. The vines, we see, take hold on props with their tendrils, as if with hands, and raise themselves as if they were animated; it is even said, that they shun cabbages and coleworts, as noxious and pestilential to them, and if planted by them, will not touch any part.

But what a vast variety is there of animals and how wonderfully is every kind adapted to preserve itself! Some are covered with hides, some clothed with fleeces, and some guarded with bristles; some are sheltered with feathers, some with scales; some are armed with horns, and some are furnished with wings to escape from danger. Nature hath also liberally and plentifully provided for all animals their proper food; I could expatiate on the judicious and curious formation and disposition of their bodies for the reception and digestion of it, for all their interior parts are so framed and disposed, that there is nothing superfluous, nothing that is not necessary for the preservation of life. Besides, nature has also given these beasts appetite and sense; in order that by the one they may be excited to procure sufficient sustenance, and by the other they may distinguish what is noxious from what is salutary. . . .

But to those beasts which live by preying on others, nature has given either strength or swiftness. On some animals she has even bestowed artifice and cunning; as on spiders, some of which weave a sort of net to entrap and destroy whatever falls into it, others sit on the watch unobserved to fall on their prey and devour it. The naker, by the Greeks called

Pinna, has a kind of confederacy with the prawn for procuring food. It has two large shells open, into which when the little fishes swim, the naker, having notice given by the bite of the prawn, closes them immediately. Thus, these little animals, though of different kinds, seek their food in common; in which it is matter of wonder whether they associate by any agreement, or are naturally joined together from their beginning. . . .

I could produce many instances of this kind, but these may suffice. Let us now proceed to things more familiar to us. The care of beasts for their own preservation, their circumspection while feeding, and their manner of taking rest in their lairs, are generally known, but still they are greatly to be admired.

Dogs cure themselves by a vomit, the Egyptian Ibis by a purge; from whence physicians have lately, I mean but few ages since, greatly improved their art. It is reported that panthers, which in barbarous countries are taken with poisoned flesh, have a certain remedy that preserves them from dying; and that in Crete, the wild goats, when they are wounded with poisoned arrows, seek for an herb called dittany, which when they have tasted, the arrows (they say) drop from their bodies. . . . Beasts, when they receive any hurt, or fear it, have recourse to their natural arms: the bull to his horns, the boar to his tusks, and the lion to his teeth. Some take to flight, others hide themselves; the cuttle-fish vomits blood, the cramp-fish benumbs; and there are many animals that, by their intolerable stink, oblige their pursuers to retire.

But that the beauty of the world might be eternal, great care has been taken by the providence of the Gods to perpetuate the different kinds of animals, and vegetables, and trees, and all those things which sink deep into the earth, and are contained in it by their roots and trunks; in order to which, every individual has within itself such fertile seed that many are generated from one; and in vegetables this seed is inclosed in the heart of their fruit, but in such abundance, that men may plentifully feed on it, and the earth be always replanted.

With regard to animals, do we not see how aptly they are formed for the propagation of their species? Nature for this end created some males and some females. Their parts are perfectly framed for generation, and they have a wonderful propensity to copulation. When the seed has fallen on the matrix, it draws almost all the nourishment to itself, by which the fœtus is formed; but as soon as it is discharged from thence, if it is an animal that is nourished by milk, almost all the food of the mother turns into milk, and the animal, without any direction, but by the pure instinct of nature, immediately hunts for the teat, and is there fed with plenty. What makes it evidently appear that there is nothing in this fortuitous, but the work of a wise and foreseeing Nature, is, that these females which bring forth many young, as sows and bitches, have many teats, and those which bear a small number, have but few. . . .

But we may yet more easily comprehend that the Gods have taken great care of the interests and welfare of men, if we examine thoroughly into the structure of the body, and the form and perfection of human nature. There are three things absolutely necessary for the support of life; to eat, to drink, and to breathe; for these operations the mouth is most aptly framed, which, by the assistance of the nostrils, draws in the more air.

The teeth are there placed to divide and grind the food. The fore-teeth, being sharp and opposite to each other, cut it asunder, and the hind-teeth (called the grinders) chew it; in which office the tongue seems to assist. At the root of the tongue is the gullet, which receives whatever is swallowed; it touches the tonsils on each side, and terminates at the interior extremity of the palate. When by the motions of the tongue the food is forced into this passage, it descends, and those parts of the gullet, which are below it, are dilated, and those above are contracted. There is another passage, called by physicians the rough artery, which reaches to the lungs for the entrance and return of the air we breathe; and as its orifice is joined to the roots of the tongue a little above the part to which the gullet is annexed, it is furnished with a sort of coverlid, lest, by the accidental falling of any food into it, the respiration should be stopped.

As the stomach, which is beneath the gullet, receives the meat and drink, so the lungs and the heart draw in the air from without. The stomach is wonderfully composed, consisting almost wholly of nerves; it abounds with membranes and fibres, and detains what it receives, whether solid or liquid, till it is altered and digested. It sometimes contracts, sometimes dilates. It blends and mixes the food together, so that it is easily concocted and digested by its force of heat, and by the animal spirits is distributed into the other parts of the body.

As to the lungs, they are of a soft and spongy substance, which renders them the most commodious for respiration; they alternately dilate and contract to receive and return the air, that what is the chief animal sustenance may be always fresh. The juice, by which we are nourished, being separated from the rest of the food, passes the stomach and intestines to the liver, through open and direct passages, which lead from the mesentery to the gates of the liver (for so they call those vessels at the entrance of it). There are other passages from thence, through which the food has its course when it has passed the liver. When the bile, and those humours which proceed from the kidneys, are separated from the food, the remaining part turns to blood, and flows to those vessels at the entrance of the liver, to which all the passages adjoin. The chyle, being conveyed from this place through them into the vessel called the hollow vein, is mixed together, and, being already digested and distilled, passes into the heart; and from the heart it is communicated through a great number of veins to every part of the body.

It is not difficult to describe how the gross remains are detruded by the motion of the intestines, which contract and dilate; but that must be declined, as too indelicate for discourse. . . .

To this skill of nature, and this care of providence, so diligent and so ingenious, many reflections may be added, which show what valuable things the Deity has bestowed on man. He has made us of a stature tall and upright, in order that we might behold the heavens, and so arrive at the knowledge of the Gods; for men are not simply to dwell here as inhabitants of the earth, but to be, as it were, spectators of the heavens and the stars, which is a privilege not granted to any other kind of animated beings. . . .

Again, he who does not perceive the soul and mind of man, his reason, prudence, and discernment, to be the work of a divine providence, seems himself to be destitute of those faculties. . . .

And it will appear incredible, unless you carefully observe the facts, how complete the work of nature is in giving us the use of speech; for, first of all, there is an artery from the lungs to the bottom of the mouth, through which the voice, having its original principle in the mind, is transmitted. Then the tongue is placed in the mouth, bounded by the teeth. It softens and modulates the voice, which would otherwise be confusedly uttered; and, by pushing it to the teeth and other parts of the mouth, makes the sound distinct and articulate. We Stoics, therefore, compare the tongue to the bow of an instrument, the teeth to the strings, and the nostrils to the sounding-board.

But how commodious are the hands which nature has given to man, and how beautifully do they minister to many arts! For, such is the flexibility of the joints, that our fingers are closed and opened without any difficulty. With their help, the hand is formed for painting, carving, and engraving; for playing on stringed instruments, and on the pipe. These are matters of pleasure; there are also works of necessity, such as tilling the ground, building houses, making cloth and habits, and working in brass and iron. It is the business of the mind to invent, the senses to perceive, and the hands to execute; so that if we have buildings, if we are clothed, if we live in safety, if we have cities, walls, habitations, and temples, it is to the hands we owe them. . . .

But what shall I say of human reason? Has it not even entered the heavens? Man alone of all animals has observed the courses of the stars, their risings and settings. By man the day, the month, the year is determined. He foresees the eclipses of the sun and moon, and foretells them to futurity, marking their greatness, duration, and precise time. From the contemplation of these things, the mind extracts the knowledge of the Gods,—a knowledge which produces piety, with which is connected justice, and all the other virtues; from which arises a life of felicity, inferior to that of the Gods in no single particular, except in immortality, which is not absolutely necessary to happy living. In explaining these things, I think that I have sufficiently demonstrated the superiority of man to other animated beings; from whence we should infer, that neither the form and position of his limbs, nor that strength of mind and understanding, could possibly be the effect of chance.

I am now to prove, by way of conclusion, that every thing in this world, of use to us, was made designedly for us. . . .

Does the earth bring forth fruit and grain, in such excessive abundance and variety, for men, or for brutes? The plentiful and exhilarating fruit of the vine and the olive-tree are entirely useless to beasts. They know not the time for sowing, tilling, or for reaping in season and gathering in the fruits of the earth, or for laying up and preserving their stores; man alone has the care and advantage of these things.

Thus, as the lute and the pipe were made for those, and those only, who are capable of playing on them, so it must be allowed that the produce of the earth was designed for those only who make use of them; and though some beasts may rob us of a small part, it does not follow that the earth produced it also for them. Men do not store up corn for mice and ants, but for their wives, their children, and their families; beasts, therefore, as I said before, possess it by stealth, but their masters openly and freely; it is for us therefore that nature hath provided this abundance. Can there by any doubt that this plenty and variety of fruit, which delight not only the taste, but the smell and sight, was by nature intended for men only? Beasts are so far from being partakers of this design, that we see that even they themselves were made for man; for of what utility would sheep be, unless for their wool, which, when dressed and woven, serves us for clothing? for they are not capable of anything, not even of procuring their own food, without the care and assistance of man. The fidelity of the dog, his affectionate fawning on his master, his aversion to strangers, his sagacity in finding game, and his vivacity in pursuit of it, what do these qualities denote, but that he was created for our use? Why need I mention oxen? We perceive that their backs were not formed for carrying burdens, but their necks were naturally made for the yoke, and their strong broad shoulders to draw the plough. . . .

Besides, the Gods not only provide for mankind universally, but for particular men. You may bring this universality to gradually a smaller number, and again you may reduce that smaller number to individuals.

For if the reasons which I have given prove to all of us that the Gods take care of all men, in every country, in every part of the world separate from our continent, they take care of those who dwell on the same land with us, from east to west. . . . Rome also and Greece have produced many illustrious men, who we cannot believe were so without the assistance of the Deity; which is the reason that the poets, Homer in particular, joined their chief heroes, Ulysses, Agamemnon, Diomedes, Achilles, to certain Deities, as companions in their adventures and dangers. Besides, the frequent appearances of the Gods, as I have before mentioned, demonstrate their regard for cities and particular men; this is also apparent indeed from the foreknowledge of events, which we receive either sleeping or waking. We are likewise forewarned of many things by the entrails of victims, by presages, and many other means, which have been long observed with such exactness, as to produce an art of divination.

There never, therefore, was a great man without divine inspiration. If a storm should damage the corn or vineyard of a person, or any accident should deprive him of some conveniences of life, we should not judge from thence that the Deity hates or neglects him. The Gods take care of great things, and disregard the small. But to truly great men all things ever happen prosperously; as has been sufficiently asserted and proved by us Stoics, as well as by Socrates, the prince of philosophers, in his discourses on the infinite advantages arising from virtue.

This is almost the whole that hath occurred to my mind on the nature of the Gods, and what I thought proper to advance. Do you, Cotta, if I may advise, defend the same cause. Remember that in Rome you keep the first rank; remember that you are Pontifex; and as your school is at liberty to argue on which side you please, do you rather take mine, and reason on it with that eloquence which you acquired by your rhetorical exercises, and which the Academy improved; for it is a pernicious and impious custom to argue against the Gods, whether it be done seriously, or only in pretence and out of sport.

Book III

When Balbus had ended this discourse, then Cotta, with a smile, rejoined,—You direct me too late which side to defend: for during the course of your argument I was revolving in my mind what objections to make to what you were saying, not so much for the sake of opposition, as of obliging you to explain what I did not perfectly comprehend; and as every

one may use his own judgment, it is scarcely possible for me
to think in every instance exactly what you wish.

You have no idea, O Cotta, said Velleius, how impatient I
am to hear what you have to say. For since our friend Balbus
was highly delighted with your discourse against Epicurus, I
ought in my turn to be solicitous to hear what you can say
against the Stoics; and I therefore will give you my best attention, for I believe you are, as usual, well prepared for the
engagement.

I wish, by Hercules, I were, replied Cotta; for it is more
difficult to dispute with Lucilius than it was with you. Why
so? said Velleius. Because, replied Cotta, your Epicurus, in
my opinion, does not contend strongly for the Gods; he
only, for the sake of avoiding any unpopularity or punishment, is afraid to deny their existence; for when he asserts
that the Gods are wholly inactive and regardless of everything, and that they have limbs like ours, but make no use of
them, he seems to jest with us, and to think it sufficient if
he allows that there are beings of any kind happy and eternal.
But with regard to Balbus, I suppose you observed how many
things were said by him, which, however false they may be,
yet have a perfect coherence and connexion; therefore, my
design, as I said, in opposing him, is not so much to confute
his principles, as to induce him to explain what I do not
clearly understand. . . . But before I enter on the subject, I
have a word to say concerning myself; for I am greatly influenced by your authority, and your exhortation at the conclusion of your discourse, when you desired me to remember
that I was Cotta and Pontifex; by which I presume you in-
timated that I should defend the sacred rites and religion and
ceremonies which we received from our ancestors. Most undoubtedly I always have, and always shall defend them, nor
shall the arguments either of the learned or unlearned ever
remove the opinions which I have imbibed from them concerning the worship of the immortal Gods. In matters of
religion I submit to the rules of the high priests, not to the

sentiments of Zeno, Cleanthes, or Chrysippus; and I pay a greater regard to what C. Lælius, one of our augurs and wise men, has written concerning religion, in that noble oration of his, than to the most eminent of the Stoics: and as the whole religion of the Romans at first consisted in sacrifices and divination by birds, to which have since been added predictions, if the interpreters of the Sibylline oracle or the aruspices have foretold any event from portents and prodigies, I have ever thought that there was no point of all these holy things which deserved to be despised. I have been even persuaded that Romulus, by instituting divination, and Numa, by establishing sacrifices, laid the foundation of Rome, which undoubtedly would never have risen to such an height of grandeur, if the Gods had not been made propitious by this worship. These, Balbus, are my sentiments both as a priest and as Cotta. But you must bring me to your opinion by the force of your reason; for I have a right to demand from you, as a philosopher, a reason for the religion which you would have me embrace; but I must believe the religion of our ancestors without any proof. . . .

Let us examine every proposition. The first one, that there are Gods, is never contested but by the most impious of men; nay, though it can never be rooted out of my mind, yet I believe it on the authority of our ancestors, and not on the proofs which you have brought. Why do you expect a proof from me, said Balbus, if you thoroughly believe it? Because, said Cotta, I come to this discussion as if I had never thought of the Gods, or heard anything concerning them. Take me as a disciple wholly ignorant and unbiassed, and prove to me all the points which I ask.

Begin, then, replied Balbus. I would first know, said Cotta, why you have been so long in proving the existence of the Gods, which you said was a point so very evident to all, that there was no need of proof? In that, answered Balbus, I have followed your example, whom I have often observed, when pleading in the Forum, to load the judge with all the arguments which the nature of your cause would permit. This also is the practice of philosophers, and I have a right to follow it. . . .

You shall judge then yourself, said Cotta, if this is a very just comparison; for, when I plead, I do not dwell upon any point agreed to be self-evident, because long reasoning only serves to confound the clearest matters; besides, though I might take this method in pleading, yet I should not make use of it in such a discourse as this, which requires the nicest distinction. . . . But the truth is, that it was because you did not think that the existence of the Gods was so evident as you could wish, that you therefore brought so many proofs. It was sufficient for me to believe it on the tradition of our ancestors; and since you disregard authorities, and appeal to reason, permit my reason to defend them against yours. The proofs on which you found the existence of the Gods, tend only to render a proposition doubtful, that, in my opinion, is not so. . . . The first was, that when we lift up our eyes towards the heavens, we immediately conceive that there is some divinity that governs those celestial bodies . . . intimating . . . that it is evident to the whole world that these bodies are Gods, which Velleius and many others do not place even in the rank of animated beings.

Another strong proof, in your opinion, was that the belief of the existence of the Gods was universal, and that mankind was daily more and more convinced of it. What! should an affair of such importance be left to the decision of fools, who, by your sect especially, are called madmen?

But the Gods have appeared to us, as to Posthumius at the lake Regillus, and to Vatienus in the Salarian Way. . . . Do you believe that the Tyndaridæ, as you called them, that is, men sprung from men, and who were buried in Lacedæmon, as we learn from Homer, who lived in the next age,— do you believe, I say, that they appeared to Vatienus on the road mounted on white horses, without any servant to attend them, to tell the victory of the Romans to a country fellow rather than to M. Cato, who was at that time the chief person of the senate? Do you take that print of a horse's hoof, which is now to be seen on a stone at Regillus, to be made by Castor's horse? Should you not believe what is probable, that the souls of eminent men, such as the Tyndaridæ, are divine and immortal, rather than that those bodies, which had been reduced to ashes, should mount on horses, and fight in an army? If you say that was possible, you ought to show how it is so, and not amuse us with fabulous old women's stories. . . .

We are now to speak of predictions. No one can avoid what is to come, and indeed it is commonly useless to know it; for it is a miserable case to be afflicted to no purpose, and not to have even the last, the common comfort, hope, which, according to your principles, none can have; for you say that fate governs all things, and call that fate, which has been true from all eternity. What advantage, then, is the knowledge of futurity to us, or how does it assist us to guard against impending evils, since it will come inevitably?

But whence comes that divination? To whom is owing that knowledge from the entrails of beasts? Who first made observations from the voice of the crow? Who invented the Lots? Not that I give no credit to these things, . . . but I ought to be informed how these things are understood by philosophers, especially as the diviners are often wrong in their conjectures. But physicians, you say, are likewise often mistaken. What comparison can there be between divination, of the origin of which we are ignorant, and physic, which proceeds on principles intelligible to every one? You believe that the Decii, in devoting themselves to death, appeased the Gods. How great, then, was the iniquity of the Gods, that they could not be appeased but at the price of such noble blood! . . . .

I do not, then, O Balbus, from anything that you have said, perceive as yet that it is proved that there are Gods. I believe it, indeed, but not from any arguments of the Stoics . . . since, then, you have divided the whole question into four parts, and I have said all that I had to say on the first, I will take the second into consideration; in which, when you attempted to show what the character of the Gods was, you seemed to me rather to prove that there are none; for you said that it was the greatest difficulty to draw our minds from the prepossessions of the eyes; but that as nothing is more excellent than the Deity, you did not doubt that the world was God, because there is nothing better in nature than the world, and so we may reasonably think it animated, or rather perceive it in our minds as clearly as if it were obvious to our eyes.

Now, in what sense do you say there is nothing better than the world? If you mean that there is nothing more beautiful, I agree with you; that there is nothing more adapted to our wants, I likewise agree with you: but if you mean that nothing is wiser than the world, I am by no means of your opinion. Not that I find it difficult to conceive anything in my mind, independent of my eyes; on the contrary, the more I separate my mind from my eyes, the less I am able to comprehend your opinion.

Nothing is better than the world, you say. Nor is there, indeed, anything on earth better than the city of Rome; do you think, therefore, that our city has a mind, that it thinks and reasons; or that this most beautiful city, being void of sense, is not preferable to an ant because an ant has sense, understanding, reason, and memory? You should consider, Balbus, what ought to be allowed you, and not advance things because they please you.

For that old, concise, and, as it seemed to you, acute syllogism of Zeno, has been all which you have so much enlarged upon in handling this topic: "That which reasons is superior to that which does not; nothing is superior to the world; therefore the world reasons." If you would prove also that the world can very well read a book, follow the example of Zeno, and say, "That which can read is better than that which cannot; nothing is better than the world; the world therefore can read." After the same manner you may prove the world to be an orator, a mathematician, a musician, that it possesses all sciences, and, in short, is a philosopher. You have often said that God made all things, and that no cause can produce an effect unlike itself. From hence it will follow, not only that the world is animated, and is wise, but also plays upon the fiddle and the flute, because it produces men who play on those instruments. . . . But if the world, considered as one great whole, is not God, you should not surely deify, as you have done, that infinite multitude of stars, which only form a part of it, and which so delight you with the regularity of their eternal courses; not but that there is something truly wonderful and incredible in their regularity, but this regularity of motion, Balbus, may as well be ascribed to a natural as to a divine cause. . . .

Consider, I pray, if everything which is regular in its motion is deemed divine, whether it will not follow that tertian and quartan agues must likewise be so, as their returns have the greatest regularity. These effects are to be explained by reason; but, because you are unable to assign any, you have recourse to a Deity as your last refuge.

The arguments of Chrysippus appeared to you of great weight; a man undoubtedly of great quickness and subtlety. . . . "If," he said, "there is anything which is beyond the power of man to produce, the being who produces it is better than man. Man is unable to make what is in the world; the being, therefore, that could do it is superior to man. What being is there but a God superior to man? Therefore there is a God."

These arguments are founded on the same erroneous principles as Zeno's, for he does not define what is meant by being better or more excellent, or distinguish between an intelligent cause and a natural cause. Chrysippus adds, "If there are no Gods, there is nothing better than man; but we cannot, without the highest arrogance, have this idea of ourselves." Let us grant that it is arrogance in man to think himself better than the world; but to comprehend that he has understanding and reason, and that in Orion and Canicula there is neither, is no arrogance, but an indication of good sense. . . .

But your school, Balbus, allows fire only to be the sole active principle; an opinion which I believe you derive from Heraclitus, whom some men understand in one sense, some in another; but since he seems unwilling to be understood, we will pass him by. You Stoics then say that fire is the universal principle of all things; that all living bodies cease to live on the extinction of that heat, and that throughout all nature whatever is sensible of that heat lives and flourishes. Now I cannot conceive that bodies should perish for want of heat, rather than for want of moisture or air, especially as they even die through excess of heat; so that the life of animals does not depend more on fire than on the other elements. . . .

If I am not mistaken, you believe that in all nature there is nothing but fire, which is self-animated. Why fire rather than air, of which the life of animals consists, and which is called from thence *anima*, the soul? But how is it that you take it for granted that life is nothing but fire? It seems more probable that it is a compound of fire and air. . . .

You Stoics hold that all fire has need of nourishment, without which it cannot possibly subsist; that the sun, moon, and all the stars, are fed either with fresh or salt waters; and the reason that Cleanthes gives why the sun is retrograde, and does not go beyond the tropics in the summer or winter, is, that he may not be too far from his sustenance. This I shall fully examine hereafter; but at present we may conclude, that whatever may cease to be, cannot of its own nature be eternal; that if fire wants sustenance, it will cease to be, and that therefore fire is not of its own nature eternal.

After all, what kind of a Deity must that be who is not graced with one single virtue, if we should succeed in forming this idea of such an one? Must we not attribute prudence to a Deity? a virtue, which consists in the knowledge of things good, bad, and indifferent. Yet what need has a being for the discernment of good and ill, who neither has nor can have any ill? Of what use is reason to him? of what use is understanding? We men, indeed, find them useful to aid us in finding out things which are obscure by those which are clear to us; but nothing can be obscure to a Deity. As to justice, which gives to every one his own, it is not the concern of the Gods; since that virtue, according to your doctrine, received its birth from men, and from civil society. Temperance consists in abstinence from corporeal pleasures, and if such abstinence hath a place in heaven, so also must the pleasures abstained from. Lastly, if fortitude is ascribed to the Deity, how does it appear? In afflictions, in labour, in danger? None of these things can affect a God. How then can we conceive this to be a deity, that makes no use of reason, and is not endowed with any virtue? . . .

Let us proceed to the two other parts of our dispute: first, "whether there is a divine providence which governs the world"; and lastly, "whether that providence particularly regards mankind"; for these are the remaining propositions of your discourse; and I think that, if you approve of it, we should examine these more accurately. With all my heart, said Velleius, for I readily agree to what you have hitherto said, and expect still greater things from you.

I am unwilling to interrupt you, said Balbus to Cotta, but we shall take another opportunity, and I shall effectually convince you. But[3] . . .

This now is reason; that reason, which you say the divine goodness has denied to the brute creation, kindly to bestow it on men alone. How great, how immense the favour! Observe Medea flying from her father and her country:—

> The guilty wretch from her pursuer flies.
> By her own hands the young Absyrtus slain,

[3] A large part of Cotta's arguments against providence appears to have been lost.

> His mangled limbs she scatters o'er the plain;
> That the fond sire might sink beneath his woe,
> And she to parricide her safety owe.

Reflection, as well as wickedness, must have been necessary to the preparation of such a fact; and did he too, who prepared that fatal repast for his brother, do it without reflection?—

> Revenge, as great as Atreus' injury,
> Shall sink his soul and crown his misery.

Did not Thyestes himself, not content with having defiled his brother's bed . . . did he not, I say, by that adultery, aim at the possession of the crown? . . . .

Do you not perceive that Thyestes must have had a share of reason proportionable to the greatness of his crimes; such crimes as are not only represented to us on the stage, but such as we see committed, nay often exceeded, in the common course of life? The private houses of individual citizens, the public courts, the senate, the camp, our allies, our provinces, all agree that reason is the author of all the ill, as well as of all the good which is done; that it makes few act well, and that but seldom, but many act ill, and that frequently; and that, in short, the Gods would have shown greater benevolence in denying us any reason at all, than in sending us that which is accompanied with so much mischief; for as wine is seldom wholesome, but often hurtful in diseases, we think it more prudent to deny it to the patient, than to run the risk of so uncertain a remedy; so I do not know whether it would not be better for mankind to be deprived of wit, thought, and penetration, or what we call reason, since it is a thing pernicious to many and very useful to few, than to have it bestowed upon them with so much liberality, and in such abundance. But if the divine will has really consulted the good of man in this gift of reason, the good of those men only was consulted on whom a well-regulated one is bestowed; how few those are, if any, is very apparent. We cannot admit, therefore, that the Gods consulted the good of a few only; the conclusion must be that they consulted the good of none.

You answer that the ill use which a great part of mankind make of reason, no more takes away the goodness of the Gods, who bestow it as a present of the greatest benefit to them, than the ill use which children make of their patrimony, diminishes the obligation which they have to their parents for it. We grant you this; but where is the similitude? It was far from Deianira's design to injure Hercules, when she made him a present of the shirt dipped in the blood of the Centaurs. . . . For it has often happened that people have served a man whom they intended to injure, and have injured one whom they designed to serve; so that the effect of the gift is by no means always a proof of the intention of the giver; neither does the benefit which may accrue from it prove that it came from the hands of a benefactor. For, in short, what debauchery, what avarice, what crime amongst men is there which does not owe its birth to thought and reflection, that is, to reason? For all opinion is reason; right reason, if men's thoughts are conformable to truth; wrong reason, if they are not. The Gods only give us the mere faculty of reason, if we have any; the use or abuse of it depends entirely upon ourselves; so that the comparison is not just between the present of reason given us by the Gods, and a patrimony left to a son by his father; for after all, if the injury of mankind had been the end proposed by the Gods, what could they have given them more pernicious than reason; for what seed could there be of injustice, intemperance and cowardice, if reason were not laid as the foundation of these vices . . . we should wish that the Gods had never bestowed this ability on man; the abuse of which is so general, that the small number of those who make a good use of it are often oppressed by those who make a bad use of it; so that it seems to be given rather to help vice, than to promote virtue amongst us.

This, you insist on it, is the fault of man, and not of the Gods. But should we not laugh at a physician or pilot, though they are weak mortals, if they were to lay the blame of their ill success on the violence of the disease, or the fury of the tempest? Had there not been danger, we should say, who would have applied to you? This reasoning has still greater force against the Deity. The fault, you say, is in man, if he commits crimes. But why was not man endued with a reason incapable of producing any crimes? . . . How could the Gods err? When we leave our effects to our children, it is in hopes that they may be well bestowed; in which we may be deceived; but how can the Deity be deceived? As Phœbus, when he trusted his chariot to his son Phaëthon, or as Neptune, when he indulged his son Theseus in granting him three wishes, the consequence of which was the destruction of Hippolytus? These are poetical fictions. But truth and not fables ought to proceed from philosophers. Yet, if those poetical Deities had foreseen that their indulgence would have proved fatal to their sons, they must have been thought blameable for it. . . .

But to conclude. If folly, by the unanimous consent of philosophers, is allowed to be the greatest of all evils, and if no one ever attained to true wisdom, we, whom they say the immortal Gods take care of, are consequently in a state of the utmost misery. . . . Telamon in our verse decides the question. If, says he, there is a Divine Providence,—

Good men would be happy, bad men miserable.

But it is not so. If the Gods had regarded mankind, they should have made them all virtuous. But if they did not regard the welfare of all mankind, at least they ought to have provided for the happiness of the virtuous. Why, therefore, was the Carthaginian in Spain suffered to destroy those best and bravest men, the two Scipios? Why did Maximus lose his son the consul? . . . But there would be no end of enumerating examples of good men made miserable, and wicked men prosperous. Why did that Marius live to an old age, and die so happily at his own house, in his seventh consulship? Why was that inhuman wretch Cinna permitted to enjoy so long a reign?

He indeed met with deserved punishment at last. But would it not have been better that these inhumanities had been prevented, than that the author of them should be punished afterwards? . . . Dionysius was thirty-eight years a tyrant over the most opulent and flourishing city; and, before him, how many years did Pisistratus tyrannize in the very flower of Greece! Phalaris and Apollodorus met with the fate they deserved; but not till after they had tortured and put to death multitudes. Many robbers have been executed; but the number of those who have suffered for their crimes is short of those whom they have robbed and murdered. . . . If, therefore, the Gods really see everything that happens to men, you must acknowledge they make no distinction between the good and the bad.

Diogenes the Cynic used to say of Harpalus, one of the most fortunate villains of his time, that the constant prosperity of such a man was a kind of witness against the Gods. Dionysius, of whom we have before spoken, after he had pillaged the temple of Proserpine at Locris, set sail for Syracuse, and, having a fair wind during his voyage, said, with a smile, "See, my friends, what favourable winds the immortal Gods bestow upon church-robbers." Encouraged by this prosperous event, he proceeded in his impiety. When he landed at Peloponnesus, he went into the temple of Jupiter Olympius, and disrobed his statue of a golden mantle of great weight, an ornament which the tyrant Gelo had given out of the spoils of the Carthaginians, and at the same time, in a jesting manner, he said, "that a golden mantle was too heavy in summer, and too cold in winter"; and then, throwing a woollen cloak over the statue, added, "this will serve for all seasons." . . . He likewise robbed the temples of the silver tables, which, according to the ancient custom of Greece, bore this inscription, "To the good Gods," saying that he was willing to make use of their goodness; and, without the least scruple, took away the little golden emblems of victory, the cups and coronets, which were in the stretched out hands of the statues, saying he "did not take, but receive them; for it would be folly not to accept good things from the Gods, to whom we are constantly praying for favours, when they stretch out their hands towards us." . . .

Yet neither did Olympian Jove strike him with his thunder, nor did Æsculapius cause him to die by tedious diseases and a lingering death. He died in his bed, had funeral honours paid to him, and left his power, which he had wickedly obtained, as a just and lawful inheritance to his son.

It is not without concern that I maintain a doctrine which seems to authorize evil, and which might probably give a sanction to it, if conscience, without any Divine assistance, did not point out, in the clearest manner, the difference between virtue and vice. Without conscience man is contemptible. For as no family or state can be supposed to be formed with any reason or discipline, if there are no rewards for good actions, nor punishments for crimes, so we cannot believe that a Divine Providence regulates the world, if there is no distinction between the honest and the wicked. . . .

But good men have sometimes success. They have so; but we cannot, with any show of reason, attribute that success to the Gods. Diagoras, who is called the atheist, being at Samothrace, one of his friends showed him several pictures of people who had endured very dangerous storms; "See," says he, "you who deny a providence, how many have been saved by their prayers to the Gods." "Aye," says Diagoras, "I see those who were saved, but where are those painted who were shipwrecked?" At another time, he himself was in a storm, when the sailors, being greatly alarmed, told him they justly deserved that misfortune for admitting him into their ship; when he, pointing to others under the like distress, asked them if they believed Diagoras was also aboard those ships?

In short, with regard to good or bad fortune, it matters not what you are, or how you have lived. The Gods, like kings, regard not everything. What similitude is there between them? If kings neglect anything, want of knowledge may be pleaded in their defence; but ignorance cannot be brought as an excuse for the Gods.

Your manner of justifying them is somewhat extraordinary, when you say, that if a wicked man dies without suffering for his crimes, the Gods inflict a punishment on his children, his children's children, and all his posterity. O wonderful equity of the Gods! What city would endure the maker of a law, which should condemn a son or a grandson for a crime committed by the father or the grandfather? . . . those eyes of the maritime coast, Corinth and Carthage, were plucked out, the one by Critolaus, the other by Hasdrubal, without the assistance of any divine anger, since you yourselves confess, that a Deity cannot possibly be angry on any provocation.

But could not the Deity have assisted and preserved those eminent cities?—Undoubtedly he could; for, according to your doctrine, his power is infinite, and without the least labour; and as nothing but the will is necessary to the motion of our bodies, so the divine will of the Gods, with the like ease, can create, move, and change all things. This you hold, not from a mere phantom of superstition, but on natural and settled principles of reason; for matter, you say, of which all things are composed and consist, is susceptible of all forms and changes, and there is nothing which cannot be, or cease to be, in an instant; and that divine providence has the command and disposal of this universal matter, and consequently can, in any part of the universe, do whatever she pleases: from whence I conclude, that this providence either knows not the extent of her power, or neglects human affairs, or cannot judge what is best for us. Providence, you say, does not extend her care to particular men; there is no wonder in that, since she does not extend it to cities, or even to nations, or people. If, therefore, she neglects whole nations, is it not very probable that she neglects all mankind? . . .

This is the purport of what I had to say concerning the nature of the Gods; not with a design to destroy their existence, but merely to show what an obscure point it is, and with what difficulties an explanation of it is attended.

Balbus, observing that Cotta had finished his discourse,— You have been very severe, he said, against a divine providence, a doctrine established by the Stoics with piety and wisdom; but as it grows too late, I shall defer my answer to another day. Our argument is of the greatest importance; it concerns our altars, our hearths, our temples, nay, even the walls of our city, which you priests hold sacred; you, who by religion defend Rome better than she is defended by her ramparts. This is a cause which, whilst I have life, I think I cannot abandon without impiety.

There is nothing, replied Cotta, which I desire more than to be confuted. I have not pretended to decide this point, but to give you my private sentiments upon it; and am very sensible of your great superiority in argument. No doubt of it, said Velleius; we have much to fear from one who believes that our dreams are sent from Jupiter, which, though they are of little weight, are yet of more importance than the discourse of the Stoics concerning the nature of the Gods.

The conversation ended here, and we parted. Velleius judged that the arguments of Cotta were truest; but those of Balbus seemed to me to have the greater probability.

THE OFFICES*

Book I

[2. . . . . Of all those useful and important subjects, which philosophers have handled so largely and accurately, the precepts they have delivered about Offices or Duties seem of the

---

* Translated by Thomas Cockman.

largest extent and comprehension; for they take in every part of our lives, so that whatever we go about, whether of public or private affairs, whether at home or abroad, whether considered barely by ourselves, or as we stand in relation to other people, we lie constantly under an obligation to some duties: and as all the virtue and credit of our lives proceed from the due discharge of this, so all the baseness and turpitude of them result from the non-observance of the same. Now, though this be a subject which all philosophers have employed themselves about (for, who ever dared to assume that name without laying down some instructions about duty?), yet have some sects of them given such accounts of man's happiness and misery, as destroy the very being of virtue and honesty[1]: for he that makes any thing his chiefest good, wherein justice or virtue does not bear a part, and sets up profit, not honesty, for the measure of his happiness; as long as he acts in conformity with his own principles, and is not overruled by the mere dictates of reason and humanity, can never do the offices of friendship, justice, or liberality: nor can he ever be a man of courage, who thinks that pain is the greatest evil; or he of temperance, who imagines pleasure to be the sovereign good. Which things are all so obvious and plain, that one would think they could never stand in need of a dispute: however, I have largely discoursed on them in another work. These sects, therefore, unless they are resolved to be inconsistent with themselves, ought wholly to abstain from speaking anything about duties; nor indeed can any constant, unalterable, rational rules of them at all be given, unless it be by those who go on this principle—that it is virtue alone, or at least that chiefly, which ought to be desired for its own sake. So that only the Stoics, Academics, and Peripatetics have a right to lay down any rules on this subject; for as to the opinion of Aristo, Pyrrho, and Herillus,

---

[1] The word *honestas*, translated here as "honesty," has really a broader connotation than "honesty" suggests. "Moral rightness" might be better. (Ed.)

that has been exploded a good while ago; who might have
claimed a privilege to treat about duties, as well as the former three, had they but left the possibility of choosing, and
allowed at least so much difference between things, as to put
us into a capacity of finding out our duty, and distinguishing
it from that which is not so. I shall follow therefore at this
time, and on this subject more especially, the Stoics; not as
a bare translator of them, but, according to my usual custom,
shall take out of their stores so much, and after such a manner, as in my own judgment I shall think most convenient.
Seeing then the whole of our following discourse is designed
to be about Offices or Duties, I think it will be necessary for
me, in the first place, to determine and fix the signification of
the word "Office," which I cannot but wonder to find omitted
by Panaetius: for every clear and rational discourse on any
subject ought first to begin with an explication of that subject, so that we may have a distinct conception of what we
are afterwards to discourse about.

[3. The whole subject of duties then, in its greatest latitude,
comprehends under it these two parts: the first is taken up in
explaining what is good, and what our greatest good; the second in certain direction and precepts, according to which on
all occasions it is our duty to govern our lives and actions. To
the first part belong such questions as these, whether all duties
are perfect or not? and, whether one can be greater or less
than another? with several others to the same purpose. Not
but that the duties of this second part, the rules and precepts
of which are laid down, have some tendency and relation to
our chiefest good; but only it does not so plainly appear, because they seem to concern more immediately the government of our lives and regulation of our manners; and these
are they which I design to explain in the following treatise.
There is also another distribution of duties, some of them being called middle or ordinary, and others perfect or complete.
To the latter, I think, we may give the name of right or
straight. By that which we have called right or straight, is

meant a virtue that is wholly complete in all its parts, without any manner of flaw or imperfection; and by that which we have called ordinary, such a one as a fair and reasonable account may be given for the doing of it. Now these fair and reasonable accounts are all to be drawn from several heads, which are by Panaetius reduced to three, and may be called general heads of deliberating or doubting concerning any action, whether it should or should not be done. The first is, when it is consulted or doubted, whether the action that is under consideration be honest or dishonest; in which inquiry men are often divided between several opinions. The second is when it is inquired and consulted, whether the action that is under deliberation will supply us with the pleasures and conveniences of life, furnish us with plenty of outward things, such as riches, honors, power, etc., which may put us into a capacity of doing good to ourselves, and to all those for whom we are more nearly concerned; all which inquiry comes under the general head of profit. The third ground or reason of doubting is, when that thing which seems to be profitable for us comes into competition with that which is honest; for then our interest drawing us one way and honesty pulling us back another, the wavering mind is, as it were, torn in sunder between the two, and is racked with doubting and anxious thoughts. There is no greater fault in any division, than not to take in all the several parts of the matter to be divided; and yet two are omitted in the now-mentioned one of Panaetius: for men not only consult and deliberate whether such an action be honest or dishonest; but also of two honests that are both proposed to them, which is the most so; and in like manner of two profitables, which is the most profitable. From whence it appears, that what he thought was contained in three, ought rather to be divided into five heads. We must then, in the first place, discourse about honesty, and this we shall do under these two inquiries: whether the thing proposed be honest or dishonest? and, of two that are honest, which is the most so? which will make up the subject of our first book. We shall treat in our second of profit or interest under the same heads. And lastly, in our third we shall endeavor to show, when a seeming advantage and honesty come into competition, how a good man should determine his judgment.

[4. The first thing to be taken notice of is this, that every creature doth by nature endeavor to preserve its own self, its life and body; and to shun and avoid those things which appear prejudicial and hurtful to it; but to seek and procure whatever is necessary for the support of its being, and advancement of its happiness, such as food, shelter, and the like. There is likewise common to all sorts of animals a desire for the continuance and propagation of their several species; together with a love and concern for their young ones. Now there is this special difference betwen men and brutes; that the latter are governed by nothing but their senses, never look any farther than just to what strikes and affects them at present, and have a very little, or hardly any concern, for what is past or to come: but the former are creatures endowed with reason, which gives them a power to carry their thoughts to the consequences of things, to discover causes before they have yet produced their effect; to see the whole progress, and even the first seeds, as it were, and appearances of them; to compare like occurrences with like, and by joining what is past and what is to come together, to make a just estimate of the one from the other; whereby they are able at once to take a view of their whole lives, and accordingly to make provision for the necessities of them. And the same force of reason makes all men by nature to love one another, and desire an intercourse of words and actions. It begets in them, likewise, a somewhat extraordinary love and affection for their own children; and strongly inclines them to frequent public meetings, and keep up societies one amongst another. For the same reason also they are very industrious to provide for the necessaries and conveniences of life; and that not only for themselves in particular, but for their wives, their children, and others whom they have a kindness for, and are obliged to take care of; which concern is very proper to rouse up the spirits, and make them more vigorous and active in business. But of all the properties and inclinations of men, there is none more natural and peculiar to them than an earnest desire and search after truth. Hence it is that our minds are no sooner free from the thoughts and engagements of necessary business, but we presently long to be either seeing, or hearing, or learning of something; and esteem the knowledge of things secret and wonderful as a necessary ingredient of a happy life. Whence it appears that nothing is more agreeable and suited to the nature and minds of men than undisguised openness, truth, and sincerity. Next to this love and affection for truth, there follows in the soul an impatient desire and inclination to pre-eminence; so that whoever has the genuine nature of a man in him, will never endure to be subject to another, unless he be one that instructs or advises, or is invested with a just and lawful authority for the benefit of the public: whence there arises a greatness of soul, which sets it above all the petty concerns and trifling enjoyments of this present world. It is another, and that too no mean prerogative of our reasonable nature, that man alone can discern all the beauties of order and decency, and knows how to govern his words and actions in conformity to them. It is he alone that, of all the creatures, observes and is pleased with the beauty, gracefulness, and symmetry of parts in the objects of sense; which nature and reason observing in them, from thence take occasion to apply the same also to those of the mind; and to conclude that beauty, consistency, and regularity, should be much more kept up in our words and actions; and therefore command us, that nothing be done that is effeminate or unbecoming; and that so strict a guard be kept over every thought and action, as that no indecency be either conceived or practiced by us. From these inclinations and instincts of nature arises and results that honesty we are seeking for; which, however little valued and esteemed it may be, is nevertheless virtuous and amiable in itself; and which we may justly say, though it were commended by no one, is yet in its own nature truly commendable.

[5. Thus, son Marcus,[2] have I given you a rough draft, and just the outlines, as it were, of honesty; which, could she be seen in her full beauty with mortal eye, would make the whole world (as Plato has said) be in love with wisdom. Now whatever is contained under the notion of honesty arises from one of these four heads; first, a sagacious inquiry and observation for the finding out of truth, which may be called by the general name of prudence: secondly, a care to maintain that society and mutual intercourse which is between them; to render to every man what is his due; and to stand to one's words in all promises and bargains; which we call justice: thirdly, the greatness and unshaken resolution of a truly brave and invincible mind, which goes by the name of magnanimity or fortitude: and lastly, a keeping of our words and actions within the due limits of order and decency; under which are comprehended temperance and moderation. Now every one of these several heads, though they all have a mutual connection and dependence on one another, has yet its peculiar class, as it were, and respective set of duties arising from it. From that, for example, which is mentioned first, and under which prudence and wisdom are contained, arises the duty of seeking, contemplating, and finding out of truth, which is the proper and peculiar business of those virtues: for it is then, and then alone that we justly esteem a man prudent and wise, when we find that he is able to see and discover the truth of things; and of an active, vigorous and piercing mind, to give an account of the reasons of them; so that it is truth that is the proper object of both these virtues, and that about which they are only concerned. The other three heads more peculiarly belong to the active life, and their business lies in procuring and keeping what

---

[2] *The Offices* is written in the form of a letter to Cicero's son, a student of philosophy under Cratippus in Athens.

is useful and necessary for the preservation of it; as in holding up mutual love and correspondence among mankind; in an elevated greatness and strength of mind; which appears, as in getting things profitable and pleasant for ourselves and dependents, so more especially in despising and being above them. Then, as for the last, viz. order, uniformity, moderation, and the like, it is plain they belong not only to contemplation, but have also a respect to our outward actions; since from keeping of these within the bounds and limits of order and moderation, we are said to observe what is virtuous and becoming.

[6. Having thus explained how the whole nature and power of honesty is deduced from some one of these four parts, we are now to discourse of them each in particular. And, first, of Prudence, which is wholly taken up in the knowledge of truth, and has the nearest affinity of any with the reasonable nature of man. For how are we all of us drawn and enticed with the desire of wisdom! how noble and glorious a thing do we imagine it to excel in knowledge! and how mean and reproachful do we count it, on the other hand, to slip, to be in error, to be ignorant, or to be imposed on? In gratifying this so natural and virtuous inclination in the mind of man, there are two grand faults to be carefully avoided: the first is an over-great hastiness and rashness in giving up our assent, presuming that we know things before we really do so. Whoever desires (as I am sure all ought) to avoid this error, must in all his inquiries allow himself time, and diligently consider the matter with himself, before he proceeds to pass his judgment on it. The second fault is, that a great many men bestow abundance of study, and a world of pains, on very difficult and obscure subjects; and such as, perhaps, when they are found out, are of but very little, or no concernment. Would men but be careful to shun these two mistakes, whatever study or pains they might spend on virtuous, worthy, or profitable subjects, it would not without reason be highly commended. Thus Caius Sulpicius was heretofore praised for his skill in astronomy: Sextus Pompeius, since my memory, for his in geometry: many have been famous in the study of logic, and more in that of the civil laws: the more peculiar business of all which parts of learning is the finding out of truth. No man, however, should be so taken up in the search of truth, as thereby to neglect the more necessary duties of active life: for, after all is done, it is action only that gives a true value and commendation to virtue. Not that we are able to be always employed without intermission, but often retire from business to study; beside that the mind, which is in perpetual motion and agitations, of itself will supply us with study and thinking, whether we set ourselves to it or not. In a word, the general aim and design of our thought, and application of mind, is either the attainment of such things as are honest, and tend to a virtuous and happy way of life, or else the improvement of our reason and understanding in wisdom and knowledge. And this may suffice for the first of our general heads of duty.

[7. Of the other remaining three, that which consists in upholding society, and keeping up mutual love and good nature amongst mankind, seems of the largest and most diffusive extent. It comprehends under it these two parts: first justice, which is much the most glorious and splendid of all virtues, and alone entitles us to the name and appellation of good men; and secondly, beneficence, which may also be called either bounty or liberality. Now the first thing that justice requires of us is this; that no one should do any hurt to another, unless by way of reasonable and just retribution for some injury received from him: and whatever belongs either to all in common, or particular persons as their own property, should not be altered, but made use of accordingly. Now no man can say that he has anything his own by a right of nature; but either by an ancient immemorial seizure, as those who first planted uninhabited countries; or, secondly, by conquest, as those who have got things by the right of the sword; or else by some law-compact, agreement, or lot. It is by some of these means that the people inhabiting Arpinum and Tusculum came to have those lands, which are now called theirs; and the same may be said as to private men's estates. However, since at present, by some of these ways, each particular man has his personal possessions, out of that which by nature was common to all, it is but just that each should hold what is now his own; which, if any one endeavor to take away from him, he directly breaks in on common justice, and violates the rights of human society. "But seeing," (as is excellently said by Plato,) "we are not born for ourselves alone; but that our native country, our friends and relations, have a just claim and title to some part of us"; and seeing whatsoever is created on earth was merely designed (as the Stoics will have it) for the service of men; and men themselves for the service, good, and assistance of one another; we certainly in this should be followers of Nature, and second her intentions; and by producing all that lies within the reach of our power for the general interest, by mutually giving and receiving good turns, by our knowledge, industry, riches, or other means, should endeavour to keep up that love and society, that should be amongst men. Now the great foundation of justice is faithfulness, which consists in being constantly firm to your word, and a conscientious performance of all compacts and bargains. The vice that is opposite to justice is injustice, of which there are two sorts: the first consists in the actual doing an injury to another; the second, in tamely looking on while he is injured, and not helping and defending him though we are able: for he that injuriously falls on another, whether prompted by rage or other violent passion, does as it were leap at the throat of his companion; and he that refuses to help him when injured, and to ward off the wrong if it lies in his power, is as plainly guilty of baseness and injustice as though he had deserted his father, his friends, or his native country. Now that former injustice, which consists in the willful and actual wronging of another, has oftentimes no other cause but fear; when he, who designedly does a man an injury, is afraid lest he himself should be forced to undergo one, if he does not secure himself by doing it beforehand. But, generally speaking, the great source and fountain of all such injustice is the satisfying of some irregular and exorbitant appetite; and in a more especial manner, the desire of riches; of which we shall therefore say something in particular. . . .

[9. As for the second, which only consists in seeing another injured, and being wanting to our duty, by not defending him; the causes of that are wont to be several: for some are afraid of offending others, or of bringing a trouble and charge on themselves: others are negligent, idle, or meanspirited: and a third sort there is, who are so taken up with their own concerns, that they have no time left to regard the oppressed, whom yet it is their duty to save and protect. I am therefore of opinion, that Plato's consequence will hardly hold good where, speaking about the philosophers, he says, "They are wholly taken up in the seeking out of truth, and perfectly neglect and make light of those things which the rest of the world are so eager after, and so contend about; and that therefore they are just." This, I say, I am afraid is a bad consequence; for though, it is true, they keep the first sort of justice, inasmuch as they actually do no wrong; yet they run perfectly counter to the other; for being engaged in their learning and studies, they abandon their friends to be injured by others, whom in justice they ought to have protected and defended. So that it is believed they hardly ever trouble themselves so far, as at all to intermeddle with the business of the public, if it was not altogether, as it were, forced on them. But it were a great deal better would they do it voluntarily; for an action, though honest, is not therefore truly virtuous, unless it be done out of choice, and with a good will. There are others yet, who out of a desire of improving their own estates, or else a morose and unsociable sort of temper, cry, they meddle with nobody's business but their own, that so they may seem to be men of strict honesty, and to injure nobody; and they do indeed avoid the one sort of injustice, but directly run themselves into the other; for they desert the common good and society of mankind, while they bestow neither study, pains, nor money toward the preservation of it. Thus have I laid down the two sorts of injustice, and pointed out to you the causes of each; and have also endeavored to explain the true nature and extent of justice; from all which account it will be easy to judge, unless we are extremely fond of our own ease, what those several duties are, which at several times are required of us. I say, unless we are fond of our own ease; for the truth of it is, it is a troublesome thing to be concerned in the business of other people: however, old Chremes in Terence thinks "That he ought to be concerned for the good of all men." But be that as it will, forasmuch as the success of our own affairs, whether good or ill, more nearly concerns us, and makes us more sensible than that of another, which appears to us small, as a thing at a great distance; therefore we pass a quite different judgment on the one and the other. And, on this account, it is a very good rule that is given by some men, "that we should never venture on any action, of which we doubt whether it is honest or dishonest"; for honesty quickly would show itself by its own native brightness; and the doubting about it a plain intimation that at least we suspected some injustice when we did it.

[10. But here it is observable, that the limits of justice are not so fixed, but that they may be altered by an alteration of circumstances; so that what at one time appears to be the duty of an honest and good man, at another is altered and becomes the quite contrary; to deliver up a trust, for example, or perform a promise, and other things relating to truth and faithfulness, are duties which justice itself will allow us, in several cases, to neglect or omit: for respect must be had to those general rules we before laid down, as the ground and foundation of all justice—first, that no injury be done to another; and secondly, that we make it our earnest endeavor to promote the good and interest of all mankind: so that our duty is not always the same, but various, according to a variety of circumstances. There may be a contract or promise, for instance, the performance of which would bring very great damage, either to the person himself that made it, or the other party to whom it was made. Thus, had Neptune not granted what he promised to Theseus, Theseus had not suffered the loss of his son Hippolytus: for, as the story goes, Neptune having granted him any three wishes, for the third he once in a very great passion desired the death of his own son; by obtaining of which he was afterwards brought into the greatest afflictions. Such promises therefore are not to be kept, as will but bring a mischief on him they were made to; no more are those which tend to the damage of the promiser himself, more than to the profit of him they were promised to.—Again, even justice itself requires us to perform a greater before a lesser duty: you promise, for example, a friend of yours, to assist him in a cause that he has depending, but your son grows dangerously sick in the meantime: here it would be no breach of duty in you, if you should not make good what you promised to your friend; and he himself rather would be much to blame, should he complain of being disappointed by you. Farther, it is plain to any one's sense, that such sort of promises can never be binding as are made by people overawed by fear, or overreached by deceit. . . .

[11. There are certain duties also to be strictly observed, even toward those that have injured us; for we ought not to go beyond certain bounds, in exacting revenge and punishment of another: in which particular it may, perhaps, be enough to make him that has wronged us repent of the wrong done; so that both he himself may abstain from the like, and others may be discouraged from injuring us for the future. There are certain peculiar laws of war also, which are of all things most strictly to be observed in the commonwealth; for there being two sorts of disputing in the world, the one by reason, and the other by open force; and the former of these being that which is agreeable to the nature of man, and the latter to that of brutes; when we cannot obtain what is our right by the one, we must of necessity have recourse to the other. It is allowable therefore to undertake wars, but it must always be with design of obtaining a secure peace: and when we have got the better of our enemies, we should rest content with the victory alone, and show ourselves merciful and kind to them afterwards, unless they are such as have been very cruel, and committed inhuman barbarities in the war. . . .

[14. We have now gone through with the subject of justice; it remains, in the next place, to go on according to our method proposed, that we say something likewise of bounty and liberality, than which there is nothing more nearly allied to the nature of man. But then we must observe these following cautions—first, that we take care in all acts of bounty, that they be not prejudicial to those we would oblige by them, nor to any other body; secondly, that we do not in our bounty and liberality go beyond our estates; and, thirdly, that we duly proportion our kindness, according to every man's merit and deserts. And first of the former, which is grounded on the great and fundamental principle of all justice, to which this duty in all its particular instances should be referred—for he who, pretending to do one a kindness, does that which is really a prejudice to him, is indeed so far from being kind and obliging, as that he ought to be counted a most pernicious flatterer; and to do any manner of injury to one, that you may show your generosity and bounty to another, is just one and the same sort of roguery and injustice, as to enrich yourself by the spoils of your neighbor. Yet this is the fault of a great many people, and especially those who are desirous of glory, to take away from some that which justly belongs to them, that so they may have to bestow on others; and they are apt to think themselves extremely bountiful if they enrich their adherents by any manner of means. But this is so far from being a duty of liberality, that nothing in the world can be more contrary to it. It ought to be therefore our first care in giving, that what we bestow be a real advantage and kindness to our friend, and no ways an injury to any third person. That action therefore of Caesar and Sylla's, in taking away estates from the rightful proprietors, and giving them to others, who had no right to them, ought by no means to be accounted liberal; for nothing can ever be truly such that is not at the same time just and honest. A second caution to be observed was this: that our bounty be not suffered to exceed our abilities: for they who give more than their estates will allow of, are, in the first place, injurious to their own relations, by spending that wealth on other people which should rather have been given or left to them. Beside that this over-great bounty in giving is usually accompanied with an answerable desire and greediness of getting; which often proceeds even to downright oppression, that so men may have wherewithal to supply this extravagant humor. One may also observe in a great many people, that they take a sort of pride in being counted magnificent, and give very plentifully, not from any generous principle in their natures, but only to appear great in the eye of the world; so that all their bounty is resolved into nothing but mere outside and pretense, and is nearer of kin to vanity and folly, than it is to either liberality or honesty. The third caution was, that our bounty should be proportioned to the merits of the receiver; in judging of which, we are first to consider the man's honesty or manners; secondly, the good-will he bears towards us; thirdly, the nearness of relation, or society that is between us; and, lastly, the benefits we have formerly received from him. It is desirable that all these inducements might concur in the same person; but when they do not, we should bestow our kindness more expecially on him, in whom we find the most and weightiest of them. . . . [16. The fourth inducement remaining to be spoken of is the nearness of relation, or society that is amongst men; for the maintenance of which, we cannot do better than to give most to those that stand nearest related to us. But that we may consider, with greater distinctness, the natural principles of human society, we shall here trace it down from the fountain head. The first thing then to be taken notice of is this: that there is such a thing as a fellowship or society between all men in general: the bond or cement that holds this together is reason and discourse, which, by teaching, learning, communicating one with another, etc., easily make men agree together, and unite them all in one natural sort of conjunction and community: nor does anything set us at a greater distance from the nature of beasts; for we oftentimes talk of the courage of them, such as lions and horses; but never a word of their equity, justice, or goodness: and why is this, but because they are destitute of reason and discourse? This is then the largest and most comprehensive of all societies, being made up of men considered barely as such, and so taking in even the whole race and kind of them one with another; the duties of which are, to let every one have a share in those things which by nature were produced for the common advantage and benefit of all; to let what is already determined by laws and civil constitutions remain as it is, without breaking in on any man's right; as to which things, however, we should remember a rule, which is now among the Greeks become a usual proverb, "All things in common amongst friends." But perhaps you may ask what kind of things we suppose them to be which ought to be common to all mankind: Ennius has given us one instance of them, which may easily be applied to a great many others—

> He that directs the wandering traveller,
> Doth, as it were, light another's torch by his own;
> Which gives him ne'er the less of light, for that
> It gave another.

By this one case he sufficiently teaches us, that whatever kindness can be done for another, without any damage or loss to ourselves, it is our duty to do it, though to a stranger. From hence have arisen those general maxims and principles of humanity not to deny one a little running water; or, the lighting his fire by ours, if he has occasion; to give the best counsel we are able to one who is in doubt or distress: which are things that do good to the person that receives them, and are no loss or trouble to him that confers them. Such things, therefore, being by nature common, should accordingly be kept open for the free use of all men; and of those which are our own we should always be giving something that may contribute to the benefit and welfare of the whole. But because the revenues of particulars are small, and there are infinite numbers of those that want, therefore is this universal bounty to be kept within the limits prescribed by Ennius, "It gives him never the less of light"; that so we may have it still within our power to be liberal to those who are more nearly allied to us.

[17. But there are several degrees of society and fellowship amongst mankind; for to take now our leave of that general and universal one already mentioned, there is a nearer among those who are all of the same country, nation, or language, than which nothing more knits and unites men to one another. There is a closer yet among those who are all of the same city; for a great many things are in common to fellow-citizens, such as markets, temples, walks, ways, laws, privileges, courts of justice, freedom of votes, besides common meetings and familiarities, and abundance of business and intercourse with one another. But there is a stricter bond of alliance still between those who belong to the same family, as taking into it but a very small part of the vast and immense one of all mankind. The closest and nearest of all societies is between man and wife; then follows that between them and their children, and afterwards that of the whole family, who inhabit together and have all things in common; which is, as it were, the first beginning of a city, and ground or seed-plot of a whole commonwealth. Next to this comes the bond of relation between brothers, as also between first and second cousins; who, growing too numerous to live in the same house, are sent out to others, as it were into new colonies. Next after this follow marriages and alliances, and so a new stock of relations that way; from whence comes a new propagation and offspring, which serves to give rise, as was said, to commonwealths. Now that nearness of blood, and the natural love which arises from it, cannot but endear men to one another, is past all doubt; it is a very great matter to have the same relics and monuments of our ancestors, to make use of the same religious ceremonies, and be laid, after death, in the same place of burial. But of all the societies and unions amongst men, there is none more excellent, or more closely knit, than when such as are men of real virtue and honesty, from a certain agreement and likeness of their manners, contract a familiarity and friendship one with another: for virtue and goodness (as we often observe) of necessity moves us wherever we see it, and makes us all have a love and respect for that person in whom we discover it; and as every virtue thus wins in our hearts, and even forces us to love those we believe to possess it, so more especially do justice and beneficence. But when several persons are all like one another in honesty and good manners, then no society can ever be more loving, or more closely united: for where there are many of the same humor and same inclinations, every one sees, in some measure, his own self, and is accordingly delighted in the person of another; and that is brought about, which Pythagoras thought the perfection of all friendship, that a great many severals are made into one. There is another remarkable fellowship or community, arising from an intercourse of doing and receiving benefits; which, while it is kept up by a mutual gratitude

and kindness of all the parties, cannot but occasion a firm
and very lasting agreement between them. But when we have
gone over all the relations that are in the world, and thoroughly considered the nature of each, we shall find that there
is no one of greater obligation, no one that is dearer and
nearer to us, than that which we all of us bear to the public.
We have a tender concern and regard for our parents, for our
children, our kindred, and acquaintance, but the love which
we have for our native country swallows up all other loves
whatsoever; for which there is no honest man but would die,
if by his death he could do it any necessary service. How detestable, then, must the wickedness and barbarity of those
people be, who have mangled and rent this their native country by all manner of villainies, and have made it their business (nay, and still do so) to bring it to ruin and utter desola-
tion. Now if there should happen any contest or competition
between these relations, which of them should have the
greatest share of our duty, we should pay the first regard to
our country and parents, from whom we have received the
most endearing obligations; the next to our children and
family, who all have their eyes on us alone, and have nobody
else on whom they can depend; next in order to these come
our kindred and relations, whose fortune is generally the
same with our own. To each of these, therefore, whom I
have just now mentioned, we most of all owe what is necessary for their subsistence: but then, as for living and eating
together, for mutual advising, discourse, exhortation, com-
forting, and sometimes (if occasion serves) rebuking, friendship is the properest soil for them; and of all kinds of friendship, there is none so pleasant as that which is cemented by
a likeness of manners.

[18. . . . It is to be observed, that whereas there were laid
down four general heads, from which all virtue and honesty
is derived, whatever proceeds from a brave and exalted mind,
that is raised above fortune and all the little chances and

accidents of the world, is usually made most account of amongst men. Hence, in reproaches, we find there is nothing more common than such things as these—

> For shame! Young men, and yet have women's hearts!
> While this brave woman plays the man—

Or something like this—

> Dear Salmacis, give spoils that cost no sweat or blood!

Whereas, on the contrary, in praises or panegyrics, those things that are done with a bravery of mind, and have something of extraordinary courage in them (I know not how), we commend in a nobler and loftier strain than we do anything else. Hence Marathon, Salamis, Plataea, etc., are so common a field for all the rhetoricians: hence our Cocles; hence the Decii, the Scipios, Marcellus, and a great many others; and especially the people of Rome itself, are particularly famous for greatness of courage. But the value that is set on military glory appears from this, that almost all statues are done in the habit and garb of a soldier.

But that sort of courage which is seen in the dangers and fatigues of war, unless a man be governed by the rules of justice, and fight for the safety and good of the public, and not for particular ends of his own, is altogether blamable; and so far from being a part of true virtue, as that it is indeed a piece of the most barbarous inhumanity. Fortitude is therefore very well defined by the Stoic philosophers, when they call it "a virtue contending for justice and honesty." No man, therefore, by baseness and treachery, has ever got the name and reputation of true courage; for nothing can ever be virtuous or creditable that is not just. To which purpose that of Plato was admirably well said: "As that sort of knowledge, which is not directed by the rules of justice, ought rather to have the name of design and subtlety, than wisdom and prudence; just so that bold and adventurous mind, which is hurried by the stream of its own passions, and not for the good and advantage of the public, should rather have the name of foolhardy and daring, than valiant and courageous." The first thing therefore I would have in a truly courageous man is, that he be a follower of goodness and fair dealing, of truth and sincerity; which are the principal and constituent parts of justice. But here it is one very unhappy thing, that, most times, these great and exalted minds are naturally ungovernable and desirous of rule: so that what Plato observed of the Spartans, that all their customs had no other aim but to get the superiority, may fitly enough be applied to these persons: for the more any man has of this greatness of soul, the more eager he is of being a sharer in the government, or rather of obtaining it wholly to himself: and it is no easy matter to be fair and equitable in all one's actions, which is the proper and peculiar office of justice, while one is endeavoring to make himself uppermost. Hence it comes to pass, that they never will be conquered in any debates, nor overruled by the laws and constitutions of the public; but make it their business, by factions and bribery, to get a strong party and interest in the republic; and rather choose to be uppermost by force and injustice, than equal to others by fair and upright dealing. But the difficulty of it can only serve to make it more honorable, but never its contrary more excusable: for no sort of case or circumstance whatever can excuse any man for being guilty of injustice. Those are therefore your truly brave and courageous men, not who rob, plunder, and injure others, but those who secure and protect them from injuries. But that greatness of mind which is truly such, and under the direction of wisdom and prudence, makes that honor and credit, which we naturally desire, not consist in the outward imaginary applause, but in the real intrinsic goodness of its actions; and is not so eager of appearing to be greater and better than others, as of really being so: for he that is so mean as to depend on the giddy and ignorant multitude, ought never to be accounted of a truly great and exalted spirit; besides that, there is nothing so easily draws men to acts of injustice as a loftiness of mind, when joined with this foolish desire of applause. This is indeed a very dangerous place, and requires our greatest concern and watchfulness; because you shall hardly find any man, who, when he has gone through labors and difficulties, does not expect this honor and applause, as a kind of reward for his courage and achievements.

[20. Now all true courage and greatness of mind is more especially seen in these two things: the first is a generous contempt or disregard of all outward goods, proceeding from an opinion, that it is unworthy of a man to admire, or wish for, or endeavor after anything, unless it be that which is honest and becoming; to make himself subject to any one's will; to be a slave to his own irregular passions, or any ways depend on the caprices of fortune. When he has got such a temper of mind as I have now been describing, then the second thing is, that he perform such actions as are glorious and profitable, but withal very full both of labor and difficulty; and extremely dangerous to his life itself, as well as to those things that are requisite for its preservation. Now all the luster and dignity of these two parts, nay, and I add all their usefulness too, is lodged only in the latter; but the groundwork, as it were, and foundation of all true greatness, is laid in the former: for in that are contained those generous principles, which exalt men's minds, and raise them to a contempt of all worldly things. But that former itself is made up of two parts: the first is an opinion that nothing is truly and really good, but only what is honest; the second, a freedom from all sort of passion or disturbance of mind: for what can more discover a man of a brave and heroic spirit, than to make no account in the world of those things which seem so glorious and dazzling to the generality of mankind; but wholly to despise them, not from any vain and fantastic humor, but from solid and firm principles of reason and judgment? Or what can more show a robust mind and unshaken constancy, than to bear those heavy and numerous calamities, which are incident to mankind in this life, with such a firm temper and fixedness of soul, as never to offend against nature and right reason, or do anything that is unworthy the dignity and character of a wise man? Now it would not at all be consistent or agreeable, that he who bore up so courageously against fear should be afterwards unable to resist desire; or that he who could never be conquered by pain, should suffer himself to be captivated by pleasure. These things therefore should well be considered, and of all desires, that of money should be avoided; for nothing is a greater sign of a narrow, mean, and sordid spirit, than to dote on riches; nor is anything, on the contrary, more creditable and magnificent than to contemn wealth, if you have it not; and if you have it, to lay it out freely in acts of bounty and liberality. The desire of glory, as I before observed, ought also to be avoided; for it robs a man wholly of his freedom and liberty, which generous spirits ought of all things in the world to maintain and contend for. Neither ought places of power to be sought after; but at some times rather to be refused when offered, at others to be laid down if they can conveniently. We should free ourselves, in short, from all vehement passions and disorders of mind, not only those of desire and fear, but also of sorrow, of joy, and of anger; that so the state of the mind may be calm and undisturbed; which will make the whole life become graceful and uniform. Now there both are and have been many, who, to gain this repose of which I am speaking, have betaken themselves to a life of retirement, and wholly withdrawn from all business of the public. Among these the noblest and most eminent of the philosophers; and some men of rigid and severe lives, who disliked the manners of the people of their governors; others have withdrawn themselves into the country, being pleased with the management of their own private fortunes. These men proposed the same end to themselves that kings and princes do, viz. the living so as to want for nothing; to be under the power and control of none, but to enjoy a full and perfect freedom; which consists in living so as one's self best pleases.

[21. This then being the common design and end of them both, those who are ambitious of power and authority, think to obtain it by enlarging their fortunes and interests in the world; but these whom I have mentioned as men of retirement, by contenting themselves with their own condition, though but humble and mean. In which they are neither of them wholly in the wrong; but the life of the latter, I mean the retired, is both easier and safer, and begets less of trouble and disturbance to others, whereas that of the former, who give themselves up to affairs of state, and the management of great and important concerns, is more adapted to the benefit and good of mankind, and the getting of credit and reputation in the world. Those people therefore are perhaps excusable, who, being of parts and capacities for learning, give themselves wholly to the study of it, and never at all meddle with public business; and so are those also, who, being disabled by sickness and infirmities, or on any other good and allowable account, have separated themselves from the administration of affairs, leaving the power and reputation of it in the hands of others: but as for those people who have none of these reasons, and pretend to despise those commands and honors, which most men admire; I am so far from thinking it a virtue in them, that I rather esteem it a very great fault. Thus far, it is true, one can hardly condemn them, in that they despise, and make little account of glory and applause; but their true reason seems to be rather this, that they do not care to suffer the labor and fatigue of them, and are afraid of encountering with rubs and repulses, as things that are attended with some shame and dishonor: for you shall often find there are a great many men, who are very inconsistent with themselves in things of a contrary nature: as for pleasure, they despise it with all the severity of a Stoic; but yet are so effeminate, as not to be able to bear the least trouble; are mighty contemners of fame and applause;

but extremely concerned at anything of disgrace: which are things that do not very well agree together. These people then, whom Nature has endowed with abilities for that purpose, should forthwith endeavor to procure themselves places, and manage the business of the commonwealth; otherwise how should the city be well governed, or the greatness of their endowments be made known to the world? But that greatness of soul, and contempt of all human things, which we have often mentioned, together with that calmness and serenity of mind, is requisite in those of a public station, as much, if not more than it is in philosophers, if ever they hope to be free from anxieties, and arrive at any steadiness or uniformity in their lives. Now these things are easier to philosophers than to them; forasmuch as their lives being led in private, require for their support a less number of things, and have fewer within the power and reach of fortune: and if any ill accident should befall them, it is impossible their sufferings can be very considerable. Those men, therefore, that are in public stations, having things of more weight and importance to be taken care of, must in reason be supposed to lie much more open to the assaults of the passions than those who spend their days in privacy and retirement. On which account they should take the more care to fortify themselves with this greatness of spirit, and to free their minds from the grievous torments and disturbances of them. But he who takes on him a public trust, should not only look that the business be honest, but that he himself be qualified for the management of it; in considering which there is a double extreme to be carefully avoided, that he neither despair through a mean timidity, nor yet be overconfident through eagerness of desire: and, lastly, in whatever he sets about, let all things be diligently and carefully put in order, before he goes on to the execution of it. . . .

[26. Another great duty of fortitude is, not to be haughty, disdainful, and arrogant when Fortune favors us, and all things go forward according to our wishes: for it shows as

much meanness and poorness of spirit to be transported
with good, as it does with ill fortune; whereas, on the other
hand, nothing is more brave than an evenness of temper in
every condition, and (as is reported of Socrates and Laelius)
a constant retaining the same air in one's countenance, without ever seeming puffed up or dejected. I find that Philip,
the king of Macedonia, was inferior to his son in the outward glory and splendor of his achievements, but very far
above him in good nature and condescension: therefore the
father kept always the character of a great person, whereas
the son often was guilty of base and dishonorable actions.
It is a good rule therefore, I think, which is given by some
men that the higher our station in the world is, the more
care we should take of our lives and actions, that they be
kept within the compass of lowliness and humility. Panaetius
tells us it was a usual saying with his scholar and familiar
friend Africanus,—"that men who give the reins to their
vicious appetites, and are high and presuming on the greatness of their fortunes, should be dealt with like horses,
when grown fierce and unruly by frequent engagements;
for as these are delivered to breakers to tame, and to be made
fit for riding; so those should be brought within the barriers
and limits of reason and philosophy, to teach them the uncertainty of all human things, and the great volubility and
changeableness of fortune." . . .

[27. We are now in the next place to speak of the fourth,
and only remaining part of virtue or honesty, under which
are comprehended bashfulness, temperance, modesty, government of the passions, and the observing a just order as to
time and place in our words and actions; from all which
arises a certain engaging kind of beauty and gracefulness,
which serves to set off and adorn our lives. Under this head
is contained that becomingness, which is in its nature so
closely united and riveted to honesty, that there is no way
left of pulling them asunder; for whatever is becoming is likewise honest, and whatever is honest is likewise becoming.

The difference between them is so very small that we may better conceive what it is, than explain it; for whatever becomingness there is in any action, it immediately arises from the honesty of it. From hence it appears that becomingness does not peculiarly belong to this one part of honesty, whereof we are now undertaking to discourse, but shows itself also in each of the three former. To reason, for instance, and discourse according to the rules of prudence; to go about nothing but after due consideration, and on every occasion to be quick at espying and defending the truth, are things that are becoming; whereas to be deceived, to be in an error or mistake, and to be imposed on, are very unbecoming; as well as to be mad or beside oneself. So again, all actions of justice are becoming; but those of injustice are both scandalous and unbecoming. The same may be said as to the actions of fortitude: whatever is done with a manly courage and bravery of mind, as it is worthy of, so it becomes a man; but whatever, on the other hand, shows any cowardice or meanness of spirit, is as contrary to becomingness as it is to true virtue. I conclude therefore that the decency whereof I am now discoursing appertaineth to each of the four parts of honesty; and so appertaineth, as not to stand in need of any mighty reach of understanding to perceive it, but is easily discoverable at the first view; for there is something of becoming contained in the very notion and idea of all virtue, from which it is distinguished by the mind alone, and not by the nature of the thing itself. Just as the beauty and good color of the countenance can never be separate from the health of the body, so this becomingness of which we are speaking, in itself is all one, and, as it were, incorporate with virtue and honesty, but may be distinguished from it by thought and imagination. Now there are two kinds or sorts of it; the one universal, which belongs to the nature of honesty in general; the other particular, and contained under this, which belongs to the several parts of it. The former is used to be thus defined; decorum, or becoming, is that which is congruous or agreeable to that excellent part of the nature of man, by which he is distinguished from the rest of the creation. As for the latter, which is contained under this, it is usually described and defined to be that which is in such manner agreeable to the nature of man, as withal to show something of temper and moderation, with a certain sweet air of gentility and good manners.

[28. That this is so, will more plainly appear, if we consider that decorum or convenience of manners, which the poets aim at in all their writings; concerning which, were it anywise necessary to my present purpose, I might largely discourse. Suffice it at present for me only to observe that the poets are then said to keep this decorum, when each of their persons is brought in saying and doing those things which are suitable to the character he bears in the world. Should Aeacus, for example, or Minos say,

> Ev'n let them hate me, whilst they dread me too;

or,

> The child's entombed in its own parent's bowels;

it would be an offence against the rules of decency, because they pass in the world for men of justice and honesty; but let the same be said by a cruel Atreus, and the whole theater shall clap and applaud it, because it is a saying very agreeable to his character. Now the poet can judge what is becoming and convenient for every person, according to the character which he bears in the poem: but Nature has given every one of us a character, by endowing us with that nobleness and excellence of being, whereby we are set above all other creatures. The poets, then, there being so great a variety of characters, can see what is becoming and convenient for all, even the most vicious; but we have got only one character to to live up to,—I mean that which is assigned us by Nature herself; a character of temperance and modesty, of constancy and moderation. And the same Nature having also taught us that we ought to be careful of our carriage and demeanor toward the rest of men, hence it appears of how large an extent that becomingness is, which belongs to the nature of honesty in general, and also that other, which is seen in the exercise of the several kinds of it: for as the beauty and comeliness of the body draw the eyes to it by the fit composure of all its members, and please us only on this account, because all its parts correspond with a kind of proportion and harmony; so this decorum, which gives a sort of luster and grace to our lives, engages the approbation and esteem of all we live with, by that just and due order, consistency, and regularity, which it keeps up and maintains in our words and actions. We ought to have, therefore, a certain respect and reverence for all men, and desire to be approved not only by the best, but by all the world; for not to care a farthing what it is people think of one, is a sign not only of pride and conceitedness, but indeed of having perfectly abandoned all modesty. But here we must observe, that there is a great deal of difference between that which justice, and that which this modesty, respect, or reverence demands, in relation to other people. It is the duty of justice, not to injure or wrong any man; of respect, or reverence, not to do anything that may offend or displease him; wherein more especially the nature of that decorum we are speaking of consists. These things then being thus explained, I suppose it may clearly enough appear what that is which we mean by becoming. As for the duties prescribed by it, the first thing to which it conducts us is, to demean ourselves suitably and agreeably to our nature, and do nothing that may anyways stain or deface it; for whilst we take this for our guide and conductress, it is impossible we should ever go out of the way; but by her shall be led through all the paths of wisdom, truth, and understanding; of justice and beneficence toward the society of mankind; and of true magnanimity and greatness of soul. But the nature of decency is more peculiarly seen in the fourth part of honesty, concerning which we are now discoursing; and relates not only to the motions of the body, but more especially to those of the mind also; each of which then are approved and becoming, when they are such as are proper and suitable to nature. Now the whole of the nature or mind of man is made up of only these two parts: the first consists in the sensitive appetite; by the blind and extravagant impulse of which he is hurried and transported from one thing to another; the second is reason, which shows and instructs him in the way of his duty, telling him what he should do, and what not do: whence it follows that it is reason which ought to be the governing faculty, and the appetite to be subject to the commands of it.

[29. Every action therefore should be free, as from precipitancy and rashness on the one hand, so from all carelessness and negligence on the other; nor should anything be done for which we cannot give a sufficient reason; which is almost the very definition of duty. In order to do this the passions must be brought under the power of reason, so as neither through hastiness to run before its orders, nor through coldness and heaviness to disregard them when given; but all their motions must be so quieted and restrained, as to bring no uneasiness or disturbance to the mind: and from this calm and peaceable state of the soul arises that constancy and moderation we have mentioned; for when once the passions grow unruly and extravagant, and refuse to be guided in their desires and aversions by the rules of prudence, they will run without question beyond all bounds and measure; for they abandon and cast off their allegiance to reason, which they ought to obey by the constitution of nature. By this means are all things turned topsy-turvy; and not the mind only, but even the body also, put very much into disorder and confusion. Do but mark those who are inflamed with a vehement anger or desire; who are transported with fear, or an overgreat joy; and you will see an alteration in their countenances, voices, gestures, and all their actions; which sufficiently gives us to understand (that we may return again to the duty now before us) how necessary it is to restrain and give check to the movements of the appetite, and to be always watchful and standing on our guard, that so we may neither be careless and inconsiderate, nor do anything rashly and at all adventures: for mankind were never designed by Nature merely to sport and idle away their time, but to follow after grave and serious studies, and business of greater importance than play is. Not but that jesting and diversion are allowable, provided we use them but as we do sleep, and other such necessary refreshments of nature, viz. after the discharge of our serious and more important duties. And even then we must see that our jesting be neither excessive nor immodest, but such as is handsome and becoming a gentleman; for as boys are allowed not all kinds of sports, but only such as have nothing that is vicious or ill in them; so in this jesting we should allow ourselves nothing but what is agreeable to honesty and good manners. We may therefore observe that jesting or merriment is of two sorts; the one clownish, abusive, scandalous, and obscene; the other handsome, genteel, ingenious, and truly pleasant. Of this kind are several instances to be met with, as in our Plautus, and the old Greek comedians; so in the writings of the Socratic philosophers: to which we may add the ingenious sayings of several men, such as are collected by the senior Cato, and usually go by the name of Apothegms. There is no great difficulty then to distinguish between a genteel and a clownish jest; the one, if brought in at a seasonable time, and when a man's mind is disengaged from business, is becoming for a gentleman; the other, for no man at all indeed, when base and unhandsome things are dressed up in filthy and obscene expressions. Our plays and recreations must also be kept within their due bounds; and care should be taken that we do not run out into great excesses, and suffer the pleasure which we take in them to carry us into anything that is base or unbecoming. Hunting, and the exercises of the Campus Martius, supply us with examples enough of creditable and manly recreations.

[30. But in all inquiries concerning what becomes us, it is of very great moment to be constantly reflecting how much man's nature excels that of beasts and inferior animals. These have no taste or relish for anything but the pleasures of the body, toward which they are carried with a great deal of eagerness; whereas nothing is more agreeable and nourishing, as it were, to the mind of man, than learning and contemplation. Hence he is always seeking or contriving something that is new, and is greatly delighted with seeing and hearing, for the increase of his knowledge: and if there is any one too much addicted to sensual pleasures, unless he is transformed into a mere brute; (for some such there are, who are men in name, and not in reality) but if, I say, any one is too much addicted, and suffers himself to be conquered by pleasure; yet, for very shame, he will hide and conceal his propensities toward it as much as possible. And what is this now but a plain indication that sensual pleasures are unbecoming the dignity of a reasonable creature, and ought to be despised and rejected by him? and that whoever sets any value on them should be sure to take care that he keep within the limits of reason and moderation? Hence it follows that we should not have any respect to pleasure, but only to the preservation of our health and strength, in our victuals, clothes, and other conveniences belonging to the body. And does not the consideration of the same dignity and excellence of our natures plainly inform us how base and unworthy a thing it is to dissolve in luxury, softness, and effeminacy; and how brave and becoming it is, on the other hand, for a man to lead a life of frugality and temperance, of strictness and sobriety? And here we must observe that Nature has given us, as it were, a double part to be acted in the world: the first is extended to all men in common, forasmuch as we are all of us partakers of reason, and that prerogative of our nature, whereby we are exalted above other animals; it is this that conducts us in the finding out our duty, and from it all honesty and becomingness arises: the second is appropriate to each in particular; for as there is a great deal of difference in bodies, some being nimble and proper for running, others more lusty, and fitter for wrestling; some of a noble and majestic air, others of a sweet and engaging kind of beauty; so there is no less, or rather a far greater variety in humors. . . .

[31. The more easily then to arrive at that decorum of which we are speaking, let every one stick to his own peculiar character and humor, provided it has nothing that is vicious in it: I say, provided it has nothing that is vicious in it; for we should always take particular care to do nothing that is contrary to that universal character which Nature has imprinted on every one of us; but, saving the reverence we owe to that, then to live according to our own particular one, so as to follow after that kind of study, and apply ourselves to that course of life which is most suitable and agreeable to our own inclinations, though others perhaps may be more useful and important; for it is in vain to struggle against the bias of your nature, or to engage in that sort of business in which you can never arrive at any perfection. From what has been said it more fully appears what that is which we call becoming; since nothing can be such that is done, as we say, in despite of nature, i.e. contrary to the bent and tendency of a man's genius. Now it is certain, if anything in the world is becoming, it is a constant uniformity in our whole lives and particular actions; which it is utterly impossible we should ever maintain, so long as we run counter to our own inclinations, and foolishly follow after those of other people: for as we should use our own native language, which all are supposed to understand best, and not lard our talk, as a great many do, with expressions out of Greek, who are therefore deservedly laughed at by others; so we should keep to one constant tenor and regular conduct in our lives and actions, so that nothing may be in them which is not well suited and of a piece with the rest. And this difference in the characters or natures of men is of so great moment, as that in consequence of it one man may be obliged to make away with himself, whilst another, though like him as to all other circumstances, may be obliged to the contrary. Cato, for instance, and those who in Africa surrendered themselves to Caesar, were all of them under the same condition; and yet any of the rest mght perhaps have been blamed for it, had they murdered themselves as Cato did, because they were men of less strictness in their lives and less severity in their manners. But Cato was a person whom Nature had endowed with incredible firmness and strength of soul, which he had augmented by perpetual constancy, and unalterably adhering to his once undertaken designs and resolutions: it became his character therefore to die, rather than to see the face of the tyrant. . . .

[42. As for trades and the ways of getting money, which of them are creditable and which otherwise, I have only these few things to observe: first, all those are unworthy ways of gaining which procure one a general hatred and ill-will: as that of the usurers and tax-gatherers, for instance: secondly, those arts are mean and ungenteel, in which a man is paid for his work, not his skill, for the very receiving a reward for one's labor is like taking of earnest to bind himself a slave. Nor are they to be esteemed as better than mean and ordinary people, that buy things up by wholesale of the merchants, to retail them out again by little and little: for what they gain is but a very poor business, unless they are guilty of abominable lying, than which there is nothing in the world more scandalous. Again, all handicraftsmen have but a mean sort of calling: and it is impossible that a workhouse should have anything that is genteel in it. Farther yet, all those trades are pitiful and low, that purvey and cater for the satisfying men's pleasures: fishmongers, butchers, cooks, etc., as Terence reckons them up: to which we may add, if you please, perfumers, dancing-masters, and those who supply us with dice or cards. But arts that have something of knowledge and skill in them, or those that are useful and necessary for the public; such as physic, for instance, or architecture, or the instruction and education of youth in good manners;—these are very creditable and commendable in those whose rank and condition is suited for such employments. As for merchandise, it is sordid and mean, when the trade that is driven is little and inconsiderable; but when it takes in a great quantity of business, and, bringing home goods from every country, sells them out again without lying or deceiving, we can hardly say but that it is creditable enough: Nay, it is most certainly very commendable, when those who are concerned in it only design (after they are sated, or rather contented with what they have gained), to betake themselves wholly from the haven to the country, as before they had done from the sea to the haven, and there enjoy quietly their private possessions. But among all the methods of enriching oneself, there is no one better, no one more profitable, and pleasant, and agreeable, no one more worthy of a man and a gentleman, than that of manuring and tilling the ground. . . .

Book III

[3. . . . . Whether, according to the opinion of the Stoics, we take virtue or honesty to be the only good; or, according to that of the Peripatetics, acknowledge it so to be the chief good, as that all things else are just as nothing against it;—it is certain, on either of these suppositions, that profit cannot be put in balance against honesty. We are therefore told that Socrates used even to curse those people who disjoined these things in thought and conception, which are one and the same in nature and reality: and, the Stoics are so far of his opinion, as constantly to maintain, that whatever is honest must be also profitable, and whatever is profitable must also be honest. It is true, had Panaetius been one of those who assert that virtue is therefore only desirable, because it brings something of profit along with it; like some, who think nothing any farther worth seeking for, than as it begets pleasure, or exemption from pain; we could then have allowed him the liberty of saying that profit is sometimes repugnant to honesty: but seeing he was one who thought nothing to be good except that which is honest, and avows, that whatever is contrary to honesty, and appears to us under the notion of profit, can neither, if we have it, make life ever the better, nor if we have it not, ever the worse;—he should not, methinks, have brought in such a deliberation, wherein that which seems profitable comes into competition with that which is honest: for that which the Stoics call their sovereign good (to live in conformity with the dictates of nature), means, I suppose, no more than this: that we should always live agreeably to the rules of virtue; and should use other things, which are suited and adapted to our natural inclinations, no farther than virtue permits and allows them. Now this being so, there are several of opinion that this general head, wherein profit and honesty are compared with one another, was improperly brought in, and that there ought not to have been given any rules or directions on this subject. . . .

[4. . . . I am therefore of opinion, when Panaetius tells us that men use to deliberate, in considering which of these two they should choose, that he meant no more than what his words strictly signify, viz. that they use to do this, and not that really they ought to do it: for it is infinitely scandalous, not only to prefer a pretended advantage before duty and conscience; but so much as to bring them to the contest and competition, and to doubt whether the one of them should be chosen before the other. If this be so, you will be ready to ask me, "How then comes there to be any doubt at all? And what is it that requires consideration on this subject?" I suppose it is this; that it sometimes happens men are not so very certain whether the action deliberated on be honest or not honest; for that which is usually counted a piece of villainy, is frequently changed by the times or circumstances, and is found to be the contrary. To lay down one instance, which may serve to give some light to a great many others; pray, what greater wickedness can there be on earth, if we speak in general, than for any one to murder, not only a man, but a friend? And shall we therefore affirm that he is chargeable with a crime, who has murdered a tyrant, though he were his familiar? The people of Rome, I am sure, will not say so, by whom this is counted amongst the greatest and most glorious actions in the world. You will say then, does not interest here carry it against honesty? No, but rather honesty voluntarily follows interest. If therefore we would, on all emergencies, be sure to determine ourselves aright, when that which we call our advantage or interest seems to be repugnant to that which is honest, we must lay down some general rule or measure, which, if we will make use of in judging about things, we shall never be mistaken as to points of duty. Now this measure I would have to be conformable to the doctrines and principles of the Stoics, which I principally follow throughout this work: for though I confess that the ancient Academics and your Peripatetics, which were formerly the same, make honesty far preferable to that which seems one's interest; yet those who assert that whatever is honest must be also profitable, and nothing is profitable but what is honest, talk much more bravely and heroically on this subject, than those who allow that there are some things honest which are not profitable, and some things profitable which are not honest: and we have very great liberty given us by our academy, so as never to be tied up to certain tenets, but are left free to defend what we think most probable.

[5. But to return to our general rule or measure: there is nothing on earth then so contrary to nature, neither death, nor poverty, nor pain, nor whatever other evil can befall a man, either in his body or fortune, as to take away anything wrongfully from another, and do oneself a kindness by injuring one's neighbor: for, in the first place, it ruins all manner of society and intercourse amongst men; since it is plain, that if once men arrive at such a pass as to plunder and injure the rest of their neighbors, out of hopes to procure some advantage to themselves, there must follow of course a dissolution of that society which of all things in the world is most agreeable to nature. Should we suppose, for example, that the bodily members had every one of them got an opinion, that to draw to itself all the vigor of its neighbors would very much serve to increase its own; it is certain the whole body must decay and perish: and just so, should every one amongst us deprive other people of their profits and advantages, and take away all he could get from them, with design of applying it only to his own use, the general society and fellowship of mankind must of necessity be broken: for though it is no more than what Nature will allow of, that each man should look after himself in the first place, and furnish himself with the necessaries of life, before he takes care to provide for other people; yet the same Nature will by no means permit that any one should rise by his thrusting down another, and increase his own fortune by the spoils of his neighbors: and not only Nature, that is the universal law or consent of nations, but particular laws, by which several countries and commonwealths are governed, have commanded likewise, that no one be suffered to do an injury to another for the sake of procuring any advantage to himself: for the very design and end of laws is to keep up agreement and union amongst citizens; which whoever destroys, is by them punished, not with the loss of his goods alone, but with prisons, banishment, or even death itself. But nature and right reason, as being at once both a human and divine law too, command this duty with much greater authority; and whoever obeys them (as all men must, who propose to live according to the rules of nature), will never be guilty of coveting what is another's, or applying to his own use what had first been injuriously taken from his neighbor: for certainly greatness and elevation of soul, as also the virtues of courtesy, justice, and liberality, are much more agreeable to nature and right reason, than pleasure, than riches, than even life itself; to despise all which, and regard them as nothing, when they come to be compared with the public interest, is the duty of a brave and exalted spirit: whereas, to rob another for one's own advantage is (as has been shown) more contrary to nature than death, than pain, or any other evil whatever of that kind. Again, those men live much more according to nature, who suffer perpetual troubles and labors for the good and preservation, were it possible, of all men (like Hercules of old, whom men, as a grateful requital for his benefits, report to be placed among the number of the gods), than those who consume all their lives in retirement, where they are not only free from disturbances and vexations, but are furnished with all the pleasures and conveniences of life; and have, moreover, the advantages of strength and comeliness superadded to them: and accordingly we find it to be so in effect, that all the most great and extraordinary geniuses have preferred all the troubles and difficulties of the former before the quiet and ease of this latter way of living. From all which laid together, it unanswerably follows, that whoever lives agreeably to the dictates of nature can never be guilty of injuring another. In fine, he that injures another to do himself a kindness, either thinks he does nothing that is contrary to nature, or that the doing an injury is a less degree of evil than death, or poverty, or pain, or loss of children, friends, or relations. If he thinks that in wronging and abusing others he doth not do anything that is contrary to nature, it is in vain to dispute any longer with such a one, who takes away from man the distinguishing part, and very characteristic, as it were, of his nature: but if he allows that it is indeed an evil; only thinks that some others, such as poverty, pain, or death, may be worse, he is grossly mistaken, in being of the opinion that the ills which touch nothing but the body or fortune can be greater than those which affect the soul.

[6. We should all of us therefore propose the same end, and every one think his own interest, in particular, to be the same with that of the community in general: which, if each one endeavor to draw solely to himself, all union and agreement amongst men will be dissolved. And if Nature enjoin us, that every man should desire and procure the advantage of another, whoever he be, though for no other reason than because he is a man, it necessarily follows that all men are joined by the self-same nature in one common interest; which, if it be true, then all men are subject to, and live equally under the same law of nature: and if this be true, too, then certainly they are forbid, by that same law of nature, any ways to injure or wrong one another; but the first of these is undoubtedly certain, therefore the last must needs be so likewise: for as to what is usually said by some men, that they would not take anything away from a father or brother for their own advantage, but that there is not the same reason for their ordinary citizens, it is foolish and absurd: for they thrust themselves out from partaking of any privileges, and from joining in common with the rest of their citizens, for the public good; an opinion that strikes at the very root and foundation of all civil societies. Others there are, who are ready to confess that they ought to bear such a regard to fellow-citizens, but by no means allow of it in relation to strangers: now these men destroy that universal society of all mankind, which, if once taken away, kindness, liberality, justice, and humanity must utterly perish; which excellent virtues whoever makes void, is chargeable with impiety toward the immortal gods; for he breaks that society which they have established and settled amongst men; the closest cement or bond of which is the being of opinion, that for men to injure and wrong one another for their private interests, is an evil that nature is much more averse from than all those which happen either to the body or fortune; nay, and I might add to the mind also, provided only they be not contrary to justice, queen of all the rest. But what (perhaps some men will be apt to say)—if a wise man be ready to perish for hunger, must not he take away victuals from another, though a perfectly useless and insignificant fellow? Not at all; for life itself is not so dear to me, as a settled resolution of doing no wrong for my private advantage. But suppose this good man, almost dead with cold, should have it in his power to take Phalaris's clothes away, one of the most savage and inhuman tyrants, would not you have him to do it? There is no great difficulty in determining such cases; for it is certain, if you take away anything from another, though never so useless and insignificant a creature, for no other end but to benefit yourself by it, it is an inhuman action, and plainly contrary to the laws of nature: but if you are one, who by living will do very great service to the republic, or perhaps to society of mankind in general, and for that only reason take something from another, it is an action that is not to be found much fault with: but in all other cases, every man is bound to bear his own misfortunes rather than to get quit of them by wronging his neighbor. You will say then, is it not more contrary to nature to covet or seize what belongs to another, than to be in sickness, or want, or any such evil? Yes; but withal it is as contrary to nature to abandon all care of the public interest; for it is a piece of injustice: whence it follows, that an honest, prudent, and valiant person, whose death would bring a great disadvantage to the public, may take from an idle and useless citizen such things as are necessary for the maintenance of life, without any offence against the laws of nature, which aim at the preservation and interest of the public; provided that he do not make the love of himself, and conceit of his own more than ordinary merits, an occasion of injuring and oppressing others: for he will perform but the duties which justice requires of him, by thus taking care to be serviceable to the public, and upholding that (which I am often forced to mention) universal society between all mankind. As for the question proposed about Phalaris, it is easily answered;

for tyrants are not members of human society, but rather its greatest and most pestilent enemies; nor is it unnatural, if it lie in one's power to rob that man, whom it is even a virtue and glory to murder. And it were heartily to be wished, that this whole destructive and impious race were utterly banished and excluded from amongst men. Just as we cut off those members of the body which have got no longer either blood or spirits in them, and serve but to infect and corrupt the rest; so should those monsters, which under the shape and outside of men, conceal all the savageness and cruelty of beasts, be cut off, as it were, and separated from the body and society of mankind. Of much the same nature are all those questions, in which the knowledge and understanding of our duty depends on the knowledge of times and circumstances.

[7. . . . I shall follow the method of the geometricians: and as they do not use to demonstrate everything, but demand to have some things allowed them beforehand, by the help of which they more easily explain and demonstrate their designs; so I demand of you, son Marcus, if you can, to grant me this following postulate; that nothing is desirable for itself alone, but that which is honest: or, however, if Cratippus will not permit you to do that, yet at least, I am sure, you must grant me this which follows; that honesty is desirable for its own sake, above all things in the world: either of the two is sufficient for my purpose, and the one is probable as well as the other, and nothing else besides them is so on this subject. And here in the first place, we must do right to Panaetius, who does not say, as indeed he ought not, that that which is profitable could ever be contrary to that which is honest, but only that which has the appearance of such: and he often avows that nothing is profitable but that which is honest, and that whatever is honest is at the same time profitable; and declares their opinion, who first made a difference between those two, to be the greatest evil that ever yet spread itself abroad amongst men. Therefore, when he speaks of a contrariety between them, he means an apparent, and not a real one; which he therefore laid down for one of the heads of his discourse: not as though it were lawful for men ever to give profit the preference before honesty; but only that they might be able to determine themselves aright, if these two at any time should seem to interfere and be inconsistent with one another. . . .

[10. . . . Men are not bound to be careless of their own interest, or to part with that to others which themselves stand in need of; but everyone may do what he thinks for his own advantage, provided it be no injury or prejudice to another person. Chrysippus, amongst a great many very good sayings, has this one in particular: "He that is running a race ought to strive and endeavor," says he, "as much as he is able, to get before his antagonist; but must not trip his heels up, or thrust him aside with his hands: so in life it is allowable that every one should get what is useful and convenient for his comfortable subsistence, but it is not so to take it away from other people." But it is nowhere more difficult to keep to one's duty, than in the affair of friendship; for as not to do everything that one handsomely can for the sake of a friend, so to do anything that is base or dishonest, are both of them equally contrary to one's duty. But there is one very short and yet easy rule, which may serve to direct us in all cases of this nature; and it is this; never to prefer that which only seems profitable, such as honors, riches, pleasure, and the like, before a kindness to a friend; but never to do anything for the sake of a friend that is an injury to the public, or a breach of one's oath, or other solemn engagement. . . .

[12. Let us lay down this therefore as a standing maxim, that whatever is dishonest can never be profitable; no, not though we should arrive at the full possession of all those advantages which we propose to obtain by it. Nay, this very persuasion, that a thing may be profitable, though it is base and dishonest, is one of the greatest misfortunes and calamities that could ever have happened to the life of man. But there often fall out, as was before observed, some peculiar cases, wherein that which is honest has a seeming repugnance with that which is profitable; so that it requires some further consideration to know whether this repugnance be certain and real, or whether they may not be brought to a fair agreement. To this head belong such examples as these: suppose we, for instance, an honest merchant when corn was scarce and extremely dear at Rhodes, to bring a large quantity thither from Alexandria; and withal to know, that a great many ships, well laden with corn, were on their way thither from the same city; should he tell this now to the people of Rhodes, or say nothing of it, but sell his own corn at the best rate he could? We suppose him a virtuous and honest man, and do not here discourse of the deliberation of one, that would hold his peace if he thought it were dishonest; but of one that doubts whether it be dishonest or not. In such sort of cases Diogenes the Babylonian, a man of great credit and note among the Stoics, is of one opinion; and Antipater his scholar, an extraordinarily smart and ingenious man, of just the contrary. Antipater would have everything be plainly told, that so the buyer might be ignorant of nothing in what he buys, that the seller himself knows of: Diogenes thinks it enough in the seller to tell the faults of his goods as far as the laws require it; and as for the rest, though, to use no cozening, yet since he is come with design to sell them, to get as much money for them as he can. "Here," may the merchant say, "I have brought my corn; I have exposed it to sale; and sell it no dearer than other people do" (nay, perhaps he will say cheaper, there being now a greater quantity than there was before), "and, pray, where is now the wrong I have done to anybody?" Antipater argues on a different principle: "What say you?" quoth he: "Are not you obliged to do good to mankind, and be serviceable to the society of all men in general? Were you not born under such an obligation? And had not you such principles ingrafted into you by Nature, which it is always your duty to follow and

obey, that your single interest should be the same with that of
all men; and again, that of all men should be the same with
yours? And will you, notwithstanding this, conceal from
the people what plenty there is coming, the knowledge of
which might be of so great use and advantage to them?"
Diogenes perhaps will reply to him thus: "It is one thing to
conceal, and another not to tell; nor can I be said to conceal
from you now, though I do not tell you, what the nature and
essence of the gods is, and what the happiness or chief good
of men; things which it would do one much more kindness
to know, than that corn will be cheaper, because great
quantities are like to be here shortly. But if anything be
profitable for you to hear, it is none of my duty to come and
tell it you immediately."—"Nay, but you will find that it
is your duty," may the other reply, "if you will please but to
remember that there is such a kind of thing as a mutual relation and society amongst all men."—"Well, I do remember
it," may the other reply again; "but, I pray you, is that
society of such a nature, as that no man who lives in it must
have anything that is his own? If this be so, then there is no
more selling, but we must even give everything away that
we have."

[13. . . . . And thus you see there are some doubtful cases, in
which on the one hand men argue for honesty, and on the
other are advocates for profit, so far as to show that it is not
only honest to do that which is profitable, but even dishonest
to neglect and omit it; and this is that seeming opposition we
spoke of, which often falls out between profit and honesty.
But let us now proceed to determine these cases; for we did
not propose them for mere question's sake, but that we might
give them a fair decision. I am then of opinion, that the
corn-merchant ought not to have concealed from the Rhodians . . . the several things that are mentioned in their cases.
It is true, not to tell a thing, is not properly to conceal it; but
not to tell that which people are concerned to know, merely
for the sake of some advantage to yourself, I think is: and

there is nobody but knows what kind of concealing this is, and who they are that make a custom of it; I am sure not your plain, sincere, ingenuous, honest, and good sort of people; but rather your shifting, sly, cunning, deceitful, roguish, crafty, foxish, juggling kind of fellows. And must it not necessarily be unprofitable for any man to lie under this, and a much longer catalogue of such black and most odious names of vices?

[20. But when people expect great advantages from their roguery, it is a mighty temptation for them to be guilty of it. Thus, for instance, when Marius was far from any hopes of obtaining the consulship, and had remained in obscurity seven years from the time of his being praetor, so that no one suspected his standing for that honor, being despatched to Rome by Q. Metellus, whose lieutenant he was, an extraordinary man, and a brave member of the republic,—he accused his general to the people of Rome of protracting the war; and told them, that if they would but choose him consul, they should soon have Jugurtha, either dead or alive, delivered into their power. It is true, by this artifice he got to be chosen consul, but he paid for it the price of his honesty and fidelity; who could thus bring a useful and excellent citizen, whose lieutenant he was, and by whom he was sent, into hatred and ill-will by false accusations. . . .

[26. . . . Regulus, then a second time consul, was surprised in Africa by Xanthippus, the Lacedaemonian, and made a prisoner (Amilcar, father of Hannibal, being the general of the Carthaginians), and was sent by the Carthaginians to the Roman senate on solemn oath given, that, unless some remarkable prisoners were restored them, he should himself return back again to Carthage. Now, as soon as this man arrived at Rome, he could not but perceive what appeared to be his interest; but withal was persuaded, as the event declared, that it only appeared so. The case was thus: here he might have stayed in his native country, and have lived at home quietly with his wife and children; might have judged his misfortune, received in the war, no more than what all men in that state are liable to; and might still have continued in his old degree of honor among those of consular dignity. "And who can deny now," will any one say, "that all these things are expedient and profitable?" Who do you think? Why, greatness of soul and true courage deny it. Can you desire any greater and more illustrious authorities?

[27. These are the virtues by which we are taught to be afraid of nothing, to despise all the outward concerns of life, and count nothing intolerable that can possibly befall a man. Well, but pray what did this Regulus do then? He came into the senate, and told them what it was he was sent about, and refused to give his own vote in the case, forasmuch as he was not to be counted a senator, as being by oath under the enemy's power; and in his speech, which he spoke to the senate on that subject ("fool that he was," some will be ready to say, "and an enemy to his own interest!"), he told them it was best not to give up their prisoners; that they were young men, and might make able leaders; but that he, for his part, grown almost useless, and worn away with old age. The senate were so persuaded by his speech, that they resolved the prisoners should be detained in custody; and he himself returned back again to Carthage; not all the love which he had for his country, his friends and relations, being able to detain him: and though he knew well enough what a barbarous enemy and what exquisite torments he was going to return to, yet he thought it his duty, whatever came of it, not to violate his oath. I think he was in a better condition therefore, even whilst he was murdered by being kept from sleeping, than ever he could have been had he stayed at home, and lived under the scandal of being an old captive and a perjured nobleman. "But was not it very great folly and madness, if he would not persuade the releasing of the prisoners, yet to go and dissuade it as much as he could?" Pray, how folly and madness? What! Though it were conducive to the good of the republic? Or can anything be profitable to a private citizen, which brings disadvantage to the commonwealth in general?

[28. Those men who separate profit from honesty wholly pervert the first principles of nature; for we all of us naturally desire our interest, toward which we are carried with so strong a bias, as that it is not in our power to turn the other way: for who is averse from, or rather, who does not most eagerly follow his own advantage? But since we can find out no real advantage, except in what is honest, becoming, and commendable, therefore we count these the principal things; and take the word *profit* to signify something which only relates to our outward necessities, and the supplying of them, without all that glorious and shining excellence which appears in the actions of virtue and honesty. "But after all is done," perhaps some men will say, "pray, what is there in an oath, that he[3] should be afraid thus to break it? What! was it Jupiter's anger that he dreaded?" But this is agreed on by all philosophers; not only those who maintain that the gods lead an idle life, neither busying themselves, nor disturbing others; but those who affirm they are always busy, and always doing something that relates to the world;—in this thing, I say, they are all agreed, that the Deity neither hurts nor is angry with any one. But supposing the worst, pray what hurt could Jupiter's vengeance have done Regulus, greater than what Regulus did to himself? It could not be anything of religion therefore that hindered him from following what appeared to be his interest. Again was he afraid of the baseness and dishonesty of the action? As to that, in the first place, always of two evils choose the least; and where was any evil in the baseness of the thing so great as was that of the torments which he endured? Besides, pray, remember that

---

[3] Cicero is referring to the story of Regulus, who was captured by the Carthaginians and sent back to Rome, on the promise that either a number of Carthaginian prisoners would be returned, or that Regulus himself would come back. Regulus persuaded the Roman Senate not to accept the exchange, and then voluntarily returned to Carthage, in order not to break his oath.

sentence of Accius, which, however it might be said by an impious king, is yet generally acknowledged to be very well said;
who, when one told him, "You have broken your oaths to
me," answered, "I neither am, nor have been tied by oath
to any treacherous deceiver." Again, they tell us, that as we
affirm some things seem profitable which are not so; so they
affirm some things seem honest which are not so: as this, for
example, of returning to be tormented, rather than break one's
oath; which is not honest, though it may seem to be so; because no man is obliged to perform that oath which was ex-
torted from him by the force of his enemies. And lastly, they
argue, that whatever makes very much for one's profit and advantage, thereby becomes honest, though before it did not
seem to be so. This is what is generally brought against Regulus; but let us see and examine all the parts in order.

[29. First, then, they say, he could fear no harm from the
anger of Jupiter, who neither can be angry, nor do harm to
anybody. This proves as strongly against all oaths in general,
as it does in particular against this of Regulus. But the thing
to be considered in people's taking of oaths, is not what danger
they are in, should they break them; for every oath is a religious affirmation; and whatever is promised after such a manner, as it were calling God for a witness to your words, ought
certainly to be performed: for now faith and justice require
it of us, and not any fear of that anger of the gods, which is
not incident to their divine natures;—the faith I mean, of
which Ennius has got these incomparable words:—

> O Faith, all-glorious and divine,
> In lofty temples fit to shine!
> Ev'n Jove himself by thee doth swear.

Whoever therefore doth not perform his oath affronts the
deity of that divine faith, which was (as Cato in his speech
informs us) set up by our fathers in the Capitol itself, even
next to the statue of the great god Jupiter. But, secondly, they
tell us, supposing Jupiter had been angry with Regulus, he

could not have brought any evil on him greater than what
Regulus brought on himself. This, I confess, would be very
true, if there were no other evil but pain: but that is so far
from being the greatest evil, as that it is not so much as any
evil at all, if we may credit some of the chief philosophers;
among whom, I pray you, let Regulus be counted of no small
authority, if I may not rather say of the greatest and most
weighty: for what greater testimony can any one desire, than
that of a principal man among the Romans, who, rather than
be wanting in any point of his duty, chose to undergo the
most exquisite torment? "But of two evils," say they, "always
choose the least"; that is, in plain words, rather be a rogue
than undergo any calamity. Can any calamity, then, be greater
than that of baseness and injustice? For if even the filth and
deformity of the body be loathsome and offensive; how much
more so must that of the mind needs be, when it is covered
and polluted with shame and dishonesty? Those philosophers,
therefore, who discourse of these things with most closeness
and severity, venture boldly to affirm that nothing is evil but
what is dishonest; and even those who do it more loosely, yet
always acknowledge that it is the greatest of all evils. That
saying of the poet is indeed good, "I neither am nor have been
tied by oath to a treacherous deceiver"; but it is therefore so,
because when Atreus was brought on the stage, he was to
make him speak that which was suitable to his character: but
if once they begin to lay this down for a maxim, that faith,
when given to those who are treacherous, is not to be kept—
they had best have a care that this be not made a refuge and
cover for perjury. As for his oaths being made to an enemy;
even war itself has laws that belong to it; and faith, except
in some very few cases, is always to be kept, even with our
greatest adversaries: for whatever you swear, for example, in
such a manner as that your conscience tells you it ought to
be done, you are bound most inviolably to perform it; but
where it is otherwise, you do not lie under any such obligation; and are not perjured, though you should not perform it.

Suppose, for instance, you had sworn to a pirate that you would pay him such a sum if he would spare your life; it would not be perjury, though you should not pay it him: for a pirate is by no means a lawful adversary, but rather a common pest and enemy of mankind; so that no one is obliged to keep his faith or oath with him: for to swear to a thing, and yet not perform it, is not immediately to forswear oneself; but then a man is properly said to be perjured when he swears, on his conscience (as our form runs), to do such and such things, and yet does not do them: for that saying of Euripides may be said in some cases to be very good—"My tongue indeed swore, but my conscience did not assent." But had Regulus, in his case, done anything contrary to the laws and conditions that are kept between enemies, it had been downright perjury: for the Carthaginians, with whom he had then to do, were a lawful adversary, between whom and us there is all the fecial, and several other laws that are common to nations: for had it been otherwise, it is certain the senate would never have delivered up some eminent persons in chains to their enemies.

[30. . . . another thing urged by his adversaries is this; that he should not have performed what was forcibly put on him. As though a man of courage could be wrought on by force! "But why," they say, "did he go at all to the senate, being resolved to dissuade the delivery of the captives?" This is to blame him for that, which particularly deserves commendation. He would not depend on his own judgment; but pleading for that which he thought most expedient, left it to be determined by the judgment of the senate: and had it not been for his counsel in the case, the prisoners had surely been sent again to Carthage, and he remained safe in his native country: but this he concluded would be prejudicial to the public, and therefore esteemed it to be no more than his duty to speak what he thought, and endure what might come of it. Lastly, they add that whatever makes highly for one's profit and advantage thereby becomes honest. I answer, that it may indeed antecedently be such, but can never become such: for nothing is profitable but what is honest; and things do not become honest by their first being profitable, but become profitable by their first being honest. I conclude, therefore, that of all those great and wonderful examples, which might easily be brought on this subject, it will be hard to find any more illustrious and commendable than this of Regulus. . . .

SUGGESTED READINGS

For the fullest treatment in English of the subjects dealt with in our Appendix on Cicero, see E. Zeller's *Stoics, Epicureans and Sceptics*; see also his *Eclectics*. Zeller's monumental work requires supplementing however. Recent works of value are E. V. Arnold's *Roman Stoicism*; R. D. Hicks', *Stoic and Epicurean*; and E. E. Bevan's *Stoics and Sceptics*.

Cicero's political philosophy is brilliantly handled by G. H. Sabine, *History of Political Theory*, Pt. II, Ch. IX.

For a most readable and stimulating treatment of Cicero, see E. Hamilton, *The Roman Way*.

MODERN LIBRARY GIANTS

A series of sturdily bound and handsomely printed, full-sized library editions of books formerly available only in expensive sets. These volumes contain from 600 to 1,400 pages each.

THE MODERN LIBRARY GIANTS REPRESENT A
SELECTION OF THE WORLD'S GREATEST BOOKS